SIZE, CAUSES AND CONSEQUENCES OF THE UNDERGROUND ECONOMY

Size, Causes and Consequences of the Underground Economy

An International Perspective

Edited by

CHRISTOPHER BAJADA
School of Finance and Economics,
University of Technology Sydney, Australia

FRIEDRICH SCHNEIDER
Department of Economics,
Johannes Kepler University of Linz, Austria

Routledge
Taylor & Francis Group

LONDON AND NEW YORK

First published 2005 by Ashgate Publishing

Reissued 2018 by Routledge
2 Park Square, Milton Park, Abingdon, Oxon, OX14 4RN
711 Third Avenue, New York, NY 10017, USA

Routledge is an imprint of the Taylor & Francis Group, an informa business

First issued in paperback 2018

A Library of Congress record exists under LC control number: 2005015264

Notice:
Product or corporate names may be trademarks or registered trademarks, and are used only for identification and explanation without intent to infringe.

Publisher's Note
The publisher has gone to great lengths to ensure the quality of this reprint but points out that some imperfections in the original copies may be apparent.

Disclaimer
The publisher has made every effort to trace copyright holders and welcomes correspondence from those they have been unable to contact.

ISBN 13: 978-0-815-39708-3 (hbk)
ISBN 13: 978-1-138-62057-5 (pbk)
ISBN 13: 978-1-351-14904-4 (ebk)

Contents

List of Contributors vii

1   Introduction 1
     Christopher Bajada and Friedrich Schneider

PART 1   TAXPAYER BEHAVIOUR AND MOTIVATIONS

2   Illegal, Immoral, Fattening or What?: How Deterrence and
     Responsive Regulation Shape Tax Morale 15
     Lars P. Feld and Bruno S. Frey

3   Explaining Taxpayer Non-Compliance through Reference
     to Taxpayer Identities: A Social Identity Perspective 39
     Natalie Taylor

4   Getting On or Getting By? Australians in the Cash Economy 55
     Valerie Braithwaite, Monika Reinhart and Jenny Job

**PART 2   MEASURING THE UNDERGROUND ECONOMY –
          INTERNATIONAL EVIDENCE**

5   An International Comparison of Underground Economic Activity 73
     Friedrich Schneider and Christopher Bajada

6   On the Estimation and Updating of the Hidden Economy
     Estimates: The UK Experience 107
     Dilip Bhattacharyya

7   The Shadow Economy in OECD and EU Accession Countries –
     Empirical Evidence for the Influence of Institutions,
     Liberalization, Taxation and Regulation 123
     Dominik H. Enste

8   The Shadow Economy in Norway 1980-2003: Some Empirical
     Evidences from Voluntary Sample Surveys 139
     Kari Due Andresen, Tone Ognedal and Steinar Strøm

9   The Underground Economy in Canada   157
         Lindsay M. Tedds

PART 3   DETECTION, PREVENTION AND PROGRESS

10   Tax Policy and the Underground Economy   179
         Peter S. Spiro

11   Tax Noncompliance in the United States: Measurement and
         Recent Enforcement Initiatives   203
         Kim M. Bloomquist, Alan H. Plumley and Eric J. Toder

12   Tackling the Underground Economy in the UK:
         A Government's Response   223
         Christopher Bajada

13   Recent Government Initiatives in Tackling the Underground
         Economy in Australia   243
         Christopher Bajada

14   Tax Compliance Strategies to Tackle the Underground Economy   275
         Simon James

Index   *291*

List of Contributors

Kari Due Andresen is a Masters student in Economics at the University of Oslo, Norway.

Christopher Bajada (editor) is a Senior Lecturer of Economics at the University of Technology Sydney and Deputy Head of the School of Finance and Economics. He started his teaching career at the University of New South Wales, from which he holds a PhD. He has taught Economics in a variety of undergraduate and post-graduate courses and has published a number of books and refereed journal articles. Dr. Bajada's research is primarily in applied macroeconomics, with a special interest in the underground economy. His research on the underground economy has attracted national publicity and has been featured on numerous radio and television programs. His research on the underground economy is also part of his work with the Australian Taxation Office as a member of the Cash Economy Task Force.

Dilip Bhattacharyya has a MSc degree in Statistics from Calcutta University and MA and PhD in Economics from the University of Essex. He has taught in a number of universities in the United States including University of Michigan, Indiana University and Wayne State University. He was also a visiting fellow at CORE, Belgium and is currently a fellow at IZA, Bonn, Germany. Dilip has also been convenor of the ESRC/Development Economics Study Group for many years. He has published a book as well as a number of papers in reputable economics journals including *The Economic Journal, De Economist, Public Finance, Public Choice* and *Economic Letters*.

Kim M. Bloomquist is a Senior Economist in the Office of Research at the US Internal Revenue Service, a position he has held since 1999. He conducts research on a wide range of issues related to taxpayer compliance. Recently, these issues have included agent-based computational models of income tax evasion, taxpayer burden modeling, and experimental approaches to measuring the indirect effects of audits. In 2003, Mr. Bloomquist was awarded first prize in the Organization for Economic Cooperation and Development's (OECD) Jan Francke Tax Research competition for his paper, 'Income Inequality and Tax Evasion: A Synthesis'.

Valerie Braithwaite is Director of the Centre for Tax System Integrity, which is part of the Regulatory Institutions Network (RegNet) at the Australian National University. She is also a Senior Fellow in the Research School of Social Sciences. Her research focuses on the micro-processes of governance, inclusive democratic practices, and defiance. She is editor of *Taxing Democracy: Understanding Tax Avoidance and Evasion* (Ashgate, 2003).

Dominik H. Enste studied Economics and Social Science at the University of Cologne (1990-96), at the University of Dublin – Trinity College (1992-93) and at George Mason University, Fairfax, Virginia (1998). He completed his PhD in Economics in 2002. During the period 1999-2001 he was Assistant Lecturer at the Department for Economic Policy, University of Cologne and at the Department of Insurance Management, University of Applied Science, Cologne. From 2001 to 2003 he was Human Resource Manager on Strategic HR topics at Gerling Insurance Group, Cologne. Since 2003 he has been Head of the Department of 'Institutional and Ethical Economics' at the Cologne Institute of Business Research (IW Cologne). Dominik has written three books including *The Shadow Economy – An International Survey*, with Friedrich Schneider (Cambridge University Press, 2003), as well as published several articles in refereed journals including the *Journal of Economic Literature*.

Lars P. Feld is Full Professor of Economics in Public Finance at the Philipps-University of Marburg, Dean of the Faculty of Business Administration and Economics at the Philipps-University of Marburg; Member of the Council of Scientific Advisors to the German Federal Finance Ministry, Permanent Guest Professor at the University of Rennes 1 (France) and Member of the CESifo Research Networks; Managing Editor of the *Perspektiven der Wirtschaftspolitik* of the Verein für Socialpolitik (Association of Economists in German Speaking Countries). Professor Feld received his Master in Economics (Diplom-Volkswirt) from the University of Saarland, Saarbrücken in 1993, and his PhD (Dr. oec.) from the University of St. Gallen in 1999. In 1998 he was Visiting Fellow at the Marshall School of Business, University of Southern California (Los Angeles) and at the Université de Rennes 1 (France). In 1996 he received the Wicksell-Prize of the European Public Choice Society, the Young Scholar Award of the IIPF in 1999 and the Best Paper Prize of the IIPF in 2001. He has published numerous articles in reputable journals such as the *Journal of Public Economics, Public Choice, Kyklos, Economic Policy, Regional Science and Urban Economics* and *European Journal of Political Economy*.

Bruno S. Frey was born in Basle, Switzerland in 1941. He studied Economics in Basle and Cambridge (England), and had a two-year stay in the United States. Since 1969 he has been an Associate Professor of Economics at the University of Basle. He was Professor of Economics at the University of Constance between 1970-77, and since 1977 has been Professor of Economics at the University of Zurich. He is also Research Director of the Centre for Research in Economics, Management and the Arts. He received an honorary doctorate in economics from the University of St. Gallen (Switzerland, 1998) and the University of Goeteborg (Sweden, 1998). He is the author of numerous articles in professional journals, as well as books, some of which have been translated into nine languages. His most recent books include *Not Just for the Money* (1997), *Economics as a Science of Human Behaviour* (1999), *The New Democratic Federalism for Europe. Functional, Overlapping and Competing Jurisdictions* (together with Reiner Eichenberger, 1999), *Arts and Economics* (2000), *Inspiring Economics* (2001),

Successful Management by Motivation. Balancing Intrinsic and Extrinsic Incentives (together with Margit Osterloh, 2001), *Happiness and Economics* (together with Alois Stutzer, 2002) and *Dealing with Terrorism – Stick or Carrot?* (2004).

Simon James is Reader in Economics, School of Business and Economics, University of Exeter, a Chartered Tax Adviser and Fellow of the Chartered Institute of Taxation. He holds an MBA as well as masters degrees in Economics, Educational Management, Education and Law and the subject of his PhD was 'Taxation and Economic Decisions'. He has published over 50 research papers mainly concerned with taxation and his 15 books include *The Economics of Taxation: Principles, Policy and Practice*. He has also edited a four-volume collection of tax papers entitled *Taxation: Critical Perspectives on the World Economy* published by Routledge in 2002 and is co-editor of *Taxation: An Interdisciplinary Approach to Research* (Oxford University Press, 2005).

Jenny Job is a PhD student at the Centre for Tax System Integrity at the Regulatory Institutions Network (RegNet) at the Australian National University. She is also a public (civil) servant on leave from the Australian Taxation Office. Jenny's research focuses on the creation and maintenance of trust in government and includes an interest in social capital, organizational culture change, organizational ethics, and responsive regulation. As part of the Cash Economy Task Force, she was a key player in integrating academic and tax office thinking to develop the ATO Compliance Model.

Tone Ognedal is Associate Professor in Economics at the University of Oslo, Norway and Research Fellow at the Frischcentre, Oslo, Norway.

Alan H. Plumley is a Technical Advisor to the Director of Headquarters Research at the Internal Revenue Service. In his 19 years in IRS Research, Alan has focused on estimating the extent and composition of taxpayer noncompliance, estimating the impact of the IRS and other factors on taxpayer compliance, and modelling for optimal resource allocation and workload selection. He earned a PhD in Public Policy from Harvard University.

Monika Reinhart is a research psychologist with extensive experience in survey development and analysis. She advises and teaches research and statistical analysis to academic staff and PhD students at the Centre for Tax System Integrity. Her current research interests focus on the legitimacy of the tax system and its implications for the regulation of taxpaying behaviour.

Friedrich Schneider (editor) is Full Professor of Economics and Vice-President of Foreign Affairs at Johannes Kepler University of Linz, Austria. He obtained his PhD in Economics from the University of Konstanz in 1976 and has since held numerous visiting and honorary positions at a number of universities. During 1991 to 1996 he was Dean of Social Science and Economics at Johannes Kepler

University of Linz and President of the Austrian Economic Association during 1997 to 1999. He has also been a consultant to numerous organisations including the Brussels EU Commission. He has published extensively in leading Economics journals including, *The American Economic Review*, *The Quarterly Journal of Economics*, *The Economic Journal* and the *Journal of Economic Literature*. He has also published numerous book chapters and books including *The Shadow Economy* (with Dominik H. Enste, Cambridge University Press, 2002), *The Encyclopaedia of Public Choice Vol. I and II* (with Charles Rowley, Kluwer, 2004) and *Changing Institutions in the European Union* (Edward Elgar, 2004). He was the editor of the *Journal of Public Choice* from 1991 to 2004 and *Perspektiven der Wirtschaftspolitik* from 2000 to 2004.

Peter S. Spiro has extensive experience in economic research with a number of public and private sector institutions in Canada, and has been on the faculty of the Economics Department at the University of Toronto. He has post-graduate degrees in Economics from the University of Toronto and the University of Chicago. He has published extensively in the fields of public finance and macroeconomic analysis. He is the author of the book *Real Interest Rates and Investment and Borrowing Strategy* (1989), which is widely used as a reference in long-run analysis of the cost of capital.

Steinar Strøm is Professor of Economics at the University of Oslo, Norway and Turin, Italy. He is also a Research Fellow at Friscentre, Oslo, Norway; IZA, Bonn, Germany; CES, Munich, Germany; CHILD, University of Turin, Italy.

Natalie Taylor is a Senior Research Analyst at the Australian Institute of Criminology, Canberra. During 2000 and 2001 she was a Postdoctoral Fellow at the Centre for Tax System Integrity at the Australian National University where she applied the social psychological principles of social identity to her research into links between taxpayer attitudes and tax compliance. The importance of social identity to understanding behaviour is a central theme both in her research on taxpayer (non)compliance as well as crime and justice more generally.

Lindsay M. Tedds is currently a PhD candidate in the Department of Economics at McMaster University in Hamilton, Ontario, Canada. Lindsay's primary research areas are public economic issues, with particular focus on the underground economy and tax evasion. Prior to attending McMaster University, Lindsay held several posts with the Government of Canada in Ottawa in the areas of public economics and policy implementation. She also holds an MA and a BA in Economics from the University of Victoria in Victoria, British Columbia, Canada and a BA in political science from Carleton University in Ottawa, Ontario, Canada.

Eric J. Toder is a Senior Fellow at the Urban Institute and an Associate in the Urban-Brookings Tax Policy Centre. In those positions, he performs and supervises research on tax policy and retirement policy. Between 2001 and 2004, he served as Director, National Headquarters Office of Research, at the Internal

Revenue Service. Dr. Toder previously held a number of positions in tax policy offices in the US government and overseas, including service as Deputy Assistant Secretary for Tax Analysis at the US Treasury Department, Deputy Assistant Director of the Congressional Budget Office, and consultant to the New Zealand Treasury. He received his PhD in Economics from the University of Rochester in 1971.

Chapter 1

Introduction

Christopher Bajada and Friedrich Schneider

Background and Objectives

As crime and other underground economic activities (including shadow economy ones) are a fact of life around the world, most societies have attempted to control these with measures ranging from education to punishment and prosecution. Gathering statistics about who is engaged in underground activities, the frequencies with which these activities are occurring and the magnitude of the problem is crucial for making effective and efficient policy decisions for the allocation of a country's resources to tackling this problem. Unfortunately, it is very difficult to get accurate information about these activities in terms of value added or from a labour market perspective because all individuals engaged in these activities do not wish to be identified. Thus the estimation of the size and development of the underground economy can be considered as a scientific passion for knowing the unknown. Public discussions of illicit work, tax evasion and all other activities in the underground economy have grown increasingly overtime. In a number of countries, initiatives to tackle the underground economy have been implemented (to varying degrees), highlighting the fact that in recent years politicians have felt the need to act as well.

However politicians are faced with a dilemma. While wealthy individuals are evading taxes, which has prompted widespread public indignation, the relatively poorer illicit workers are often much less criticized for doing the same thing even though some politicians argue that they are behaving anti-socially and are contributing to unemployment and social injustice in our society. This opinion is broadly shared by the community particularly in relation to social fraud and illegal employment. But what about part-time illicit work in the evenings (moonlighting) which, for example, about half of the population in Germany would tolerate or even take advantage of, if they had the opportunity to make use of it? Can more sanctions and controls, combined with more regulation, be the ultimate solution to combat illicit work and the underground economy? What is the right way to deal with undeclared work?

In the popular scientific media and daily newspapers and magazines, such questions are often given little attention. More often than not the discussions on the underground economy fluctuate between two extremes: either the underground economy is blamed for the many problems related to economic management, such as unemployment or a growing public debt, or it is treated as a consequence of an economic system that is characterized by high taxes and too much regulation.

There are several important reasons why policy makers should be especially concerned about the growth of the underground economy. Among the most important of these are:

1.   A growing underground economy can be seen as the reaction of individuals who feel overburdened by the state and who choose the 'exit option' rather than the 'voice option' to express their dissatisfaction. If the growth of underground activities is caused by a rise in the overall tax and social security burden, together with institutional sclerosis, then the consecutive 'flight' into the underground economy may erode the tax and social security bases further adversely affecting the future provision of public goods and services. The result can be a vicious circle of further increases in budget deficits or tax rates as a result of continuing growth of the underground economy.

2.   A growing underground economy may cause severe difficulties for politicians, particularly their use of official indicators – unemployment rates, labour force participation rates, income and consumption figures, just to mention a few – that are unreliable in the presence of a growing underground economy. Policy based on erroneous official indicators is likely to be ineffective or in the worse case, counter-productive.

3.   The effects of a growing underground economy on legitimate activity is quite important to consider. On the one hand, a prospering underground economy may attract (domestic and foreign) workers away from legitimate employment and create competition for legitimate firms. On the other hand, a significant portion of income (at least 2/3) earned in the underground economy is immediately spent in the legitimate economy, generating a positive impact in the legitimate sector that may otherwise not have come about.

Hence, the major goal of this book is to shed some light on how we might attempt to answer the questions posed earlier. In addition the book provides a comprehensive overview of the size and development of the underground economy, its major causes and motivations and its effects on the legitimate economy. This book brings together the latest research on tax evasion, tax morale and other underlying factors which have so significantly influenced participation in the underground economy. Finally, this book reviews some of the recent strategies a number of countries have undertaken in their attempts to tackle the underground economy problem. In this regard these countries are 'leaders' amongst the other nations in their pursuit to limit the growth in their domestic clandestine activities.

In the rest of this chapter we provide a brief overview of the various consequences that come from a large and growing underground economy. We conclude this discussion with a brief summary of the various chapters that make up this collection of works.

Consequences of an Underground Economy

The underground economy serves as the vehicle by which economic agents escape the inspections and regulations of government. It is also the same vehicle that creates economic 'anarchy' to the extent that it undermines 'the stability and responsibility of political, legal and economic institutions that might otherwise serve to facilitate the (economic) development process' (Priest, 1994). An analysis of the underground economy is incomplete without discussing its consequences on legitimate economic activity. Whichever motive fosters active participation, the consequences of a large underground economy may turn out to be quite significant. For this reason it is important to improve our understanding of these consequences to help identify strategies to discourage clandestine activities. The consequences may be summarized as follows.

Declining Taxation Revenue

The overwhelming interest in the underground economy is with the extent of uncollected tax revenue. Although this is not the only serious consequence of tax evasion, it nevertheless warrants significant attention. Whenever participation in the underground economy expands, tax revenue losses add to the financial pressures of government to satisfy the service needs of the community. Daunted with spending decisions and commitments the government, in response to falls in revenue, may cut its expenditures, raise taxes or finance its expenditures by running larger deficits. Doing so may drive more individuals into the underground economy or encourage existing underground participants to work more extensively (Carter, 1984). The effect may be further compounded as higher taxes reduce investment and savings, inhibiting the growth of the legitimate economy. For example, conservative estimates for Canada have shown that the Canadian government is loosing an average of $6 billion annually in tax revenue from the underground economy (Berger, 1986). Estimates for New Zealand portray a similar scenario. Estimates suggest that the New Zealand government is loosing between 6.4 percent and 10.2 percent of total tax liability from the underground economy (Giles, 1999).

Distortions of Economic and Social Data

Individuals and businesses that participate in the underground economy not only contribute to lowering tax revenue collections, they also bias economic and social information which policymakers use to gauge their economic policies. The fact that the underground economy in many countries has been estimated to be quite large suggests national accounts information is significantly under-estimated. Immediately this distorts measures of economic growth (Houston, 1990), the rate of inflation (Reuter, 1982), the size of the business cycle (Bajada, 2003), the rate of unemployment (McDonald, 1984), productivity (Carson, 1984), the size of the tax base (Hansson, 1982), and the volume of savings (Greenfield, 1993). Incorrect policy prescriptions can only follow from such data distortions. For example, the fact unemployment may be consistently upward biased because of the underground economy may result in policies that are too expansionary and generate inflationary pressures.

Tax Morality

If the community acknowledges that the underground economy is growing and not being detected, there is an incentive to encourage a more active involvement or motivate new participants to join in. Unfortunately the incentives that encourage a participant to join usually have to be followed by strong deterrence policies to have them quit. Generally once a participant crosses over to the underground economy it may be quite difficult to bring them back, particularly since the financial gains to those who participate are immediate.

Unfair Price Competition

By its very nature, the underground economy promotes unfair price competition. If a business sub-contracts labour from the underground economy at significantly lower costs, the firm is in a better position to price compete with its competitors, who may not be participating in the underground economy. Alternatively the firm may engage in selling goods and services in the underground economy while concealing all or part of its income. Unfortunately active participation in the underground economy may force some small legitimate businesses out of the market or force their survival by driving them to participate also.

Welfare Effects

Those who participate in the underground economy may be contributing far less than honest taxpayers for the rights to use government goods and services. The government provides a vast array of goods and services including law enforcement, defence, education, hospitals, roadwork, transport and emergency services. In order that these services may be provided, it is expected that everybody pays their fair share of taxes. If there are a large number of individuals who are participating in the underground economy and not paying their fair share of tax, yet continue to expect the provision of public goods and services, they impose on honest tax payers the burden of raising the finances for their provision. As long as illicit activities are growing, the resource flow from the legitimate to the underground economy implies significant welfare losses.

The competitive advantage that the underground economy offers without doubt contributes considerably to efficiency and productivity losses (see Hansson, 1982). A growth in the underground economy may mean the closure of a large number of small legitimate businesses.

Implications for Efficiency

The underground economy may distort the allocation of economic resources particularly if it channels them into sectors of the economy where tax evasion is more pronounced. The inefficiencies may become larger if the inefficient redistribution of resources impacts on the methods of production, for example, changing to small-scale production techniques, employing fewer workers, fewer tools and equipment and less specialization (see Kesselman, 1997). There may also be further implications for efficiency if decisions to consume or invest are distorted as a consequence. Kesselman (1997) argues that individuals who participate in the underground economy are more likely to increase their consumption rather than their savings or expenditure on consumer durables because doing so would attract the tax administration's attention. They may even invest very small amounts of human capital in their underground employment in fear that it may only have a short lifespan.

Unregulated Activities

There is also the inevitable consequence of poor work place practices in the underground economy. Goods and services that are provided in the underground economy do not offer the same guarantees of workmanship as one would expect of goods and services provided in the legitimate sector. Unfortunately there are many goods and services that are provided in the legitimate economy under strict health and safety guidelines which ensure adequate consumer protection. However goods and services provided in the underground economy are unlikely to conform in the same way to these guidelines. For example, hairdressers operating legitimately are expected to meet health and safety standards as prescribed in their code of practice. Yet the same hairdresser operating from their backyard after hours may ignore these rules and regulations particularly if it adds to their costs or limits the time the participant has to earn an income in the underground economy. Other examples may include poor plumping and electrical services that may produce significant costs in repairs or pose a fire risk to the occupants.

Income Distribution

Those who are presently on a low income could increase their disposable income by working in the underground economy and claiming to be unemployed in order to receive welfare assistance. The combined income could in most cases exceed the wage received for similar (low paid) work in legitimate economy. The flow of welfare benefits to those who are actively engaged in clandestine activities implies not only an inefficient redistribution of income, but it may also imply that measures of income inequality may be far from what the official statistics suggest (Skolka, 1984).

Are there any Benefits?

Needless to say, there are also some benefits that have been advocated as a consequence of the underground economy. A notable remark by a former Italian Prime Minister highlights the point:

> It is a bad thing to say, but these 'deviations' are a positive thing, at least as far as employment is concerned. If the taxman was to intervene in the underground economy he would be acting in accordance with the principles of distributive justice but would be ruining not only a host of small businessmen and their workers, but perhaps the country's economy and social peace as well. (De Grazia, 1982)

With the exception of employment, a number of others have suggested potential benefits that may accrue from an underground economy. These include:

*   Portes et al. (1989) suggests that the underground economy may adapt faster to changes in economic conditions thereby helping to accelerate structural changes necessary for economic development;
*   Skolka (1984) has suggested that the underground economy may generate positive welfare effects by redistributing income;
*   Prager (1983) has credited the underground economy with the provision of goods that may not otherwise be available in the legitimate economy. Such a statement may be true of less developed economies that may have deficient planning for reallocating resources (Carter, 1984). However for the more developed countries this proposition is unlikely to be true;
*   Harding and Jenkins (1989) argue that not only does the underground economy foster competition, it reduces pressure on wages, stimulating economic growth while keeping inflation low;
*   Operators that have a monopolistic control on the market for the goods and services that they provide, may be made more efficient in the production and distribution as a consequence of those who are operating in the underground economy in the same market for their goods and services (Kesselman, 1997).

As appealing as these may sound, the efficiency gains may only be small and insignificant to outweigh the costs from non-compliance described earlier. There appears to be no evidence at all to suggest that the underground economy does foster structural change that may take place in the legitimate economy. In fact evidence from audits suggests that there is nothing innovative in the underground economy. The activities found to operate in the underground economy are very similar, if not identical, to those occupations found in the legitimate economy. Neither is there any evidence that the underground economy promotes competition. It appears that there are more disadvantages from having a sizeable underground economy than there can be from any benefits that it may have to offer.

Plan of this Book

This book is divided into three parts. *Part 1* contains three chapters that discuss the important topic of taxpayer behaviour and motivations. In Chapter 2, Lars Feld and Bruno Frey deal extensively with what shapes tax morale and what is its interaction with the underground economy. In Chapter 3, Natalie Taylor examines the effects of tax payer identities on voluntary self reporting of tax obligation and in Chapter 4, Valerie Braithwaite, Monika Reinhart and Jenny Job provide an insight into the social demographics that make up those participating in the underground economy in Australia.

Part 2 contains five chapters on measuring the underground economy. In Chapter 5, an extensive international comparison of underground economic activity is given by Friedrich Schneider and Christopher Bajada. In Chapter 6, Dilip Bhattacharyya deals with issues often confronting those researchers attempting to estimate the size of the underground economy. In this work Dilip presents estimates of the underground economy for the United Kingdom. In Chapter 7, Dominik Enste examines the causes of the underground economy for countries in the OECD as well as the EU accession countries. In Chapters 8 and 9, two case studies on the size and development of the underground economy for Norway (by Kari Due Andresen, Tone Ognedal and Steinar Strom) and for Canada (by Lindsay M. Tedds) are presented.

Part 3 contains five chapters on detection, prevention and progress by governments in dealing with underground economic activities. In Chapter 10, Peter S. Spiro provides a survey of how the presence of a sizeable underground economy will effect decisions concerning tax policy and in Chapter 11, Kim M. Bloomquist, Alan H. Plumley and Eric J. Toder analyse the extent of non-tax compliance in the US. In Chapter 12, Christopher Bajada examines, how the UK government has responded to the recommendations made in the Grabiner Report on dealing with underground economic activities and in Chapter 13, he examines the Australian government's attempts to deal with what anecdotal evidence suggests is a growing underground economy. In Chapter 14, Simon James discusses various tax compliance strategies by identifying different risks of non-compliance as a way of tackling the underground economy.

In the remainder of this section is a brief summary of each chapter.

Chapter 2   In this chapter Lars Feld and Bruno Frey take as a starting point that a fundamental result of the tax evasion literature is the mystery why people actually pay taxes given the rather low levels of fines and auditing probabilities. According to their line of argument, the deterrence model of tax evasion cannot explain the high tax compliance rates without specifically referring to an exogenously given tax morale. Feld and Frey show quite convincingly, that tax morale in Switzerland is a function of (1) the fiscal exchange, where tax payers get public services in return for the taxes they pay, (2) the political procedure that leads to this exchange and (3) the personal relationship between tax payers and tax administrators.

Chapter 3   This chapter examines the effects of taxpayer identities on voluntary self reporting of tax obligations. Natalie Taylor finds that taxpayers perceptions of themselves in relation to the tax authorities, the behaviour of other tax payers and the tax system itself, affects the way they comply with their tax paying obligations. One of the most important factors found to be affecting the degree of compliance is the fairness and the integrity of the tax system and those who administer it. When these are not present, the tax authority must depend heavily on threat and coercion as a means to enforce compliance. However more often than not such compliance is not only costly but is likely to be ineffective because effective surveillance is not possible in the underground economy.

Chapter 4   This chapter provides an insight into the social demographics that make up those participating in the underground economy in Australia. Purchasers of underground economy services tend to be educated, full-time male employees while suppliers of underground services tend to be younger, less educated consumers. The authors find that the underground economy is not only widespread and visible in the community, but surprisingly tolerated. This is despite personal beliefs of those surveyed that suggests participating in the underground economy is wrong.

Chapter 5   This chapter provides an international comparison of the size and development of the underground economy for 145 countries during the period 1999/2000 to 2002/2003. The results suggest that the underground worldwide has been growing steadily during this period: from 33.6 percent of official GDP during 1999/2000 to 35.2 percent of official GDP by 2002/2003. The major driving forces behind the growing underground economy are the tax and social security burden, combined with an increased government regulation, particularly in the labour market.

Chapter 6   In this chapter, Dilip Bhattacharyya discusses the issues often confronting those researchers attempting to estimate the size of the underground economy. The application and extensions of his earlier work (see Bhattacharyya, 1990), produces a number of interesting results than may interest researchers in this area. His application to the UK suggests that the underground economy is an important public policy issue for the government to address.

Chapter 7   This chapter examines the causes of the underground economy for countries in the OECD as well as the EU accession countries. Confirming earlier results, this paper finds that the burden of taxation and social security contributions as well as the burden of regulation has contributed to an increase in the underground economy in the OECD countries. For those countries in economic transition, the influence of corruption, economic freedom and the quality of institutions add to this earlier list of factors influencing the size of the underground economy. Interestingly two thirds of the variance of the underground economy in the OECD and in the transition countries is explained by the quality of the institutions.

Chapter 8   In this chapter, survey data from Norway spanning the period between 1980 and 2003 provides an insight into the development of the underground economy. The findings suggest that unreported work over this time has gone down from 20 percent to 10 percent. Interestingly the marginal tax rate reform was not found to be a significant factor driving down the extent of undeclared work. Some important factors found to influence this result include the growth in jobs in the public sector and in large corporations as well as the growth in labour market participation by women.

Chapter 9 This chapter presents an updated estimate of the underground economy in Canada. It extends on the earlier work of Giles and Tedds (2002) by (i) modelling additional explanatory variables suggested by the literature to contribute to underground economy participation and (ii) improving on the econometric technique previously developed. The results clearly suggest that the size of the underground economy in Canada has increased substantially in recent years.

Chapter 10 This chapter provides a survey of how the presence of a sizeable underground economy will affect decisions concerning tax policy. This chapter considers the important distinction between income and consumption taxes and their effects on the underground economy, as well as a comparison of the effects of a Value Added Tax versus a Retail Sales Tax. A number of other important issues are discussed in the context of the underground economy and tax policy including, the scope of commodity substitution and the structure of the business sector. The emphasis on both microeconomic and macroeconomic estimates of the underground economy for tax policy purposes is argued to be an important exercise researchers should engage themselves in.

Chapter 11 This chapter provides some insight into the extent of tax non-compliance in the US, particularly the areas where non-compliance is of greatest concern. The use of a tax gap map may not only help visualise the structural composition of the tax gap but provide a relative comparison of the various sources of tax-non compliance affecting the revenue sources of the IRS. This chapter also discusses at some length the recent initiatives undertaken by the IRS to tackle underground economic activity in the United States, particularly for offshore financial transactions and tax shelters.

Chapter 12 This chapter examines the UK government's response to the recommendations made in the Grabiner Report on dealing with underground economic activities in the UK. This discussion highlights the fact that the majority of the recommendations of the Grabiner Report have since been implemented and the results are beginning to have a positive impact on reducing the growth of underground activities particularly in a number of problematic areas such as welfare and housing benefit fraud, tobacco and alcohol fraud and VAT missing trader fraud.

Chapter 13 This chapter examines the Australian government attempts to deal with what anecdotal evidence suggests is a growing underground economy in Australia. With the institution of the Cash Economy Task Force (CETF) in 1996, the Australian Tax Office has been guided by its recommendations (as well as from business and community input) in its attempt to deal with illicit activities. Although efforts are still on-going, a number of CETF recommendations have been implemented. The evidence provided by the Australian Taxation Office suggests that its renewed efforts are beginning to impact positively on underground economy activities in Australia. This chapter reviews the various recommendations published in its three reports, followed by a discussion on the government's progress in addressing these recommendations.

Chapter 14 In this chapter Simon James discusses various tax compliance strategies to tackle participation in the underground economy. He raises an important issue that is sometimes often overlooked: that tax compliance strategies need to be carefully crafted so that one area of compliance is not compromised by vigilant enforcement action in another area. This chapter provides a general approach to developing an effective tax compliance strategy by way of identifying different risks of non-compliance, analysing compliance behaviour and implementing strategies.

References

Bajada, C. (2003), 'Business Cycle Properties of the Legitimate and Underground Economy in Australia', *Economic Record*, Vol. 79. pp. 397-411.

Berger, S. (1986), 'The Unrecorded Economy: Concepts, Approach and Preliminary Estimates for Canada 1981', *Canadian Statistical Review*, Statistics Canada, Cat 11-003E.

Bhattacharyya, D.K. (1990), 'An Econometric Method of Estimating the Hidden Economy, United Kingdom (1960-1984): Estimates and Tests', *The Economic Journal*, Vol. 100, September, pp. 703-17.

Carson, C.S. (1984), 'The Underground Economy: An Introduction', *Survey of Current Business*, Vol. 64(5), pp. 21-37.

Carter, M. (1984), 'Issues in the Hidden Economy – A Survey', *Economic Record*, Vol. 60, No. 170, pp. 209-21.

De Grazia, R. (1982), 'Clandestine Employment: A Problem of Our Times', in V. Tanzi (1982), pp. 29-44.

Giles, D.E.A. (1999), 'Modeling the Hidden Economy and the Tax-Gap in New Zealand', *Empirical Economics*, Vol. 24. pp. 621-40.

Giles, D.E.A. and Tedds, L.M. (2002), *Taxes and the Canadian Underground Economy*, Canadian Tax Foundation, Paper No.106, Canada.

Greenfield, H.I. (1993*), Invisible, Outlawed and Untaxed: America's Underground Economy*, Praeger Publishers, London.

Hansson, I. (1982), 'The Underground Economy in a High Tax Country: The Case of Sweden', in V. Tanzi (1982), pp. 233-43.

Harding, P. and Jenkins, R. (1989), *The Myth of the Hidden Economy*, Open University Press, Philadelphia.

Houston, J.F. (1990), 'The Policy Implications of the Underground Economy', *Journal of Economics and Business*, Vol. 42(1), pp. 27-37.

Kesselman, J.R. (1997), 'Policy Implications of Tax Evasion and the Underground Economy', in O. Lippert and M. Walker (1997), pp. 293-317.

Lippert, O. and Walker, M. (1997), *The Underground Economy: Global Evidence of its Size and Impact*, The Fraser Institute, Vancouver, BC, Canada.

McDonald, R.J. (1984), The Underground Economy and BLS Statistics Data, *Monthly Labour Review*, January, pp. 4-18.

Portes, A., Castells, M. and Benton, L. (1989), *The Informal Economy: Studies in Advanced and Less Developed Countries*, Johns Hopkins University Press, Baltimore.

Prager, J. (1983), 'Two Cheers for the Underground Economy', *Economic Policy Papers*, Centre for Applied Economics, New York University.

Priest, G. (1994), 'The Ambiguous Moral Foundations of the Underground Economy', *Yale Law Journal*, Vol. 103(8), pp. 2259-88.

Reuter, P. (1982), 'The Irregular Economy and The Quality of Macroeconomic Statistics', in V. Tanzi (ed.) (1982), pp. 125-43.

Skolka, J. (1984), 'A Few Facts About the Hidden Economy Seminar – The Unofficial Economy, Consequences and Policies in the West and East', cited in Mirus, R., Smith, R.S. and Karoleff, V. (1984), *Canadian Public Policy*, Vol. 20(3), pp. 235-52.

Tanzi, V. (1982), *The Underground Economy in the United States and Abroad*, Lexington Books, Massachusetts.

PART 1

TAXPAYER BEHAVIOUR AND MOTIVATIONS

PART I

TAXPAYER BEHAVIOR AND
MOTIVATIONS

Chapter 2

Illegal, Immoral, Fattening or What?: How Deterrence and Responsive Regulation Shape Tax Morale

Lars P. Feld and Bruno S. Frey

There should be no place in our organization for brusqueness, incourtesy, or arrogance. We want the bureau representative to meet the taxpayer and discuss his problems sympathetically, understandingly, frankly and fairly ... Secretary of the U.S. Treasury (1929)

Introduction

The puzzle of the economic theory of tax compliance is why people do pay taxes. According to the seminal study by Allingham and Sandmo (1972), which in turn is based on Becker's (1968) economic theory of crime, the extent of deterrence, as the product of the probability of being detected and the size of the fine imposed, determines the amount of income evaded. However, in view of the low deterrence applied in most countries, either because of a low intensity of control or small penalties, taxpayers should evade more than they actually do, i.e. compliance is too high. For the United States, Alm, McClelland and Schulze (1992, p. 22) argue: *A purely economic analysis of the evasion gamble implies that most individuals would evade if they are 'rational', because it is unlikely that cheaters will be caught and penalized.* Arrow-Pratt measures of risk aversion of more than 30 must exist in order to account for the present compliance rate in the U.S. Graetz and Wilde (1985) or Alm, McClelland and Schulze (1992) report however a range of between one and two for the U.S.

Two strands of arguments can be explored in order to close the gap between theory and facts (see the extensive surveys on tax compliance by Andreoni, Erard and Feinstein 1998, Slemrod and Yitzhaki 2002 and Torgler 2003). On the one hand, the probability of being detected is subjective. This might first imply that individual perceptions of being caught when cheating on the tax code are much higher than objective probabilities of detection. Such misperceptions of risk by individuals (which is supported by experimental research) are however unsustainable over a longer time horizon where people can infer control intensities from friends and relatives. Second, subjective probabilities of being caught exist in the sense that the individual ability to evade taxes strongly varies among subgroups of the population. For example, withholding taxes strongly reduce auditing costs of tax administrations because auditing of firms suffices to obtain information on employees' labor incomes. Moreover, it can be conjectured that income generated in the industrial sector can be less easily evaded than those in the services sector, that capital income is more easily evaded than labor income and so on. Adding socio-demographic structure and details of the auditing process could hence help to explain the poor performance of traditional economic tax compliance models.

On the other hand, tax morale serves as an explanation for high compliance rates in OECD countries.[1] In the approach of Allingham and Sandmo (1972), tax morale residually explains the level of tax compliance independent of tax policy and the behavior of state authorities. This argument is consistent with the view that fundamental social norms, like religion or civic duty, shape tax morale. Moreover, informal social control independent from auditing efforts by the tax office might increase compliance rates. For example, the leisure class might exaggerate the exposition of wealth such that envy of less affluent taxpayers leads to investigations by the tax administration.[2] In contrast to these supposedly policy-independent norms, four different types of reciprocity norms that depend on government policy, tax authorities' behavior and state institutions might increase tax morale: first, citizens pay their taxes if their fellow citizens contribute their fair share (Feld and Tyran 2002). In that respect, traditional deterrence policy is rather delicate, because the tax office can mistakenly forego to audit tax cheaters (who additionally tell their friends and relatives about it). Continued public discussion about the decline of tax morale serves the same purpose: honest taxpayers arrive at the perception that they are the last to remain so stupid to comply with the tax code.

Second, the government provides public services to citizens in exchange for their tax payments. If the fiscal equivalence between public goods and tax prices is violated by setting those prices too high, citizens think they have a justification for evading taxes.[3] Third, citizens perceive their tax payments as contributions to the '*bonum commune*' such that they are willing to honestly declare their income even if they do not receive a full public good equivalent to their tax payments. For example they might be net contributors to the welfare state. Income redistribution is the more accepted by affluent citizens the more the political process is perceived to be fair and the more policy outcomes are legitimate.[4] In that respect, a classic second mistake of traditional deterrence policy should be mentioned. The tax authority might erroneously audit honest taxpayers who then feel unhappy about the violation of their privacy. Fourth, the way the tax office treats taxpayers in auditing processes plays a role. As Frey and Feld (2002) and Feld and Frey (2002, 2002a) argue, taxpayers and tax authorities are engaged in a psychological tax contract in which fiscal exchange is implicitly specified. The implicit contract about fiscal exchange presupposes that taxpayers and the tax authority treat each other as partners of a contract, i.e. with mutual respect and honesty. If tax administrations instead treat taxpayers as inferiors in a hierarchical relationship, this psychological tax contract is violated and citizens have good reason not to stick to their part of the contract and to evade taxes. Braithwaite (2003) is speaking of responsive regulation in this context.

Because the traditional economic approach to tax evasion does not appear to be successful in explaining tax compliance and since reciprocity norms that establish an exchange relationship between the state and the citizens shape tax morale, a case study of Switzerland appears to be particularly useful. The reason for such an assessment was already emphasized by Georg von Schanz (1890, I, p. 114) who argued that Switzerland should provide fertile ground for tax compliance analysis because the small size of the cantons and their direct democratic political systems establish a close exchange relationship between taxpayers and tax authorities. In the next section of this chapter, the analysis by Schanz is hence briefly summarized in order to trace the traditional Swiss approach to tax compliance. Many of the arguments that are systematically analyzed in subsequent research already show up in this historical account. How tax evasion in Switzerland evolved over time according to different estimates in the literature is discussed in the subsequent section. The impact of traditional economic and legal, socio-demographic, psychological and institutional factors on Swiss tax evasion is analyzed next by summarizing the studies by Feld and Frey (2002) and Frey and Feld (2002). These results are put into perspective in the final section by relating them to the existing literature.

Early Accounts of Tax Evasion in Switzerland

Georg von Schanz, who invented comprehensive individual income for taxation purposes, published his five volumes on taxation in Switzerland in 1890. Until today it is the most comprehensive collection of Swiss tax provisions and their analysis. It covers all tax laws of the then 25 cantons as well as their development in the 19th century. It goes without saying that this collection is providing precious insights into Swiss tax culture.[5] To understand Swiss tax history of the 19th century, it is worth noting at the outset that the main power to tax income and wealth originated with the Swiss cantons at that time. The federation founded in 1848 only received contributions from the cantons, tariff and indirect tax revenues. The historic situation in Switzerland was hence not much different from that of other federal states like Germany or the U.S. in the 19th century. What may be surprising however to many observers is the fact that today the cantons still have the basic power to tax (personal and corporate) income, property and wealth while the federal level has its own (highly progressive) income tax and the local jurisdictions levy a surcharge on cantonal taxes.[6]

Five features of Swiss tax culture as described by Schanz mainly shape individual tax compliance until today. First, with the exception of a withholding tax on capital income introduced together with the federal income tax during the Second World War, individual and corporate income is not taxed at source. Taxable income is derived on the basis of a system of individual self-assessment. Documents of the canton of Basel provide early evidence for such a system when (a kind of) income taxation in 1804 started with voluntary tax payments: 'The

Great Council chose a method of tax collection which did not reveal how much each individual paid' (Schanz 1890, II, p. 6, our translation). The cantonal government of Basel was however not satisfied with that method and increased the intensity of control since 1812 by demanding taxpayers to declare their income under oath (Schanz 1890, II, p. 9). A similar method was chosen by the canton of Geneva in 1815 (Schanz 1890, IV, p. 204) which additionally introduced a commission for the income assessment of taxpayers in 1864 and penalties in 1871 because of unsatisfactory results of the method of voluntary tax payment (Meier 1984, p. 498). Auditing efforts were subsequently intensified in all cantons in the second half of the 19th century. Self-assessment forms required a detailed balance of income and wealth in the cantons of Zurich since 1871 and of Fribourg in 1862 for example (Schanz 1890, II, p. 414, IV, pp. 7 and 21). In other cantons, like e.g. Schaffhausen from 1862 to 1879, the assignment of responsibilities in tax auditing switched from the local to the cantonal level in order to reduce the personal involvement of tax commissioners (Schanz 1890, II, pp. 178 and 183). Interestingly enough, self-assessment remained the rule of income reporting until recent times. Swiss cantons have still not switched to a system of withholding taxation. Even when individuals do not submit their tax forms at all, the tax authorities only estimate income or assets (Kucher and Götte 1998). A switch to withholding taxation is not seriously considered.

Second, Swiss taxpayers are well aware of the fiscal exchange between public goods or services, and tax prices. It is interesting to note that a voluntary school tax in the canton of Glarus provided sufficient revenue to finance education services over a longer period (Schanz 1980, III, p. 98), while a voluntary welfare tax to redistribute income in the canton of Appenzell i. Rh. had to be quickly turned into coercive taxation (Schanz 1890, III, p. 10). Moreover, new taxes were more easily introduced in Swiss cantons when the additional revenue could be justified by financing needs from new public goods or services. This was the case in Appenzell i. Rh. in 1804 where it was argued that the additional revenue was needed to finance law enforcement measures – and a visit of the bishop of the Roman-Catholic church (Schanz 1890, III, p. 3). Similarly, Basel-County received the popular consent to levy direct taxes again in 1871 in order to finance cantonal investments. However, the tax increase in 1876 that was supposed to cover budget deficits politically failed. Another attempt in 1887 was finally adopted in order to finance the cantonal hospital (Schanz 1890, II, pp. 116).

Third, in the majority of cases tax laws must be decided by citizens in an obligatory referendum. The examples of tax changes just mentioned were also politically decided in referendums or cantonal assemblies. Schanz was reluctant to acknowledge the usefulness of these political procedures. On the one hand, he mourned that concessions to citizens in referendums violated principles of just taxation. On the other hand, he realized that peoples' consent to an introduction of new taxes or to tax increases did not lead to any major problems in the cantons (Schanz 1890, I, pp. 49 and 52). Meier (1984, p. 496) shows some understanding for Schanz' perspective as he was a tax expert who viewed direct democracy as an unnecessary restriction to rational taxation. Meier also criticized that referendums entailed a stressful bargaining process with uncertain and often stochastic outcomes. Meanwhile, instruments of direct democracy are however positively assessed with respect to their impact on tax morale. Pommerehne and Weck-Hannemann (1996) argue that governments in direct democratic cantons provide public goods and services that are more strongly in line with citizens' preferences which in turn reduces taxpayers' incentives to evade taxes. The evidence described by Schanz indicates that direct democracy in Switzerland established a process of mutual learning between the government (and its bureau) and citizens in which cantonal governments had to find out citizens' preferences for public services and citizens realized their willingness to pay for them. In that process an exchange relationship between the state and the citizens could develop without any major disturbances. Institutions of direct democracy indeed served to procedurally establish the Wicksellian (1896) connection between public services and tax prices.

Fourth, increases in deterrence measures are often coupled with positive incentives. When Schaffhausen increased deterrence in 1879 by shifting auditing responsibilities from the local to the cantonal level, increasing penalties and publishing tax registers, it also reduced the administrative pressure on taxpayers. Taxpayers obtained the benefit of a doubt by conceding that they may erroneously declare up to 4 percent less than true income without any penalty. Moreover, no penalties were imposed if taxpayers voluntarily declared a higher income or wealth in their periodic tax declaration. Hence a standing tax amnesty was introduced in the case of self-declaration of taxpayers (Schanz 1890, II, p. 180). The government of Glarus did not consider a penalty because it was supposed to induce taxpayers to evade wealth in the case of bequests. After several experiments to enhance tax compliance by increased deterrence, Neuchâtel started to differentiate between tax evasion and tax fraud in 1867 and subsequently decreased penalties by nearly half for tax evasion (Schanz 1890, IV, pp. 63-82). The distinction between tax evasion as an administratively investigated offense that does not entail previous conviction, and tax fraud as a criminal offense, when forgery of a document can be proved, still prevails in Switzerland. It is a distinction unique in OECD countries today.

Fifth, in some cases Swiss tax authorities rely on social control in addition to official audits in order to increase tax compliance rates. In the 19th century, several cantons started to publish the tax registers in which the taxes paid by Swiss residents in each community of the canton were denoted. It was an attempt to increase the probability of detection with social control in the community as a complement to auditing by government authorities. A mixture of moral suasion by and envy of their fellow citizens was supposed to increase tax morale of tax cheaters. For example, Schaffhausen hoped to increase tax compliance by publication of tax registers in 1879. In addition, taxpayers that were found guilty of tax evasion were prohibited to enter bars and restaurants for up to 5 years. The names of those people were also published in all bars and restaurants in that area (Schanz 1890, II, p. 182). Similar measures were imposed by the canton of Bern in 1889 (Schanz 1890, III, p. 310). Schanz was very pessimistic about the success of published tax registers because he conjectured that honest taxpayers would reduce their tax compliance once they realized that their neighbors successfully evaded taxes (Schanz 1890, I, p. 120). Today, a few cantons still publish tax registers, like e.g. Bern, Luzern, Fribourg or Vaud, while the success has never been systematically assessed.

All in all, these early discussions of Swiss tax culture by Georg von Schanz pretty well reveal basic principles of tax compliance in Switzerland. Taxpayers are fundamentally taken seriously as partners in a (psychological) tax contract. The first institution that ensures this contractual relationship is the procedural establishment of fiscal exchange by direct democratic decision-making that subsequently shapes the material existence of fiscal exchange in the Swiss cantons. Second, taxpayers are not treated as inferiors in a hierarchical relationship. Increases in deterrence in the 19th century were often accompanied by a relaxation of government intrusion in individual privacy. Taxpayers were and still are given the benefit of a doubt. Third, Swiss cantons (more or less consciously) establish a relationship of trust by sticking to self-assessment procedures. While a major source of under-declaration of income became less important by the introduction of the withholding tax on capital income during the Second World War, sufficient possibilities to evade different forms of income still exist. However, taxation of labor income at source is not seriously discussed in Switzerland. Finally, the reliance on social control as a complement to auditing by tax authorities is typical for a society in which state institutions evolved from self-organized communities over time. The Swiss federation is a bottom up polity such that it appears natural to use the strong social ties existing at the local level. However, the usefulness of the publication of tax registers is ambiguous.

The Level of Tax Evasion in Switzerland

The measurement of income tax evasion is necessarily difficult because individual incentives to truthfully reveal the share of income evaded are minimal. With the exception of eliciting a general attitude to tax morale, like it is asked in the World Value Survey (see again Torgler's 2003 outstanding dissertation), surveys among the population are not useful to assess the level of tax evasion. Hence indirect measurement methods have to be developed. In 1864, the tax office of Geneva estimated that only half of the taxable individual wealth was effectively declared (Meier 1984, p. 497) without saying anything about the measurement method. During the period 1860 to 1869, the canton of Zurich estimated about the same amount of evaded wealth on the basis of public assessments of bequeathed assets (Schneider 1929). About a century later in 1962, the federal government estimated the extent of tax evasion again in a widely recognized report on 'tax defraudation' in Switzerland. Based on that capital income for which a tax credit from the withholding tax on capital income was not claimed, tax evasion was estimated to amount to 645 million SFR which is about 2 percent of official GDP in 1962 (Higy 1962/63, p. 510, Pommerehne 1983, p. 267).[7] According to Higy (1962/63), the federal government in this report expected that labor income of between 1.3 and 1.5 billion SFr was evaded. The Commission Justitia and Pax (1981) of the Swiss bishops' conference estimated tax evasion from capital income in 1978 to be again

600 million SFr by using the same method as the federal government in 1962. In the last general tax amnesty in Switzerland of 1969 however, 1.15 billion SFr could be additionally taxed. The additional revenue was about 6 percent of income and wealth tax revenue in that year (Pommerehne and Zweifel 1991, Feld 2003, Torgler, Schaltegger and Schaffner 2003).

These early estimates are more or less unsystematic and incomplete, they often focus too strongly on capital income, they are not very transparent and appear to be rather ad hoc. A very popular indirect method to estimate the level of tax evasion is the GAP method according to which the difference is calculated between national accounts measures of primary income and income reported to the tax authorities in percent of the national accounts measure of primary income (Schneider and Enste 2000).[8] While the national accounts data compute the purchasing side, the tax data indicate income accrual. Differences between both reveal that more is spent than is officially earned and thus raise the suspicion of tax evasion. This method can only be employed if both measures are calculated independently from each other. Pommerehne and Weck-Hannemann (1996) have used this approach to analyze the factors influencing the level of income tax evasion in Switzerland for the years 1965, 1970 and 1978. Feld and Frey (2002) and Frey and Feld (2002) have extended their data set to the years 1985, 1990 and 1995. In all of these years, the independent accounting of primary national income by the federal tax administration and the federal statistical office could be ensured.

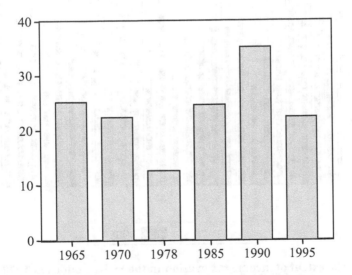

Figure 1   The average level of income tax evasion in the Swiss cantons from 1965 to 1995 (in percent of gross household income)

Figure 1 shows the level of income tax evasion according to these estimates between 1965 and 1995. It is evident that tax evasion is much larger according to these estimates than is suggested by the informed guesstimates discussed before. Tax evasion varies between 12.6 percent in 1978 and 35.1 percent in 1990. Figure 2 indicates the variation of these estimates across the cantons for 1970 and 1995. As can be seen, there are substantial differences between the 26 cantons. In 1995, tax evasion was highest in the cantons Uri, Thurgau, Schaffhausen, Zug and Geneva, and lowest (with less than 15 percent) in the cantons Appenzell a. Rh., Appenzell i. Rh. and the Valais. The average for all the cantons in 1995 is 22.3 percent. It is important to note that tax evasion has changed considerably over time in many cantons. While tax evasion decreased in some cantons, like in Schwyz, Obwalden, Nidwalden and Graubünden, it has risen sharply in others, most notably in the two city cantons of Basle-City and Geneva. In both cantons, tax compliance declined steadily over time leading to a large difference between the first and last year of the observation period.

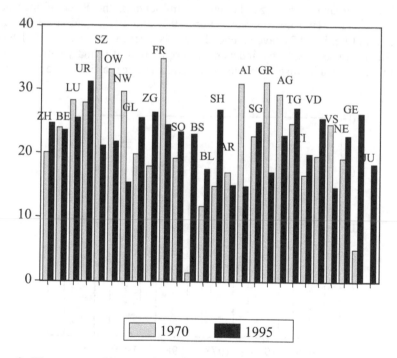

Figure 2   The extent of income tax evasion in the Swiss cantons in 1970 and 1995 (in percent of gross household income)

To put these estimates into perspective, it is useful to confront them with the development of the shadow economy in Switzerland. Since the preferred estimates of Schneider (2000) are based on the currency demand approach it can be argued that it captures labor income to a larger extent than capital income. If this were correct, the size of the shadow economy should be lower than that of tax evasion because capital income supposedly makes up for a larger share of tax evasion. Figure 3 shows the estimates for the Swiss shadow economy from 1975 to 2002. In contrast to the estimates of tax evasion in Figure 1, the variation of the shadow economy over time much less follows a cyclical pattern, but is characterized by a steady increase since 1985. In addition, the size of the shadow economy is less than half the extent of tax evasion. Figure 4 contains the size of the shadow economy in the Swiss cantons in 1995 according to Schneider's (2000) estimates on the basis of currency demand. What is interesting in reflecting the cantonal variation is the fact that the cantons with the largest shadow economies in 1995 are also those that have high levels of tax evasion in 1970. According to Figure 2, the cantonal structure of income tax evasion in 1995 however markedly differs reflecting the fact that tax evasion is not as common in rural or mountainous areas as in earlier times. This development supports the conjecture that tax evasion is nowadays more heavily driven by capital income tax evasion than it was in the sixties or seventies.

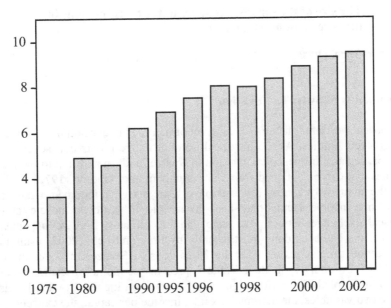

Figure 3   The size of the shadow economy in Switzerland from 1975 to 2002 (in percent of national income)

Source: Schneider (2000)

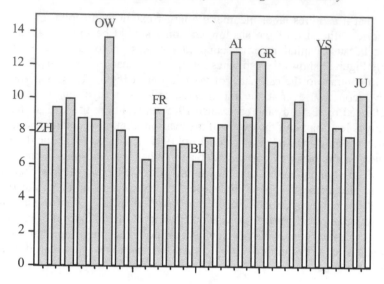

Figure 4   The size of the shadow economy in the Swiss cantons in 1995 (in percent of national income)

Source: Schneider (2000)

Determinants of Swiss Tax Evasion

The impact of different factors on the level of income tax evasion has been realized only in a few studies. As the historical account above points out, several factors might particularly influence tax evasion in Switzerland. In addition to the standard variables that can be obtained from the Allingham and Sandmo (1972) model, i.e. fines, the intensity of control of the taxpayers, the marginal income tax rate and the level of true income, factors that shape tax morale, in particular those establishing the fiscal exchange between the state and the citizens, need to be taken into account. This has been done most recently by Frey and Feld (2002) using pooled cross section time series data for the 26 cantons of Switzerland over the period 1970-1995. Column (1) in their Table 1 presents econometric estimates for the effect of the probability of detection and of the fine on income evaded. In addition to these two variables, the marginal tax rate, income per capita, the existence of tax indexation to inflation, population size, the proportion of people older than 65 years, the share of self-employment from total employment, the share of employment in the agricultural sector and time dummies are also included as explanatory variables. The OLS regression in column (1) of Table 1 indicates that the basic tax evasion model is not performing in a satisfactory way. While more than 70 percent of tax evasion in the cantons can be traced, only the size of the fine for tax evasion is statistically significant at the 5 percent level in the OLS estimate, and only at the 10 percent level in the TSLS estimate in column (2). The probability of detection is far from being statistically significant and moreover has a theoretically unexpected positive sign suggesting that people evade more taxes the more intensively they are controlled. In addition, the marginal tax rate has a significant positive impact on tax evasion on the 1 percent significance level.

These results are disappointing for the standard model of tax evasion because the main deterrence variables are only weakly significant if at all and partly have theoretically unexpected signs. The results are not due to outliers as the Jarque-Bera-test statistics indicate. In all equations, the hypothesis of normal distribution of the residuals cannot be rejected according to those test statistics. Only demographic variables like the proportion of people older than 65 years, the share of self-employment from total employment and the share of employment in the agricultural sector have an additional statistically significant influence on tax evasion. All in all, it has to be concluded that the crucial explanatory variables of the standard model of tax evasion do not fare well in empirical tests. This is not a specific feature of an application of the model to the case of Switzerland but has also been observed in a great number of empirical studies for the U.S. (Clotfelder 1983 for a positive impact of the marginal tax rate; Beron, Tauchen and Witte 1992 and Slemrod, Blumenthal and Christian 2001 for a sometimes even significant positive impact of the probability of detection on tax evasion in some income groups). Hence, an investigation on the factors influencing the fiscal exchange relationship is necessary to understand Swiss tax evasion.

The Treatment of Taxpayers

As contended above, the way tax administrations treat taxpayers has an impact on taxpayers' behavior. Based on Crowding Theory (Frey 1997a), Frey and Feld (2002) argue that a systematic relationship between external intervention (in this case, how the tax officials deal with taxpayers) and intrinsic motivation (in this case, individuals' tax morale) exists. Deterrence is only one of the motivational forces in getting people to pay their taxes. Quite another is the set of policies available to the tax authority to bolster taxpayers' tax morale. A 'respectful' relationship of the tax authorities to the taxpayers crowds in tax morale while an 'authoritarian' relationship using instruments of deterrence has two countervailing effects: on the one hand the change in relative prices (the higher probability of being punished) reduces the incentives to evade taxes, but on the other hand tax morale is crowded out. Which effect dominates depends on specific circumstances. The tax officials can choose between these extremes in many different ways. For instance, when they detect an error in the tax declaration, they can immediately suspect an intention to cheat, and impose legal sanctions. Alternatively, the tax officials may give the taxpayers the benefit of a doubt and inquire about the reason for the error. If the taxpayer in question indeed did not intend to cheat but simply made a mistake, he or she will most likely be offended by the disrespectful treatment of the tax authority. The feeling of being controlled in a negative way, and being suspected of tax cheating, tends to crowd out the intrinsic motivation to act as an honorable taxpayer and, as a consequence, tax morale will fall. In contrast, if the tax official makes an effort to locate the reason for the error by contacting the taxpayer in an informal way (e.g. by phoning him or her), the taxpayer will appreciate this respectful treatment and tax morale will be upheld.

Table 1   Unbalanced panel regressions of cantonal share of income evaded in percent of true income upon treatment by the tax authority and control variables, 1970 to 1995

Variables	OLS (1)	TSLS (2)
Probability of Detection Measured as the Number of Tax Auditors per Taxpayer (in %)	0.021 (1.56)	0.024 (1.15)
Standard Fine as a Multiple of the Evaded Tax Amount (in %)	-0.030* (2.19)	-0.041(*) (1.86)
Maximum Marginal Tax Rate (in %)	0.470** (3.19)	0.442** (2.84)
Gross Effective Primary Income per Capita (in 1'000 SFr)	0.199 (1.31)	0.186 (1.11)
Tax Indexation, Dummy = 1 if there is an indexation to inflation, and 0 otherwise	-0.791 (0.85)	-0.709 (0.76)
Population (in 1'000)	-0.001 (0.28)	-0.001 (0.56)
Proportion of People older than 65 (in %)	-0.579** (2.72)	-0.610* (2.45)
Share of Self-Employment from Total Employment (in %)	-0.605* (2.34)	-0.661* (2.26)
Share of Employment in the Agricultural Sector (in %)	0.482** (3.74)	0.416* (2.52)
F-Test: Time Dummies	45.179**	48.841**
$\bar{R}^2$	0.719	0.750
SER	4.915	4.718
J.-B.	2.705	0.053

Source: Frey and Feld (2002), Table 1

Notes: instruments are the amount of evaded income from true income, the probability of detection and the standard fine all three of the former period. OLS has 128, TSLS 102 observations. The numbers in parentheses are the t-statistics of the estimated parameters based on White heteroscedasticity consistent standard errors. The F-statistics test the joint significance of the mentioned variables. SER is the standard error of regression, J.-B. is the value of the Jarque-Bera-Statistic for normality of the residuals. '(*)', '*', or '**' denotes significance at the 10, 5, or 1 percent level, respectively. The computations were performed in EViews, Version 3.1.

Table 2   **Unbalanced panel regressions of cantonal share of income evaded in percent of true income, exogenous government behavior, 1970 to 1995**

Variables	TSLS (3)	TSLS (4)	TSLS (5)
Typical Procedure if No Tax Declaration	2.908**	3.712**	2.153*
	(2.97)	(3.49)	(2.21)
Respectful Procedure	-4.574*	-5.726**	5.783
	(2.61)	(3.84)	(0.86)
'Authoritarian' Procedure	-3.888*	-6.673*	-7.129
	(2.06)	(3.31)	(0.88)
Respectful Procedure * Direct Democracy	–	–	-2.529*
			(2.01)
'Authoritarian' Procedure * Direct Democracy	–	–	0.844
			(0.49)
Index of Direct Democracy	–	-2.291**	-0.462
		(3.14)	(0.33)
Probability of Detection (in ‰)	0.057*	0.066**	0.035
	(2.43)	(2.74)	(1.50)
Standard Fine (in %)	-0.059**	-0.055*	-0.064**
	(3.00)	(2.48)	(2.72)
Marginal Tax Rate (in %)	0.475**	0.709**	0.718**
	(3.37)	(4.92)	(5.26)
Income per Capita (in 1'000 SFr)	0.428*	0.353*	0.423**
	(2.40)	(2.20)	(2.65)
Tax Indexation	-0.321	-1.038	-0.365
	(0.30)	(0.91)	(0.32)
Population (in 1'000)	-0.002	-0.005(*)	-0.006*
	(0.96)	(1.94)	(2.26)
Proportion of People older than 65 (%)	-0.420(*)	-0.463(*)	-0.778**
	(1.71)	(1.95)	(3.09)
Share of Self-Employment from Total Employment (in %)	-0.605*	-0.687*	-0.581*
	(2.12)	(2.61)	(2.34)
Share of Employment in the Agricultural Sector (in %)	0.329(*)	0.403**	0.329*
	(1.95)	(2.69)	(2.14)
Dummy for French and Italian Speaking Cantons	–	-7.432**	-6.786**
		(3.10)	(3.08)
F-Test: Respectful Equals Authoritarian	0.284	0.315	7.829*
F-Test: Direct Democracy	–	–	9.485**
F-Test: Respectful Procedure	–	–	18.284**
F-Test: 'Authoritarian' Procedure	–	–	1.222
$\overline{R}^2$	0.767	0.798	0.814
SER	4.559	4.242	4.072
J.-B.	0.535	1.846	0.877

Source: Frey and Feld (2002), Table 2

Notes: see Table 1.

In order to investigate the relationship between taxpayers and tax authorities, Feld and Frey (2002) sent a survey to the tax authorities of the 26 Swiss cantons which asked detailed questions about the legal background of tax evasion, like the use and size of fines, whether an explicit link is established between tax payments and the provision of public services, the perceived feedback effect of tax evasion on the level of public services, the intensity of control by tax authorities, the existence of tax amnesties, and whether the tax register is published in a jurisdiction. The survey also included questions on the treatment of taxpayers by tax authorities in day-to-day audits, in particular when a taxpayer is suspected of not declaring his or her true taxable income.

In particular the extent of respectful treatment of the taxpayers is captured by (1) Fully observing procedures based on formal and informal rules, i.e. what happens typically if a taxpayer does not declare taxable income at all (procedures, fines), if a tax declaration is mistakenly filled out or, in a second stage, if taxpayers do not react?; (2) Acknowledgment of individual citizens' rights and personality, i.e. what does the tax administration do if taxpayers declared taxable income by mistake too high? Are there any differences in the treatment whether these mistakes are formally wrong, e.g. mistakes in adding up columns of figures, or possibilities for legal tax avoidance, e.g. tax deductions, are not used? Are there attempts to find out whether taxpayers intentionally or mistakenly declare too low a taxable income? Are mistakes in the tax declaration to the advantage or to the disadvantage of taxpayers?; (3) Avoidance of high penalties for minor offenses and giving taxpayers the benefit of a doubt: what are the minimum, maximum and standard fines for tax evasion, the fines in the case of inheritances and of self-declaration, as a multiple of the tax payment (or in percent of the tax payment)? Deterrence is considered by clearly establishing taxpayers' legal duties and penalties for not complying: is the criminal code applied in the case of tax fraud, i.e. is it possible to impose a prison sentence or a monetary fine? Which is the maximum monetary fine in the case of tax fraud (maximum fine in thousands of Swiss Francs)? What is the average monetary fine for tax fraud? Are the monetary fines for tax fraud added to the fine for tax evasion if tax fraud is part of the criminal code? What is the maximum prison sentence for tax fraud? What is the average prison sentence for tax fraud?

The way taxpayers are treated by tax authorities reveals interesting differences between the Swiss cantons. Only 58 percent of Swiss cantonal tax authorities believe that mistakes in reported incomes are, on average, in favor of taxpayers. 31 percent believe that mistakes are neither to the advantage nor to the disadvantage of taxpayers, and 12 percent believe that mistakes are to the disadvantage of taxpayers. These answers indicate a general lack of distrust towards taxpayers. If a taxpayer does not report his or her true taxable income, tax authorities can contact her in several ways. 54 percent of the cantons phone the person concerned and ask how the mistake(s) occurred in the tax reporting form and what explanation the taxpayer has. All of the cantons send a letter to the taxpayer, half of them with a standard formulation. Nearly 85 percent ask the taxpayer to visit the tax office, but only half of the cantons mention the possibility of punishment. Thus, tax authorities rarely adopt the strategy of explicit deterrence, but rather seek to gain additional information. 96 percent of the cantonal tax authorities correct reported incomes that are too high, i.e. reduce taxable incomes when taxpayers commit mistakes that are to their disadvantage. 27 percent of the tax authorities correct reported taxable income even if taxpayers fail to profit from legal tax savings.

The impact of the treatment of taxpayers on tax evasion is considered in the estimated equations presented in Table 2. Two variables in column (3) capture the respectful treatment of taxpayers by the tax authority. The typical procedure if no tax declaration is coded 0 if a reminder is sent and direct income assessment follows, 1 if a reminder is followed by a penalty and an assessment by the tax authority, 2 if a direct income assessment by the authority without any other contact to taxpayers follows, 3 if there is a penalty and an official assessment without a reminder and without an attempt to check out the situation. The respectful procedure obtains if taxpayers are first called on the phone, then a written reminder is sent, and finally the taxpayer is invited to visit the tax administration. The variable 'Typical procedure if no tax declaration' in column (3) of Table 2 indicates that there is a statistically significant (1 percent level) positive influence on tax evasion when the tax authority becomes less respectful. The variable 'respectful procedure' captures the other aspects of how the tax authority deals with the taxpayers collected by our survey. The effect is again statistically significant (5 percent level) and indicates that tax evasion is reduced when taxpayers are treated more respectfully. The authoritarian treatment is captured by a dummy variable that is one if taxpayers are directly invited to pay a visit to the tax administration and additionally threatened by potential fines. According to the estimates in column (3) of Table 2, the 'authoritarian' procedure reduces tax evasion. This effect is statistically significant at the 5 percent level.

Column (3) also contains the two standard variables for deterrence already included in Table 1 as well as the control variables used there. The probability of detection is statistically significant (at the 5 percent level) and has a theoretically unexpected positive sign. It suggests that a higher probability of being caught raises (rather than decreases) tax evasion. An increase in the standard fine reduces tax evasion in a statistically significant way (1 percent level), which corresponds to theoretical expectations.

Establishing Fiscal Exchange by Political Decision-Making Procedures

The fiscal exchange relationship between taxpayers and the state also depends on the politico-economic framework within which the government acts. It has, in particular, been argued that the extent of citizens' political participation rights systematically affects the kind of tax policy pursued by the government and its tax authority. Empirical studies by Weck-Hannemann and Pommerehne (1989), Pommerehne and Weck-Hannemann (1996), Pommerehne and Frey (1992) and Frey (1997) focus on the impact of constitutional differences of the cantons on tax evasion. The more direct democratic the political decision-making procedures of a canton are, the lower is tax evasion according to those studies. Feld and Frey (2002a) have found that the treatment of taxpayers by the tax authority can partly be explained by these constitutional differences between the Swiss cantons as well. The more strongly developed citizens' participation rights are the more respectfully they are treated by the tax authority.

The extent of direct democratic participation rights of the citizens is measured by an index proposed by Stutzer (1999) and successfully used by Frey and Stutzer (2002) in an analysis of subjective well-being of citizens and by Schaltegger and Feld (2001) in an analysis of government centralization in Switzerland. Although the index is extensively discussed in these papers, it is necessary to at least note the following: this index is constructed on the basis of the different constitutional provisions concerning the extent of direct democracy at the Swiss cantonal level. All Swiss cantons have mandatory constitutional referendums, but already in the case of an optional constitutional referendum the number of signatures and the time span in which they have to be collected vary across cantons. The variation between the cantons is even higher in the cases of constitutional and statutory initiatives, mandatory and optional statutory referendums, and fiscal referendums. All this information is used by Stutzer (1999) to construct the index employed in this paper.

In addition to the index of direct democracy, a regional dummy variable is included that measures whether a canton has a majority of German or of French and Italian speaking citizens.[9] It is often argued that the cultural differences between Swiss cantons, most visible in the language differences among the Swiss population, are strongly reflected in Swiss politics as well. The French and Italian speaking cantons in the West and South of Switzerland appear to be internationally more open, e.g. reflected by their position towards the European Union, and appear to favor government solutions to a larger extent than the German speaking cantons. It is thus also argued that this translates into fiscal policies. In addition, the French and Italian speaking cantons usually have lower rankings in the index of direct democracy such that this variable could well indicate the impact of cultural differences when they are not controlled for. Therefore, this regional dummy variable is included in the econometric model for testing robustness.

The estimation results in column (4) of Table 2 suggest again that the respectful treatment and the authoritarian treatment have about the same effect on tax evasion. Moreover, direct democracy and thus higher participation rights have a significant negative impact on tax evasion. Including political participation rights in the analysis does however not affect the results. Higher audit rates are still associated with higher tax evasion, while a higher fine and the authoritarian procedure successfully deter taxpayers from evading taxes. In addition, the respectful procedure reduces tax evasion as well.

The most interesting point shows up when the interaction between higher participation rights and treatment by the tax authority are considered in column (5) of Table 2. The respectful procedure has indeed a negative impact on tax evasion in more directly democratic cantons while it increases tax evasion in more representative democratic cantons. And vice versa for the 'authoritarian' procedure: it has a dampening effect on tax evasion in more representative democratic cantons and increases tax evasion in more direct democratic cantons. While the single effects of the interaction terms with the respectful procedure do not reach any conventional significance level, they are individually significant in the case of the interaction terms with the 'authoritarian' procedure. Nevertheless, the tests on the joint significance of the respectful procedure variables and the direct democracy variables, reported on the bottom of Table 2, indicate that each of these variables has a significant impact on tax evasion while that of the 'authoritarian' procedure is not significant at any conventional significance level according to that Wald test. In addition, the hypothesis that the effects of respectful and authoritarian treatment are equal can now be rejected at the 5 percent significance level. The dampening effect of the 'authoritarian' procedure on tax evasion mainly arises in representative democracies while the dampening effect of the respectful procedure mainly occurs in direct democracies. Distinguishing both constitutional systems underlines the dominance of a respectful as compared to an authoritarian treatment.

Putting the Results into Perspective

These results are fully in line with the existing literature on tax evasion in Switzerland and also with the historical study of Schanz (1890). The studies by Frey and Feld (2002) and Feld and Frey (2002) corroborate the earlier findings of Weck-Hannemann and Pommerehne (1989), Pommerehne and Weck-Hannemann (1996), Pommerehne and Frey (1992) and Frey (1997) with respect to the impact of direct democracy on tax evasion. Torgler (2003a) uses an alternative approach to study tax morale in the Swiss cantons by investigating two micro data sets, the World Value Survey and the International Survey Programme, that contain questions about tax morale of respondents. His results provide evidence that direct democracy shapes tax morale. According to his estimates, tax morale is significantly higher in direct democratic cantons. Distinguishing between different instruments of direct democracy, he finds that the fiscal referendum has the highest positive influence on tax morale. In addition, tax morale of respondents is higher if they have a higher trust in government, or in the courts and the legal system. Finally, local autonomy as an indicator of fiscal federalism has a marginally significant positive impact on tax morale. Since studies for the U.S. (Gerber 1999) and Switzerland (Pommerehne 1978) show that policies in direct democratic jurisdiction are more strongly in line with citizens' preferences, institutions of direct democracy can be seen as a means to establish a relationship of fiscal exchange between taxpayers and the government. While Schanz (1890) was pessimistic about the usefulness of direct democracy in tax compliance, it becomes evident that the possibility to decide on tax rates and the level of public services shows taxpayers what they get in exchange for their tax payment. This method helps to reveal citizens' preferences for public goods.

The impact of the treatment of taxpayers by the tax office on tax evasion has not yet been investigated for Switzerland. The studies by Frey and Feld (2002) and Feld and Frey (2002) are the first to investigate it. There is however similar evidence for Australia reported by Braithwaite (2003) according to which responsive regulation by the tax office pays off in the form of lower tax evasion.

Again quite interestingly Swiss citizens are the more respectfully treated by the tax authority the more strongly developed citizens' participation rights (Feld and Frey 2002a). Respectful treatment is subsequently more successfully reducing tax evasion in direct democratic cantons. In addition, tax authorities in more direct democratic cantons appear to give taxpayers more frequently the benefit of a doubt. Feld and Frey (2002a) report evidence that tax authorities in more direct democratic cantons believe to a significantly lesser extent that mistakes in the tax declaration are in favor of taxpayers. Moreover, a publication of tax registers occurs less often in direct democratic cantons. In light of the doubts by Schanz (1896) on the effectiveness of these measures in the 19th century this is an interesting result.

That a friendly and respectful treatment of taxpayers by the tax authorities is an important means to reduce tax evasion has been recognized for a long time in Switzerland. Again the historical account by Schanz (1890) as summarized at the outset indicates that citizens are frequently given the benefit of a doubt. If deterrence measures were increased, additional measures to reduce the administrative interference in the private sphere of individuals were taken. Schneider (1929) strongly argues in favor of a respectful treatment of taxpayers. In form of the tax administrator the state is personalized to the citizens. A too strong emphasis on deterrence would accordingly lead to a distrust of citizens and finally crowd out tax morale. Moral suasion does however not lead to increases in tax morale, as Torgler (2003b) finds in a controlled experiment in a Swiss community. The simple normative appeal by the tax commissioner in a letter did not have any significant impact on tax morale. These results corroborate those for the U.S. provided by Blumenthal, Christian and Slemrod (2001).

The evidence for Switzerland is also pretty consistent with respect to the impact of traditional deterrence measures, like the fine or the intensity of control, on tax evasion: there is no robust effect of deterrence on tax evasion or tax morale in Switzerland. In most cases, both variables are insignificant. Sometimes, like in the studies by Feld and Frey (2002) and Frey and Feld (2002) as well as Torgler (2003a), the intensity of control even has an unexpected positive sign. Weck-Hannemann and Pommerehne (1989) provide evidence that the intensity of control has the expected negative sign and is statistically significant for highly educated taxpayers only. They interpret it as evidence for the complexity of risk assessment in the evasion gamble. Feld and Frey (2002) exploit the Swiss distinction between tax evasion and tax fraud and find evidence that penalties for tax fraud have a quantitatively stronger negative impact on tax evasion than fines for tax evasion. Feld and Frey (2002a) report evidence that penalties for not submitting the tax declaration are significantly higher, while fines for tax evasion are significantly lower in direct democratic cantons. Kucher and Götte (1998) employ a ratio of concurrence between the government's recommendation to vote in referendums and the actual referendum outcome as a measure of trust in the government. According to their time series analysis for the city of Zurich from 1964 to 1996, the share of submitted tax declarations from all tax declarations is significantly higher, the higher is trust. All these results reflect that tax compliance in Switzerland is affected by deterrence in a non-linear way. Smaller offenses are punished relatively lightly. If citizens do not stick to the rules of the game, they are more strongly punished. This policy pays attention to the fact that nobody's perfect and to cheat a little bit does not undermine the underlying psychological tax contract. Meier (1977) discusses evidence from a survey among the Swiss population that indicates a general tolerance to minor forms of tax evasion. The evidence is fully in line with the allowance of individual errors in the tax declaration in some cantons up to a certain amount during the 19th century.

Conclusion for Economic Policy

A fundamental result of the tax evasion literature is that it remains a mystery why people actually pay taxes, given the rather low levels of fines and auditing probabilities. The deterrence model of tax evasion cannot explain the high tax compliance rates without referring to an exogenously given tax morale. The case of Switzerland indicates that tax compliance results from a complicated interaction of deterrence measures and a psychological tax contract that establishes fiscal exchange between taxpayers and tax authorities. Tax morale in Switzerland is a function of (1) the fiscal exchange where taxpayers get public services for the tax prices they pay, (2) the political procedure that leads to this exchange and (3) the personal relationship between the taxpayers and the tax administrators.

The tax authority takes into account that the way it treats the taxpayers systematically affects the latter's tax morale, and therefore their willingness to pay taxes, which in turn affects the costs of raising taxes. When the auditors detect incorrectly reported income in the tax declaration, they can immediately be suspicious of an intent to cheat, and impose legal sanctions. Alternatively, the auditors may give the taxpayers the benefit of the doubt and inquire into the reasons for the mistake. If the taxpayer in question did not intend to cheat but simply made a mistake, he or she will most likely be offended by the disrespectful treatment of the tax authority. The feeling of being controlled in a negative way, and being suspected of tax cheating, tends to crowd out the intrinsic motivation to act as an honorable taxpayer and, as a consequence, tax morale will fall. In contrast, when the auditor makes an effort to locate the reason for the error by contacting the taxpayer in an informal way (e.g. by phoning him or her), the taxpayer will appreciate this respectful treatment and tax morale is upheld.

Studies on Swiss tax evasion provide evidence for such a view of responsive regulation. They moreover show that this interaction between taxpayers and tax authorities is shaped by direct democratic decision-making. Responsive regulation is particularly successful and significantly more frequently employed in direct democratic cantons. Direct democracy as such leads to lower tax evasion and higher tax morale. In addition, deterrence occurs in a complicated fashion such that smaller offenses are only punished lightly. Taxpayers are often given the benefit of a doubt. The whole system appears to be made for the creation of trust between citizens and between citizens and the state. This creates an environment in which it pays for citizens to follow their civic duty. It is not merely a matter of Swiss culture that tax evasion is relatively low, but a characteristic that can be attributed to the existence of a psychological tax contract between tax authorities and taxpayers. This is likely to be relevant in all democracies. Tax commissioners should be well aware of the existence of such a contract just as the Secretary of the U.S. Treasury stated in 1929: 'We want the bureau representative to meet the taxpayer and discuss his problems sympathetically, understandingly, frankly and fairly.'

Notes

1   See e.g. Schwartz and Orleans (1967), Roth, Scholz and Witte (1989), Alm, McClelland and Schulze (1992), Cullis and Lewis (1997), Torgler (2003).
2   This argument is not totally unrealistic. By commenting on a survey on Swiss taxpayers conducted by Strümpel (1965) according to which Swiss citizens demand a punishment of tax cheaters, Keller (1966/67, p. 245) argued that this demand might as well be interpreted as envy instead of a sense of civic duty.
3   See Spicer and Lundstedt (1976), Spicer and Becker (1980) and Becker, Büchner and Sleeking (1987). Alm, McClelland and Schulze (1992) and Alm, Jackson and McKee (1993) find that the introduction of a public good in exchange for the taxes paid increases compliance rates in experiments. See also Lewis (1978), Falkinger (1988), Bordignon (1993) and Reckers, Sanders and Roark (1994).
4   Tyler (1990) analyses procedural fairness in the context of experiments. A broader survey is given by Frey, Benz and Stutzer (2004). For an analysis which political institutions shape the perception of procedural fairness, see Pommerehne, Hart and Frey (1994), Pommerehne and Weck-Hannemann (1996), Frey (1997), Pommerehne, Hart and Feld (1997), Feld and Frey (2002) and Feld and Tyran (2002). According to their analysis, direct democratic institutions increase tax morale. The final paper argues that this is not only due to reciprocity but also to the legitimacy.
5   See Meier (1984) who is the only more recent account of Schanz' work.
6   Hence cantons can set tax rates and define tax bases autonomously. Both leads to a strong variation in (effective) tax rates among cantons and local jurisdictions. See Feld (2000) for a more detailed description of the Swiss fiscal system. Tax evasion laws form part of the legal power of the Swiss cantons as well.
7   Strümpel (1965) and Keller (1966/67) erroneously contend that about 300 million SFr were evaded which would imply a compliance rate of about 96 to 97 percent. Still a compliance rate of 91 percent is high.
8   Many arguments can be brought forward against this method. See Schneider and Enste (2000). Slemrod and Yithzaki (2002) for example criticize that, first, some of the national accounts data are based on tax return data, and second, there are many inconsistencies in the definition of both income measures. Engel and Hines (1999) find however that the GAP measure of tax evasion performs extraordinarily well to capture the dynamics of tax compliance in the U.S. from 1947 to 1993. Since the indirect method of calculating income evaded poses an error in the variables problem, it is necessary to include socio-demographic variables that capture the opportunity of evading taxes of different taxpayers.
9   It should be noted that aside the respective and 'authoritarian' treatment variables, the typical procedure if no tax declaration and the dummy for French and Italian speaking cantons, all variables vary over time. The direct democracy index does so only moderately, but the fine, the probability of detection, tax indexation and so on vary considerably. Thus, sufficient degrees of freedom remain in the cross section domain despite of the reduced number of Swiss cantons.

References

Allingham, M.G. and Sandmo, A. (1972), 'Income Tax Evasion: A Theoretical Analysis', *Journal of Public Economics*, Vol. 1, pp. 323-38.

Alm, J., Jackson, B.R. and McKee, M. (1993), 'Fiscal Exchange, Collective Decision Institutions and Tax Compliance', *Journal of Economic Behavior and Organization*, Vol. 22, pp. 285-303.

Alm, J., McClelland, G.H. and Schulze, W.D. (1992), 'Why Do People Pay Taxes?', *Journal of Public Economics*, Vol. 48, pp. 21-38.

Andreoni, J., Erard, B. and Feinstein, J. (1998), 'Tax Compliance', *Journal of Economic Literature*, Vol. 36, pp. 818-60.

Becker, G.S. (1968), 'Crime and Punishment: An Economic Approach', *Journal of Political Economy*, Vol. 76, pp. 169-217.

Becker, W., Büchner, H.-J. and Sleeking, S. (1987), 'The Impact of Public Transfer Expenditures on Tax Evasion: An Experimental Approach', *Journal of Public Economics*, Vol. 34, pp. 243-52.

Beron, K.J., Tauchen, H.V. and Witte, A.D. (1992), 'The Effect of Audits and Socioeconomic Variables on Compliance', in J. Slemrod (ed.), *Why People Pay Taxes*, University of Michigan Press, Ann Arbor, pp. 67-89.

Blumenthal, M., Christian, C. and Slemrod, J. (2001), 'Do Normative Appeals Affect Tax Compliance? Evidence from a Controlled Experiment in Minnesota', *National Tax Journal*, Vol. 54, pp. 25-138.

Bordignon, M. (1993), 'A Fairness Approach to Income Tax Evasion', *Journal of Public Economics*, Vol. 52, pp. 345-62.

Braithwaite, V. (ed.) (2003), *Taxing Democracy*, Ashgate, London.

Commission Justitia Pax (1981), *Die Bankeninitiative*, Paulusdruckerei, Fribourg.

Clotfelder, C.T. (1983), 'Tax Evasion and Tax Rates: An Analysis of Individual Returns', *Review of Economics and Statistics*, Vol. 65, pp. 363-73.

Cullis, J.G. and Lewis, A. (1997), 'Why People Pay Taxes: From a Conventional Economic Model to a Model of Social Convention', *Journal of Economic Psychology*, Vol. 18, pp. 305-21.

Engel, E. and Hines, J.R. (1999), 'Understanding Tax Evasion Dynamics', NBER Working Paper No. 6903, NBER, Cambridge.

Falkinger, J. (1988), 'Tax Evasion and Equity: A Theoretical Analysis', *Public Finance*, Vol. 43, pp. 388-95.

Feld, L.P. (2000), 'Tax Competition and Income Redistribution: An Empirical Analysis for Switzerland', *Public Choice*, Vol. 105, pp. 125-64.

Feld, L.P. (2003), 'Rückführung von Fluchtkapital als Voraussetzung für den fiskalischen Erfolg einer Abgeltungssteuer?', in G. Schick (ed.), *Veranlagung – Abgeltung – Steuerfreiheit: Besteuerung von Kapitalerträgen im Rechtsstaat*, Stiftung Marktwirtschaft, Berlin, pp. 43-53.

Feld, L.P. and Frey, B.S. (2002), 'The Tax Authority and the Taxpayer: An Exploratory Analysis', Unpublished Manuscript, University of St. Gallen 2002.

Feld, L.P. and Frey, B.S. (2002a), 'Trust Breeds Trust: How Taxpayers Are Treated', *Economics of Governance*, Vol. 3, pp. 87-99.

Feld, L.P. and Tyran, J.-R. (2002), 'Tax Evasion and Voting: An Experimental Analysis', *Kyklos*, Vol. 55, pp. 197-222.

Frey, B.S. (1997), 'A Constitution for Knaves Crowds Out Civic Virtues', *Economic Journal*, Vol. 107, pp. 1043-53.

Frey, B.S. (1997a), *Not Just for The Money. An Economic Theory of Personal Motivation*, Edward Elgar, Cheltenham.

Frey, B.S. and Feld, L.P. (2002), 'Deterrence and Morale in Taxation: An Empirical Analysis', CESifo Working Paper No. 760, August 2002.

Frey, B.S. and Stutzer, A. (2002), *Happiness and Economics*, Princeton University Press, Princeton.

Frey, B.S., Benz, M. and Stutzer, A. (2004), 'Introducing Procedural Utility: Not Only What but also How Matters', *Journal of Theoretical and Institutional Economics*, Vol. 160, pp. 377-401.

Gerber, E.R. (1999), *The Populist Paradox: Interest Group Influence and the Promise of Direct Legislation*, Princeton University Press, Princeton.

Graetz, M.J. and Wilde, L.L. (1985), 'The Economics of Tax Compliance: Facts and Fantasy', *National Tax Journal*, Vol. 38, pp. 355-63.

Higy, C. (1962/63), 'Die finanz- und steuerpolitische Entwicklung in der Schweiz in den Jahren 1958/62', *Finanzarchiv N.F.*, Vol. 22, pp. 505-20.

Keller, T. (1966/67), 'Der Schweizer als Steuerzahler', *Finanzarchiv N.F.*, Vol. 26, pp. 242-46.

Kucher, M. and Goette, L. (1998), 'Trust Me: An Empirical Analysis of Taxpayer Honesty', *Finanzarchiv N.F.*, Vol. 55, pp. 429-44.

Lewis, A. (1978), 'Perceptions of Tax Rates', *British Tax Review*, Vol. 6, pp. 358-66.

Meier, A. (1977), 'Steuern und Staatsausgaben im Urteil von Schweizerbürgern: Ergebnisse und Konsequenzen einer Pilotstudie', *Archiv für Schweizerisches Abgaberecht*, Vol. 45, pp. 273-98.

Meier, A. (1984), 'Die Bekämpfung der Steuerhinterziehung in der Schweiz: Georg Schanz' "Die Steuern der Schweiz" und die Gegenwart', *Finanzarchiv N.F.*, Vol. 44, pp. 490-508.

Pommerehne, W.W. (1978), 'Institutional Approaches to Public Expenditure: Empirical Evidence from Swiss Municipalities', *Journal of Public Economics*, Vol. 9, pp. 255-80.

Pommerehne, W.W. (1983), 'Steuerhinterziehung und Schwarzarbeit als Grenzen der Staatstätigkeit', *Schweizerische Zeitschrift für Volkswirtschaft und Statistik*, Vol. 119, pp. 261-84.

Pommerehne, W.W. and Frey, B.S. (1992), 'The Effects of Tax Administration on Tax Morale', Unpublished Manuscript, University of Zurich.

Pommerehne, W.W. and Zweifel, P. (1991), 'Success of a Tax Amnesty: At the Poll, for the Fisc?', *Public Choice*, Vol. 72, pp. 131-65.

Pommerehne, W.W. and Weck-Hannemann, H. (1996), 'Tax Rates, Tax Administration and Income Tax Evasion in Switzerland', *Public Choice*, Vol. 88, p. 161-70.

Pommerehne, W.W., Hart, A. and Feld, L.P. (1997), 'Steuerhinterziehung und ihre Kontrolle in unterschiedlichen politischen Systemen', *Homo Oeconomicus*, Vol. 14, pp. 469-87.

Pommerehne, W.W., Hart, A. and Frey, B.S. (1994), 'Tax Morale, Tax Evasion and the Choice of Policy Instruments in Different Political Systems', *Public Finance*, Vol. 49 (Supplement: *Public Finance and Irregular Activities*): pp. 52-69.

Reckers, P.M.J., Sanders, D.L. and Roarke, S.J. (1994), 'The Influence of Ethical Attitudes on Taxpayer Compliance', *National Tax Journal*, Vol. 47, pp. 825-36.

Roth, J.A., Scholz, J.T. and Witte, A.D. (1989) (eds), *Taxpayer Compliance: An Agenda for Research*, University of Pennsylvania Press, Philadelphia.

Schaltegger, Ch.A. and Feld, L.P. (2001), 'On Government Centralization and Budget Referendums: Evidence from Switzerland', CESifo Working Paper No. 615, December.

Schanz, G. von (1890), *Die Steuern der Schweiz in ihrer Entwicklung seit Beginn des 19. Jahrhunderts*, Vol. I to V, Stuttgart.

Schneider, F. (2000), 'Die Entwicklung der Schattenwirtschaft in der Schweiz sowie in den 26 Kantonen über die Periode 1995-1999', Unpublished Manuscript, Johannes-Kepler University of Linz.

Schneider, F. and Enste, D. (2000), 'Shadow Economies: Size, Causes, Consequences', *Journal of Economic Literature*, Vol. 38, pp. 77-114.

Schneider, S. (1929), 'Steuer und Moral', *Schweizerische Zeitschrift für Volkswirtschaft und Statistik*, Vol. 65, pp. 309-45.

Schwartz, R.D. and Orleans, S. (1967), 'On Legal Sanctions', *University of Chicago Law Review*, Vol. 34, pp. 282-300.

Secretary of the Treasury (1929), *An Open Letter to the American Taxpayer*, U.S.A. Government Printing Office.

Slemrod, J. and Yitzhaki, S. (2002), 'Tax Avoidance, Evasion and Administration', in A.J. Auerbach and M. Feldstein (eds), *Handbook of Public Economics*, North-Holland, Amsterdam, Vol. 3, pp. 1423-70.

Slemrod, J., Blumenthal, M. and Christian, C.W. (2001), 'Taxpayer Response to an Increased Probability of Audit: Evidence from a Controlled Experiment in Minnesota', *Journal of Public Economics*, Vol. 79, pp. 455-83.

Spicer, M.W. and Becker, L.A. (1980), 'Fiscal Inequity and Tax Evasion: An Experimental Approach', *National Tax Journal*, Vol. 33, pp. 171-75.

Spicer, M.W. and Lundstedt, S.B. (1976), 'Understanding Tax Evasion', *Public Finance*, Vol. 31, pp. 295-305.

Strümpel, B. (1965), 'Der Schweizer als Steuerzahler: Ein Beitrag zum internationalen Vergleich der Steuermoral', *Finanzarchiv N.F.*, Vol. 24, pp. 244-58.

Stutzer, A. (1999), 'Demokratieindizes für die Kantone der Schweiz', Working Paper No. 23, Institute for Empirical Research in Economics, University of Zurich.

Torgler, B. (2003), *Tax Morale: Theory and Empirical Analysis of Tax Compliance*, Ph.D. Thesis, University of Basel.

Torgler, B. (2003a), 'Tax Morale and Institutions', forthcoming in *European Journal of Political Economy*, 2004.

Torgler, B. (2003b), 'Moral Suasion: An Alternative Tax Policy Strategy? Evidence from a Controlled Experiment in Switzerland', Unpublished Manuscript, University of Basel.

Torgler, B., Schaltegger, C.A. and Schaffner, M. (2003), 'Is Forgiveness Divine? A Cross-Cultural Comparison of Tax Amnesties', *Schweizerische Zeitschrift für Volkswirtschaft und Statistik*, Vol. 139, pp. 375-96.

Tyler, T.R. (1990), *Why People Obey the Law*, Yale University Press, New Haven.

Weck-Hannemann, H. and Pommerehne, W.W. (1989), 'Einkommensteuerhinterziehung in der Schweiz: Eine empirische Analyse', *Schweizerische Zeitschrift für Volkswirtschaft und Statistik*, Vol. 125, pp. 515-56.

Wicksell, K. (1896), *Finanztheoretische Untersuchungen nebst Darstellung und Kritik des Steuerwesens Schwedens*, Gustav Fischer, Jena.

Chapter 3

Explaining Taxpayer Non-Compliance through Reference to Taxpayer Identities: A Social Identity Perspective

Natalie Taylor

Introduction

Despite an abundance of research over several decades into the reasons for taxpayer non-compliance, researchers, practitioners and policymakers around the world are still trying to grapple with the issue of how to improve taxpayer compliance. In countries where voluntary self-reporting of tax obligations is encouraged, particularly where computerised tracking of income may be limited, voluntary and truthful reporting of income and legitimate deductions is an important component to ensuring that tax systems remain viable and continue to function appropriately. Tax systems after all are the foundations on which democratic societies can flourish, safe in the knowledge that public goods and services will be maintained and that those less fortunate will be looked after.

However for tax systems to operate effectively it is necessary that all lawful revenues are collected. In a climate of increasing reliance on self-reporting the collection of revenues depends in many ways upon the truthful reporting by taxpayers. This is particularly so in the underground economy where paperwork for money changing hands is non-existent and there is no simple way of monitoring financial transactions. The percentage of Gross Domestic Product (GDP) represented by the underground economy is estimated to be substantial and increasing on a global level (Braithwaite et al. 2003). In Australia, for example, it is estimated that the average percentage of GDP in 2001/2002 due to the shadow economy was about 14 percent. This potentially represents a substantial amount of revenue not being collected by tax authorities and redistributes the tax burden solely amongst those who do not operate in the underground economy. Paying tax is not popular at the best of times, so what can we do when transactions cannot be traced – how can taxpayers be encouraged to report their taxable earnings in the absence of surveillance and monitoring?

This dilemma underlies much of the research that has been conducted into understanding tax non-compliance. Earlier theoretical models emphasised the purely economic nature of tax compliance (Allingham and Sandmo 1972) whereby individuals are motivated by self-interest and cost/benefit considerations.

Basically, the benefits of not declaring income (more money in the pocket) are weighed against the probabilities of being caught and punished. If the probability of being caught is perceived to be too high then individuals will choose to declare their income. Conversely if the risks of being caught are perceived to be low then individuals will not declare income. The underlying assumption is that individuals will not voluntarily pay taxes unless their hand is in some way forced through surveillance, monitoring and the threat of punishment. This argument of course leads to the view that where income cannot be easily traced it will not be reported to tax authorities. A natural extension of this argument is that individuals will seek out opportunities, which might allow them to avoid paying tax (such as *choosing* to operate in the underground economy).

While some evidence certainly does exist for this cost benefit approach (Beck and Jung 1989), more recent research has shown that taxpaying behaviour is also affected by other factors such as appeals to conscience and perceptions of justice and fairness (Cowell 1992; McGraw and Scholz 1991). Taxpayer compliance increases when the system is perceived as fair, just and legitimate and decreases when it is not (Roberts and Hite 1994). In particular this occurs even when deterrence measures and personal gain are controlled for (Wenzel 2002). Further, those who choose to operate within the underground economy are more likely to be disengaged from the tax system, have no commitment to it and show less shame and remorse about tax evasion than those who do not operate within the underground economy (Braithwaite et al. 2003). These findings imply that a simple cost benefit analysis is not adequate to explain taxpayer behaviour. Rather it is necessary to look beyond self-interest to variables that might explain tax compliance through social influences and mediators. Why is it that some taxpayers see the tax system as fair and legitimate while others are totally disengaged from it, *regardless of self-interest outcomes?* Why is it that some taxpayers actively seek out opportunities to evade tax while others do not? Why is it that conscience and moral obligation to pay tax affect some taxpayers but not others? The answers to these questions, and the social influences driving them, will be argued in this chapter to revolve around attitudes and behaviours toward paying tax which stem from how taxpayers perceive themselves in relation to tax authorities, the tax system and other groups of taxpayers. Understanding these influences should be important to tax authorities who are unable in the underground economy to obtain compliance through monitoring and tracking.

Beyond Self-interest

Prior to any discussion about what these social influences might be and how they operate, it is worthwhile thinking first about why people voluntarily comply with rules and laws set down by others, particularly when those rules do not benefit self or may be contrary to one's self-interest. In order to maintain effective social order and ensure that rules and decisions are followed, authorities need to be influential (Smith and Tyler 1996; Tyler 1997). While this can sometimes be achieved through the use of reward and coercion (cf. French and Raven 1959), these methods can be time consuming and costly to implement. Further, their effectiveness is far from established (Turner 1991; Tyler 1997) both because it is simply not possible to monitor the activities of every single person 24 hours a day and coercion can sometimes result in the opposite behaviour from that being advocated (Brehm and Brehm 1981; Taylor 2003).

A persuasive authority, however, which wields influence rather than coercion has the capacity to induce voluntary compliance through being perceived as legitimate and representative of those over whom it has power. It obtains its influence by being perceived to enact those values which are important and central to those being ruled (Haslam and Platow 2001). In essence people who voluntarily comply with rules laid down by authorities (even when such compliance is against their self-interest and in the absence of sanctions) do so because they believe that it is right to do so and that the authority making the rules is a legitimate one. Conferring legitimacy on an authority means that people will be willing to follow the rules of that authority because it is perceived that the authority is acting in the best interests of those it represents and is treating everyone fairly and with respect (Tyler 1997). Further, a legitimate authority is associated with being fairer and less coercive than an illegitimate authority (Taylor and McGarty 2001) even when outcomes are held constant (Ellemers et al. 1998). Clearly then, it is in the interests of tax authorities to project themselves as representative so that they will be seen as legitimate, allowing voluntary compliance with their rules to emerge rather than having to rely on threat and coercion.

How do Perceptions of Fairness and Justice Affect Tax Compliance?

It is not unreasonable to expect that if I am required to pay tax then so should others. That is, I have a right to expect that I will be treated exactly the same way as any one else who earns taxable income. Such treatment (with consistent enforcement of appropriate sanctions for those who do not pay their rightful taxes) implies that the tax authority is trustworthy, neutral and respectful (Tyler et al. 1997). Even if paying tax means less money in my pocket I know that everyone else who earns income is also paying their share of taxes.

This procedure breaks down however when there are different methods and opportunities for taxpayers to pay tax. In Australia, for example, many wage and salary earners have tax deducted from their salary automatically on a fortnightly or monthly basis (known as Pay-As-You-Go). Other people do not have tax automatically deducted and are required to declare their tax obligations at the end of the financial year. This means that for the former there is little choice about payment of tax from salary while for the latter there may be more possibilities for avoidance and evasion. If wage and salary earners think about themselves and other wage and salary earners in comparison with those for whom tax is not automatically deducted, it is possible and indeed quite likely that they will perceive the tax system to be unfair and inequitable (Spicer and Lundstedt 1976; Wallschutzky 1984). Again, where perceptions exist that the rich find loopholes to evade their tax obligations, dissatisfaction with the tax system is likely to increase

(Taylor 2001). Perceptions of unfairness and inequity are naturally associated with a reluctance to comply with tax requirements ('Why should I pay tax when others do not?'). Where evasion is not possible because tax is automatically deducted, people perceiving an inequitable and unfair tax system may well seek evasion opportunities elsewhere (such as through not declaring cash payments, rental income etc.).

So far, none of this is new. But perceptions of fairness and inequity are not objectively determined (Tyler, Boeckmann, Smith and Huo 1997). That is, whether people perceive a tax system or their tax burden or distributive outcomes to be unfair or inequitable and the degree to which people will be willing to declare their taxable income voluntarily, will depend on how they perceive themselves within the tax system and their relationship to both the tax authority and other groups of taxpayers. Traditionally, fairness and justice have been investigated by looking at the way individuals judge outcomes and procedures specifically in relation to themselves (Wenzel 2002). Such an approach, however, neglects the important point that individuals can and often do categorize themselves as members of social groups and larger social categories (Smith and Tyler 1996; Turner 1991). This means that perceptions about fairness and justice are not always based on 'is it fair for me?' but can also be based on 'is it fair for us?'. The answers to these two questions will not necessarily always coincide.

Taxpayer Identities: A Social Identity Approach

When people think about themselves they may think of themselves as unique and different from others (me, you) or they may think of themselves as being members of social categories (male, American). The latter does not simply mean that someone who thinks of himself as male continues to regard himself as unique and different from other males. Rather, this social categorization involves a psychological transformation from 'me' to 'we' and 'him/her' to 'them' and occurs from changes in situational context (the issue, those involved, the frame of reference). If someone thinks of themselves as belonging to the category 'male' this is likely to be in a context which makes salient the differences between males and females. An example of such a context might be where the issue of 'equality between the sexes' is being discussed. As the discussion deepens stereotypical beliefs and behaviours associated with being male or female will begin to dominate perceptions – males will become more 'male' in their attitudes and behaviour while females will become more 'female'. This results from the psychological transformation taking place from seeing oneself as a unique individual to seeing oneself as belonging to a social category (Turner et al. 1987).

In the above scenario a male will begin to judge the issue from the perspective of 'males' rather than himself alone. As part of this process he will begin to perceive other males as being psychologically more similar to himself (ingroup) while females will become more differentiated psychologically from both himself and other males (outgroup). From a social identity approach this means that attitudes, behaviours, perceptions of fairness, legitimacy, what is right and what is wrong are outcomes of, and vary with, self-categorisation. Influence is argued to be an outcome of self-categorisation and is specific to ingroups (who are perceived as representative, legitimate and trustworthy) while outgroups possess no ability to influence because they are perceived as illegitimate and untrustworthy (Turner 1991).

If we apply this reasoning to the realm of tax it is clear that tax authorities need to be perceived as representative, legitimate and trustworthy (ingroup authority) by taxpayers if voluntary tax compliance is to be achieved. Trustworthiness, neutrality and respectfulness imply that the tax authority is treating all taxpayers fairly and appropriately, increasing its legitimacy and ability to obtain voluntary compliance. In this context of taxation I will be likely to see myself as being similar to all other taxpayers and will expect the treatment given to me by the tax authority to be similar to the treatment given to any other taxpayer. That is, regardless of whether I agree with the system *per se* (variation in tax brackets, levels of tax etc.) I am likely to view myself as a 'taxpayer' when paying tax assuming that I also perceive the tax authority to be legitimate, behaving appropriately and enforcing the rules systematically.

If, however, I perceive that certain groups of taxpayers are being treated differently (Pay-As-You-Go paying taxes while others evade taxes, the 'rich' evading taxes through loopholes which the 'poor' cannot access, penalties being applied to some taxpayers but not others) or that the tax authority is in some other way behaving inappropriately then the legitimacy of both the tax authority and tax system are substantially reduced. It is likely that I will begin to think of myself not as 'a taxpayer' but, for example, as 'a poor taxpayer' compared with 'the rich' or a 'Pay-As-You-Go taxpayer' versus 'those who don't automatically have tax deducted'. Such sub-group identification, based on perceptions of unfairness and inequity between 'us' and 'them' can lead to collective relative deprivation (see Walker and Mann 1987); that is, a subjective sense of collective, group-based injustice. 'We' have been treated unfairly compared to 'them'. Such perceptions of group-based injustice can generate anger, resentment, resistance and a strong desire to remedy the perceived injustice. Perceived injustice may be remedied through unjust behaviour becoming just; but if this is not possible then attitudes and behaviour are likely to result in resistance and disengagement from the tax system (Braithwaite et al. 2003). The tax authority may even be perceived as being part of, or representing, the interests of the outgroup (perception of bias and discrimination in its behaviour) in which case the authority's ability to influence is dramatically reduced and even rejected outright (Taylor 2003).

Taxpayers and their Social Identities

To illustrate how taxpayers might think of themselves in terms of social identities, a qualitative study was undertaken in which the content of 'letters to the editor' on a contentious tax issue were analysed (Taylor 2001). This issue concerned the proposed introduction of a new tax levy to be imposed on those Australian taxpayers earning more than $A50,000 per annum (0.5 percent for those earning between \$50-\$100,000, and 1 percent for those earning above \$100,000). The justification for the levy was to provide extra funding for Australia's continuing military involvement in East Timor, a region in political and economic strife, and Australia's involvement was part of the UN peacekeeping agreement.

The announcement was made by the Prime Minister, John Howard, on 23 November 1999, in which he stated that 'The levy I have announced is the fair and decent way to deal with this unexpected Budget difficulty'. By definition, the new tax was discriminatory in that it applied to only a subset of the population (those earning above A\$50,000). Further, it did not take into consideration that a couple, each earning A\$45,000 and therefore coming in under the income threshold, would not pay the levy whereas a single income earner on A\$50,000 with a dependent wife and children would have to pay the levy. There was also controversy surrounding the manner in which the cutoff for the levy had been decided. There was an implicit assumption that those earning above A\$50,000 were wealthy and therefore could afford to pay the tax, which had caused a backlash from those who disagreed with being labeled in this manner. The fact that businesses and corporations were not required to pay the levy also caused much discontent.

Secondly, the imposition of the new tax was to be placed under the banner of an existing healthcare tax levy (Medicare), which most Australians pay to assist in financing the national health system. That is, the new tax levy was to be paid under the rubric of an existing levy. This also had the potential to create perceptions of injustice because the Medicare levy, supposedly for supporting healthcare in a national system which was arguably underfunded, was being used inappropriately by subsuming a new and unrelated tax levy. From the date of the announcement of the tax levy (23 November 1999), newspaper clippings were scanned for letters to the editor which referred explicitly to the introduction of the new tax levy. Fifty letters to the editor were identified over a two-week period.

To determine whether the letters to the editor reflected personal or social identity, the content of the letters was coded by two independent coders according to whether a personal identity or a social identity could be detected. When social identity was detected, the coders were required to determine from the content who comprised a psychological ingroup for the writer and who represented a psychological outgroup. The options given for the ingroup were: high income, middle income, poor, small business people, hard working, Pay-As-You-Go taxpayers, government, Australians, other or unclear. The options given for the outgroup were: rich, poor, unemployed, big business/high wealth individuals, government or unclear. In the event that coders were unable to allocate one of these categories, they were asked to note down extra categories which they felt were applicable.

Social identities were detected by both coders in all letters. The most dominant ingroup category was Australians, followed by Pay-As-You-Go taxpayers and high income earners. The most dominant outgroup category was the government, followed by big business/high wealth individuals. Of those who saw themselves primarily as Australian, 86 percent perceived the government to be outgroup. Inequitable outcomes were focused on more in the letters when a distinction was being made between sub-groups of taxpayers than when this distinction was less apparent. It seems that perceived inequities in outcomes lead those who feel disadvantaged to focus on what their subgroup does not have in comparison with another subgroup, and to be concerned with improving outcomes for their own group rather than themselves. An example of one of the letters (where Pay-As-You-Go was the ingroup social identity identified and big business was the outgroup identity) follows:

> So now we have an East Timor levy. Why is it always the PAYE taxpayer who must carry government spending? How many big businesses, with defence force contracts, are making good profits from our peacekeeping involvement? A short time ago we heard that the big three banks turned over record-breaking profits. Why is there no business levy?

In looking at this letter it is important to note the word 'we' and the direct reference to the group 'PAYE taxpayer'. Anger and resentment about perceived unfairness in who carries the tax burden is clearly evident in this letter. The author clearly perceives unfairness in the tax system whereby one group of taxpayers (which s/he belongs to) is being asked to carry the tax levy while big businesses (which make big profits) are exempted. While the decision in this case about the levy and who was to pay it stemmed from government (and government was identified as an outgroup in the letters) the anger and resentment about the perceived unfairness undoubtedly impacts negatively on both perceptions of the tax authority (since it would be enforcing the levy) and the tax system more generally.

Similarly, another study which analysed the content of unsolicited comments written by 155 taxpayers at the end of a self-completion survey relating to attitudes toward tax in 2000 (Taylor 2003) found that social identities were identified in 74 percent of cases. Specific comments referred to the fact that 'the tax system is inequitable', 'the system benefits the wealthy', 'too many loopholes in the system', 'little people pay while the rich don't' and the 'rules are applied inconsistently'. Further, those who perceived the tax authority as being unrepresentative regarded being an honest taxpayer as less important, felt more resentment about paying tax, felt less obligated to obey the rules and were more disengaged from and resistant toward the tax system than those who perceived the tax authority to be representative.

Representativeness of Tax Authorities and Voluntary Tax Compliance

The above findings show that taxpayers can define themselves in terms of sub-groups of taxpayers and that perceptions of unfairness can stem from this social identity ('it is unfair for us'). Perceptions of an unrepresentative tax authority and an illegitimate tax system can lead to resistance and disengagement from that system (Braithwaite et al. 2003). Indeed it is precisely under these conditions that it is argued that people will actively begin to seek out ways to avoid paying tax (entering the underground economy, cash payments etc.). These findings imply that the degree to which voluntary tax compliance will occur will depend upon the perceived legitimacy of the tax system overall and the degree to which the tax authority is perceived as legitimate and representative of self as a taxpayer, *not from surveillance or the risk of being caught per se*. To the degree that surveillance and risk of detection drive tax compliance this will occur as *a result of* how the tax authority and tax system are perceived. One way to measure voluntary tax compliance in this context is to investigate the degree to which 'extra' income not ordinarily subject to automatic tax deductions and not always easy to track is declared to the tax authority. Such income would include eligible terminal payments, government allowances, government and superannuation pensions, interest, and dividends. These items in Australia are regarded as 'extra income' as tax is not automatically deducted from these types of income – they therefore provide an indication of the degree to which taxpayers choose to declare these items on their tax returns.

Given the preceding argument it is hypothesised that declaration of this type of income will increase the more that a tax authority is perceived to be representative of and acting in the interests of all taxpayers. This should occur while holding constant the perceived risk of detection for non-compliance and previous experience with audits and fines. Further, as ingroups are perceived as more persuasive, legitimate and fair than outgroup members (Ellemers et al. 1998; Haslam 2001; Turner et al. 1987; Tyler 1997), a representative tax authority should be associated with greater legitimacy, greater fairness and less threat than an unrepresentative tax authority. This is because an unrepresentative authority loses influence as it loses legitimacy, and can become associated with perceptions of threat and coercion (Taylor and McGarty 2001).

These hypotheses were investigated through analysis of data from a self-completion survey conducted with Australian taxpayers in 2000 by the Centre for Tax System Integrity at the Australian National University (Braithwaite 2000).[1] The research presented in this section comprises part of a much larger research project conducted by the Centre, in which a survey was mailed out randomly to 7754 Australian taxpayers drawn from the Australian electoral roll. 2040 taxpayers returned their questionnaires. This chapter deals only with those survey questions relevant to the issues being investigated, and relates only to those respondents who provided complete data on the variables being investigated (N=1173). In addition to demographic variables, scales were constructed from items in the questionnaire to reflect perceptions relating to representativeness of the tax office, legitimacy, threat, fairness of tax burden, power of the tax office over individuals and big business, and self-reporting of 'extra' income.

Construction of Scale Items

Measuring Perceived Representativeness of the Australian Tax Office (ATO)

An eight-item scale was constructed from the questionnaire reflecting the degree to which the ATO was perceived as representative of the taxpayer (Taylor, 2003). Responses were made on a scale ranging from 1 (strongly disagree) to 5 (strongly agree). The items were: 'The tax office listens to powerful interest groups, not to ordinary Australians', 'The tax office can be trusted to administer the tax system so that it is right for the country as a whole', 'The tax office's decisions are too influenced by political pressures', 'The tax office has acted in the interests of all Australians', 'The tax office has turned its back on its responsibility to Australians', 'The tax office has caved in to pressure from special interest groups', 'The tax office is trusted by you to administer the tax system fairly', and 'The tax office takes advantage of people who are vulnerable'. Some of these items were reverse scored so that a higher score on this scale reflects a more representative tax authority. This scale is referred to as 'ATO-self' ($\alpha = .84$).

Measuring Legitimacy of the Australian Tax Office

Tyler (1997, p.323) defines legitimacy as 'the feeling of obligation to defer and accept that authorities are entitled to be obeyed'. Two items measuring obligation to obey authority (see Tyler, 1997) were combined to reflect perceived legitimacy of the tax office. These were 'People should follow the decisions of the Tax Office even if they go against what they think is right' and 'I should accept decisions made by the Tax Office even when I disagree with them' ($\alpha = .61$). Although inter-item reliability was not particularly high, this finding is consistent with some of the inter-item reliabilities found by Tyler, 1997. This scale is referred to as 'legitimacy' with a higher score reflecting greater perceived legitimacy of the ATO.

Measuring Perceived Threat of the Australian Tax Office

A four-item scale was constructed to reflect how threatening the tax office was perceived to be. These were 'The tax office is more interested in catching you for doing the wrong thing, than helping you do the right thing', 'The tax office has too much power', 'The tax office treats people as if they will only do the right thing when forced to', and 'The tax office treats people as if they can be trusted to do the right thing' (reverse scored). This scale is referred to as 'threat' ($\alpha = .74$), with a higher score on this scale reflecting a perception that the ATO is threatening.

Measuring Fairness of Tax Burden

A three-item scale was constructed to measure perceived fairness of the tax burden for oneself and similar others. These were: 'In your opinion, do the following people/groups pay their fair share of tax? (a) You, yourself (b) your industry/occupation group'. These items were responded to on a 1 (much more than fair share) to 5 (much less than fair share) scale. A third item asked 'Think about the people who are in the same boat as you when it comes to paying tax. In your opinion, do they pay … ?' with the same response scale as before. This scale is referred to as 'fairness' ($\alpha = .75$) with a higher score reflecting the perception that the tax burden is fair.

Measuring Perceived Power of the Australian Tax Office to Obtain Compliance

Five items were factor analysed to reflect the perceived power of the ATO to obtain compliance. These were 'The Tax Office can't do much if a large company decides to defy it', 'The Tax Office can't do much if a small business decides to defy it', 'The Tax Office can't do much if a wealthy individual decides to defy it', 'The Tax Office can't do much if an ordinary wage and salary earner decides to defy it', 'The Tax Office can't do much if a self-employed taxpayer decides to defy it'. So that high power was associated with higher scores, all five items were reverse scored. These five items were factor-analysed using Principal Components Analysis with Varimax rotation. The analysis yielded two components with eigenvalues greater than 1, accounting for 81 percent of the variance. As expected, large companies and wealthy individuals loaded onto one component, while small business, ordinary wage and salary earners and self-employed taxpayers loaded onto the second component. All loadings were at .8 or higher. The first component is referred to as Power over Large Business ($\alpha = .88$), while the second component is referred to as Power over Individuals ($\alpha = .82$).

Measuring Voluntary Tax Compliance

Voluntary tax compliance was measured by the degree to which respondents indicated that they had declared all (a) eligible terminal payments, (2) Australian government allowances, (3) government and superannuation pensions, (4) interest, and (5) dividends. These items are regarded as 'extra income' as tax is not automatically deducted from these types of income and so provide an indication of the degree to which taxpayers choose to declare these items on their tax returns. A principal components analysis revealed all items to load onto one factor, accounting for 58 percent of the variance, ($\alpha = .79$).

Factors that Correlate with a Representative Tax Authority

Table 1 shows the inter-item correlations for each of these variables, as well as means and standard deviations. It can be seen that, in terms of straight bivariate correlations, a more representative tax authority was significantly associated with a more legitimate, fair and unthreatening tax authority. A representative tax authority was also perceived as one which possessed power over big business and high wealth individuals (psychological outgroup) while no relationship with power over individuals (psychological ingroup) existed.

Table 1   Means, standard deviations and inter-item correlations for perceptions of power, threat, legitimacy, fairness, representativeness of the tax office, and reporting of income

	Mean	SD	ATO-self	Legit	Threat	Fair-ness	Power (indiv)	Power (bus)
ATO-Self	2.97	.65						
Legitimacy	2.67	.83	.22*					
Threat	3.00	.72	-.69*	-.15*				
Fairness	2.63	.63	.29*	.13*	-.25*			
Power (ind)	4.13	.66	-.04	.12*	.04	-.07		
Power (bus)	3.17	1.20	.40*	-.15*	-.27	.16*	.23*	
Tax compliance	0.98	.10	.04	-.04	-.02	-.02	.14*	.02

Representativeness of the ATO and Willingness to Declare Extra Income

To investigate which variables affected taxpayers' willingness to declare extra income, and the role of taxpayer identity in this process, a hierarchical regression analysis was undertaken. In a first step, the demographic variables of age, sex and income were entered as well as whether taxpayers had ever been audited or fined, and perceived likelihood of getting caught by the tax office for not declaring income. With these variables controlled for, the second step entered legitimacy, threat, fairness, power over individuals, power over business and representativeness of the ATO. A third step entered interaction terms between representativeness of the ATO and legitimacy, threat, fairness, power over individuals and power over big business/high wealth individuals.

Voluntary tax compliance was found to be significantly greater with respondents who were older and had higher incomes. This correlation between age and tax compliance has been found in previous research (see Wenzel and Taylor 2004), as has the correlation between higher income and tax compliance (see Wenzel 2002). Further and as predicted, the more representative the tax office was perceived to be, the more compliant taxpayers were. It was also found that the more the tax office was perceived to possess power over individuals the greater the tax compliance. However, while this latter finding might at first glance support a surveillance/threat explanation for compliance, this main effect was mediated by a significant interaction between the representativeness of the tax office and perceived power over individuals (see Figure 1). That is, when the tax office was perceived as *unrepresentative* of self, power over individuals was associated significantly with greater tax compliance ($\beta=0.18$, p<.01), reflecting the standard deterrence explanation of tax behaviour. However, when the tax office was perceived as *representative* of self, tax compliance was not significantly associated with the degree to which the tax office was perceived to have power over individuals ($\beta=0.04$, ns). Consistent with the earlier theorising, tax authority power over individuals is not a driver of tax compliance when the authority is perceived to represent the interests of taxpayers. It only increases tax compliance when the tax authority is perceived as unrepresentative of taxpayers.

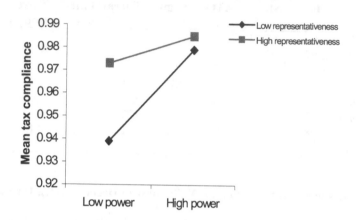

Figure 1   Relationship between power over individuals, representativeness of tax office and tax compliance

A Social Identity Perspective for Understanding Voluntary Tax Compliance

Clearly, a tax authority which embodies (or is perceived to embody) the norms and values of those over whom it rules (taxpayers) has many advantages over an authority which does not. It is much more likely to be judged favourably and hence to have its decisions and actions viewed as legitimate and fair by taxpayers. This means it is well placed to obtain voluntary compliance, as a legitimate authority engenders a sense of willingness and obligation to obey rules (Tyler 1997). When taxpayers are willing to follow rules and declare their taxable income voluntarily, a much more effective system of taxation is able to operate because time and resources which would otherwise be required by a tax authority to enforce compliance are not necessary and can be utilised elsewhere.

The fact that a representative authority is persuasive and not coercive (Haslam 2001; Turner et al. 1987) also means that that authority is not associated with threat. This is important for authorities trying to obtain compliance as the use (or perceived use) of threat can lead to the opposite behaviour from that advocated (Brehm and Brehm 1981). An example where the use of threat with taxpayers may well have backfired stem from findings reported by Slemrod et al. (2001). In this study, in collaboration with the Minnesota Department of Revenue, a random sample of Minnesota taxpayers, stratified by income (low, medium, high) were either sent a letter from the Commissioner of Revenue informing them that they had been randomly selected for close examination of their individual tax returns or were not contacted at all (control group). The aim was to determine whether an audit threat would increase tax compliance. Changes in self-reported taxable income were compared between the previous and current returns, as well as between the experimental and control groups. While the low and medium income taxpayers reported an increase in taxable income compared with the control group, the high income taxpayers who were sent an audit letter reported *less* income than the comparable control group. Although the authors suggest the possibility that high income earners may have reacted to the audit threat by entering into what they perceived as a process of 'negotiation' with the tax authority, it is equally possible that these high income earners reacted against what they may have perceived to be an illegitimate, unfair and unwarranted use of authority power.

When threat and coercion are perceived to be used against self and ingroup members, people can react against such threat by resisting or adopting behaviour in the opposite direction from that advocated (Brehm and Brehm 1981). If an intergroup context is salient (e.g., 'us taxpayers' versus 'the tax authority'), the relationship between taxpayers and the tax authority is likely to be increasingly characterized by perceptions of threat and coercion (Haslam 2001; Taylor and McGarty 2001), resulting in greater resistance, hostility and counter attack (Kemmelmeier and Winter 2000). Such attitudinal and behavioural responses are clearly detrimental for tax authorities attempting to obtain compliance with rules and regulations. They are also potentially detrimental to the morale of tax authority staff, particularly those who have to deal with disgruntled taxpayers on a daily basis. Although further research is needed to tease out how different taxpayers may respond to the use of threat, tax authorities would do well to err on the side of caution and be very careful about when and how they use threat and coercion with taxpayers.

Conclusion

Tax non-compliance (particularly in the underground economy and in countries which rely on self-reporting) is a major concern for governments and tax authorities on a global scale. Non-compliance erodes the tax base, reduces the revenue available for maintenance of public goods and services, redistributes the tax burden unfairly and increases the likelihood of dissatisfaction with, and resentment toward, tax authorities and the tax system in general. Such attitudes can lead to disengagement with the tax system and actively striving to find ways to avoid paying taxes.

It has been argued in this chapter that voluntary tax compliance revolves primarily around how taxpayers perceive themselves in relation to tax authorities, the tax system and other groups of taxpayers. While satisfaction or dissatisfaction with tax systems cannot be divorced from governments (tax systems operate in order to provide revenue for governments and how taxes are spent are determined by governments) tax authorities are the lawful collector of these monies. They are also the intermediary between governments and the taxpayer, meaning that much of the focus (attitudes, resentments) will naturally fall on tax authorities. Further, as tax authorities are charged with the administration of the tax system and the collection of taxes they play a key role in the integrity and legitimacy of that system. Hence, while tax authorities may have no control over levels of tax or how taxes are spent they do have considerable control over the degree to which the tax system is administered fairly and with integrity. Of foremost importance is the degree to which the tax system and the tax authority are seen as legitimate and representative of taxpayers. Legitimacy and representativeness will be very much based on the degree to which taxpayers feel that they are being treated fairly, respectfully, neutrally and appropriately. Contrary to the view that self-interest, surveillance and threat dominate decisions about tax compliance, voluntary tax compliance was shown in this paper to be strongly affected by factors other than self-interest.

A representative tax authority was clearly shown in this paper to be perceived as legitimate, fair and unthreatening – it was only when the authority was perceived as *unrepresentative* that perceptions of its power was associated with tax compliance. This reflects the fact that an unrepresentative authority loses its legitimacy and influence – as people distance themselves from the system and seek ways to avoid paying tax threat and coercion are all that is left as a tool for tax authorities. As mentioned, however, threat and coercion are unlikely to work when surveillance and monitoring are not possible (as in the underground economy); they are also highly inefficient tools because they are time and resource intensive. Further, given that threat and coercion can actively work against the goals that they are meant to achieve, authorities would do well to expend their resources on trying to improve their legitimacy and representativeness in the eyes of taxpayers rather than rely on surveillance and threat to improve tax compliance.

Note

1. The author was a post doctoral fellow at the Centre for Tax System Integrity between April 2000 and August 2001. Approval has kindly been given by the Centre for Tax System Integrity to reproduce findings from the survey data here.

References

Allingham, M. and Sandmo, A. (1972), 'Income Tax Evasion: A Theoretical Analysis', *Journal of Public Economics*, Vol. 1, pp. 323-38.

Beck, P.J. and Jung, W. (1989), 'Taxpayers' reporting decisions and auditing under information asymmetry', *Accounting Review*, Vol. 64(3), pp. 468-87.

Braithwaite, V. (2000), 'Community Hopes, Fears and Actions Survey. Canberra: Centre for Tax System Integrity', Research School of Social Sciences, The Australian National University.

Braithwaite, V., Schneider, F., Reinhart, M. and Murphy, K. (2003), 'Charting the Shoals of the Cash Economy', in V. Braithwaite (ed.), *Taxing Democracy: Understanding Tax Avoidance and Evasion*, pp. 93-108.

Brehm, S.S. and Brehm, J.W. (1981), *Psychological reactance: A theory of freedom and control*. Academic Press, New York.

Cowell, F.A. (1992), 'Tax evasion and inequity', *Journal of Economic Psychology*, Vol. 13(4), pp. 521-43.

Ellemers, N., Van Rijswijk, W., Bruins, J. and De Gilder, D. (1998), 'Group commitment as a moderator of attributional and behavioural responses to power use', *European Journal of Social Psychology*, Vol. 28, pp. 555-73.

French, J.R.P. and Raven, B.H. (1959), 'The bases of social power', in D. Cartwright (ed.), *Studies in Social Power*, Ann Arbor, Mich: Institute of Social Research, pp. 150-67.

Haslam, S.A. (2001), *Psychology in Organizations: The social identity approach*. Sage Publications, London.

Haslam, S.A. and Platow, M.J. (2001), 'The link between leadership and followership: How affirming social identity translates vision into action', *Personality and Social Psychology Bulletin*, Vol. 27, pp. 1469-79.

Kemmelmeier, M. and Winter, D.G. (2000), 'Putting threat into perspective: Experimental studies on perceptual distortion in international conflict', *Personality and Social Psychology Bulletin*, Vol. 26, pp. 795-809.

McGraw, K.M. and Scholz, J.T. (1991), 'Appeals to civic virtue versus attention to self-interest: Effects on tax compliance', *Law and Society Review*, Vol. 25, pp. 471-98.

Roberts, M.L. and Hite, P.A. (1994), 'Progressive taxation, fairness and compliance', *Law and Policy*, Vol. 16, pp. 27-47.

Slemrod, J., Blumenthal, M. and Christian, C. (2001), 'Taxpayer response to an increased probability of audit: evidence from a controlled experiment in Minnesota', *Journal of Public Economics*, Vol. 79, pp. 455-83.

Smith, J. and Tyler, T.R. (1996), 'Justice and power: when will justice concerns encourage the advantaged to support policies which redistribute economic resources and the disadvantaged to willingly obey the law?', *European Journal of Social Psychology*, Vol. 26, pp. 171-200.

Taylor, N. (2001), 'Experiencing social injustice: When subordinate and superordinate identities exclude authorities'. Unpublished manuscript.

Taylor, N. (2003), 'Understanding taxpayer attitudes through understanding taxpayer identities', in V. Braithwaite (ed.), *Taxing Democracy: Understanding Tax Avoidance and Evasion*, pp. 71-92.

Taylor, N. and McGarty, C. (2001), 'The role of subjective group memberships and perceptions of power in industrial conflict', *Journal of Community and Applied Social Psychology*, Vol. 11, pp. 389-93.

Turner, J.C. (1991), *Social Influence*. Open University Press, UK.

Turner, J.C., Hogg, M.A., Oakes, P.J., Reicher, S.D. and Wetherell, M.S. (1987), *Rediscovering the Social Group: A self-categorization theory*. Basil Blackwell, Oxford.

Tyler, T.R. (1997), 'The psychology of legitimacy: A relational perspective on voluntary deference to authorities', *Personality and Social Psychology Review*, Vol. 1, pp. 323-45.

Tyler, T.R., Boeckmann, R.J., Smith, H.J. and Huo, Y.J. (1997), *Social Justice in a Diverse Society*. Westview, Boulder, CO.

Walker, I. and Mann, L. (1987), 'Unemployment, relative deprivation, and social protest', *Personality and Social Psychology Bulletin*, Vol. 13, pp. 275-83.

Wenzel, M. (2002), 'The impact of outcome orientation and justice concerns on tax compliance: The role of taxpayers' identity', *Journal of Applied Psychology*, Vol. 87 (4), pp. 629-45.

Wenzel, M. and Taylor, N. (2004), 'An experimental evaluation of tax-reporting schedules: a case of evidence-based tax administration', *Journal of Public Economics*, Vol. 88, pp. 2785-99.

Chapter 4

Getting On or Getting By?
Australians in the Cash Economy[*]

Valerie Braithwaite, Monika Reinhart and Jenny Job

Introduction

Economic transactions that are undertaken to escape the attention of tax and financial regulators attract interest. On the one side are those looking to emulate the latest ruse; on the other side are those whose job it is to crack down on tax evasion and crime; and in the middle are the masses who simultaneously are entertained and shocked by tales of bold, illegal financial wizardry. Unfortunately, displays of defiance involving money laundering, overseas bank accounts, and major fraud are not the subject of the analysis undertaken in this chapter. Nor are we including in our analysis the hidden economic transactions that occur at the other end of the spectrum – the common kinds of bartering that flourish in any community with a modicum of social capital. Our focus is on economic transactions that lie between these two extremes where individuals pay others or are paid by others in cash for work that has been done, and where the understanding is that tax is not paid on the earned income. These are activities that are part of what is variously referred to as the 'hidden', 'underground', 'shadow', 'grey' or 'cash' economy. Drawing on Feige's (1996, 1999) typology of such activities, the focus of our attention falls mainly in the *unreported economy* in which rules regarding the declaration of income are violated to evade tax, and the *unrecorded economy* in which income producing activities are concealed and not represented through normal accounting conventions, and therefore, cannot be appropriately included in the national accounts.

The domain of enquiry, therefore, involves fairly ordinary activities that most people engage in – paying for household maintenance or home improvements in cash; paying cash for child care, out-of-school tuition, car repairs, laundry, cleaning and meals; being the recipient of cash for helping out in a business; or being paid cash for a second job. As we suggest in this chapter, whether or not people code these activities and payments as significant, in so far as they make tax evasion a little easier remains an open question in Australia. After all, paying or being paid in cash is not a crime. It only becomes illegal and of concern to a tax authority when the income generated by this transaction is not declared or is 'hidden'.

This chapter aims to provide a snapshot of the ways in which Australians routinely think about the cash economy and contribute to its apparently increasing presence (Schneider, 2002). Schneider has ranked Australia 14 among 21 OECD countries in terms of the size of its cash economy. Based on a figure of 14.1 percent of GDP (see Schneider, 2002), Australia's cash economy sits about 2.6 percent below the OECD average of 16.7 percent. It is less than the size of the cash economy in Canada, but more than that of Great Britain, New Zealand and the USA.

From a macro economic perspective, interest in the cash economy revolves around the contentious issue of size, the macro drivers of increased cash economy activity, and the implications for the projection of economic growth and economic policy. From a micro economic perspective, the question is why do individuals become involved in the cash economy: Are they aware of what they are doing, do they actively choose or passively drift into this behaviour, what is the reasoning that lies behind their actions, and how do they make sense of the cash economy more generally? Understanding and identifying the micro triggers is the purpose of the work reported in this chapter.

The chapter is organized around three key issues. In the next section, we use survey data collected from a random sample of 2040 Australians in 2000 to answer the following questions:

(a)   Are Australians tolerant of cash economy activity?
(b)   Do Australians share an understanding that cash economy activity is illegal and unacceptable?
(c)   Do Australians feel responsible for doing something about cash economy activity?
(d)   How likely is it that Australians are unintentionally complicit in cash economy activity; or at the very least, turn a blind eye to their own involvement and of those with whom they transact business?

Next we bring together previous work on the attitudinal drivers of cash economy activity (Braithwaite, Schneider, Reinhart and Murphy, 2003; Reinhart, Job and Braithwaite, 2004; Schneider, Braithwaite and Reinhart, 2001). In particular, we hypothesise that tax morale and the social and legal practices that nurture tax morale determine level of engagement in the cash economy. The data used to test these hypotheses combine survey responses from 2000 and 2001-2.

Finally we use the same data set to explore the prevalence of cash economy activity and ask whether or not cash economy payments and earnings are localized in particular social demographic groups. Of particular interest are questions of whether cash economy earnings are more likely to be found among the young, the poor, the unemployed, those supporting families, and those receiving social security or other government benefits.

Australians Reflect on the Cash Economy

Database

The data used in this section came from a national survey, the Community Hopes, Fears and Actions Survey (CHFAS) (Braithwaite and Reinhart, 2001; Braithwaite, Reinhart, Mearns and Graham, 2001). CHFAS was conducted between June and December 2000, and was a tax omnibus designed to collect baseline data on how Australia's tax system was faring at the time of the introduction of the GST. A sample of 7754 randomly selected citizens from the publicly available electoral rolls received a questionnaire and reply paid envelope. Reminders were sent at varying intervals over the following six months to those with whom we had had no contact. Included in this process was a mail out with a new questionnaire after 5 weeks. In all, 2040 questionnaires were collected for analysis. The response rate, after adjusting for out-of-scope respondents (no longer at the address or deceased), was 29 percent. While low in comparison with other surveys, this response rate is consistent with other research reports based on single topic tax surveys (Kirchler, 1999; Pope, Fayle and Chen, 1993; Wallschutzky, 1996; Webley, Adams and Elffers, 2002). Detailed analyses of early versus late respondents and comparisons with census data on social demographic indicators suggested that the sample provided a relatively representative cross-section of the Australian population. Under-represented were young males and overrepresented were those in scribing occupations (see Mearns and Braithwaite 2001 for details on the methodology and the sampling).

Findings

When asked about the morality of cash economy activity, only a minority of Australians was prepared to condone it. In response to the question, 'do you think you should honestly declare cash earnings on your tax return?', 72 percent said yes, they thought they should. Only 15 percent gave an unequivocal no, and 13 percent opted for a 'don't know' response.

Further evidence of the moral overtones associated with not declaring cash income to the tax authority was evident in another set of questions about 'how you would feel if you were caught and fined for not declaring $5000 that you had earned outside your regular job?'. The overwhelming majority responded with feelings of wrongdoing (82 percent), guilt (70 percent), shame (72 percent), and embarrassment (74 percent), with a high 89 percent expressing concern to put matters right. Australians know the law and have been well socialised into thinking that they should abide by it.

But is the theory reflected in practice? There are a number of pieces of evidence from the CHFAS that suggest that some slippage is tolerated. Australians were asked how they would respond if they found out an acquaintance was working for cash-in-hand payments. The majority said that they would think it was wrong (52 percent), but it was just a majority by a whisker, and the percentage fell short of what we might expect given the moral sentiments expressed above.

Furthermore, 35 percent said they would not care, only 23 percent said they would voice disapproval directly to their acquaintance, and a low 7 percent said they would report it to the Tax Office. In fact, a higher proportion, 13 percent, said they would respond by thinking their acquaintance was clever. In situ, moral constraints seem to evaporate for many people. Perhaps the slippage occurs because there is not deep commitment to the moral principle. It is worth noting, in this regard, that 32 percent thought that working for cash-in-hand payments was a trivial offence, and only 48 percent were clearly of the opinion that the government should actively discourage participation in the cash economy. An unusually high 29 percent said that they just didn't know if the government should do anything or not.

    The picture that emerges from these data is of a society where a moral code and a law regarding cash economy activity remain intertwined and where citizens openly acknowledge what is right and what is morally acceptable. At the same time, there is a story of the desirable and the practicable coming apart. In practice, there appears to be a shift away from the ideal code of practice. Helping explain this shift are responses to questions about what other people are doing. In addition to asking 'what do YOU think' about the cash economy, we asked 'what do you think MOST people think?'. The data were striking in showing how most people thought that others were far more free of the constraints of morals and law than they were. Only 20 percent of Australians thought that MOST people believed in declaring cash earnings (compared to 72 percent in response to what do YOU think), and 56 percent thought that most people considered cash-in-hand tax evasion to be a trivial offence (compared to 32 percent for what do YOU think). We see from these data that the personal norms regarding the right thing to do are at odds with the same people's perceptions of social norms, that is, perceptions of what others think. People believe the social norms to be far more lax and permissive on cash economy matters than their own personal norms.

    Both personal and social norms play a role in shaping tax behaviour (Wenzel, 2004a, b). Some people might be expected to stick by their moral position regardless of what others are doing. Others look to their environment for cues and do their best to fit in. In the area of cash economy, there is every reason to believe that, when relatively small amounts of money are involved (less than $50), the path of least resistance is to 'go with the flow' – at least 'go with *what one believes is* the flow'. We know from the CHFAS that most Australians will use cash for transactions that involve a sum of less than $50 (Braithwaite et al., 2001). In supermarkets, 75 percent of Australians reported using cash if their purchases were below the $50 mark, in stores selling sporting goods, books, clothes or gifts, 66 percent used cash for purchases below $50, and in restaurants, 77 percent used cash if the bill was less than $50. Thus, we might infer that it would be common practice for most Australians to use cash for the run-of-the-mill activities that we have found to be associated with the cash economy (see Schneider et al., 2001) for details of these activities). Having handed over the cash, they can only surmise whether the provider declares it as income to the Tax Office. We suspect that most Australians assume it is not declared, on the basis of their responses about what most people think, but there usually is no hard evidence. When we asked the question, 'In the past 12 months have you paid anyone cash-in-hand for goods and services?' – knowing that they were going to evade tax – only 14 percent said that they had.

Our final question on Australians' reflections on the cash economy was 'why, in your opinion, do people do it?'. A set of options was provided. Most Australians thought that people worked for cash-in-hand to avoid paying tax (92 percent), to get more disposable income (88 percent), and because they needed extra money from a second job (84 percent). The reasons they gave were financial and personal – there was less agreement on people working for cash-in-hand to avoid entering the government system (61 percent) or because the tax rates were too high (67 percent).

There appeared to be less agreement on why people were paid cash-in-hand. Most agreement emerged for employers wanting to avoid insurance, superannuation and other compensatory payments for their employees (74 percent), preferring to stay clear of government and its red tape (67 percent), and reducing costs (62 percent). The CHFAS, unfortunately, did not include questions on why ordinary citizens paid suppliers cash-in-hand for the services and goods they received.

Attitudes that Predict Cash Economy Participation

In the previous section, we explored the ways in which Australians understand the cash economy, regardless of whether or not they participate in it themselves. How we interpret, understand and talk about the cash economy, however, does not necessarily tell us why some people become involved and why others do not. In the remainder of the chapter, our goal is to identify some of the key factors that lead some people into cash economy activity, while others stay away.

The reasons for tax non-compliance are complex and multifaceted (Collins, Milliron and Toy, 1992; Jackson and Milliron, 1986; Richardson and Sawyer, 2001), but one of the most important attitudinal factors to emerge at the macro analytic level is tax morale (Torgler, 2003). Using cross-national data sets, Torgler has been able to show that countries that have low tax morale also have higher tax evasion and tax avoidance.

Within the context of the cash economy, tax morale has been singled out as a constraint in situations where opportunity beckons (Brooks, 1998; Schneider and Enste, 2000; Wallschutzky, 1993). Tax morale has been defined broadly by Frey and his colleagues (for example, see Frey and Feld, 2002) as the 'intrinsic motivation to pay taxes' (Torgler, 2003: 5). Others refer to a similar phenomenon when they state that people pay tax voluntarily (Alm et al., 1995; Andreoni et al., 1998; Lewis, 1982), because they believe it is a desirable thing to do (Schwartz and Orleans, 1967; McGraw and Scholz, 1991; Richardson and Sawyer, 2001; Weigel, Hessing and Elffers, 1987).

Database

In order to test the hypothesis that tax morale constrains people in their cash economy activity, seven variables that are thought to reflect tax morale were selected from the Community Hopes, Fears and Actions Survey (CHFAS) and from the follow-up Australian Tax System: Fair or Not Survey (ATSFONS). The surveys were conducted 18 months apart, with the ATSFONS following up respondents from the CHFAS and adding 1213 new cases to the sample (response rate for this new sample was 38 percent). For the present analysis, the new cases from the ATSFONS are added to the CHFAS sample to give a total of 3253 respondents, of whom 184 had worked for cash-in-hand payments (suppliers) and 455 had paid others cash-in-hand (purchasers).

The seven variables thought to reflect tax morale are listed in Table 1. These variables are measured through a set of multi-item scales, the details of which can be obtained from Braithwaite and Reinhart (2001). For present purposes, it is important to note that the scales reflect the degree to which individual respondents endorse each of the attitudinal concepts listed in Table 1. Thus, the higher the score, the stronger the attitude.

The first five variables in Table 1 represent internal constraints. By internal constraint we mean an attitude that boosts the individual's sense that engaging in the cash economy is wrong, and is something that will and should generate feelings of discomfort, shame, guilt, or disapproval. In addition to asking directly about such feelings and beliefs (1-3 in Table 1), respondents were asked to predict their behaviours towards an acquaintance engaged in cash economy activity (4-5 in Table 1). The assumption was that people with high tax morale themselves, in particular with a deep sense of moral commitment, would be more likely to report cash economy 'wrongdoing' to the authorities and would be less likely to approve of such behaviour.

The final two measures in Table 1 (6-7) are external (as opposed to internal) constraints that are required to legitimise and nurture tax morale. Internal constraints are learnt and reinforced by the community that shares them. As that community disappears, and as internal constraints like tax morale lose value and fail to elicit respect, individuals 're-define' doing the right thing so that they can adapt to their changing environment without feeling fearful or guilty about the consequences. Some psychologists and criminologists refer to this as rationalization (Thurman, St John and Riggs, 1984), implying that wrongful actions are undertaken against the backdrop of an enduring moral code. In the domain of taxation, our rapidly changing world makes the moral foundations less solid. 'The right thing to do' is constantly being challenged, if not re-defined, by changing laws, changing technologies, changing norms, and changing codes for survival. Thus, tax morale is unlikely to remain high if the community perceives flouting of the law and little likelihood of sanctioning from the authorities.

Findings

In Table 1, correlations are reported between tax morale and working in the cash economy (supplier) (Column 2) and tax morale and paying others who are working in the cash economy (purchaser) (Column 3). With one exception, the five measures of internal constraints were significantly correlated with cash economy participation in the direction that one would expect. Participation was higher among those who did not feel shame or guilt, who felt little pride in being an honest taxpayer, and who were tolerant, if not approving, of acquaintances working for cash-in-hand. The one exception involved taxpayer ethics. One could *believe* that one should be honest in one's tax dealings, yet pay someone in cash, knowing that they would not declare it to the Tax Office. The other important observation to make regarding the correlations in Table 1 is that all the relationships are quite low. Thus, tax morale constrains cash economy activity, but only to a small degree, whether one is a supplier or a purchaser.

Table 1 Measures that are associated with tax morale and their relationships with participation in the cash economy as a supplier (person who works for cash-in-hand = 1, other = 0) or purchaser (person who pays cash-in-hand = 1, other = 0)[a]

	Pearson product-moment correlation coefficient	
Measures linked to tax morale	Working for cash-in-hand (supplier)	Paying cash-in-hand (purchaser)
Internal constraints		
1. Personal norm of being honest on tax	-.17***	-.03
2. Pride in being an honest taxpayer	-.12***	-.08***
3. Feelings of shame, guilt and embarrassment if caught for not declaring cash payments	-.11***	-.09***
4. Approving of an acquaintance working cash-in-hand – thinking they were clever	.17***	.10***
5. Willing to dob-in an acquaintance working cash-in-hand	-.11***	-.13***
External constraints		
6. Perceptions of a social norm of being honest	-.09***	-.10***
7. Perception of enforcement by the tax authority – chances of being caught	-.12***	-.18***

[a] The questions asked were: 'Have you worked for cash-in-hand payments in the last 12 months? By cash-in-hand we mean cash money that tax is not paid on'; and 'Have you paid anyone cash-in-hand payments in the last 12 months for work or services they provided to you? By cash-in-hand we mean cash money that tax is not paid on'. Notes: *** $p < .001$.

For the external constraints of the perceived norms of others in the community (6 in Table 1) and the likelihood of getting caught (7 in Table 1), the correlations again are significant though small, and are in the direction predicted. As hypothesised, when external constraints are perceived to be strong, be they social or legal, the likelihood of being involved oneself as a supplier or purchaser is lower.

In summary, tax morale is important as a base for containing cash economy activity. Tax morale like conscience is a self-regulatory device. As with all self-regulatory devices, tax morale needs the support of social and legal infrastructure. Tax morale is likely to flag if society's major institutions and citizenry show signs of not taking tax compliance seriously. Thus, we find that perceptions of how other people are responding to the cash economy (perceptions of the social norms), and the likelihood of being caught also play a role in containing individual participation in the cash economy. While the consistency in the statistics associated with various indicators of tax morale is impressive, we should not be deceived into thinking that the story is all about tax morale. The amount of variation in cash economy behaviour that is explained by tax morale remains notably small. Tax morale provides a base for containment. It is not sufficient by any means. There are other factors at work that trigger cash economy involvement. In the next section, we consider some other explanations.

Social Demographic Dispersion of Cash Economy Participation

The media have popularised the notion that cash economy activity occurs mainly within certain social groups. Tradespersons, taxi drivers and welfare beneficiaries are regularly targeted for cash economy crackdowns (*The Age*, 2003; Clark, 2003). The assumption has always been that material self-interest prevails particularly when opportunity presents itself and needs demand satisfaction (Brooks, 1998; Schneider and Enste, 2000). In this section we ask whether there is evidence to support the idea that cash economy activity occurs in pockets or is restricted to certain social demographic groups. We ask whether those who supply cash economy labour or purchase cash economy labour are predominantly: (a) male or female; (b) young or old; (c) married or not married; (d) with or without children at home; (e) Australian born or born elsewhere; (f) with high income or low income; (g) with basic educational qualifications or highly educated; (h) in the official paid workforce or outside of it; and (i) employed by others or self-employed? Finally, we examine the occupational profile of cash economy workers, asking what kinds of jobs do they do officially, and does this correspond to their cash economy work.

Data Set

The analyses presented in this section are based on the aggregated data set used in the previous section that combines the random sample from the CHFAS in 2000 and the new random sample from the ATSFONS in 2001-2. In earlier work, analyses were carried out on a sample of people who responded to the CHFAS in

2000 and later these same people responded to the ATSFONS in 2001-2. Results from this panel study are reported in Braithwaite et al. (2003). Where these findings are referred to below, they are identified as 'panel study findings' to distinguish them from the aggregated data set used for this chapter.

Findings

Based on the aggregated data set, the percentage of Australians who reported that they had worked in the cash economy in the past 12 months was 6 percent. The average amount earned in the cash economy was in the vicinity of $2000, with 62 percent earning less than $1,000 and 11 percent earning more than $5,000. The kinds of jobs that people most commonly reported doing for cash-in-hand involved household services (34 percent), home repairs (22 percent), teaching and training (19 percent), and garden work (8 percent).

The pattern for purchasers was similar, but with a higher rate of involvement. The percentage paying for cash economy services in the past 12 months was 14 percent, but again the average paid out was in the vicinity of $2,000. Of the purchasers, 66 percent estimated their expense as being less than $1,000, and 6 percent reported paying out more than $5,000. The jobs that purchasers paid for primarily involved home repairs (45 percent), followed by household services (23 percent) and gardening (21 percent).

From panel data findings reported in Braithwaite et al. (2003), most of this activity was transient from one year to the next, with only 2 percent of those working for cash-in-hand being 'stayers'. Most took work of this kind at one time point, but not the other: 4 percent in 2000, and 4 percent in 2001-2 (Braithwaite et al., 2003). The same story of being a transient applied to purchasers. While 8 percent reported being repeat players from one year to the next, 8 percent purchased cash economy services only in 2000, and 9 percent only in 2001-2 (Braithwaite et al., 2003).

The transient and, as we will see below, dispersed nature of cash economy activity is perhaps the most surprising finding from this research. Not only is cash economy work undertaken by different people at different times, but these people come from all different walks of life. If we are to believe the data presented here, cash economy activity can pop up anywhere and everywhere – we may think it is wrong, but we live happily in its midst. Before pursuing this argument further, however, let us return to the data summarized in Table 2, showing variation and similarity across different social demographic groups.

Looking at the supply column (Column 3) in Table 2, most of the percentages showing cash economy activity fall in the 4 to 7 range. The differences that emerged between groups, while statistically significant, are not dramatic. Working for cash-in-hand payments was significantly more common in some social demographic groups than others, but the percentages indicating participation rates show its presence in all groups to some degree.

Table 2   Percent of the sample who provide labour in the cash economy (suppliers) and who purchase labour in the cash economy (purchasers) broken down by social demographic characteristics

Social demographic variable	Category	% supplying labour		% purchasing labour	
Sex	male	7	***	16	**
	female	4		13	
Age	30 yrs or less	13	***	8	***
	31-54 years	6		16	
	55 yrs or more	2		14	
Marital status	married	5	***	16	***
	not married	9		11	
Dependants	no child at home	6		14	
	child at home	6		16	
Australian born	no	4	*	17	*
	yes	6		14	
Education level[a]	primary/intermediate	2	***	7	***
	leaving, year 12	7		12	
	trade, diploma	9		18	
	university	6		22	
Personal income	less than $12,000	7		8	***
	$12,000 to $18,999	6		11	
	$19,000 or more	6		18	
Official work status	full-time	6	*	17	***
	part-time	8		15	
	none	5		12	
Work sector	self-employed	10	**	20	*
	employee private	7		14	
	employee public or non-profit	4		16	

[a] The sample used for this particular analysis came from the CHFAS. The question was not asked in ATSFONS. All other analyses are based on the aggregated data set. Notes: $* p < 0.05$; $** p < 0.01$; $*** p < 0.001$.

From Table 2, the most marked differences for working for cash-in-hand emerge in relation to education, age and work sector. Those who were older and more poorly educated were *not* prominent in the ranks of cash economy workers. Indeed, those who left school at 15 years of age or less were the least represented of all groups as workers in the cash economy (2 percent). The young, however, were overrepresented, as were the self-employed. Filling this picture out a little more are results depicting the cash economy worker as an unmarried Australian-born male. In 2000, this person was far more likely to be in the official work force either as a full-time or part-time worker, but by 2001-2, the relationship was less marked. Thus, we see only a weak relationship emerge in the aggregated data set summarized in Table 2. At this stage, it remains unclear whether this change is due to sampling fluctuation or to the impact of the GST.

If we turn our attention now to those who purchased the labour of the cash economy worker, the social demographic profile is reversed in some important respects. Purchasers were older, wealthier, and married. They were well-educated with full-time jobs. They were also somewhat more likely to be self-employed and not born in Australia, although both these relationships weakened from 2000 to 2001-2002.

These research findings associate cash economy activity with mainstream Australia. There is little evidence in the analyses presented to date of such activity being the preferred option of socially marginalised or economically disadvantaged groups in society. Nevertheless, we can use the aggregated CHFAS and ATSFONS data set to look more deeply at those in receipt of a government benefit and those whose work in the official economy is unskilled. First, we explore the data for evidence of recipients of government benefits working for cash-in-hand more often than others in the community. Second, we examine the source of cash economy labour: Is it more likely to be drawn from particular occupational groups, in particular unskilled groups?

Neither the 2000 nor the 2001-2 surveys were designed to address specifically issues of government benefits. From the survey data, however, we were able to group respondents into one of three categories: (a) those in receipt of a government allowance such as Youth Allowance, Austudy or Newstart who had lodged a tax return; (b) those not in receipt of a government allowance such as Youth Allowance, Austudy or Newstart who had lodged a tax return; and (c) other. Since lodgement is expected of all Australians whose annual income exceeds $6,000, the numbers comprising the first two groups were quite respectable for the purposes of this analysis. A comparison of these groups in terms of who worked in the cash economy and who did not produced significant findings (see Reinhart et al., 2004 for full report). Of those who received an allowance, 11 percent were employed in the cash economy. Of those who did not receive an allowance, 5 percent were cash economy workers. The percentage was the same for the 'other' category. A disproportionate number of beneficiaries under these schemes would have been younger Australians. Thus, support emerges for increased cash economy work being undertaken by beneficiaries of government benefits in circumstances where the beneficiary is relatively young. The age qualification is important because when this analysis was repeated for older Australians, no significant differences emerged. Participation rates were 5 percent for those who lodged a tax return and received a pension, 7 percent for those who lodged a tax return and did not receive a pension, and 5 percent for those in the 'other' category.

Finally, we ask the question where does the cash economy labour come from? Statistically, there is a relationship between the jobs held in the official economy and those performed in the cash economy (see Reinhart et al., 2004 for details of the analysis). Those who are managers or professionals are more likely than other occupational groups to be working as managers or professionals in the cash economy. Similarly, those officially in clerical, sales and trades are proportionally overestimated in cash economy activities in clerical, sales and trades. And transport, production and labouring work in the official economy is more likely to be carried out by the same people in the cash economy. But the other observation that can made from the data in Table 3 is that while cash economy skilled work (either managerial/professional or trades/clerical/sales) is more likely to be done by those with the relevant skills in the official economy, most skilled cash economy workers find work outside their main occupation. In contrast, unskilled workers who venture into the cash economy stay within the category of unskilled labour.

Table 3   Do Australians stay within their occupational group or diversify when they work in the cash economy

	% staying within	% going outside
Professional, managerial	37	63
Trade, clerical, sales, hospitality	38	62
Transport, production, labourers	69	31

Conclusion

Australians engage in the cash economy as suppliers of labour and purchasers of labour. The social demographic profiles of these groups differ. Purchasers tend to be older, married, employed full-time, highly educated and highly paid. Suppliers are more likely to be male, young, not married, and to have a diploma or a secondary qualification. Both groups were overrepresented among the self-employed, particularly suppliers. Suppliers were also more likely to be receiving a youth or student allowance or a government benefit designed for the unemployed. These profiles suggest that those who profit from the cash economy are the privileged in our society and those who are trying to get a foothold on the ladder of opportunity. Through involvement in the cash economy, Australians both line their wallets and meet their needs.

These differences, however, do not polarise social-demographic groups. Cash economy activity is widely dispersed and highly visible in the population. The visibility is reflected in Australians' perceptions of community tolerance of cash economy activity, a tolerance that is accompanied by a personal belief that it really is the wrong thing to do. The tension that has been documented between Australians' perceptions of social norms and their personal ethics would appear to be an unstable psychological state. Either Australians compartmentalize cash economy activity as something over which they have little control – as something they deal with by going with the flow – or they are in the process of bringing their personal beliefs in line with social realities. Presumably this process involves looking more kindly on those engaging in the cash economy, even if it seems wrong, and re-defining cash economy activity as a way of showing initiative, making one's way in the world and getting ahead, particularly among the young.

As for the role of tax authorities in this climate, the challenge appears to be one of containment rather than elimination of cash economy activity. A surprising number of Australians are unsure whether the government should or should not be cracking down on such activity. The links between the cash economy and the official economy are strong. People work in both, sometimes in the same job, sometimes not. The relationships between the two economies suggest that at the individual level, getting a job in one may be an advantage in getting a job in the other. For many Australians, cash economy activity may simply be a response to the challenge of the times – to work hard, to reap the rewards of their efforts, to save for retirement, and to express their individualism through self-reliance. Within the confines of this newly emerging and prized self-image, tax authorities, for many Australians, have yet to convincingly stake their claim.

Note

*   The research reported in this paper was funded by the Australian Taxation Office, the Commonwealth Department of Family and Community Services and the Australian National University.

References

Alm, J., Sanchez, I. and De Juan, A. (1995), 'Economic and Non-economic Factors in Tax Compliance', *Kyklos*, Vol. 48(1), pp. 3-18.

Andreoni, J., Erard, B. and Feinstein J. (1998), 'Tax Compliance', *Journal of Economic Literature*, Vol. 36, pp. 818-60.

Braithwaite, V. and Reinhart, M. (2001), *The Community Hopes, Fears and Actions Survey: Goals and Measures*, Centre for Tax System Integrity Working Paper No. 2, Australian National University and Australian Taxation Office, Canberra.

Braithwaite, V., Reinhart, M., Mearns, M. and Graham, R. (2001), *Preliminary Findings from the Community Hopes, Fears and Actions Survey*, Centre for Tax System Integrity Working Paper No. 3, Australian National University and Australian Taxation Office, Canberra.

Braithwaite, V., Schneider, F., Reinhart, M. and Murphy, K. (2003), 'Charting the Shoals of the Cash Economy', in V. Braithwaite (ed.), *Taxing Democracy: Understanding Tax Avoidance and Evasion*, Ashgate, Aldershot.

Brooks, N. (1998), 'The Challenge of Tax Compliance', in C. Evans and A. Greenbaum (eds), *Tax Administration: Facing the challenges of the future*, Prospect Media, St Leonards, Australia.

Clark, D. (2003), 'Insight: Nothing for Little Johnny', *Business Review Weekly*, December, www.brweekly.com/stories/20031201/21095.aspx.

Collins, J.H., Milliron, V.C. and Toy, D.R. (1992), 'Determinants of Tax Compliance: A Contingency Approach', *Journal of the American Taxation Association*, Vol. 14, pp. 1-29.

Feige, E. (1996), 'Overseas Holdings of U.S. Currency and the Underground Economy', in S. Pozo (ed.), *Exploring the Underground Economy: Studies of Illegal and Unreported Activity*, WE Upjohn Institute for Employment Research, Kalamazoo, Michigan.

Feige, E. (1999), 'Underground Economies in Transition: Noncompliance and Institutional Change', in E. Feige and K. Ott (eds), *Underground Economies in Transition*, Ashgate, Aldershot.

Frey, B. and Feld, L. (2002), 'Deterrence and Morale in Taxation: An Empirical Analysis', CESifo Working Paper No. 760.

Jackson, B.R. and Milliron, V.C. (1986), 'Tax Compliance Research: Findings, Problems, and Prospects', *Journal of Accounting Literature*, Vol. 5, pp. 125-65.

Kirchler, E. (1999), 'Reactance to Taxation: Employers Attitudes towards Taxes', *Journal of Socio-Economics*, Vol. 28, pp. 131-38.

Lewis, A. (1982), *The Psychology of Taxation*, Martin Robertson, Oxford.

McGraw, K.M. and Scholz, J.T. (1991), 'Appeals to Civic Virtue versus Attention to Self-Interest: Effects on Tax Compliance', *Law and Society Review*, Vol. 25(3), pp. 471-98.

Mearns, M. and Braithwaite, V. (2001), *The Community Hopes, Fears and Actions Survey: Survey Method, Sample Representativeness and Data Quality*, Centre for Tax System Integrity Working Paper No. 4, Australian National University and Australian Taxation Office, Canberra.

Pope, J., Fayle, R. and Chen, D.L. (1993), *The Compliance Costs of Employment-Related Taxation in Australia*, Australian Tax Research Foundation, Sydney.

Reinhart, M., Job, J. and Braithwaite, V. (2004), *Untaxed Cash Work: Feeding Mouths, Lining Wallets*, Report for the Department of Family and Community Services, Canberra.

Richardson, M. and Sawyer, A.J. (2001), 'A Taxonomy of the Tax Compliance Literature: Further Findings, Problems and Prospects', *Australian Taxation Forum*, Vol. 16(2), pp. 137-320.

Schneider, F. (2002), 'The Value Added of Underground Activities: Size and Measurement of the Shadow Economies of 110 Countries All over the World', Paper presented at the Centre for Tax System Integrity Workshop on Economic Integrity in the Tax System, The Australian National University, 17 July, Canberra.

Schneider, F. and Enste, D.H. (2000), 'Shadow Economies: Size, Causes, and Consequences', *Journal of Economic Literature*, Vol. XXXVIII, pp. 77-114.

Schneider, F., Braithwaite, V. and Reinhart, M. (2001), *Individual Behaviour in Australia's Shadow Economy: Facts, Empirical Findings and Some Mysteries*, Centre for Tax System Integrity Working Paper No. 19, Australian National University and Australian Taxation Office, Canberra.

Schwartz, R. and Orleans, S. (1967), 'On Legal Sanctions', *University of Chicago Law Review*, Vol. 34, pp. 282-300.

The Age (2003), '70,000 Face New Tax Blitz', August 19.

Thurman, Q.C., St John, C. and Riggs, L. (1984), 'Neutralization and Tax Evasion: How Effective would a Moral Appeal be in Improving Compliance to Tax Laws?', *Law and Policy*, Vol. 6, pp. 309-27.

Torgler, B. (2003), 'Tax Morale: Theory and Empirical Analysis of Tax Compliance', Doctoral Dissertation, Universität Basel.

Wallschutzky, I. (1993), 'Taxpayer Compliance – Issues in Research Methods', Paper presented at the ATO Conference on Taxpayer Compliance Research, 2-3 December, Canberra.

Wallschutzky, I. (1996), 'Issues in research methods: with reference to income tax research', Department of Commerce, University of Newcastle, Newcastle.

Webley, P., Adams, C. and Elffers, H. (2002), *VAT Compliance in the United Kingdom*, Centre for Tax System Integrity Working Paper No. 41, Australian National University and Australian Taxation Office, Canberra.

Weigel, R., Hessing, D. and Elffers, H. (1987), 'Tax Evasion Research: A Critical Appraisal and Theoretical Model', *Journal of Economic Psychology*, Vol. 8(2), pp. 215-35.

Wenzel, M. (2004a), 'An Analysis of Norm Processes in Tax Compliance', *Journal of Economic Psychology*, Vol. 25, pp. 213-28.

Wenzel, M. (2004b) 'Motivation or Rationalization? Causal Relations between Ethics, Norms and Tax Compliance', *Journal of Economic Psychology*, forthcoming.

PART 2

MEASURING THE UNDERGROUND ECONOMY – INTERNATIONAL EVIDENCE

An International Comparison of Underground Economic Activity

Friedrich Schneider and Christopher Bajada

Introduction

Despite continuous government attempts to increase taxpayer compliance, the underground economy continues to offer an avenue for taxpayers to evade their tax paying obligations. The consequences are clear: policymakers have imperfect knowledge on the state of economic affairs, more so as underground economic activities increase.

Estimating the size of the underground economy is an onerous task. Any serious attempt to gauge its size should be able to measure a broad range of activities. These activities may include income generated from (say) babysitting, bartering of services, income evaded by (say) a mechanic who chooses to report only part of their income, businesses that overstate their expenses, legitimate income earned and laundered abroad, and income concealed by welfare recipients. Many academic studies have simply focused on some aspects of the vast array of underground activities, and in doing so provide only a lower bound estimate of its size. Part of the problem is the complexity involved in attempting to capture the various facets of these activities. Most authors trying to measure the underground economy face the difficulty of how to define it. One commonly used working definition is all currently unregistered economic activities that contribute to the officially calculated (or observed) Gross Domestic Product.[1]

Although quite a large literature[2] on single aspects of the underground economy exists, including a comprehensive survey on the topic by Schneider and Enste (2000), the subject is still quite controversial.[3] There are disagreements about the definition of the underground economy, the estimation procedures used and the use of their estimates in economic and policy formulation.[4] Nevertheless international estimates of the size of the underground economy appear to suggest that there has been an increase in its size over time.

Why is it so important to know something about the size of the underground economy? In principle the underground economy has a number of important implications. These include:

- Unreliable data affects the credibility of any statistical estimates attempting to model an economic phenomenon;

- It may give rise to inefficient policy prescriptions particularly if it is driven by changes in the published data. The gauge most commonly used to measure the functioning of the economy, namely the behaviour of economic variables, can be significantly distorted by the existence of a non-negligible underground economy and undoubtedly this has a serious implication for the measurement of the business cycle in general;
- Significant underground activity deprives the government of much needed tax revenue to fund public works;
- Honest businesses face the threat of closure with unfair price competition coming from businesses that actively participate in the underground economy in an attempt to cut costs.

This chapter has two objectives in mind. First, to update the estimates of the underground economy in 145 countries first presented by Schneider and Enste (2000), using the DYMIMIC and currency demand approach. Second, to gauge the extent of the size of the underground economy in countries at similar stages of their economic development and to make some policy recommendations. We demonstrate in this chapter that not only has the size of the underground economy grown in a large number of these countries during the three years over which the estimates are undertaken (1999/2000, 2001/02 and 2002/2003), but countries with relatively thin tax compliance initiatives and monitoring (or auditing) strategies experience the greatest underground economic activities.

Methodologies Used to Estimate the Underground Economy

Voluntary Survey and Samples

Using this approach for estimating the size of the underground economy, individuals are interviewed and asked whether they have actively participated in the underground economy. Some surveys take the form of direct contact between the interviewer and the respondents selected for the survey. In other surveys the respondents are requested to complete a questionnaire and to mail back their responses. Other surveys use combinations of the two methods for eliciting information. Typically the questions ask the respondent if they acted as a buyer or seller in the underground economy. Others may use more indirect questioning in an attempt to overcome the bias in responses that result from directly asking the respondent whether they have failed to meet their tax obligations.

Although susceptible to significant bias from the sensitive nature of the topic (Hansson, 1989), surveys have typically been favoured by government departments interested to know the extent of illicit economic behaviour. Typically surveys are in the form of interviews in which a representative sample of the population is asked whether they have participated as buyers or sellers of labour and/or goods in the underground economy. Surveys from Italy (Censis, 1976), the United States (Ross, 1978), Britain (Dilnot and Morris, 1981), Belgium (Pestiau, 1983), Norway (Isachsen and Strom, 1989), Netherlands (Van Eck and Kazemier,

1988), and Germany (Frey, Weck and Pommerehne, 1982), each reached the conclusion that the extent of illicit economic behaviour has been growing over time and is likely to continue to do so in future.

Although such surveys have the potential to uncover detailed information about the quality of work and the characteristics of employment (see Frey and Pommerehne, 1984), it is doubtful whether in fact such techniques have the potential to uncover most of the underground activities taking place at any one time.

Tax Auditing

Unlike the voluntary nature of surveys, a tax auditing approach is a non-voluntary method by which the tax authorities may uncover concealed income earned by those participating in irregular activities. This approach, as with voluntary surveys, has been used extensively in many countries to detect subterranean activities: the United States (Simon and Witte, 1982), Sweden (Frey and Pommerehne, 1984), United Kingdom (IRS, 1979; and O'Higgins, 1989), Holland (Kinsey, 1987), and France (OECD, 1980).

However the method of non-voluntary tax auditing is probably more important in identifying over-estimation of deductible expenses rather than under-reporting of income because expenses require receipts and concealed earnings need to be proven (see OECD, 1978). As a result only a small part of the underground economy is probably captured using this approach. This small proportion includes those who work and pay some of their tax obligations. It excludes all those who do not work and who are still actively supplying their labour services in the underground economy. It is unlikely that this approach will give reliable information about the true trend of non-compliance over time as the procedure is susceptible and sensitive to changes in tax structure, tax legislation and methods of auditing. Nevertheless this approach is more likely to uncover a larger proportion of the underground economy than those that would be detected based on the voluntary responses of samples and surveys, particularly if individuals fear being punished if detected concealing income (Mirus, Smith and Karoleff, 1994). See also Thomas (1992) for a detailed discussion of fiscal auditing and the implications for measuring illicit activities.

Using National Accounts

This method relies on a 'residual' approach rather than the direct approach of surveys and tax audits. The method assumes than concealed income will find its way back into the legitimate economy in the form of legitimately measured expenditure. The difference between legitimate income and expenditure may be used to proxy the extent of underground activities (see Matthews, 1984; and Macafee, 1980). This discrepancy approach can be applied at the national or at the household level. At the national level O'Higgins (1981) for the United Kingdom and Macafee (1980) for the United States found rising trends in this discrepancy and concluded that the underground economy was growing. Park (1979) and

Hansson (1982) found no such trend for Sweden, and for Germany, Langfelt (1989) found the underground economy to be declining between 1961 and 1974. At the household level, the methodology is somewhat similar but the focus is on disaggregate measures in the discrepancy between income and expenditure. Similarly Yoo and Hyun (1998) use micro-level data to produce estimates of the underground economy for a number of countries.

Monetary Methods

A very popular methodology for estimating the size of the underground economy is the so-called 'monetary methods' (see Gutmann, 1977 and Tanzi, 1983). Because those who work in the underground economy make every attempt to remain unobserved from the authorities by explicitly requesting cash as payment for their services, 'monetary' approaches seem to suggest an efficient way to uncover the trail of these participants.

This led to a new 'generation' of models that made every effort to identify the 'extra' currency that may be attributed to the factors which may explain the size of the underground economy. The advantage of this methodology is that it permits an evaluation of, and the change in, the size of the underground economy which may be attributed to the burden of taxation, presumed to be the major factor driving such illicit activities.

The currency demand approach introduced by Cagan (1958) calculated a correlation between currency demand and the tax pressures (as one cause of the underground economy) for the United States over the period 1919 to 1955. Some twenty years later, Gutmann (1977) used a similar approach, (without statistical methods) to estimate the underground economy for the United States. He specifically looked at the ratio between currency and demand deposits over the years 1937 to 1976 as a basis for his inference about what had happened to the size of the US underground economy overtime.

Tanzi (1980, 1983) extended Cagan's approach by estimating a currency demand equation for the United States for the period 1929 to 1980 as the basis for calculating the underground economy. His approach assumed that underground (or hidden) transactions are predominantly undertaken in the form of cash payments, because such activities leave no observable traces for the authorities to follow up and prosecute. An increase in the size of the underground economy will therefore show up as an increase in the demand for currency (more so now in light of growing currency substitutes). A number of causal factors, such as the direct and indirect tax burden, which are assumed to be the major factors causing people to work in the underground economy, were included in the estimation equation, in addition to the usual variables namely, income and interest rates.[5]

The basic regression equation for the currency demand, proposed by Tanzi (1983), is as follows:

$$ln\left(\frac{C}{M_2}\right)_t = \beta_0 + \beta_1 ln(1+TW)_t + \beta_2 ln\left(\frac{WS}{Y}\right)_t + \beta_3 ln(R)_t + \beta_4 ln\left(\frac{Y}{N}\right)_t + u_t \qquad (1)$$

with $\beta_1 > 0$, $\beta_2 > 0$, $\beta_3 < 0$, $\beta_4 > 0$
where

ln denotes natural logarithms;

$\dfrac{C}{M_2}$ is the ratio of cash holdings to current and deposit accounts;

TW is a weighted average tax rate (to proxy changes in the size of the underground economy);

$\dfrac{WS}{Y}$ is a proportion of wages and salaries in national income (to capture changing payment and money holding patterns);

R is the interest paid on savings deposits (to capture the opportunity cost of holding cash) and

$\dfrac{Y}{N}$ is the per capita income.

Any 'excess' increase in currency, or the amount unexplained by the conventional or normal factors (*discussed above*) is then attributed to the rising tax burden. Figures for the size and development of the underground economy can be calculated by comparing the difference between the development of currency when the direct and indirect tax burden (and government regulations) are held at their lowest value, and the development of currency with the current (much higher) burden of taxation and government regulations. Assuming in a second step the same income velocity for currency used in the underground economy as for legal M1 in the official economy, the size of the underground can be computed and compared to the official measure of GDP.

The currency demand approach is one of the most commonly used approaches. It has been applied to many OECD countries,[6] but has nevertheless been criticized on various grounds.[7] The most commonly raised objections to this method are as follows:

- Not all transactions in the underground economy are paid in cash. Isachsen and Strom (1985) used the survey method to find out that in Norway, in 1980, roughly 80 percent of all transactions in the hidden sector were paid in cash. The size of the total underground economy (including barter) may thus be even larger than previously estimated.

- Most studies consider only one particular factor, the tax burden, as a cause of the underground economy. But others (such as the impact of regulation, taxpayers' attitudes toward the state, 'tax morality' and so on) are not considered, because reliable data for most countries is not available. If, as seems likely, these other factors also have an impact on the extent of the underground economy, it might again be higher than reported in most studies.[8]

- As discussed by Garcia (1978), Park (1979), and Feige (1996), increases in currency demand deposits are due largely to a slowdown in demand deposits rather than to an increase in currency caused by activities in the underground economy, at least in the case of the United States.
- Blades (1982) and Feige (1986, 1996), criticize Tanzi's studies on the grounds that the US dollar is used as an international currency. Instead, Tanzi should have considered (and controlled for) the presence of US dollars, which is used as an international currency and held in cash abroad.[9] Moreover, Frey and Pommerehne (1984) and Thomas (1986, 1992, 1999) claim that Tanzi's parameter estimates are not very stable.[10]
- Most studies assume the same velocity of money in both types of economies. As argued by Hill and Kabir (1996) for Canada and by Klovland (1984) for the Scandinavian countries, there is already considerable uncertainty about the velocity of money in the official economy, and the velocity of money in the hidden sector is even more difficult to estimate. Without knowledge about the velocity of currency in the underground economy, one has to accept the assumption of an 'equal' money velocity in both sectors.
- Ahumada, Alvaredo, Canavese and Canavese (2004) show that the currency approach together with the assumption of equal income velocity of money in both the reported and the hidden transaction is only correct if the income elasticity is 1. As this is, for most countries, not the case so the calculation has to be corrected.
- Finally, the assumption of no underground economy in a base year is open to criticism. Relaxing this assumption would again imply an upward adjustment of the size of the underground economy.

Transactions Approach

This approach has been advocated strongly by Feige.[11] It is based upon the assumption, that there is a constant relation over time between the volume of transaction and official GNP, as summarized by the well-known Fisherian quantity equation, or $M \times V = P \times T$ (with M = money, V = velocity, P = prices, and T = total transactions). Assumptions also have to be made about the velocity of money and about the relationships between the value of total transactions ($P \times T$) and total (= official + unofficial) nominal GNP. Relating total nominal GNP to total transactions, the GNP of the underground economy can be calculated by subtracting the official GNP from total nominal GNP. However, to derive figures for the underground economy, one must also assume a base year in which there is no underground economy. This assumes the ratio of $P \times T$ to total nominal (official = total) GNP is 'normal' in the base year and would have remained constant over time, had there been no underground economy.

This method, too, has several weaknesses, particularly the assumption of a base year with no underground economy, and of a 'normal' ratio of transactions to nominal GNP. Moreover, to obtain reliable underground economy estimates, precise figures of the total volume of transactions should be available, and this might be especially difficult to achieve for cash transactions because they depend, among other things, on the durability of bank notes in terms of the quality of the papers on which they are printed.[12] Also, the assumption is made that all variations in the ratio between the total value of transaction and the officially measured GNP are due to the underground economy. This means that a considerable amount of data is required in order to eliminate financial transactions from 'pure' cross payments, which are legal and have nothing to do with the underground economy per se. In general, although this approach is theoretically attractive, the empirical requirements necessary to obtain reliable estimates are so difficult to fulfill, that its application may lead to doubtful results.

MIMIC Approach

The model approach explicitly considers multiple causes leading to the existence and growth of the underground economy over time. The empirical method used is quite different from those used elsewhere. It is based on the statistical theory of unobserved variables, which considers multiple causes and multiple indicators of the phenomenon to be measured. For the estimation, a factor-analytic approach is used to measure the underground economy as an unobserved variable over time. The unknown coefficients are estimated in a set of structural equations within which the 'unobserved' variable cannot be measured directly. The DYMIMIC (dynamic multiple-indicators multiple-causes) model consists in general of two parts, (i) the measurement model that links the unobserved (or latent) variables to observed indicators, and (ii) the structural equations model which specifies causal relationships among the unobserved variables. In this case, there is one unobserved (or latent) variable, the size of the underground economy. It is assumed to be indirectly observable by a set of indicators of the underground economy, thus capturing the structural dependence of the underground economy on variables that may be useful in predicting its movement and size in the future. The following diagram provides a representation of the structural and measurement models and the interaction between the causes, the latent variable and the indicator variables.

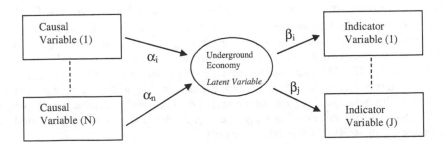

Figure 1 Development of the underground economy

Figure 1 demonstrates that there is an interwoven connection between the latent variable (θ) and the causal (X) and indicator (Y) variables. However the connections between the causal, latent and indicator variables are all unidirectional, so the causal variables determine the size and growth of the latent variable, which in turn influences the observable indicator variables. If we look at the Structural Model first we observe that at every point in time the underground economy is dependent on a number of causal variables through a number of parameter estimates denoted α_i, where i=1...n. Although we are using a latent variable (θ) which is unobservable, we can estimate these parameters (α_i) by tracing its existence through a set of indicator variables via the β_j parameters, where j=1...k. These β_j parameters form part of the Measurement Model in the overall MIMIC framework. Mathematically, Figure 1 may be represented as follows:

$$Y = \beta\theta + e^*$$ (2)

$$\theta = \alpha X + e^{**}$$ (3)

where

X and Y are the causal and indicators variables respectively;

α and β are (n×1) and (j×1) vectors of the parameters respectively;

e^* and e^{**} are the random error terms of dimension (j×1) and (n×1) respectively.

The Structural Model in Figure 1 is represented by equation (3) and the Y-Model is represented by equation (2). Both e^* and e^{**} are assumed to be normally distributed and uncorrelated with one another and that $cov(e^*) = \Psi$ and $cov(e^{**}) = \Theta$. By substituting (3) into (2), the model may be represented as follows:

$$Y = \Pi X + \xi$$ (4)

where

$\Pi = \alpha\beta$ and

$\xi = \alpha e^{**} + e^*$

Equation (4) is a matrix representation of a multivariate regression model that captures the underlying framework of the MIMIC model. The advantage offered by the model given by equation (4) is that the matrix Π can be used to produce the estimates of the parameters α_i. Knowing the α_i parameters allows us to estimate the weighted index of the path of the latent variable (or underground economy) from equation (3). Therefore as the measure of the latent variable is not given in absolute terms but as an index, an exogenous variable will need to be used to calibrate the actual size of the latent variable. The latent variable model when calibrated with information from say, a currency demand model, may be used to produce a time series of subterranean activity.

There is a large body of literature[13] on the possible causes and indicators of the underground economy, in which the following three types of causes are distinguished:

- The burden of direct and indirect taxation, both actual and perceived: a rising burden of taxation provides a strong incentive to work in the underground economy.
- The burden of regulation as proxy for all other state activities: it is assumed that increases in the burden of regulation provides a strong incentive to enter the underground economy.
- The 'tax morality' (citizens' attitudes toward the state), describes the readiness of individuals (at least potentially) to leave their official occupations or engage after hours in underground economic activities. It is assumed that a declining tax morality tends to increase the size of the underground economy.[14]

Indicators A change in the size of the underground economy may be reflected in the following indicators:

- Development of monetary indicators: if activities in the underground economy increase, additional monetary transactions are required, particularly if cash is used to avoid detection.
- Development of the labour market: increasing participation of workers in the underground economy may result in a decrease in participation in the official economy. Similarly, increased activities in the underground economy may be reflected in shorter working hours in the official economy by those heavily engaged in such activities.[15]
- Development of the production market: an increase in the underground economy means that inputs (especially labour) may move out of the official economy (at least partly), depressing the growth rate of officially measured output.

As with the other approaches, there are also a number of shortcomings arising from the use of the MIMIC approach.

- There is no assurance that the estimates produced by the MIMIC model will reflect exactly participation in the underground economy since the causes and indicators may in fact also be driving or driven by other economic phenomena (see Giles and Tedds, 2002).
- The MIMIC model does not produce an estimate of the underground economy that can be interpreted, for example, as a percentage of GDP. Rather the approach produces an index of estimated underground economic activity. In order to obtain an absolute size of the underground economy, the model requires a benchmark estimate derived from an alternative methodology. Typically the currency demand approach is used to provide this benchmark.

•   The flexibility offered by the MIMIC approach does not make it easier to use variables that are often difficult to measure. For example, the degree of government regulation impacts on underground economic activities but constructing reliable estimates of such variables are not so straightforward.

Physical Input Method

A. *The Kaufmann – Kaliberda Method*[16]   To measure overall (official and unofficial) economic activity in an economy, Kaufmann and Kaliberda (1996) assume that electric-power consumption is regarded as the single best physical indicator of overall (or official plus unofficial) economic activity. Overall economic activity and electricity consumption have been empirically observed throughout the world to move in lockstep, with electricity to GDP elasticity usually close to one. This means, that the growth of total electricity consumption is an indicator for growth of overall (official and unofficial) GDP. By having this proxy measurement for the overall economy and then subtracting from this overall measure the estimates of official GDP, Kaufmann and Kaliberda (1996) derive an estimate of unofficial GDP. This method is very simple and appealing. However, it can also be criticized on various grounds:

•   Not all underground economic activities require a considerable amount of electricity (e.g. personal services), and other energy sources can be used (gas, oil, coal, etc.). Only a part of the underground economy will be captured.
•   Over time, there has been considerable technical progress, so that both the production and use of electricity are more efficient than in the past, and this will apply in both official and unofficial uses.
•   There may be considerable differences or changes in the elasticity of electricity/GDP across countries and over time.[17]

B. *The Lackó Method*   Lackó (1996, 1998, 1999, 2000) assumes that a certain part of the underground economy is associated with the household consumption of electricity. This part comprises the so-called household production, do-it-yourself activities, and other non registered production and services. Lackó further assumes that in countries where the portion of the underground economy associated with the household electricity consumption is high, the rest of the hidden economy (or the part Lackó cannot measure) will also be high. Lackó (1996, pp.19 ff.) assumes that in each country a part of the household consumption of electricity is used in the underground economy.

Lackó's approach (1998, p.133) can be described by the following two equations:

$$\ln E_i = \alpha_1 \ln C_i + \alpha_2 \ln PR_i + \alpha_3 G_i + \alpha_4 Q_i + \alpha_5 H_i + u_i \qquad (5)$$

with $\alpha_1 > 0, \alpha_2 < 0, \alpha_3 > 0, \alpha_4 < 0, \alpha_5 > 0$

$$H_i = \beta_1 T_i + \beta_2 (S_i - T_i) + \beta_3 D_i \tag{6}$$

with $\beta_1 > 0$, $\beta_2 < 0$, $\beta_3 > 0$

where

i: the number assigned to the country,

E_i: per capita household electricity consumption in country i,

C_i: per capita real consumption of households without the consumption of electricity in country i in US dollars (at purchasing power parity),

PR_i: the real price of consumption of 1 kWh of residential electricity in US dollars (at purchasing power parity),

G_i: the relative frequency of months with the need of heating in houses in country i,

Q_i: the ratio of energy sources other than electricity energy to all energy sources in household energy consumption,

H_i: the per capita output of the underground economy,

T_i: the ratio of the sum of paid personal income, corporate profit and taxes on goods and services to GDP,

S_i: the ratio of public social welfare expenditures to GDP, and

D_i: the sum on number of dependants over 14 years and of inactive earners, both per 100 active earners.

In a cross-country study, Lackó econometrically estimates equation (5) substituting H_i by equation (6). The econometric estimation results can then be used to establish an ordering of the countries with respect to electricity use in their respective underground economies. For the calculation of the actual size (value added) of the underground economy, Lackó must know how much GDP is produced by one unit of electricity in the underground economy of each country. Since these data are not known, Lackó takes the result of one of the known underground economy estimations (the United States estimates of 10.5 percent of GDP – see Morris, 1993) and applies this proportion to the other countries, thereby using the underground economy of the United States as a base. Lackó then calculates the size of the underground economy for other the countries. This method is also subject to a number of criticisms, namely:

- Not all underground economy activities require the use of electricity. Alternative energy sources could also be used.
- Underground economy activities do not take place only in the household sector.
- It is doubtful whether the ratio of social welfare expenditures can be used as the explanatory factor for the underground economy, especially in transition and developing countries.
- It is questionable which is the most reliable base value in order to calculate the size of the underground economy in all other countries, particularly for the transition and developing countries for which their economic fundamentals are different from (say) the OECD group of countries.

International Comparisons of the Underground Economy

In order to calculate the size and development of the underground economy for the 145 countries presented here, a DYMIMIC (or latent estimation) approach is used. Econometric estimations have been undertaken for the group of African countries, South and Central American countries, the Asian, Middle Eastern and the South Pacific Island countries, those countries that still have a Communist regime and the OECD group of countries. One disadvantage from using the DYMIMIC approach is that we can only extract relative estimates of the size of the underground economy and so to obtain absolute figures we have to use an alternative approach, which in our case is the use of a currency demand model. In order to calculate absolute figures for the select group of countries we used the available estimations from the currency demand approach in combination with the DYMIMIC approach for Australia, Austria, Germany, Hungary, Italy, India, Peru, Russia and the United States (from studies of Chatterjee, Chaudhury and Schneider, 2003; Del'Anno and Schneider, 2004; Bajada and Schneider, 2003; Alexeev and Pyle, 2003; Schneider and Enste, 2002; and Lacko, 2000). When making comparisons between the estimates of the underground economy, we limit ourselves to those groups of countries that are at similar phases in their economic development. In addition one should also keep in mind the shortcomings of the DYMIMIC and currency demand approach discussed earlier in this chapter.

In the remainder of this chapter we present updated results of the size of the underground economy for 145 countries around the world.

Case Study 1: Selected OECD Countries

In Table 1 we report the results of the size of the underground economy for 21 OECD countries. With the exception of Austria, Germany and Switzerland, all the OECD countries reported in Table 1 exhibit a marginal decline in underground economic activity over this period. This is reflected in the decline of the unweighted averages, namely 16.8 percent of GDP for 1999/00, 16.7 percent of GDP for 2001/02, and 16.3 percent of GDP for 2002/03. Of these OECD countries, Greece has by far the largest underground economy sector measuring on average 28.5 percent of GDP, and this is closely followed by Italy (26.6 percent of GDP). Belgium, Portugal and Spain each have an underground economy sector that has averaged more than 20 percent of GDP over this period, while only the United States and Switzerland have an underground economy that has averaged less than 10 percent of GDP. The median estimate of the underground economy amongst this group of 21 countries is for Canada (15.7 percent of GDP) flanked on either side by Ireland (15.6 percent of GDP) and Germany (16.4 percent of GDP).

How has the ranking of the size of the underground economy for these countries changed over this time period? In 1999/00, of the OECD countries in Table 1, Switzerland had the smallest underground economy (8.6 percent of GDP) followed by the United States (8.7 percent of GDP) and Austria (9.8 percent of

GDP). By 2002/03 the ranking had changed such that United States had the smallest measured underground economy (8.4 percent of GDP), followed by Switzerland (9.4 percent of GDP) and Japan (10.8 percent of GDP). Austria had climbed to fourth place with an estimated underground economy of 10.9 percent, an increase of 1.1 percent of GDP. At the other end of the scale, Greece retained the spot for the largest estimated underground economy followed by Italy and Spain. Over these years the ranking at the higher end remained unchanged.

In Figure 2 we plot the average size of the underground economy for each of these countries.

Table 1   The size of the underground economy in 21 OECD countries for the period 1999/00, 2001/02 and 2002/03

		Underground Economy (in % of official GDP) using the DYMIMIC and Currency Demand Method		
No.	Country	1999/00	2001/02	2002/03
1	Australia	14.3	14.1	13.5
2	Austria	9.8	10.6	10.9
3	Belgium	22.2	22.0	21.0
4	Canada	16.0	15.8	15.2
5	Denmark	18.0	17.9	17.3
6	Finland	18.1	18.0	17.4
7	France	15.2	15.0	14.5
8	Germany	16.0	16.3	16.8
9	Greece	28.7	28.5	28.2
10	Ireland	15.9	15.7	15.3
11	Italy	27.1	27.0	25.7
12	Japan	11.2	11.1	10.8
13	Netherlands	13.1	13.0	12.6
14	New Zealand	12.8	12.6	12.3
15	Norway	19.1	19.0	18.4
16	Portugal	22.7	22.5	21.9
17	Spain	22.7	22.5	22.0
18	Sweden	19.2	19.1	18.3
19	Switzerland	8.6	9.4	9.4
20	United Kingdom	12.7	12.5	12.2
21	United States	8.7	8.7	8.4
Unweighted Average		**16.8**	**16.7**	**16.3**

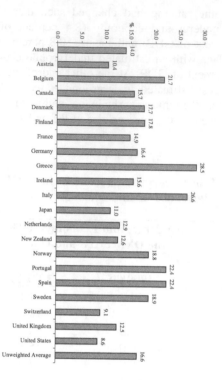

Figure 2   The size of the underground economy in 21 OECD countries for the period 1999/00, 2001/02 and 2002/03 (percent of GDP)

Case Study 2: Asia-Pacific and Middle Eastern Countries

Asian Countries   In Table 2 we report the results of the size of the underground economy for 28 Asian and Middle Eastern countries for the period 1999/00, 2001/02 and 2002/03. Unlike the OECD countries, all the Asian and Middle Eastern countries reported in Table 2 experienced a growth in the size of the underground economy. This is reflected by the rise of the unweighted averages, namely 28.5 percent of GDP in 1999/00, 29.5 percent of GDP in 2001/02 and 30.4 percent of GDP in 2002/03. The unweighted averages for each of the two categories of countries are as follows (*not individually reported in the table*): 32.9 percent of GDP for the Asian countries and 24.2 percent of GDP for the Middle Eastern countries.

Of the Asian countries Thailand has by far the largest underground economy, measuring more than half of officially reported GDP, with Cambodia following closely behind (51.3 percent of GDP). At the other end of the scale, Singapore has the smallest underground economy of the Asian countries reported in the table, measuring 13.4 percent of GDP. The median estimate of the underground economy from the selected Asian countries is for Malaysia (31.6

percent of GDP). However having said all this, it is quite difficult to make 'fair' comparisons between all these Asian countries because countries such as Singapore, which are more developed economies, cannot be compared with their less developed counterpart economies such as Thailand.

Table 2   The size of the underground economy in 28 Asian and Middle Eastern countries for the period 1999/00, 2001/02 and 2002/03

		Underground Economy (% of official GDP) using the DYMIMIC and Currency Demand Method		
No.	Country	1999/00	2001/02	2002/03
1	Bangladesh	35.6	36.5	37.7
2	Bhutan	29.4	30.5	31.7
3	Cambodia	50.1	51.3	52.4
4	Hong Kong. China	16.6	17.1	17.2
5	India	23.1	24.2	25.6
6	Indonesia	19.4	21.8	22.9
7	Iran. Islamic Rep.	18.9	19.4	19.9
8	Israel	21.9	22.8	23.9
9	Jordan	19.4	20.5	21.6
10	Korea. Rep.	27.5	28.1	28.8
11	Kuwait	20.1	20.7	21.6
12	Lebanon	34.1	35.6	36.2
13	Malaysia	31.1	31.6	32.2
14	Mongolia	18.4	19.6	20.4
15	Nepal	38.4	39.7	40.8
16	Oman	18.9	19.4	19.8
17	Pakistan	36.8	37.9	38.7
18	Papua New Guinea	36.1	37.3	38.6
19	Philippines	43.4	44.5	45.6
20	Saudi Arabia	18.4	19.1	19.7
21	Singapore	13.1	13.4	13.7
22	Sri Lanka	44.6	45.9	47.2
23	Syrian Arab Republic	19.3	20.4	21.6
24	Taiwan. China	25.4	26.6	27.7
25	Thailand	52.6	53.4	54.1
26	Turkey	32.1	33.2	34.3
27	United Arab Emirates	26.4	27.1	27.8
28	Yemen. Rep.	27.4	28.4	29.1
	Unweighted Average	**28.5**	**29.5**	**30.4**

Middle Eastern Countries   The estimates of the underground economy for the Middle Eastern countries in Table 2 are relatively smaller as a percentage of GDP when compared with the Asian estimates (24.2 percent of GDP for the Middle East compared with 32.9 percent of GDP for Asia) over this period. Of the Middle Eastern countries, Lebanon has by far the largest underground economy, estimated at 35.3 percent of the GDP over the period 1999/00, 2001/02 and 2002/03. Both Turkey and Lebanon have an underground economy estimated at more than 30 percent of GDP, while Iran, Oman and Saudi Arabia have underground economies estimated at less than 20 percent of GDP. Of these three countries Saudi Arabia has the marginally smaller estimate measuring 19.1 percent of GDP. The median estimate of the underground economy for the Middle Eastern countries reported in Table 2 is for Kuwait, estimated at 20.8 percent of GDP.

In Figure 3 we plot the average size of the underground economy for each of these countries.

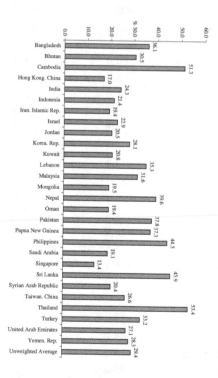

Figure 3   The size of the underground economy in 28 Asian and Middle Eastern countries for the period 1999/00, 2001/02 and 2002/03 (percent of GDP)

Pacific Island Countries   In Table 3 we report the results of the size of the underground economy for 10 South West Pacific Island countries. Each of the 10 countries in Table 3 exhibits a growth in the size of underground economy over the period 1999/00, 2001/02 and 2002/03. This growth is reflected in the unweighted average growth rate for the countries collectively – from 31.7 percent of GDP in 1999/00 to 33.4 percent of GDP in 2002/03. Of these 10 countries Tonga has the largest estimated underground economy, measuring an average 36.3 percent of GDP over this period. By contrast, the smallest underground economy was estimated for the Marshall Islands (at an average of 28.9 percent of GDP). The median estimate of the underground for these 10 countries is for Samoa, with an estimated size of the underground economy of 32.5 percent of GDP. Over this same period the ranking of the size of the underground economy across these countries changed very little.

In Figure 4 we plot the average size of the underground economy for each of these 10 countries.

Table 3   **The size of the underground economy in 10 South West Pacific islands for the period 1999/00, 2001/02 and 2002/03**

		Underground Economy (% of official GDP) using the DYMIMIC and Currency Demand Method		
No.	Country	1999/00	2001/02	2002/03
1	Fiji	33.6	34.3	35.1
2	Kiribati	34.1	35.0	35.3
3	Maldives	30.3	31.4	32.0
4	Marshall Islands	28.1	29.0	29.6
5	Micronesia. Fed. Sts.	31.3	32.1	33.2
6	Palau	28.4	29.2	30.0
7	Samoa	31.4	32.6	33.5
8	Solomon Islands	33.4	34.5	35.3
9	Tonga	35.1	36.3	37.4
10	Vanuatu	30.9	31.7	32.5
	Unweighted Average	**31.7**	**32.6**	**33.4**

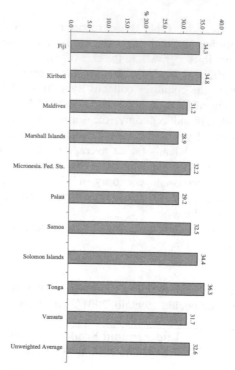

Figure 4 The size of the underground economy in 10 West Pacific islands for the period 1999/00, 2001/02 and 2002/03 (percent of GDP)

Case Study 3: Other Developing and Transition Countries[18]

In the remainder of this section we consider a broad range of countries by geographical location. The results on the size of the underground economies for the developing countries presented here (*but not discussed previously*) relate to Africa and Central and South America. The results on the size of the underground economies for the transition countries presented here (*but not discussed previously*) relate to 25 East and Central European countries. Also included in these estimates are the results of the size of the underground economy for three Communist regime countries.

Central and South American Countries In Table 4 we present the result of the size of the underground economy for 21 Central and South American countries. With the exception of Chile, Costa Rica, Argentina, Paraguay and Puerto Rico, the remaining 16 countries have an underground economy estimated to be greater than 30 percent of GDP for the period 1999/00, 2001/02 and 2002/03. The countries with the largest estimated size of the underground economy are Bolivia (67.8 percent of GDP), Panama (64.8 percent of GDP) and Peru (60.4 percent of GDP). Of the 25 countries, the smallest underground economies were estimated for Chile (20.3 percent of GDP), Costa Rica (27 percent of GDP) and Argentina (27.1 percent of GDP). The median estimate of the underground economy amongst this group of 25 Central and South American countries is for Brazil at 41 percent of GDP.

Table 4   The size of the underground economy in 21 Central and South American countries for the period 1999/00, 2001/02 and 2002/03

		Underground Economy (% of official GDP) using the DYMIMIC and Currency Demand Method		
No.	Country	1999/00	2001/02	2002/03
1	Argentina	25.4	27.1	28.9
2	Bolivia	67.1	68.1	68.3
3	Brazil	39.8	40.9	42.3
4	Chile	19.8	20.3	20.9
5	Colombia	39.1	41.3	43.4
6	Costa Rica	26.2	27.0	27.8
7	Dominican Republic	32.1	33.4	34.1
8	Ecuador	34.4	35.1	36.7
9	El Salvador	46.3	47.1	48.3
10	Guatemala	51.5	51.9	52.4
11	Haiti	55.4	57.1	58.6
12	Honduras	49.6	50.8	51.6
13	Jamaica	36.4	37.8	38.9
14	Mexico	30.1	31.8	33.2
15	Nicaragua	45.2	46.9	48.2
16	Panama	64.1	65.1	65.3
17	Paraguay	27.4	29.2	31.4
18	Peru	59.9	60.3	60.9
19	Puerto Rico	28.4	29.4	30.7
20	Uruguay	51.1	51.4	51.9
21	Venezuela. RB	33.6	35.1	36.7
Unweighted Average		**41.1**	**42.2**	**43.4**

From 1999/00 to 2002/03 each of the 21 countries in Table 4 exhibited a growth in the size of their underground economy. On average, the size of the underground economy for this collective group of countries increased from 41.1 percent of GDP in 1999/2000 to 43.4 percent of GDP by 2002/03. Over the same time period those countries that experienced the largest underground economic activity did so for each of the years covered in the estimation period. The same is true for those countries with the smallest estimated underground economic activities. Overall the relative ranking of the size of the underground economy changed only marginally.

In Figure 5 we plot the results for the average size of the underground economy for each of these countries.

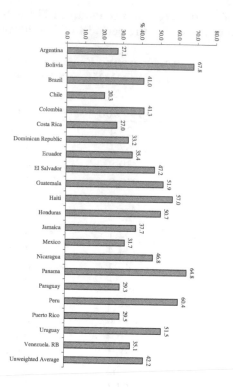

Figure 5   The size of the underground economy in 21 Central and South American countries for the period 1999/00, 2001/02 and 2002/03 (percent of GDP)

East and Central European Countries   Next we consider the estimates for 25 East and Central European (transition) countries. The results of the size of the underground economy are reported in Table 5. Each of these countries experienced a growth in their underground economic activities over the period 1999/00 to 2002/03. This is reflected by the increase of the unweighted average across all countries for this period (38.1 percent of GDP for 1999/00 to 40.1 percent of GDP by 2002/03). Of these 25 countries, Georgia had by far the largest underground economy, estimated at 67.6 percent of GDP followed by Azerbaijan (61 percent of GDP) and Ukraine (53.5 percent of GDP). On the other hand the Slovak Republic was estimated to have the smallest underground economy (19.5 percent of GDP) followed by the Czech

Republic (19.6 percent of GDP) and Hungary (25.7 percent of GDP). Only the Slovak and Czech Republic have underground economic activities measuring less that 20 percent of GDP. The median estimate of the underground economy amongst this group of 25 countries is for Bulgaria (37.4 percent of GDP).

In Figure 6 we plot the results of the average size of the underground economy for each of these 25 East and Central European countries.

Table 5   The size of the underground economy in 25 East and Central European and Former Soviet Union countries for the period 1999/00, 2001/02 and 2002/03

		Underground Economy (% of official GDP) using the DYMIMIC and Currency Demand Method		
No.	Country	1999/00	2001/02	2002/03
1	Albania	33.4	34.6	35.3
2	Armenia	46.3	47.8	49.1
3	Azerbaijan	60.6	61.1	61.3
4	Belarus	48.1	49.3	50.4
5	Bosnia and Herzegovina	34.1	35.4	36.7
6	Bulgaria	36.9	37.1	38.3
7	Croatia	33.4	34.2	35.4
8	Czech Republic	19.1	19.6	20.1
9	Estonia	38.4	39.2	40.1
10	Georgia	67.3	67.6	68.0
11	Hungary	25.1	25.7	26.2
12	Kazakhstan	43.2	44.1	45.2
13	Kyrgyz Republic	39.8	40.3	41.2
14	Latvia	39.9	40.7	41.3
15	Lithuania	30.3	31.4	32.6
16	Macedonia. FYR	34.1	35.1	36.3
17	Moldova	45.1	47.3	49.4
18	Poland	27.6	28.2	28.9
19	Romania	34.4	36.1	37.4
20	Russian Federation	46.1	47.5	48.7
21	Serbia and Montenegro	36.4	37.3	39.1
22	Slovak Republic	18.9	19.3	20.2
23	Slovenia	27.1	28.3	29.4
24	Ukraine	52.2	53.6	54.7
25	Uzbekistan	34.1	35.7	37.2
Unweighted Average		**38.1**	**39.1**	**40.1**

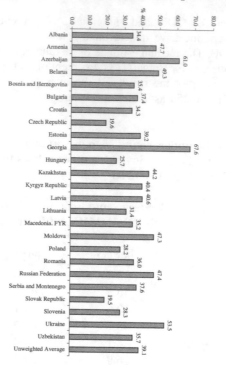

Figure 6 The size of the underground economy in 25 East and Central European countries for the period 1999/00, 2001/02 and 2002/03 (percent of GDP)

African Countries In Table 6 we present the result for 37 African countries. We arrive at a similar conclusion as we have for most of the countries examined so far (except for the majority of the OECD countries), that the size of the underground economy over the period 1999/00 to 2002/03 has grown. This is reflected in the growth of the unweighted average size of the underground economy from 41.3 percent of GDP (1999/00) to 43.2 percent of GDP (2002/03). Of these 37 African countries, Zimbabwe had the largest underground economy over this period (61.2 percent of GDP) followed by Tanzania (59.3 percent of GDP) and Nigeria (58.6 percent of GDP). At the other end of the scale South Africa exhibited the smallest underground economic activity (29 percent of GDP) followed by Lesotho (32.3 percent of GDP) and Namibia (32.5 percent of GDP). The median estimate of the underground economy amongst this group of 37 African countries is Mozambique (41.3 percent of GDP). Some caution should be placed on these estimates in particular given the relatively poorer quality of data from some of the very less developed countries (Ethiopia) in comparison with the relatively more developed African countries, (say) Egypt.

Table 6   **The size of the underground economy in 37 African countries for the period 1999/00, 2001/02 and 2002/03**

No.	Country	Underground Economy (% of official GDP) using the DYMIMIC and Currency Demand Method		
		1999/00	**2001/02**	**2002/03**
1	Algeria	34.1	35.0	35.6
2	Angola	43.2	44.1	45.2
3	Benin	47.3	48.2	49.1
4	Botswana	33.4	33.9	34.6
5	Burkina Faso	41.4	42.6	43.3
6	Burundi	36.9	37.6	38.7
7	Cameroon	32.8	33.7	34.9
8	Central African Republic	44.3	45.4	46.1
9	Chad	46.2	47.1	48.0
10	Congo. Dem. Rep.	48.0	48.8	49.7
11	Congo. Rep.	48.2	49.1	50.1
12	Cote d'Ivoire	43.2	44.3	45.2
13	Egypt. Arab Rep.	35.1	36.0	36.9
14	Ethiopia	40.3	41.4	42.1
15	Ghana	41.9	42.7	43.6
16	Guinea	39.6	40.8	41.3
17	Kenya	34.3	35.1	36.0
18	Lesotho	31.3	32.4	33.3
19	Madagascar	39.6	40.4	41.6
20	Malawi	40.3	41.2	42.1
21	Mali	42.3	43.9	44.7
22	Mauritania	36.1	37.2	38.0
23	Morocco	36.4	37.1	37.9
24	Mozambique	40.3	41.3	42.4
25	Namibia	31.4	32.6	33.4
26	Niger	41.9	42.6	43.8
27	Nigeria	57.9	58.6	59.4
28	Rwanda	40.3	41.4	42.2
29	Senegal	45.1	46.8	47.5
30	Sierra Leone	41.7	42.8	43.9
31	South Africa	28.4	29.1	29.5
32	Tanzania	58.3	59.4	60.2
33	Togo	35.1	39.2	40.4
34	Tunisia	38.4	39.1	39.9
35	Uganda	43.1	44.6	45.4
36	Zambia	48.9	49.7	50.8
37	Zimbabwe	59.4	61.0	63.2
	Unweighted Average	**41.3**	**42.3**	**43.2**

In Figure 7 we plot the results of the average size of the underground economy for each of these 37 African countries.

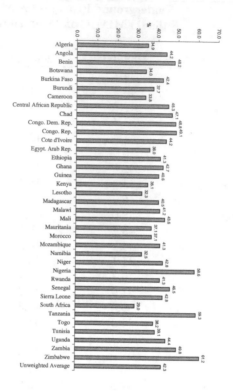

Figure 7   The size of the underground economy in 37 African Countries for the period 1999/00, 2001/02 and 2002/03 (percent of GDP)

Communist Countries   The final sets of figures are for three (3) Communist regimes. The results for the size of the underground economy for China, Lao and Vietnam are presented in Table 7 and the average estimates over the period 1999/00, 2001/02 and 2002/03 are plotted in Figure 8. Again one should be aware of the difficulty of making comparisons between these countries, especially for China, which is partly a market economy and a planning socialist economy. It is an open question whether the meaning of the underground economies can be compared to the size from other countries previously presented.

Table 7   The size of the underground economy in 3 Communist countries for the period 1999/00, 2001/02 and 2002/03

		Underground Economy (in % of official GDP) using the DYMIMIC and Currency Demand Method		
No.	Country	1999/00	2001/02	2002/03
1	China	13.1	14.4	15.6
2	Lao PDR	30.6	31.9	33.4
3	Vietnam	15.6	16.9	17.9
	Unweighted Average	**19.8**	**21.1**	**22.3**

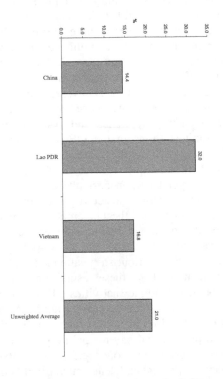

Figure 8   The size of the underground economy in 3 Communist countries for the period 1999/00, 2001/02 and 2002/03 (percent of GDP)

Summary of Findings

In Table 8 we present a summary of the results of the size of the underground economy for the 145 countries reported in the previous pages. The first number of each row contains the average estimated size of the underground economy for the various classifications given in column 1. The results are reported for the periods 1999/2000, 2001/2002 and 2002/2003. The second number (in parenthesis) identifies the number of countries within each of the broad country classifications given in column 1. The final row provides an unweighted average of the size of the underground economy for the whole sample of countries, 145 in total. This final row suggests that the underground world wide has been growing steadily during this period. As we have seen however, this has not been the case for the OECD. Part of the reason for this may be a combination of greater research efforts on the underground economy and a response by the tax authorities to the growing public sentiment and outcry that the underground economy has been growing [for example, Canada (see Chapter 9), the United States (see Chapter 11), the United Kingdom (see Chapter 12), and Australia (see Chapter 13)].

Although making cross country comparisons of the size of the underground economy over time is a difficult one, a quick glance at the numbers in Table 8 seem to suggest that the underground economy is larger in countries that have generally poorer monitoring and compliance instruments for tackling the growth in clandestine activities. Take for example the African countries, with an average estimated size of the underground economy of 43.2 percent of GDP (2002/2003). Compared with the OECD average of 16.3 percent of GDP (2002/2003), clandestine activities in Africa seem much more entrenched. This is probably no surprise given the experience and systems in place throughout the various government administrations in the OECD compared with Africa. It is important however that when making this general remark that we keep in mind the fact that production and its techniques are very different in the African countries (for example, a greater dependence on agricultural production) when compared with the OECD. The nature of economic activity itself may facilitate opportunities for concealing greater income from the tax authorities in the African countries which may not be so easily possible in the more developed ones.

What can we say about the potential policy implications if the underground economy is left to flourish unattended? There are a number of potentially serious implications from these results, particularly for countries that have larger underground economic activities. First, a vibrant underground economy not only reduces the size of the current tax base but also reduces future stream of tax collections. The loss of tax revenue may significantly undermine a government's ability to provide and pay for public goods and services necessary. Second, an unchecked underground economy fosters greater confidence that the tax authorities are unable to prevent and detect such illicit behaviour, compounding the pressures for participation. The implications are distortions in national economic data including labour market statistics and inefficient policy prescriptions from the use of such data. Third, there may be significant effects on competition and therefore the survival of (small) legitimate business operations from a growing underground economy. There are strong reasons to expect that small legitimate operators may be forced out of business by the unscrupulous trading of the illegitimate operators. Worse still, it may force those same legitimate operators to engage in underground activity in order to survive. Finally, knowledge that those who are receiving unemployment benefits while secretly engaged in underground economy activity has a significant affect on dampening general taxpayer morality, further contributing to underground economic activity. From the point of view of governments a large and growing underground economy is bad news for efficient and effective implementation of public policy. It is not until tax administrations in these countries take seriously these implications and attempt to significantly reduce these illicit activities that the efficiency and effectiveness of public policy will be improved.

Table 8   Average size of the underground economy for developing, transition and OECD countries (percent of official GDP)

Countries/Year	Average Size of the Underground Economy – Value added in % of official GDP using DYMIMIC and Currency Demand method *(Number of Countries)*		
	1999/2000	**2000/2001**	**2002/2003**
Africa	41.3	42.3	43.2
	(37)	*(37)*	*(37)*
Central and South America	41.1	42.2	43.4
	(21)	*(21)*	*(21)*
Asia and Middle East	28.5	29.5	30.4
	(28)	*(28)*	*(28)*
East and Central Europe	38.1	39.1	40.1
	(25)	*(25)*	*(25)*
Highly developed OECD	16.8	16.7	16.3
	(21)	*(21)*	*(21)*
South Pacific Islands	31.7	32.6	33.4
	(10)	*(10)*	*(10)*
Communist Countries	19.8	21.1	22.3
	(3)	*(3)*	*(3)*
Unweighted Average – 145 Countries	33.6	34.5	35.2

Source: own calculations

Conclusion

The existence of the underground economy is an important issue not only for economic policy but also tax morality. In this chapter we have provided updated estimates for the underground economy for 145 countries using the combined DYMIMIC and currency demand approaches. The average size of the underground economy (in percentage of official GDP) over the most recent estimate (2002/03) is 43.2 percent of GDP for Africa, 43.4 percent of GDP for Central and South America, 16.3 percent of GDP for the highly developed OECD, 30.4 percent for

Asia and the Middle East, 40.1 percent for East and Central Europe, 33.4 percent of GDP for the South Pacific Island countries and 22.3 percent of GDP for the communist countries. The varying estimates of underground activity reported in this chapter appear to suggest that the inefficient means of detecting underground economic activity is a major factor contributing to the larger estimates found for the less developed countries. An increase in the burden of taxation, high unemployment and low official GDP growth are major contributors to the underground economy, and our estimates (which are increasing overtime) suggest that a greater attention to this problem needs to be given to avoid the more serious consequences that may arise from these activities in future.

Notes

1. This definition is used for example, by Feige (1989, 1994), Schneider (1994a, 2003, 2005) and Frey and Pommerehne (1984). Do-it-yourself activities are not included. For estimates of the underground economy and the do-it-yourself activities for Germany see Karmann (1986, 1990).

2. The literature about the 'shadow', 'underground', 'informal', 'second', 'cash'-or 'parallel', economy is increasing. Various topics, on how to measure it, its causes, its effect on the official economy are analyzed. See for example, survey type publications by Frey and Pommerehne (1984); Thomas (1992); Loayza (1996); Pozo (1996); Lippert and Walker (1997); Schneider (1994a, 1994b, 1997, 1998); Johnson, Kaufmann, and Shleifer (1997), Johnson, Kaufmann and Zoido-Lobatón (1998a, 1998b); Belev (2003); Gerxhani (2003) and Pedersen (2003). For an overall survey of the global evidence of the size of the shadow economy see Schneider and Enste (2000, 2002), Schneider (2003, 2005) and Alm, Martinez and Schneider (2004).

3. Compare e.g. in the *Economic Journal*, Vol. 109(456), June 1999 the feature 'controversy: on the hidden economy'.

4. Compare the different opinions of Tanzi (1999), Thomas (1999), Giles (1999a,b) and Pedersen (2003).

5. The estimation of such a currency demand equation has been criticized by Thomas (1999) but part of this criticism has been considered by the work of Giles (1999a, 1999b) and Bhattacharyya (1999), who both use the latest econometric techniques. We adopt a similar approach in this paper.

6. See Karmann (1986 and 1990), Schneider (1997, 1998), Johnson, Kaufmann and Zoido-Lobatón (1998a), and Williams and Windebank (1995).

7. See Thomas (1992, 1999), Feige (1986), Pozo (1996), Pedersen (2003) and Ahumada, Alvareda, Canavese and Canavese (2004).

8. One (weak) justification for the only use of the tax variable is that this variable has by far the strongest impact on the size of the underground economy in the studies known to the authors. The only exception is the study by Frey and Weck-Hannemann (1984) where the variable 'tax immorality' has a quantitatively larger and statistically stronger influence than the direct tax share in the model approach. In the study of Pommerehne and Schneider (1985), for the U.S., besides various tax measures, data for regulation, tax immorality, minimum wage rates are available, the tax variable has a dominating influence and contributes roughly 60-70 percent to the size of the underground economy. See also Zilberfarb (1986).

9. In another study by Tanzi (1982, esp. pp. 110-113) he explicitly deals with this criticism. A very careful investigation of the amount of US-$ used abroad and the US currency used in the underground economy and to 'classical' crime activities has been undertaken by Rogoff (1998), who concludes that large denomination bills are major driving force for the growth of the underground economy and classical crime activities due largely to reduced transactions costs.

10. However in studies for European countries Kirchgaessner (1983, 1984) and Schneider (1986) reach the conclusion that the estimation results for Germany, Denmark, Norway and Sweden are quite robust when using the currency demand method. Hill and Kabir (1996) find for Canada that the rise of the underground economy varies with respect to the tax variable used; they conclude 'when the theoretically best tax rates are selected and a range of plausible velocity values are used, this method estimates underground economic growth between 1964 and 1995 at between 3 and 11 percent of GDP' (Hill and Kabir [1996, p. 1553]).

11. For an extended description of this approach, see Feige (1996); for a further application for the Netherlands see Boeschoten and Fase (1984), and for Germany see Langfeldt (1984).

12. For a detailed criticism of the transaction approach see Boeschoten and Fase (1984), Frey and Pommerehne (1984), Kirchgaessner (1984), Tanzi (1982a,b, 1986), Dallago (1990), Thomas (1986, 1992, 1999) and Giles (1999a).

13. Thomas (1992); Schneider (1994a, 1997); Schneider and Enste (2000, 2002); Pozo (1996); Johnson, Kaufmann and Zoido-Lobatón (1998a, 1998b); and Giles (1999a, 1999b).

14. When applying this approach for European countries, Frey and Weck-Hannemann (1984) had difficulty obtaining reliable data for the regulation and tax morality variables. Hence, their study was criticized by Helberger and Knepel (1988), who argued that these results were unstable with respect to changing variables in the model over the years.

15. It is possible that the participation rate as well as the number of hours worked may be unaffected by underground economy activity if such activities are undertaken after hours or on weekends when individuals are not working in the legitimate economy.

16. This method was used earlier by Lizzeri (1979), Del Boca and Forte (1982), and then was used much later by Portes (1996), Kaufmann and Kaliberda (1996), Johnson, Kaufmann and Shleifer (1997). For a critique see Lackó (1998).

17. Johnson, Kaufmann and Shleifer (1997) make an attempt to adjust for changes in the elasticity of electricity/GDP.

18. For an extensive and excellent literature survey of the research about the shadow economy in developing countries see Gerxhani (2003). In this paper Gerxhani (2003) stresses that the distinction between developed and developing countries with respect to the shadow economy is of great importance. Due to space reasons this point is not further elaborated here.

References

Ahumada, H, Alvaredo, F., Canavese A. and Canavese, P. (2004), 'The demand for currency approach and the size of the shadow economy: A critical assessment', Discussion Paper, Delta Ecole. Normale Superieure, Paris.

Alm, J., Martinez-Vazquez, J. and Schneider, F. (2004), 'Sizing the problem of the hard-to-tax', Working Paper, Georgia State University, USA.

Bajada, C. and Schneider, F. (2003), 'The size and development of the shadow economies in the Asia-Pacific', Discussion Paper, Department of Economics, University of Linz, Austria, forthcoming in the Asian Pacific Economic Journal, 2005.

Belev, B. (2003), 'The informal economy in the EU Accession Countries: Size, scope, trends and challenges to the process of EU enlargement', Center for Study of Democracy, Sofia.

Bhattacharyya, D.K. (1999), 'On the economic rationale of estimating the hidden economy', *The Economic Journal*, Vol. 109(456), pp. 348-59.

Blades, D. (1982), 'The hidden economy and the national accounts', OECD (Occasional Studies), Paris, pp. 28-44.

Boeschoten, W.C. and Fase, M.M.G (1984), 'The Volume of Payments and the Informal Economy in the Netherlands 1965-1982', M. Nijhoff, Dordrecht.

Cagan, P. (1958), 'The demand for currency relative to the total money supply,' *Journal of Political Economy*, Vol. 66(3), pp. 302-28.

CENSIS (1976), 'L'occupazione occultra-caratteristiche della partecipazione al lavoro in Italia', in B.S. Frey and W.W. Pommerehne (1984), *Review of Income and Wealth*, Vol. 30(1), pp. 1-23.

Chatterjee, S., Chaudhury, K. and Schneider, F. (2003), 'The size and development of the Indian shadow economy and a comparison with other 18 Asian countries: An empirical investigation', Discussion Paper, Department of Economics, University of Linz, Austria.

Dallago, B. (1990), *The irregular economy: The 'underground economy' and the 'black labour market'*, Dartmouth (U.K.), Publishing Company.

Del'Anno, R. and Schneider, F. (2004), 'The shadow economy of Italy and other OECD countries: What do we know?', Linz: University of Linz, Department of Economics, Discussion Paper, forthcoming in *Journal of Public Finance and Public Choice*, 2005.

Del Boca, D and Forte, F. (1982), 'Recent empirical surveys and theoretical interpretations of the parallel economy in Italy', in V. Tanzi (1982a) (ed.), *The underground economy in the United States and abroad*, Lexington (Mass.), Lexington, pp. 160-78.

Dilnot, A., and Morris C.N. (1981), 'What Do We Know About the Black Economy in the United Kingdom', *Fiscal Studies*, Vol. 2, pp. 58-73.

Feige, E.L. (1986), 'A re-examination of the Underground Economy in the United States', *IMF Staff Papers*, Vol. 33(4), pp. 768-81.

Feige, E.L. (ed.) (1989), *The Underground Economies. Tax Evasion and Information Distortion*, Cambridge, New York, Melbourne, Cambridge University Press.

Feige, E.L. (1994), 'The underground economy and the currency enigma', *Supplement to Public Finance/Finances Publiques*, Vol. 49, pp. 119-36.

Feige, E.L. (1996), 'Overseas holdings of U.S. currency and the underground economy', in S. Pozo (ed.), Exploring the Underground Economy. Kalamazoo, Michigan, pp. 5-62.

Frey, B.S. and Pommerehne, W. (1984), 'The hidden economy: State and prospect for measurement', *Review of Income and Wealth*, Vol. 30(1), pp. 1-23.

Frey, B.S. and Weck-Hannemann, H. (1984), 'The hidden economy as an unobserved variable', *European Economic Review*, Vol. 26(1), pp. 33-53.

Frey, B.S., Hannelore, W. and Pommerehne, W.W. (1982), 'Has the shadow economy grown in Germany? An exploratory study', *Weltwirtschaftliches Archiv*, Vol. 118(4), pp. 499-524.

Garcia, G. (1978), 'The currency ratio and the subterranean economy,' *Financial Analysts Journal*, Vol. 69(1), pp. 64-6.

Gerxhani, K. (2003), 'The informal sector in developed and less-developed countries: A literature survey', *Public Choice*, Vol. 114(3/4), pp. 295-318.

Giles, D.E.A. (1999a), 'Measuring the hidden economy: Implications for econometric modelling', *The Economic Journal*, Vol. 109(456), pp. 370-80.

Giles, D.E.A. (1999b), 'Modelling the hidden economy in the tax-gap in New Zealand', *Empirical Economics*, Vol. 24(4), pp. 621-40.

Giles, D.E.A. and Tedds, L.M. (2002), 'Taxes and the Canadian Underground Economy', Canadian Tax Paper No. 106, Canadian Tax Foundation, Toronto/Ontario.

Gutmann, P.M. (1977), 'The subterranean economy,' *Financial Analysts Journal*, Vol. 34(1), pp. 24-7.

Hansson, I. (1982), 'The Underground Economy in a High Tax Country: The Case of Sweden', in Tanzi, V. (1982a), pp. 233-43.

Hansson, I. (1989), 'The Underground Economy in Sweden', in Feige, E.L. (1989), Cambridge, Cambridge University Press.

Helberger, C. and Knepel, H. (1988), 'How big is the shadow economy? A re-analysis of the unobserved-variable approach' of Frey, B.S and Weck-Hannemann, H, *European Economic Journal*, Vol. 32, pp. 965-76.

Hill, R. and Kabir, M. (1996), 'Tax rates, the tax mix, and the growth of the underground economy in Canada: What can we infer?', *Canadian Tax Journal/Revue Fiscale Canadienne*, Vol. 44(6), pp. 1552-83.

IRS (1979), 'Estimates of Income Unreported on Individual Tax Reforms, Washington D.C.: Internal revenue service', U.S. Department of the Treasury.

Isachsen, A.J. and Strom, S. (1989), 'The Hidden Economy in Norway With Special Emphasis on the Hidden Labour Market', in Feige, E.L. (ed.) (1989), Cambridge, Cambridge University Press.

Johnson, S., Kaufmann, D. and Shleifer, A. (1997), *The Unofficial Economy in Transition*, Brookings Papers on Economic Activity, Fall, Washington D.C.

Johnson, S, Kaufmann, D, and Zoido-Lobatón, P. (1998a), 'Regulatory discretion and the unofficial economy,' *The American Economic Review*, Vol. 88(2), pp. 387-92.

Johnson, S., Kaufmann, D. and Zoido-Lobatón, P. (1998b), 'Corruption, public finances and the unofficial economy.', Washington, D.C.: The World Bank, discussion paper.

Karmann, A. (1986), 'Monetäre Ansätze zur Erfassung der Schattenwirtschaft: Ein Vergleich verschiedener Messansätze', *Kredit und Kapitel*, Vol. 19(3), pp. 233-47.

Karmann, A. (1990), 'Schattenwirtschaft und ihre Ursachen: Eine empirische Analyse zur Schwarzwirtschaft und Selbstversorgung in der Bundesrepublik Deutschland', *Zeitschrift für Wirtschafts- und Sozialwissenschaften (ZWS)*, Vol. 110(3), pp. 185-206.

Kaufmann, D. and Kaliberda, A. (1996), 'Integrating the unofficial economy into the dynamics of post socialist economies: A framework of analyses and evidence', in: B. Kaminski (ed.), *Economic Transition in Russia and the New States of Eurasia*, London: M.E. Sharpe, pp. 81-120.

Kinsey, K.A. (1987), 'Survey Data on Tax Compendium and Review', *American Bar Foundation Working Paper*, No. 8716, Chicago.

Kirchgaessner, G. (1983), 'Size and development of the West German shadow economy, 1955-1980', *Zeitschrift für die gesamte Staatswissenschaft*, Vol. 139(2), pp. 197-214.

Kirchgaessner, G. (1984), 'Verfahren zur Erfassung des in der Schattenwirtschaft erarbeiteten Sozialprodukts', *Allgemeines Statistisches Archiv*, Vol. 68(4), pp. 378-405.

Klovland, J. (1984), 'Tax evasion and the demand for currency in Norway and Sweden: Is there a hidden relationship?' *Scandinavian Journal of Economics*, Vol. 86(4), pp. 423-39.

Lackó, M. (1996), 'Hidden economy in East-European countries in international comparison, Laxenburg', International Institute for Applied Systems Analysis (IIASA), working paper.

Lackó, M. (1998), 'The hidden economies of Visegrad countries in international comparison: A household electricity approach', in L. Halpern, and C. Wyplosz (eds), *Hungary: Towards a market economy*, Cambridge (Mass.): Cambridge University Press, pp. 128-52.

Lackó, M. (1999), 'Hidden economy an unknown quantity? Comparative analyses of hidden economies in transition countries in 1989-95', Working paper 9905, Department of Economics, University of Linz, Austria.

Lackó, M. (2000), 'Hidden Economy – An unknown quantity: Comparative analysis of hidden economics in Transition countries 1989-95', *Economics of Transition*, Vol. 8(1), pp. 117-49.

Langfeldt, E. (1984), 'The unobserved economy in the Federal Republic of Germany', in E.L. Feige (ed.), *The Unobserved Economy*, Cambridge University Press., pp. 236-60.

Langfelt, E. (1989), 'The Underground Economy in the Federal Republic of Germany: A Preliminary Assessment', in E.L. Feige. (1989), Cambridge, Cambridge University Press.

Lippert, O. and Walker, M. (eds) (1997), *The Underground Economy: Global Evidences of its Size and Impact*, Vancouver, B.C., The Frazer Institute.

Lizzeri, C. (1979), *Mezzogiorno in controluc*, Enel, Naples.

Loayza, N.V. (1996), 'The economics of the informal sector: a simple model and some empirical evidence from Latin America', Carnegie-Rochester Conference Series on Public Policy 45, pp. 129-62.

MacAfee, K. (1980), 'A Glimpse of the hidden economy in the national accounts', *Economic Trends*, Vol. 136, pp. 81-7.

Matthews, K.G.P. (1984), 'The GDP Residual Error and the Black Economy: A Note', *Applied Economics*, Vol. 16, pp. 443-48.

Mirus, R., Smith, R.S. and Karoleff, V. (1994), 'Canada's Underground Economy Revisited: Update and Critique', *Canadian Public Policy*, Vol. 20(3), pp. 235-52.

Morris, B. (1993), 'Editorial Statement. International Economic Insides', IV, *International Statistical Yearbook*, Budapest.

OECD (1978), 'Methods Used To Estimate the Extent of Tax Evasion', Mimeo, Vol. 78(6), Paris, November 17.

OECD (1980), 'Une etude sur l'exactitude des declarations de revenus en France', Mimeo, MAS/WP.7, Vol. 80(3), March, Paris cited in B.S. Frey. and W.W. Pommerehne (1984).

O'Higgins, M. (1981), 'Aggregate Measurement of Tax Evasion: An Assessment', *British Tax Review*, Vol. 5, pp. 286-302.

O'Higgins, M. (1989), 'Assessing the underground economy in the United Kingdom', in E.L. Feige (ed.), *The Underground Economies: Tax Evasion and Information Distortion*, Cambridge: Cambridge University Press, pp. 175-95.

Park, T. (1979), 'Reconciliation between personal income and taxable income', pp. 1947-77, mimeo, Washington D.C.: Bureau of Economic Analysis.

Pedersen, S. (2003), 'The Shadow Economy in Germany, Great Britain and Scandinavia: A Measurement Based on Questionnaire Service', Study No. 10, The Rockwoll Foundation Research Unit, Copenhagen.

Pestiau, P. (1983), 'Belgium's Irregular Economy', in: Gaertner, W. and Wenig, A. (1985), 'Proceeding of the International Conference on the Economics of the Shadow Economy', University of Bielefeld, West Germany, October 10-14, 1983, Springer Verlag, Berlin.

Portes, A. (1996), 'The informal economy', in: S. Pozo (ed.), *Exploring the Underground Economy*, Kalamazoo, Michigan, pp. 147-65.

Pozo, S. (ed.) (1996), *Exploring the Underground Economy: Studies of Illegal and Unreported Activity*, Michigan: W.E. Upjohn, Institute for Employment Research.

Rogoff, K. (1998), 'Blessing or Curse? Foreign and underground demand for euro notes', *Economic policy: The European Forum* 26, pp. 261-304.

Ross, I. (1978), 'Why the Underground Economy is Booming', *Fortune*, October, pp. 92-8.

Schneider, F. (1986), 'Estimating the size of the Danish shadow economy using the currency demand approach: An attempt', *The Scandinavian Journal of Economics*, Vol. 88(4), pp. 643-68.

Schneider, F. (1994a), 'Measuring the size and development of the shadow economy. Can the causes be found and the obstacles be overcome?', in H. Brandstaetter and W. Güth (eds), *Essays on Economic Psychology*, Berlin, Heidelberg, Springer Publishing Company, pp. 193-212.

Schneider, F. (1994b), 'Can the shadow economy be reduced through major tax reforms? An empirical investigation for Austria', *Supplement to Public Finance/Finances Publiques*, Vol. 49, pp. 137-52.

Schneider, F. (1997), 'The shadow economies of Western Europe', *Journal of the Institute of Economic Affairs*, Vol. 17(3), pp. 42-8.

Schneider, F. (1998), 'Further empirical results of the size of the shadow economy of 17 OECD-countries over time', Paper to be presented at the 54 Congress of the IIPF Cordowa, Argentina and discussion paper, Department of Economics, University of Linz, Linz, Austria.

Schneider, F. (2003), 'The shadow economy', in C.K. Rowley and F. Schneider (eds), *Encyclopedia of Public Choice*, Kluwer Academic Publishers, Dordrecht.

Schneider, F. (2005), 'Shadow Economies around the World: What do we really know?', forthcoming *European Journal of Political Economy*.

Schneider, F. and Enste, D. (2000), 'Shadow economies: Size, causes, and consequences', *The Journal of Economic Literature*, Vol. 38(1), pp. 77-114.

Schneider, F. and Enste D. (2002). *The Shadow Economy: Theoretical Approaches, Empirical Studies, and Political Implications*, Cambridge (UK): Cambridge University Press.

Simon, C.B. and Witte, A.G. (1982), *Beating the System: The Underground Economy*, Boston (Mass.): Urban House.

Tanzi, V. (1980), 'The underground economy in the United States: Estimates and implications', *Banca Nazionale del Lavoro*, Vol. 135(4), pp. 427-53.

Tanzi, V. (1982a) (ed.), *The Underground Economy in the United States and Abroad*, Lexington (Mass.), Lexington.

Tanzi, V. (1982b), 'A second (and more skeptical) look at the underground economy in the United States' in V. Tanzi (1982) (ed.), *The Underground Economy in the United States and Abroad*, Lexington (Mass.), Lexington, pp. 38-56.

Tanzi, V. (1983), 'The underground economy in the United States: Annual estimates, 1930-1980,' *IMF-Staff Papers*, Vol. 30(2), pp. 283-305.

Tanzi, V. (1999), Uses and abuses of estimates of the underground economy, *The Economic Journal*, Vol. 109(456), pp. 338-40.

Thomas, J.J. (1986), 'The underground economy in the United States: A comment on Tanzi', *IMF-Staff Papers*, Vol. 33(4), pp. 782-89.

Thomas, J.J. (1992), *Informal Economic Activity, LSE*, Handbooks in Economics, London: Harvester Wheatsheaf.

Thomas, J.J. (1999), 'Quantifying the black economy: 'Measurement without Theory' Yet Again?', *The Economic Journal*, Vol. 109(456), pp. 381-89.

Williams, C.C. and Windebank, J. (1995), 'Black market work in the European Community: Peripheral work for peripheral localities?', *International Journal of Urban and Regional Research*, Vol. 19(1), pp. 23-39.

Yoo, T. and Hyun, J.K. (1998), 'International Comparison of the Black Economy: Empirical Using Micro-Level Data', Paper presented at the 1998 Congress of International Institute of Public Finance, Cordoba, Argentina.

Van Eck, R. and Kazemier, B. (1988), 'Features of the Hidden Economy in Netherlands', *Review of Income and Wealth*, Vol. 34, pp. 251-73.

Zilberfarb, B.Z (1986), 'Estimates of the underground economy in the United States, 1930-80', *IMF-Staff Papers*, Vol. 33(4), pp. 790-98.

Chapter 6

On the Estimation and Updating of the Hidden Economy Estimates: The UK Experience

Dilip Bhattacharyya

Introduction

For many years a number of Economists emphasized the importance of the estimates of the 'hidden economy' in managing and understanding the working of the modern economies. All available evidences suggest that a substantial part of the economic activities remain unrecorded in the national income statistics. This message is also clear from the recent survey by Schneider and Enste (2000). Although many researchers produced estimates of unrecorded component of the national income under different names, these estimates are rarely used in other economic research or in economic management. A list of typical criticism against these estimates is:

(a)   it is not possible to observe the unrecorded economy directly, hence the estimates are unreliable as different components of the unrecorded economy behaves differently;

(b)   the assumptions made in the estimation procedure are not realistic and open to criticism;

(c)   the estimates are obtained without theory (Thomas, 1999);

(d)   consistent updating of the 'hidden economy' estimates is almost impossible, hence the estimates have very limited value.

In this paper our primary objective is to discuss the problem of estimating and updating the 'hidden economy'. However, in the development of this paper we will comment on these criticisms and will show that these criticisms are not convincing if we accept the published national income statistics are not exposed to these criticisms.

In the next section we will present a general framework which is used in the estimation of the 'hidden economy' in the literature either explicitly or implicitly. Although a general framework justifies most methods used in the estimation of the 'hidden economy', the statistical problems associated with the estimation and updating of these estimates differs considerably from one method to other. To keep the discussion properly focused we used Bhattacharyya (1990) as the method of estimation and also discussed the updating problem within this method. As all existing methodology uses either published data or a survey data to estimate the 'hidden economy' they are described as sample-based estimates. Hence, the estimates are non-unique. This is one of the criticisms against the 'hidden economy' estimates. However, a careful examination suggests that the national income statistics are also revised with the passage of time and therefore also non-unique.

In Bhattacharyya (1990) an explicit *Data Generating Procedure* (DGP) was estimated to obtain the 'hidden economy' estimates conditional upon the recorded personal income data. Thus, in practice one could obtain the current 'hidden economy' estimates by using the *Data Generating Procedure* in Bhattacharyya (1990) and the published personal income data for the current period. However, following this approach we observe that the plausible estimates are obtained only for the years 1985 to 1987. This suggests that the DGP is robust for prediction only for a short period ahead. It is also possible that the DGP is continuously changing and that is only visible when compared between two distant periods. As our starting point is the 'hidden economy' estimates presented in Bhattacharyya (1990), the updating of the estimates can be done in two alternative ways.

Bhattacharyya (1990) presented the 'hidden economy' estimates for the period 1960 to 1984, hence one could keep these estimates fixed and obtain a new DGP for the post 1984 period. Alternatively, we can re-estimate the DGP for the total period starting from 1960.

In the following section we present a general framework which has been either implicit or explicit theoretical justification of the empirical models. The actual model and methods used in Bhattacharyya (1990) are presented in the subsequent section, along with some extension of the model. The estimated models and the 'hidden economy' estimates are discussed in the next section. In the concluding section we provide some indication of the alternative use of the DGP in obtaining the 'hidden economy' estimates for the future periods as well as few suggestion for future research.

The General Framework

Following the Chicago School we assume that the national product has a technological relation with the factors of production. Thus, we can write that

$$Y = T(L, K, M, E, Z) \tag{1}$$

where,
Y is national product;
L is labour input;
K is capital input;
M is money in circulation;
E is energy input; and
Z is a vector of other factors of production.

If we assume that the level of inputs are chosen following an optimising principle then the demand for each factors of production will depend on the factor prices (or shadow factor prices) and the level of national product. Thus, the derived demand for M is:

M = f (wages, interest rate, general price level, energy price, Y and other input prices). Similarly,

E = g (wages, interest rate, general price level, energy price, Y and other input prices).

In the existing literature these two derived demand functions are generally used although the consumer demand approach taken by some authors may be interpreted as an extension from derived demand of L.

If we assume that the technological relation T takes the Cobb-Douglas form we obtain log-linear demand functions for each inputs. As most studies on the estimation of the 'hidden economy' used log-linear model of currency demand, it appears most people used an established theory in their empirical work. Hence, the criticism of Thomas (1999) and others appears inappropriate. Bhattacharyya (1990) used a form of currency demand function, which is similar to the demand for M with some added assumptions.

Model and Methods

The underlying model and the method of estimation of the 'hidden economy' adopted in this paper is very similar to Bhattacharyya (1990), although certain minor extensions are made to improve the procedure. The assumptions used to specify the model and to derive the method of estimating the 'hidden economy' are taken as 'maintained hypothesis'. These assumptions are:

1. The size of the economy measured in terms of national income or GDP has a one to one correspondence with the notes and coin in circulation, i.e we assume that the 'Cambridge Equation' is valid;
2. The transactions in the unrecorded economy are primarily conducted in currency;
3. At any given point in time, the total currency in circulation is the sum of (a) demand for currency by the recorded economy and (b) demand for currency by the unrecorded economy;
4. There is no misspecification in the currency demand equation for the recorded economy.

Thus, from the above assumptions we write,

$$M_t = M_{Rt} + M_{URt} \tag{2}$$

where M_{Rt} and M_{URt} are the demand for currency by the recorded economy and the unrecorded economy respectively, and M_t is the total demand for currency for the whole economy.

Following Baumol and Tobin (1989) we specify the currency demand equation in a flexible form. Thus, the currency demand function for the recorded economy is

$$M_{Rt} = A(Y_{Rt})^{\beta_1} (\Pi_t)^{\beta_2} (P_t)^{\beta_3} e^{F(L)u_t} \qquad (3)$$

where Y_{Rt} is recorded income, Π_t is a short-term interest rate, P_t is the general price level, M_{Rt} is defined before and u_t is 'white noise'. A, β_1, β_2 and β_3 are parameters of the model and $F(L)$ is a polynomial in lag operator L.

The demand for currency by the unrecorded sector is

$$M_{URt} = (Y_{ht})^{\beta_4} + w_t \qquad (4)$$

where M_{URt} is defined as before, Y_{ht} is a measure of unrecorded income and w_t is 'white noise'. It is assumed that u_t and w_t are independent of each other.

The total currency in circulation M_t is observable for the economy, but M_{Rt} and M_{URt} are not observable. Hence, we substitute M_{Rt} and M_{URt} by their demand specifications in (3) and (4) into relation (2). For our empirical work we use the approximation

$$\ln(M)_t = \ln(M_{Rt}) + (M_{URt} / M_{Rt}) \qquad (5)$$

Substituting (3) and (4) in (5) and after some algebraic manipulation (5) can be written as

$$m_t = \alpha + \beta_1 y_{Rt} + \beta_2 \pi_t + \beta_3 p_t + \left((Y_{ht})^{\beta_4} / H(.)\right) + \varepsilon_t + v_t \qquad (6)$$

where small characters are logarithms of the corresponding capital characters and $H(.) = A(Y_{Rt})^{\beta_1} (\Pi_t)^{\beta_2} (P_t)^{\beta_3}$; ε_t is a 'white noise' and v_t is a serially correlated disturbance term but independent of ε_t.[1]

The equation (6) is estimable if Y_{ht} is observable. We assume that Y_{Rt} and Y_{ht} have a joint distribution where $E(Y_{ht} | Y_{Rt})$ is a non-linear function of Y_{Rt}. In the empirical work we assume

$$Y_{ht} = \sum_{i=2}^{4} \alpha_i (Y_{Rt})^i \qquad (7)$$

Substituting Y_{ht} from equation (7) into equation (6), we have an estimable equation and the estimates for the parameters α_2, α_3 and $\alpha4$ are obtainable.[2] Once we obtain these estimates the 'hidden economy' estimates can be written as:

$$\hat{Y}_{ht} = \sum_{i=2}^{4} \hat{\alpha}_i (Y_{Rt})^i \tag{8}$$

This proxy produces asymptotically desirable estimates when the conditional expectation of Y_h given Y_R is a non-linear function of Y_R.[3] The particular non-linear function used in our experiment is a fourth degree polynomial in Y_R without the linear term. This particular non-linear form also fits the RESET proxy suggested in Thursby and Schmidt (1977). Replacing Y_{ht} by a function of Y_{Rt} as in equationn (7), the regression equation in (6) becomes estimable.[4] The estimable equation is a hybrid function in the sense that one part of the specification is log-linear, the other part is non-linear and it produces non-constant income, price and interest elasticities.

The estimated standard errors of the 'hidden economy' estimates can be obtained from the estimated covariance matrix of α_2, α_3 and α_4. The conditional standard error of Y_{ht} can be written as:

$$SE\left(\hat{Y}_{ht}\middle|Y_{Rt}\right) = \left[\sum_{i=2}^{4} \sum_{j=2}^{4} cov\left(\left(\hat{\alpha}_i, \hat{\alpha}_j\right)\left(Y_{ht}\right)^i (Y_{ht})^j\middle|Y_{Rt}\right)\right]^{\frac{1}{2}} \tag{9}$$

The model specified here has one special character namely the serially correlated disturbance term is associated with the log-linear part of the specification and the serially uncorrelated disturbance is associated with the non-linear part. This particular feature of the model has some advantage in the final selection of the estimated parameters. The two-stage non-linear estimation followed here is very similar to Durbin (1970). At the first stage the whole model is estimated by a non-linear estimation procedure and in the second stage lagged residuals of the first stage are also included as additional explanatory variables of the model. Once the dynamic structure of the model is correctly specified by the lagged residuals the final estimates are chosen where,

$$DA = (1/n) \left(\sum |Z_{it} - Z_{jt}| / |Z_{it}|\right) \times 100.0 \tag{10}$$

is closest to zero. Here Z_{it} is the estimate of the hidden economy at the first stage of the estimation and Z_{jt} is the estimate obtained at the second stage.

In this model β_4 cannot be estimated freely along with other parameters of the model. Therefore, we obtained the estimate for β_4 through grid search within the range 0 to 1.[5]

Empirical Results

In Bhattacharyya (1990) the 'hidden economy' estimates are reported for the period 1960:1 to 1984:4. According to Bhattacharyya the choice of the period was dictated by the availability of data which are not subject to revision. Following similar logic we restricted our study for the period 1960:1 to 1990:4.[6] Thus to update the hidden economy estimates we face three distinct situations. Using the estimated parameters of Bhattacharyya (1990) we can use the post 1984 data and obtain the 'hidden economy' estimates for 1985:1 to 1990:4. Alternatively, we can re-estimate the model using the new data set and obtain the new estimates of the 'hidden economy' for the whole period. The third option is to obtain estimates of the parameters in a restricted way where the estimated parameters vary from the Bhattacharyya (1990) only for the period 1985:1 to 1990:4.

In our first attempt to update the 'hidden economy' estimates we used the relation (8) where the estimates for α's are taken from Bhattacharyya (1990) and Y_{Rt}'s for the years 1985:1 to 1990:4 from the Economic Trend Annual Supplement, 1996. The estimates obtained through this process were highly implausible. These results suggest that a structural change has happened in the DGP for the 'hidden economy'. In this experiment we observed that if the updating is restricted to only up to 1986, the 'hidden economy' estimates are plausible and likely to pass other indirect tests. It appears that a structural change has occurred in 1987 and coincides with stock market crash of 1987. To incorporate this structural change we replace α_i by $(\alpha_i + \delta_i D_t)$ for i = 2,3 and 4. The dummy variable D_t takes value 1 from 1988 to 1990 and for the other periods takes the value 0. To obtain the 'hidden economy' estimates and their standard errors for the period 1960 to 1990 we replace α_i by $(\alpha_i + \delta_i D_t)$ for i = 2,3 and 4; in relations (8) and (9).[7] With this specification of the currency demand equation were estimated freely for the total period 1960:1 to 1990:4 and also by restricted estimation where 1960:1 to 1984:4 estimates were kept approximately fixed at the level obtained in Bhattacharyya (1990) but freely estimated for the rest of the data. The estimated parameters of the models are presented in Table 1 and Table 2 respectively.

In terms of diagnostic tests and the standard errors of the estimates it is clear that both models fit the data well. Therefore, purely in terms of model fittings and associated statistical tests, it is not possible to infer that one model is superior to the other. However, in numerical terms, the estimated parameters are different and will produce different 'hidden economy' estimates thus requiring further investigation.[8]

Table 1   Estimated parameters of the unrestricted model for the period 1960:1-1990:4

Parameters	Estimates	Standard Errors
lnA	0.710585	0.204719
β_1	0.62213	0.066077
β_2	0.052848	0.015344
β_3	-0.444357	0.108164
ρ	0.701508	0.067222
α_2	0.835934 - 02	0.206719 - 03
α_3	-3.140243	0.651042 - 05
α_4	0. 705253 - 06	0.454546 - 07
δ_2	-2.574915	0.107107 - 02
δ_3	0.125832 - 03	0.195461 - 04
δ_4	-6.693263	0.949071 - 07
β_4	0.634	

Log likelihood = 350.715; $\overline{R}^2$ = 0.9995; $\hat{\sigma}$ = 0.01465; DW = 2.2061; Ljung-Box ($\chi^2(10)$) = 12.9; LM($\chi^2(10)$) = 15.00; ARCH-F(5,112) = 0.790; Innovation Error Test - F(15, 102) = 1.523; Mean (DA) = 0.1300; Variance (DA) = 0.02903.

Table 2   Estimated parameters of the restricted model for the period 1960:1-1990:4[9]

Parameters	Estimates	Standard Errors
lnA	0.639027	0.206021
β_1	0.621736	0.062156
β_2	0.042349	0.013757
β_3	-0.395874	0.106624
ρ	0.705071	0.06713
α_2	0.696060 - 02	0.232298 - 03
α_3	-3.116611	0.631447 - 05
α_4	0.582846 - 06	0.419720 - 07
δ_2	-2.45579	0.107107 - 02
δ_3	0.100473 - 03	0.137121 - 04
δ_4	-6.556406	0.681135 - 07
β_4	0.696	

Log likelihood = 350.009; $\overline{R}^2$ = 0.9995; $\hat{\sigma}$ = 0.01473; DW = 2.2019; Ljung-Box ($\chi^2(10)$) = 14.3; LM($\chi^2(10)$) = 16.03; ARCH-F(5,112) = 0.8265; Innovation Error Test - F(15, 102) = 1.378; Mean (DA) = 0.5125; Variance (DA) = 0.07416.

The two estimated models and the estimated 'hidden economy' series are examined in three different ways, namely:

1. by comparing the forecasting ability of the two fitted models;
2. by considering the plausibility of the two series of the 'hidden economy' estimates;
3. by assessing the relationships between the government expenditure function and the two estimated 'hidden economy' series.

A comparison of the forecasting ability of the two competing models is presented in Table 3. The forecasts are obtained for the period 1991:1 to 1994:2, using dynamic one period ahead forecasting procedure.[10] We observe that the mean forecast errors and the variance of the forecast errors are very similar for the two models and on the basis of these results it is not possible to discriminate between them.

Table 3   Forecasting results of the two competing models

	LM_0	LM_0F1	LM_0F2	DIF1	DIF2
Mean	2.81166	2.79960	2.79959	0.01206	0.01207
Variance	0.00297	0.00136	0.00136	0.00289	0.00284

LM_0 = Logarithm of currency in circulation;
LM_0F1 = Forecasts of LM_0 using estimates of Table 1;
LM_0F2 = Forecasts of LM_0 using estimates of Table 2;
DIF1 = LM_0 - LM_0F1;
DIF2 = LM_0 - LM_0F2.

Forecasting exercise was also conducted for a shorter period (first eight quarters) and we observed no qualitative differences between these forecasts and the forecasts of Table 3.

Failing to discriminate between the two fitted equations on the basis of diagnostic tests and forecasting abilities, we examined the 'hidden economy' estimates in terms of plausibility of the magnitudes and movements. The 'hidden economy' estimates obtained from the estimated parameters in Table 1 are presented in Appendix Table A. Similarly in Appendix Table B the 'hidden economy' estimates are obtained from the estimated parameters in Table 2. From these tables it is clear that the 'hidden economy' estimates were 3.59 percent of the GNP in one series and 3.15 percent of the GNP in the other series for 1960:2. After this point two series moved quite differently over the years and in Table A the estimates for 1990:4 is 11.16 percent of the GNP whereas in Table B the corresponding figure is 7.06 percent of the GNP. Thus, in numerical terms two sets of estimates are quite different and we have no extraneous information to choose one against the other. If a researcher's interest is to update an estimated economic relationship where the 'hidden economy' estimates were used from Bhattacharyya

(1990), then the estimates in Table B are more useful. On the other hand if the researcher's main interest is to obtain the hidden economy estimates where maximum sample information is utilised then the estimates in Table A more reliable. This implies that every time one intends to use the 'hidden economy' estimates in any economic analysis it will be necessary to re-estimate the 'hidden economy' series again to include all current information.[11] However, we observed that when the Bhattacharyya (1990) series were updated only for two or three years, the updating procedure for Table B is reasonably good. Hence, the most relevant question would be when should a researcher re-estimate the whole 'hidden economy' series instead of updating the existing series? To obtain an answer to this question we investigated the importance of the 'hidden economy' estimates on government expenditure function using the data in Appendix Table A and Table B.

The experiment using the 'hidden economy' estimates on government expenditure function is an elaborate exercise. A brief description of the experiment and some empirical results are presented here. The details of this experiment and the full empirical results are available in Bhattacharyya (1996). The government expenditure functions are generally estimated as a long run relationship (see Chrystal and Alt (1979), Ram (1986, 1987)). However, our experiment involves quarterly 'hidden economy' estimates and that prompted us to specify a short-run government expenditure model. We assumed that the government decides about the desired level of expenditure following the specification in Gemmell (1990) with the 'hidden economy' as an additional explanatory variable. The adjustment to the desired level produced the lag structure and the dynamics in the equation. The estimated government expenditure functions produced many interesting results. However, in terms of our objective, both estimated 'hidden economy' series produced very similar results in terms of estimated government expenditure function and its predictive capacity. Failing to discriminate between the two series by this test, we conducted a non-standard experiment where we obtained the implicit tax rate for the tax evaded income (assuming the 'hidden economy' as tax evaded income). Here, we observe that the tax rate estimated with the 'hidden economy' estimates in the Appendix Table A is more plausible than the estimated tax rate obtained the data in Appendix Table B.

Conclusion

The main aim of this paper was to examine the problems of updating the 'hidden economy' estimates. However, in the process of this investigation we obtained a few other results that would interest many empirical researchers.

(a)   We conclude that the total revision of the 'hidden economy' estimates are better than updating the series while keeping the earlier estimates fixed. This finding provides a support for the complete revision of the published data often encountered in the official publications. In fact, we found that if the earlier series were extended only for two or three years, the results were not much different from the results estimated for the whole period.

We conjecture that the data published in the 1996/1997 *Economic Trends: Annual Supplement* (presented in this paper as Appendix C) with revisions for last twenty years can be justified by reasons similar to ours.

(b)   We observed a distinct shift in the parameters of the data generating process for the 'hidden economy' after the stock market crash of 1987. This may suggest that the shock of the crash had been mainly absorbed in the 'hidden economy', therefore to study the effect of the crash on the economy will require a model which incorporates the behaviour of the 'hidden economy'.

(c)   The estimated short-run government expenditure functions were improved when the 'hidden economy' estimates are included in the specification. This suggests that the government made their expenditure plan by implicit consideration of the size of the 'hidden economy'. We also observed that the inclusion of the 'hidden economy' also supported some earlier findings of the existence of a particular form of Wagner's Law in the UK.

(d)   We suggested a new method of calculating the tax losses due to the 'hidden economy'. Traditionally, using the average tax rate implied by the published data does this calculation. However, as the relevant average tax rate for the 'hidden economy' could be anywhere between 0 percent to 100 percent, the procedure suggested in this paper is likely to be more accurate.

Data Sources

1.   Currency in circulation (M) – *Financial Statistics*, several issues, HMSO.
2.   Personal income in current prices (Y_R) – *The Economic Trends*, 1992 Annual Supplement.
3.   Retail price index (P) – *The Economic Trends*, 1992 Annual Supplement.
4.   London clearing banks' base rate (Π) – *Financial Statistics*, several issues.
5.   Gross national product in current prices (GNP) – *The Economic Trends*, 1996 Annual Supplement.
6.   Government expenditure (G) – *The Economic Trends*, 1995 Annual Supplement.
7.   Population – *Annual Abstract of Statistics*, several issues.
8.   Price indices for government output and other output – *Annual Abstract of Statistics*, several issues.

Notes

1.   Interested readers can obtain the full derivations in Bhattacharyya (1989).
2.   Statistical properties of these estimates are available in Bhattacharya and Bhattacharyya (1993).
3.   This result is available in Bhattacharya and Bhattacharyya (1993).
4.   To save space full discussion of the estimation procedure is not presented here. Interested readers may like to consult Bhattacharyya (1990) for these details.
5.   If the hidden economy is created totally by cash transactions then the β_4 should be equal to 1. However, with changing financial markets, the parameter β_4 may be changing and the structure of that change will be of great interest to the policy makers.

However, in this paper we are treating β_4 as a fixed parameter and the search has been made in the grid 0 and 1.

6. Although the data used for this study is not the most current published data, the general methodological issues discussed in this paper are still valid and yet unpublished information.

7. This particular finding has an important story to tell. Although most experts believed that the 1987 crash was larger than 1933 crash, the recorded economy did not show any noticeable change on the major macroeconomic indicators. It appears from our findings that a significant part of the shock from the crash was absorbed in the hidden economy and thus leaving the recorded economy reasonably smooth.

8. An interesting finding in this exercise is the importance of the dummy variable in the estimation of the 'hidden economy'. In both models the structural changes in the parameters that generate the 'hidden economy' may explain the relatively smooth movement of the observed consumption.

9. This restricted model produces 'hidden economy' estimates with approximately the same values as Bhattacharyya (1990) for the period 1960:2 to 1984:4.

10. This particular period is chosen for a forecasting exercise. At the time of this investigation these were the only reliable data available.

11. This tantamount to say that every time a researcher wants to use the GDP or GNP data in any contemporary economic analysis the researcher should obtain full sets of revised GDP or GNP data. In practice, this will prove any extension of empirical work almost impossible.

References

Berndt, E. and Savin, E. (1977), 'Conflict among criteria for testing hypothesis in the multivariate linear regression model', *Econometrica*, Vol. 45, pp. 1263-77.

Bhattacharyya, D.K. (1989), 'An econometric method of estimating the "hidden economy", UK (1960-1984): Estimates and Tests', Wayne State Working Paper, No. 89-11.

Bhattacharyya, D.K. (1990), 'An econometric method of estimating the "hidden economy", UK (1960-1984): Estimates and Tests', *Economic Journal,* Vol. 100, pp. 703-17.

Bhattacharyya, D.K. (1996), 'The hidden economy estimates and their implications to government expenditure: UK (1960-1990)', Paper presented at the *European Economic Associations Annual Congress,* Istanbul, Turkey.

Bhattacharyya, R. and Bhattacharyya, D. (1993), 'Proxy and instrumental variable methods in a regression model with one of the regressors missing', *Journal of Multivariate Analysis,* Vol. 47, pp. 123-38.

Chrystal, K.A. and Alt, J.E. (1979), 'Endogenous government behaviour: Wagner's Law or Gotterdammerung', in S.T. Cook and P.M. Jackson (eds), *Current Issues in Fiscal Policy,* Oxford: Martin Robertson.

Durbin, J. (1970), 'Testing for serial correlation in least squares regression when some of the regressors are lagged dependent variables', *Econometrica,* Vol. 39, pp. 410-21.

Gemmell, N. (1990), 'Wagner's Law, relative prices and the size of the public sector', *The Manchester School,* Vol. 58, pp. 361-77.

Ram, R. (1986), 'Comparing evidence on Wagner's hypothesis from conventional and "real" data', *Economics Letters,* Vol. 20, pp. 259-62.

Ram, R. (1987), 'Wagner's hypothesis in time-series and cross-section perspectives: evidence from "real" data for 115 countries', *Review of Economics and Statistics,* Vol. 69, pp. 194-204.

Appendix

Table A   The hidden economy estimates (1960:2 to 1990:4) with DA minimum

Year	$\hat{Y}_{ht}$	$S.E\left(\hat{Y}_{ht}\right)$	$\hat{Y}_{ht}/_{GNP}\times100$	Year	$\hat{Y}_{ht}$	$S.E\left(\hat{Y}_{ht}\right)$	$\hat{Y}_{ht}/_{GNP}\times100$
(1)	(2)	(3)	(4)	(1)	(2)	(3)	(4)
1960.2	0.21726	0.00494	3.35945	1971.1	0.90568	0.01830	6.52367
1960.3	0.22433	0.00509	3.42743	1971.2	0.96471	0.01933	6.70959
1960.4	0.23087	0.00523	3.44740	1971.3	1.00388	0.02000	6.76286
1961.1	0.23783	0.00538	3.48163	1971.4	1.06475	0.02102	7.00678
1961.2	0.25623	0.00578	3.76094	1972.1	1.12294	0.02198	7.28143
1961.3	0.26141	0.00589	3.69857	1972.2	1.22351	0.02360	7.57636
1961.4	0.26350	0.00593	3.77836	1972.3	1.23856	0.02384	7.54346
1962.1	0.26840	0.00603	3.78235	1972.4	1.36103	0.02573	7.88229
1962.2	0.28077	0.00630	3.84674	1973.1	1.44328	0.02697	7.85203
1962.3	0.28706	0.00643	3.90030	1973.2	1.56206	0.02869	8.42354
1962.4	0.29431	0.00658	3.98197	1973.3	1.63261	0.02968	8.61899
1963.1	0.29045	0.00650	3.95598	1973.4	1.73406	0.03106	8.79473
1963.2	0.31210	0.00696	4.05433	1974.1	1.83096	0.03233	9.44035
1963.3	0.32046	0.07131	4.08487	1974.2	1.94909	0.03382	9.32403
1963.4	0.33394	0.00741	4.12322	1974.3	2.27271	0.03755	10.32767
1964.1	0.34140	0.00757	4.17816	1974.4	2.47447	0.03962	10.72826
1964.2	0.36198	0.00799	4.31283	1975.1	2.83961	0.04284	11.48338
1964.3	0.37288	0.00822	4.38014	1975.2	2.99845	0.04403	11.46373
1964.4	0.38710	0.00851	4.41796	1975.3	3.33563	0.04612	12.24714
1965.1	0.39751	0.00872	4.45936	1975.4	3.39028	0.04640	11.97006
1965.2	0.42545	0.00929	4.72675	1976.1	3.67646	0.04761	12.18178
1965.3	0.43329	0.00944	4.71014	1976.2	3.77815	0.04793	12.24366
1965.4	0.45696	0.00992	4.87632	1976.3	4.06130	0.04851	12.71620
1966.1	0.50530	0.01088	5.33129	1976.4	4.10946	0.04856	12.14703
1966.2	0.47684	0.01031	4.93831	1977.1	4.27269	0.04864	12.28172
1966.3	0.46762	0.01013	4.78141	1977.2	4.41767	0.04858	12.30789
1966.4	0.48946	0.01056	4.96514	1977.3	4.62328	0.04828	12.49671
1967.1	0.50428	0.01086	5.06310	1977.4	4.79584	0.04782	12.43413
1967.2	0.52837	0.01133	5.17507	1978.1	5.09038	0.04662	12.70340
1967.3	0.54034	0.01156	5.27114	1978.2	5.37636	0.04495	12.81948
1967.4	0.55040	0.01176	5.30252	1978.3	5.54990	0.04370	12.90825
1968.1	0.59570	0.01263	5.54084	1978.4	5.76630	0.04191	13.00856
1968.2	0.60091	0.01273	5.53170	1979.1	6.02802	0.03944	13.21152
1968.3	0.60933	0.01289	5.45215	1979.2	6.37212	0.03588	13.06968
1968.4	0.63329	0.01335	5.56637	1979.3	6.76050	0.03210	13.13484
1969.1	0.67392	0.01411	5.77873	1979.4	7.28054	0.03033	13.58969
1969.2	0.67176	0.01407	5.69817	1980.1	7.41172	0.03111	13.35469
1969.3	0.69023	0.01442	5.76731	1980.2	7.67950	0.03481	13.50029
1969.4	0.73223	0.01520	5.97010	1980.3	7.98341	0.04257	13.57169
1970.1	0.75870	0.01568	6.08905	1980.4	8.11564	0.04707	13.44028
1970.2	0.82492	0.01688	6.37100	1981.1	8.26747	0.05302	13.38904
1970.3	0.84638	0.01726	6.37050	1981.2	8.39830	0.05878	13.31183
1970.4	0.88678	0.01797	6.48612	1981.3	8.57958	0.06769	13.23825

Table A   (continued)

Year	$\hat{Y}_{ht}$	$S.E\left(\hat{Y}_{ht}\right)$	$\hat{Y}_{ht}/_{GNP}\times100$	Year	$\hat{Y}_{ht}$	$S.E\left(\hat{Y}_{ht}\right)$	$\hat{Y}_{ht}/_{GNP}\times100$
(1)	(2)	(3)	(4)	(1)	(2)	(3)	(4)
1981.4	8.67467	0.07279	13.03442	1986.3	10.97450	0.18099	11.19310
1982.1	8.87291	0.08429	13.12406	1986.4	11.16790	0.17928	11.10096
1982.2	8.90711	0.08639	12.81764	1987.1	11.26352	0.17819	10.95215
1982.3	9.04072	0.09489	12.78383	1987.2	11.47364	0.17563	10.91314
1982.4	9.11245	0.09965	12.53742	1987.3	11.87850	0.17198	10.94721
1983.1	9.26681	0.11024	12.34357	1987.4	12.34393	0.17343	11.13812
1983.2	9.32483	0.11432	12.41457	1988.1	12.27485	0.25578	10.77317
1983.3	9.46679	0.12446	12.16499	1988.2	12.61160	0.23971	10.79871
1983.4	9.57649	0.13231	12.07932	1988.3	13.08095	0.23393	10.84926
1984.1	9.67052	0.13895	11.96254	1988.4	13.51654	0.24401	10.83933
1984.2	9.76581	0.14549	11.97671	1989.1	13.64764	0.24910	10.76159
1984.3	9.84632	0.15078	11.94709	1989.2	13.99675	0.26508	10.91228
1984.4	10.05691	0.16311	11.77643	1989.3	14.39480	0.28437	11.04175
1985.1	10.08970	0.16474	11.58665	1989.4	14.68100	0.29776	10.95532
1985.2	10.27298	0.17266	11.50081	1990.1	14.89848	0.30871	11.00306
1985.3	10.37991	0.17606	11.43024	1990.2	15.12021	0.32373	11.00244
1985.4	10.50935	0.17900	11.37006	1990.3	15.44097	0.36821	11.03722
1986.1	10.65446	0.18090	11.25848	1990.4	15.58833	0.40917	11.16171
1986.2	10.81715	0.18153	11.24596				

Table B **Updates hidden economy estimates after keeping 1960:2 to 1984:4 fixed as earlier estimates**

Year	$\hat{Y}_{ht}$	$\hat{Y}_{ht}/_{GNP}\times100$	Year	$\hat{Y}_{ht}$	$\hat{Y}_{ht}/_{GNP}\times100$
(1)	(2)	(3)	(1)	(2)	(3)
1960.2	0.18093	3.14610	1971.1	0.74236	6.18889
1960.3	0.18681	3.20594	1971.2	0.78754	6.35983
1960.4	0.19217	3.21297	1971.3	0.81879	6.33590
1961.1	0.19835	3.25856	1971.4	0.86668	6.52720
1961.2	0.21296	3.51832	1972.1	0.91475	6.77238
1961.3	0.21521	3.39992	1972.2	0.99138	7.02908
1961.4	0.21897	3.53683	1972.3	1.00371	6.94800
1962.1	0.22349	3.54191	1972.4	1.09882	7.25441
1962.2	0.23308	3.59803	1973.1	1.16511	7.18275
1962.3	0.23831	3.65107	1973.2	1.25338	7.60363
1962.4	0.24420	3.71575	1973.3	1.30784	7.80938
1963.1	0.24291	3.71940	1973.4	1.38454	7.87833
1963.2	0.26004	3.78909	1974.1	1.46107	8.37432
1963.3	0.26704	3.83465	1974.2	1.54651	8.27986
1963.4	0.27810	3.87168	1974.3	1.78638	8.93814
1964.1	0.28495	3.92439	1974.4	1.93325	9.21253
1964.2	0.30104	4.04889	1975.1	2.19897	9.75326
1964.3	0.31019	4.11226	1975.2	2.30758	9.77664
1964.4	0.32189	4.17979	1975.3	2.54285	10.36926
1965.1	0.33106	4.22752	1975.4	2.58121	10.00235
1965.2	0.35321	4.44509	1976.1	2.78016	10.27293
1965.3	0.35985	4.43113	1976.2	2.84430	10.19243
1965.4	0.37909	4.60506	1976.3	3.03168	10.52667
1966.1	0.41947	5.04783	1976.4	3.06283	10.08770
1966.2	0.39532	4.66293	1977.1	3.17407	10.15606
1966.3	0.38806	4.52184	1977.2	3.26109	10.24661
1966.4	0.40577	4.73095	1977.3	3.39060	10.35520
1967.1	0.41874	4.82034	1977.4	3.49708	10.26711
1967.2	0.43726	4.89815	1978.1	3.67034	10.21923
1967.3	0.44715	4.98937	1978.2	3.84635	10.36194
1967.4	0.45536	5.02000	1978.3	3.94664	10.33476
1968.1	0.49307	5.26895	1978.4	4.07138	10.40822
1968.2	0.49614	5.24021	1979.1	4.20761	10.40636
1968.3	0.50297	5.18418	1979.2	4.39626	10.28028
1968.4	0.52240	5.34204	1979.3	4.59279	10.26208
1969.1	0.55622	5.55834	1979.4	4.83978	10.42292
1969.2	0.55324	5.47441	1980.1	4.89662	10.16233
1969.3	0.56819	5.55415	1980.2	5.01871	10.18283
1969.4	0.60192	5.75231	1980.3	5.14525	10.08616
1970.1	0.62485	5.85394	1980.4	5.19966	9.93211
1970.2	0.67605	6.09218	1981.1	5.25537	9.79074
1970.3	0.69349	6.10247	1981.2	5.31089	9.83206
1970.4	0.72532	6.16608	1981.3	5.38379	9.72155

Table B   (continued)

Year	$\hat{Y}_{ht}$	$\hat{Y}_{ht}/\text{GNP} \times 100$	Year	$\hat{Y}_{ht}$	$\hat{Y}_{ht}/\text{GNP} \times 100$
(1)	(2)	(3)	(1)	(2)	(3)
1981.4	5.41960	9.51926	1986.3	7.72195	9.25627
1982.1	5.49569	9.54163	1986.4	8.11928	9.50001
1982.2	5.51582	9.26639	1987.1	8.17876	9.42525
1982.3	5.57255	9.22226	1987.2	8.68640	9.75824
1982.4	5.60505	9.01946	1987.3	8.88635	9.64157
1983.1	5.67600	8.80355	1987.4	7.29925	7.73086
1983.2	5.70978	8.87605	1988.1	7.38283	7.69133
1983.3	5.79138	8.66286	1988.2	7.48192	7.58047
1983.4	5.86090	8.58627	1988.3	7.61977	7.43487
1984.1	5.90871	8.50529	1988.4	7.75263	7.37201
1984.2	5.96037	8.50412	1989.1	7.78972	7.23193
1984.3	6.03870	8.51457	1989.2	7.91711	7.27201
1984.4	6.21842	8.41145	1989.3	8.01876	7.23911
1985.1	6.24642	8.29098	1989.4	8.11332	7.18540
1985.2	6.47066	8.38451	1990.1	8.22299	7.10686
1985.3	6.63219	8.51208	1990.2	8.37105	6.96705
1985.4	6.85182	8.68055	1990.3	8.56760	6.97182
1986.1	7.06703	8.77783	1990.4	8.69181	7.06479
1986.2	7.38394	9.01822			

Table C   Gross National Product and total personal income published in 1995 and 1996/97 *Economic Trends – Annual Supplements* **(figures are in current prices)**

Year	GNP1	GNP2	PI1	PI2
1984.1	80803	80840	67980	67927
1984.2	81686	81540	69733	69774
1984.3	82485	82416	70621	70785
1984.4	85222	85399	73864	73921
1985.1	87005	87075	73320	73379
1985.2	89470	89324	76453	76410
1985.3	90864	90811	77655	77687
1985.4	92301	92430	79721	79605
1986.1	94568	94635	80124	80186
1986.2	96274	96187	82748	82607
1986.3	98136	98047	84112	84073
1986.4	100487	100603	86426	86196
1987.1	102677	102843	85754	85859
1987.2	105168	105136	88448	88247
1987.3	108618	108503	91105	90912
1987.4	110675	110826	94368	94011
1988.1	113731	113939	95075	94942
1938.2	116800	116788	93322	98143
1988.3	120770	120570	101475	101475
1988.4	124545	124699	105503	105300
1989.1	126719	126818	105270	104961
1989.2	128080	128265	109257	108773
1989.3	130800	130357	112283	112198
1989.4	133746	134003	115611	115456
1990.1	135302	135403	116744	116169
1990.2	137053	137426	119730	119393
1990.3	140374	139899	123733	123410
1990.4	139370	139659	126483	126033
1991.1	140423	140663	125542	125005
1991.2	143308	143887	128642	128394
1991.3	144512	144053	130599	130478
1991.4	146861	147221	133600	132655
1992.1	146997	147473	134479	133361
1992.2	149593	150601	137168	136490
1992.3	152138	151794	138857	138355
1992.4	152686	152172	141007	139723

Notes: GNP1 and PI1 are taken from 1995 Economic Trends; GNP2 and PI2 are taken from 1996/97 Economic Trends.

Chapter 7

The Shadow Economy in OECD and EU Accession Countries – Empirical Evidence for the Influence of Institutions, Liberalization, Taxation and Regulation

Introduction

Tax evasion, illicit work and social security fraud are widely spread. Most governments focus on fighting this deviant behaviour by punitive measures. But empirical data shows contrary to standard economic theory, that this way is expensive, inefficient and, finally, unsuccessful. Governments have to change institutions (e.g. tax system) and regulations to reduce incentives for illicit work and tax evasion. An increasing burden of taxation and social security contributions are – as well as regulations and the poor quality of institutions – the driving forces for the increase of the shadow economy especially in OECD-countries, as the empirical analysis here proves. More empirical evidence is presented for the influence of working time regulation on illicit work. For transition countries, multivariate analysis provide evidence for the significant influence of corruption, economic freedom and the quality of institutions on the size if the shadow economy. The quality of institutions can for example explain two-thirds of the variance of the shadow economy in OECD and transition countries.

New Challenges for Economic and Social Policy

The causes, effects and problems generated by increasing shadow economic activities are extensively and controversially discussed in the OECD and EU-Accession countries. Owing to dramatically rising rates of unemployment (e.g. in the EU), the financing problems of public expenditure, and the rising vexation and disappointment with economic and social policies, have initiated a range of broad initiatives on behalf of the EU Commission, the EU Parliament and initiatives at the appropriate national levels.[1]

But they face a dilemma. While evasion of taxes by the wealthy leads to widespread public indignation, illicit workers receive less criticism, although, as some politicians argue, they are behaving anti-socially, contributing to unemployment and social injustice. This opinion is broadly shared with regard to social fraud, illegal employment and extensive tax evasion. But what about part-time illicit (evening) work ('moonlighting'), which roughly half of the population of Germany, Norway, Great Britain and Sweden would tolerate or even take advantage of if they had the opportunity to make use of it?[2] Can more sanctions and control combined with more regulation become the ultimate solution to fight illicit work, or is there any other option to deal with undeclared work?

The guidelines laid down by the EU Commission in their pan-European employment strategy for combating illicit work, calls for exchange of 'good practice models' and co-ordination at the EU level, including stricter controls and harsher sanctions. This is nothing new and hardly goes beyond trying to cure the symptoms. This analysis will reveal the true causes and the reasons why harsher sanctions will fail to fight illicit work.

Definition: Shadow Economy, Tax Evasion and Illicit Work

The starting point of nearly all controversies in this literature are either the different estimates of the size of the shadow economy or the 'right' definition. With this in mind, research efforts stick to questions such as the best method to estimate the extent of the shadow economy, the size of the shadow economy labour force and its changes over time. The topic of interest here an analysis of the causes of underground economic activity.[3]

Since the term 'shadow economy' comprises numerous economic activities it is difficult to provide a formal definition.[4] For example, one has to distinguish between goods and services produced and consumed within the household, 'soft' forms of illicit work ('moonlighting'), illegal employment and social fraud, as well as criminal economic activities. In general, the shadow economy can be seen as the decision of individuals against the official norms and formal institutions for economic activity. From the point of view of economic policy are those shadow economic activities particularly relevant, which are related to the added value. Concerning the evaluation of the activities in the context of an economic order, one has to distinguish between the output of illegal and legal activities, on the one hand, and legal and illegal production and distribution of these activities, on the other. Figure 1 illustrates this definition. Yet, the boundaries between the sectors are not clearly defined and they vary with the level of economic development.

Criteria \ Sectors	Household sect or	Informal sector	Irregular sector	Criminal sector
Production/ Distribution	legal	legal	illegal	illegal
Market transactions	no	yes	yes	yes
Output (goods/ services)	legal	legal	legal	illegal
NAC-conventions	Self-sufficient economy (legal)		Shadow economy (illegal)	
Examples	Do-it-yourself, home office work; baby-sitting; exchange of goods	Neighbour-hood help; counselling centres; self-help organisations; honorary activities; network help	**Illicit work:** ⇨ because of violations of distributing, handicraft and trade regulations. ⇨ because of tax evasion ⇨ and abuse of public benefits.	Trade with stolen goods and drugs; prohibited gambling; fraud; smuggling; stolen goods

Figure 1 Categorization of the underground economy

Source: Schneider and Enste (2002, p. 11)

The underground economy can be divided into four sectors. The informal economic activities may be defined in terms of the two concepts of market transactions and legality/NAC-conventions. Hence, the underground economy can be logically separated into a legal and an illegal sector. The legal sector then can be defined as the self-sufficient economy while the illegal one as the shadow or hidden economy.

As marked in grey (in Figure 1), the production of private households as well as voluntary work for charities is excluded from further analysis. Following Tanzi's line of argumentation (1999, p. 338), activities, which do not generate added value but merely imply a financial gain for the individual, are also ruled out (prostitution, smuggling, kidnapping etc.). Furthermore, pure tax evasion is not included in the following analysis either. Hence, the subject of this study is the shadow economy, especially illicit work combined with tax evasion.[5] Illicit work, carried out either on a part-time basis by individuals ('moonlighting') or as part of the activities of a firm ('sole job'), constitutes the largest element of the shadow economy.

Fighting the Symptoms

The increase of underground economies has drawn the attention of politians to this phenomenon. When asked, how to fight illicit work, politians and bureaucrats often only think of harsher sanctions and tighter control. In Germany for example both measures has been implemented to fight illicit work and illegal employment. Sanctions can now amount to 300,000 Euro for illict work and 500,000 Euro for illegal employment. According to a recent decision of the German parliament, the number of controllers will be increased by nearly fifty percent to 7,000. This will lead to costs of control amounting to half a billion euro. However, new empirical findings for Germany show that sanctions and tighter controls have not reduce illicit work.

In fact, in spite of harsher sanctions and additional input (personnel and resources), fewer investigations are undertaken and the shadow economy is still increasing, as shown in Figure 2. The fines are growing in line with the estimates of the size of the shadow economy, but the amount of penalties finally paid is constantly decreasing. 25 percent at the most are eventually paid by the illicit workers.

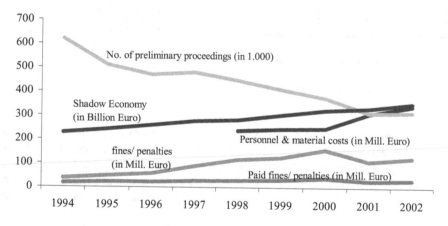

Figure 2 Fighting the symptoms in Germany

Source: Enste (2003) – detailed data sources are given there

A closer look reveals, that in Germany only one out of thousand illicit workers pay a fine or penalty (see Enste, 2003). Curing the symptoms has obviously failed. It is therefore necessary to focus on the causes. Based on broad theoretical work, empirical evidence is presented in the following sections for 21 OECD-Countries and 10 Transition Countries.

Causes in OECD-Countries

The growth of the shadow economy has been caused by many different factors but the most important and most often cited ones are:[6]

- the increasing burden of taxes and social security contributions combined with the increase in the density and intensity of regulations in the official economy, especially on labor markets;
- the (forced) reduction of weekly working time, the early retirement and the growing unemployment rate; and
- the long-term decline of civic virtue and loyalty towards public institutions combined with a declining tax morale, partly as a results of corruption and the decline of the quality of public institutions.

Tax Burden

In almost all studies the increasing burden of tax and social security contribution is one of the most important causes for the growth of the shadow economy.[7] Since taxes affect labor-leisure choices and stimulate labor supply in the shadow economy (or the untaxed sector of the economy) the distorting effect of this choice is a major concern for economists. The bigger the difference between the total cost of labor in the official economy and the after-tax earnings from work, the greater the wish to avoid this difference and to work in the shadow economy. Since this difference depends largely on the social security system and the overall tax burden, they are key factors for the existence and the growth of the shadow economy.

A growing shadow economy can be seen in this context as the reaction of individuals who feel overburdened by the state and who choose the 'exit' option rather than the 'voice' option. The increase of the shadow economy is caused by a rise in the overall tax and social security burden coupled with institutional sclerosis, but the increase of underground activities also erodes the tax and social security bases. The result is a further increase in the budget deficit or tax rates, additional growth of the shadow economy and gradual weakening of the economic and social fundament of collective arrangements.

The correlation between individual reaction and taxation is illustrated in the following figure of a modified Laffer (1979) curve, which originally shows the effect of tax evasion through additional leisure time. Gutmann (1981) modified the figure by integrating the possibility to engage in shadow economic activities. The top part of the graph shows the correlation between tax rate and tax yield. The axes show the aggregated tax rate in percentage of the income and the tax yield. The more the state increases the tax rates, the more opposition grows. If the yield maximum in S (tax rate t*) is surpassed, the internal revenue decreases despite rising tax rates as citizens try to avoid paying. Lowering the rates would in this case even result in a higher yield as the negative incentives are reduced.

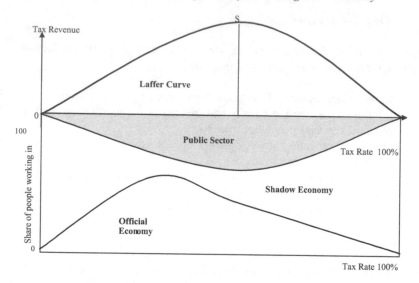

**Figure 3   Correlation between tax yield, tax rate and the growth of the
shadow economy**

The lower part of the graph shows the link to the shadow economy.[8] To simplify, the economy is divided into three sectors (public sector, official and shadow economy). With regards to the development of an economy over time we should note that at the beginning the informal sector was strong. The introduction of an extensive official economy is not possible without state activity. If the former grows, so does the latter as it requires resources. When taxes are introduced positive effects predominate. There are positive incentives to switch to the official economy if the state actually guarantees property rights in exchange for taxation. The optimum combination of taxes and supply of public goods cannot be generalised as the situation and tax culture differs from country to country. Citizens may get accustomed to the increasing use of resources by the state, so a higher tax burden does not necessarily result in a growing shadow economy.

But, since politicians and bureaucrats, as modelled in Public Choice Theory, act rationally, they try to maximise their utility. This finally leads to tax yield maximisation by politicians and budget maximisation by bureaucrats, resulting in higher tax rates to finance the growing public sector.[9] The rising tax burden means stronger incentives to work illicitly. Once the tax yield has reached its maximum, the public sector can no longer expand as taxpayers will not accept this limitation of their freedom caused by high tax rates and strict regulations any longer and will increasingly engage in shadow economic activities. A new set of rules and institutions is necessary. Revolutions or transformation processes change the established institutions, replacing those who were in power. With new government, other laws and institutions will be implemented, because a situation without any state activity – anarchy – is not desirable for anybody. In such a situation all economic activities take place in the shadow economy (see Figure 3).

At this point of institutional change, the development of regulations and supplying resources for state activity is advantageous for all. But the supply of public goods by the state (e.g. protection of property rights) requires resources, so some activities are transferred to the public sector. The process of institutional development starts again. The 'new institutions' are supported by the people, as they are perceived as legitimate and increase their welfare. These considerations show that the perception of public equivalents is an important criterion for the decision whether or not to work illicitly. If the combination of taxes and supply of public goods is perceived as legitimate, it will not result in a rise of shadow economic activity.

Figure 4 shows the correlation of the total tax burden and the size of the shadow economy, presenting some empirical evidence for the 'Gutmann Curve' for the OECD-countries.

A correlation between tax burden and shadow economy has been found in many studies on a macro- and microeconomic level (see Enste, 2002). Figure 5 presents empirical evidence for these findings. The tax burden can explain to more than one third of the variance in the size of the shadow economies. But, there is of course a vicious circle: the higher the tax burden, the larger the shadow economy. And the larger the shadow economy, the smaller the tax base. Hence, to finance a given supply of public goods, the tax rate has to rise leading to more incentives to work illicitly.

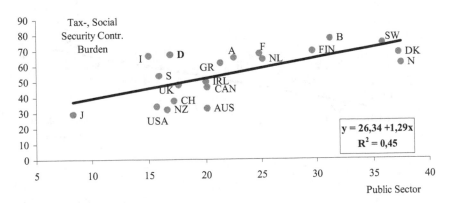

Figure 4 Public sector and tax burden

Sources: OECD (2003); ILO (2002); Enste (2004a)

Notes: Total Tax and Social Security Burden (incl. employer contributions, less cash benefits) of average single earner (in percent of labour costs) plus VAT; Public Sector (in percent of GDP).

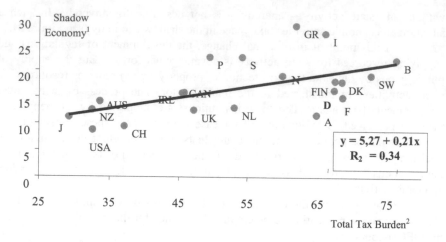

Figure 5 Tax Burden and shadow economy

Source: Enste (2004a)

Notes: (1) Shadow Economy (Monetary Demand Approach). (2) Total Tax and Social Security Burden (incl. employer contributions, less cash benefits) of average single earner (in percent of labour costs) plus VAT. Data: OECD (2003); Schneider (2003).

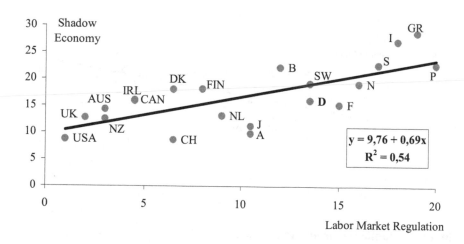

Figure 6 Labor market regulation and shadow economy

Source: Enste (2004a)

Data: OECD (1999); Schneider/Enste (2000b).

Intensity of Regulations

Another important factor, which limits the freedom of choice for individuals engaged in the official economy is the increase of the intensity of regulations, often measured by the number of laws and regulations such as license requirements, labor market regulations, trade barriers and labor restrictions for immigrants. The influence of labor regulations on the shadow economy has also been analyzed in various studies. Regulations lead to a substantial increase in labor costs in the official economy. Since most of these costs are shifted to the employees, these costs provide another motivation to work in the shadow economy, where it is possible to avoid them.[10]

Labor Market Regulations   In this context, the numerous regulations on the official labor market and the total wage costs are often discussed. Figure 6 shows a ranking of 21 OECD-Countries: the higher the rank, the more labor market regulations. According to this data, 54 percent of the variance in the size of the shadow economy can be explained by labor market regulations. This regression is robust when using different OECD-labor market regulation indices.

Table 1   Illicit work in five european countries

		Germany	Denmark	Great Britain	Norway	Sweden
1	Illicit work in Percent of GDP	4.1	3.8	1.2	2.6	2.3
2	... percent of the population have work illicitly in the last 12 months	11.7	21.6	8.7	18.2	12.0
3	... percent of the population are willing to work illictly	46.4	58.6	36.3	52.7	51.5
4	Standard working hours per year[2]	1.662	1.640	1.693	1.688	1.738
5	Illicit work (hours per year)[3]	428	268	198	226	245
6	Total working time of illicit workers (hours per year)	2.090	1.908	1.891	1.914	1.983
7	Percentage of illicit work of total working time per year	20.5	14	10.5	11.8	12.3

Source: Enste (2004a)

Notes: Representative survey (population from 18 to 66 years).

Data: Schneider and Enste (2000b); Pedersen (2003); Lamnek, Olbrich and Schäfer (2000); EIRO Observer (2003).

Working Time   An important labor market regulation is the forced reduction of working time. Labor-Leisure Models show the fatal effect of reducing regular working time, if people prefer to work longer. This leads to more illicit work. Empirical investigations in five European Countries found, that employees prefer to work between 1.891 and 2.090 hours per year. If they are not allowed to work these hours officially, they do it in the shadow economy, as Table 1 shows.

This study also reveals the minimum amount of illicit work in the five countries. According to this survey, illicit work equals 4.1 percent of GDP in Germany, 3.8 percent in Denmark, 1.2 percent in Great Britain, 2.6 percent in Norway and 2.3 precent in Sweden. In Germany an illicit worker works on average an additional 20 percent of his official working time illicitly.

Main Causes in the New Member States of the EU (and some other East European Countries)

Overview of Main Causes

In Eastern Europe the following main factors for the growth of the shadow economy are important:

- The lack of competence and trust in official institutions (e.g. legislation, administration/bureaucracy, courts) combined with an inefficient and corrupt administration;
- Property rights cannot be guaranteed by the official institutions combined with inadequate enforcement of laws and regulations;
- High costs and administrative burden for entrepreneurs hinder official economic development;
- A low probability of being caught as an illicit worker or tax evader can result in a cost-benefit calculation where illicit work is more attractive than regular and official work;
- Sometimes 'hiding in the shadows' is essential for surviving or to establish a business due to slow bureaucracy;
- Broad acceptance of illicit work (e.g. access to credits and loans in the shadow economy), makes it difficult to fight this phenomenon.

Empirical Evidence for Some Factors

Empirical evidence for some of these factors influencing the development of the shadow economy are comprehensively presented in Figure 7. The new members of the EU (without Malta and Cyprus), Bulgaria, Romania and Russia are of special interest in this context and are mentioned by name. The analysis shows that corruption, economic freedom, and the quality of institutions have a significant impact on the shadow economy.

a) Corruption and the Shadow Economy

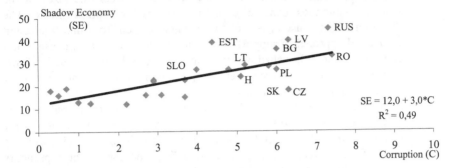

b) Economic Freedom and the Shadow Economy

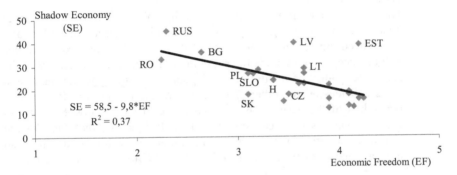

c) The Quality of Institutions and the Shadow Economy

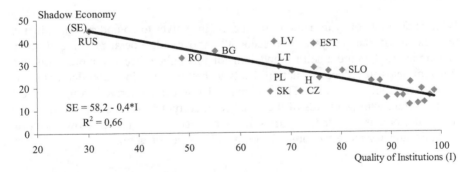

Figure 7 Causes of the shadow economy

Source: Enste (2004b)

Data: Transparency International (2003); The Heritage Foundation (2003); Worldbank (2003); Schneider (2003).

a)   There is a strong positive correlation between the shadow economy and corruption. Nearly 50 percent of the variance between the sizes of the shadow economies can be explained by the corruption index. The direction of the cause-effect-relation cannot be seen from this figure, but theoretical approaches support this notion of corruption as a cause, not a consequence of the shadow economy (Rose-Ackerman, 1999; Tanzi 1998). That means, entrepreneurs try to avoid corrupt bureaucrats by going or staying underground.

b)   Economic freedom and liberalisation can also help reduce the attractiveness of irregular activities in the black economy. Although for some countries the correlation is not very high, the overall view reveals a significant correlation and R-squared of 37 percent. If entrepreneurs and households do not feel overburdened by the state, do not have to obey too many regulations and pay too high taxes, they will not go underground.

c)   The most important factor is the quality of institutions. If the state guarantees property rights, provides a good infrastructure and public goods according to the preferences of the people, paying taxes and fees will be accepted. Crucial is the right combination of the efficiency of the state, the quality of institutions and public goods on the one hand and taxes and fees on the other. The quality of the institutions can explain two thirds of the variance between the size of the shadow economy in the 25 countries covered here. Other analysis show, that the Eastern European countries which have institutions with a higher quality also have a higher growth rate of the official GNP (Busch/Matthes, 2004).

Political Implication

What is the best policy measure to reduce the incentives to go underground, taking the results of the analysis into account? Above all, liberalization and more economic freedom are a solid foundation for this policy, because more economic freedom helps to reduce corruption, leads to better institutions and decreases the attractiveness of illicit work. This recommendation can be derived from empirical results: More than two thirds of the variance in corruption can be explained by the level of liberalisation the countries have reached, as Figure 8 shows. Hence, liberalisation and more economic freedom will reduce corruption.

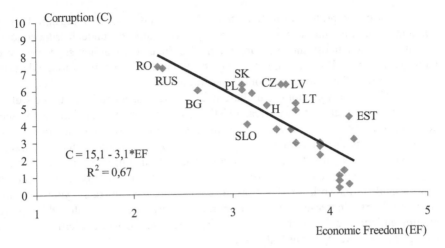

Figure 8 Corruption and economic freedom

Source: Transparency International (2003); The Heritage Foundation (2003); own calculation

Notes: (1) Corruption index for 2002. Recoded Values: 0 (no corruption) to 10 (extremly corrupt). (2) Index for economic freedom of the Heritage Foundation for 2002. Recoded Values: 1 (no freedom) to 5 (a lot freedom). Similiar results by using data of the Fraser Institut (2003).

The Shadow Economy – A Challenge for National Governments

The causes for the strong increase in shadow economic activities are rising tax burdens, regulation density and defensive labour market policy directed at a re-distribution of working hours. Especially in transition countries, the lack of clear and stable institutions are another driving force of irregular economic activities. In combination with a reduced tax moral and less loyalty to the government, these are the most important factors for the 'migration' into the shadow economy. But increasing the costs of illicit work by intensified controls and setting higher fines will not bring positive effects on the overall welfare of the state – as has been shown here for Germany.

Still, the growth of the shadow economy leads to reduced state revenues which, in turn, reduces the quality and quantity of publicly provided goods and services. Ultimately, this may lead to an increase of the tax rates for firms and individuals in the official sector. These are quite often combined with a deterioration in the quality of the public goods (such as the public infrastructure) and of public administration, the consequence of there is further incentives to participate in the shadow economy.

In many countries the government is facing the challenge to impose substantial reforms to the social security and tax systems in order to prevent the total defeat of the protective welfare state. The dilemma is the vicious circle: high tax and regulation burdens cause higher growth rates of undeclared economic activities, which boost the pressure on public finance to either save money or increase tax rates. But, high tax rates again increase the incentives to evade taxes and to escape in the shadow economy, and so on.

The shadow economy can therefore been seen as a challenge to the welfare state. Since in a cumulative process existing institutions and rules are losing their acceptance in the society, it will end up with a situation, in which democratic voting ('voice') is less attractive than using the 'exit' option to the shadow economy. Eventually, the loyalty to the democratic political institutions is abandoned or difficult to sustain. The option of improving the quality of institutions and the institutional framework may act as a circuit breaker in this cycle. Fighting corruption by increasing the transparency perfectly fits into this policy recommendation, because it will reduce the incentives to work illicitly as well as strengthen the loyality towards the state.

Notes

1. See, for example, EU Commission (1998), EU Parliament (2000); German Parliament (2004).
2. See Enste (2002).
3. The different methods are described in detail in Schneider and Enste (2000a, 2000b, 2002).
4. Here is a small selection of terms used either synonymously or in different issue areas, according to the respective author: underground economy, illicit work, informal sector, irregular sector, leisure economy, alternative economy, black economy, hidden economy, unofficial economy, parallel economy, shadow economy, unobserved economy, unrecorded economy. See, amongst others, Thomas (1992, p. 125), Dixon (1999), Giles (1999) and Tanzi (1999).
5. Nevertheless, most estimates of the size of the shadow economy include to a certain extent some of the criminal activities as a result of the specification of the method used. The difficulties of these estimates are described in OECD (2002). and discussed in Schneider and Enste (2000a). They must be considered in this analysis.
6. For an overview of studies of the causes see Frey and Pommerehne (1984), Thomas (1992) and Schneider and Enste (2000a, 2000b, 2002).
7. See, for instance, studies by Feige (1989), Pozo (1996), Lippert and Walker (1997), Schneider (1994, 1997); Giles (1999) and Tanzi (1999).
8. For a simplified figure, which ignores the effects of state activity, see for example Frey and Weck (1983a) and Neck, Schneider and Hofreither (1989).
9. Frey and Weck (1983) show that this also leads to an additional supply of jobs in the public sector.
10. See Johnson, Kaufmann and Zoido-Lobatón (1998b, p. 18) and Friedman, Johnson, Kaufmann and Zoido-Lobatón (1999).

References

Busch, Berthold and Matthes, Jürgen (2004), 'Institutional Transformation and Economic Performance', *IW Trends*, 31 (1), Köln, pp.15-21.

Dixon, H. (1999), 'Controversy: On the hidden economy', Edititorial introduction, in *Economic Journal*, Vol. 109(H.456), pp. 335-37.

EIRO Observer (2003), 'Working Time Developments in 2002', Nr. 3/03, S. 2-3.

Enste, D.H. (2002), 'Schattenwirtschaft und institutioneller Wandel – Eine soziologische', *sozialpsychologische und ökonomische Analyse*, Tübingen.

Enste, D.H. (2003), 'Ursachen der Schattenwirtschaft in den OECD-Staaten', *iw-trends*, Vol. 4, Institut der deutschen Wirtschaft Köln.

Enste, D.H. (2004a), 'Schattenwirtschaft: Boom trotz härterer Strafen – warum?', *Zeitschrift Sozialer Fortschritt*, Vol. 53(H.2), pp. 29-36.

Enste, D.H. (2004b), 'Schattenwirtschaft in Osteuropa', *iw-trends*, Vol. 1, Institut der deutschen Wirtschaft Köln.

EU-Kommission (1998), Die Kommission eröffnet eine Diskussion über die nichtangemeldete Erwerbstätigkeit'. Brüssel (COM 1998 219 – C4-0566/1998 – 1998/2082(COS)) vom 8.4.1998.

EU-Parlament (2000), Bericht zur Mitteilung der Kommission zur nichtangemeldeten Erwerbstätigkeit (Dokument A5-0220/2000) vom 30.8.2000.

Feige, E.L. (ed.) (1989), *The Underground Economies: Tax evasion and information distortion*, Cambridge University, Cambridge, New York, Melbourne.

Frey, B.S. and Pommerehne, W. (1984), 'The hidden economy: State and prospect for measurement', *Review of Income and Wealth*, Vol. 30(H.1), pp. 1-23.

Frey, B.S. and Weck, H. (1983), 'Bureaucracy and the shadow economy: a macroapproach', in Hanusch and Horst (eds), *Anatomy of Government Deficiencies*, Berlin (Springer), pp. 89-109.

Friedman, E., Johnson, S., Kaufmann, D. and Zoido-Lobatón, P. (1999), *Dodging the Grabbing Hand: The determinants of unofficial activity in 69 countries*, Washington.

German Parliament (2004), Gesetz zur Intensivierung der Bekämpfung der Schwarzarbeit und der damit zusammenhängenden Steuerhinterziehung, BMF, Berlin.

Giles, D.E.A. (1999), 'Measuring the hidden economy: Implications for econometric modelling', *Economic Journal*, Vol. 109, pp. 370-80.

Gutmann, P.M. (1981), 'Implications of the the subterranean economy', in R.X. Bove and R.D. Klingenstein (eds), Wertheim´s underground economy conference. p. 31-58.

International Labour Organisation (ILO) (2002), ILO-Yearbook of Labour Statistics – ILO Statistics on Public Sector Employment, Genf.

Johnson, S., Kaufmann, D. and Zoido-Lobatón P. (1998), *Corruption, Public Finances and the Unofficial Economy*, Washington.

Laffer, A.B. (1979), *The Economics of the Tax Revolt: A reader*, Harcourt Brace Jovanovich, New York.

Lamnek, S., Olbrich, G. and Schäfer, W. (2000), *Tatort Sozialstaat – Schwarzarbeit*, Leistungsmissbrauch, Steuerhinterziehung und ihre (Hinter) Gründe, Opladen.

Lippert, O. and Walker, M. (eds) (1997), *The Underground Economy: Global evidences of its size and impact*, Fraser Institute, Vancouver, B.C.

Neck, R., Schneider, F. and Hofreither, M.F. (1989), 'The consequences of progressive income taxation for the shadow economy: Some theoretical considerations', in B. Dieter and F. Bernhard (eds), *The Political Economy of Progressive Taxation*, Springer, Berlin, Heidelberg, New York, pp. 149-76.

Organisation for Economic Co-operation and Development (OECD) (1999), *OECD Employment Outlook*, Paris.

Organisation for Economic Co-operation and Development (OECD) (2002), *Measuring the Non-observed Economy – A Handbook*, Paris.

Organisation for Economic Co-operation and Development (OECD) (2003), *Taxing Wages 2001-2002*, Paris.

Pedersen, S. (2003), *The Shadow Economy in Germany, Great Britain and Scandinavia – A Measurement Based On Questionnaire Surveys*, Kopenhagen.

Pozo, S. (ed.) (1996), *Exploring the Underground Economy*, Kalamazoo, Michigan (Upjohn Institue for Employment Research).

Rose-Ackerman, S. (1999), *Corruption and Government: Causes, consequences, and reform*, Cambridge University Press, Cambridge.

Schneider, F. (1994), 'Can the shadow economy be reduced through major tax reforms? An empirical investigation for Austria', *Public Finance*, Vol. 49, Supplement, pp. 137-52.

Schneider, F. (1997), 'The shadow economies of Western Europe', *Journal of the Institute of Economic Affairs*, Vol. 17(H.3), pp. 42-8.

Schneider, F. (2003), Aktuelle Prognose zur Entwicklung der Schattenwirtschaft in Deutschland im Jahr 2003, Pressemitteilung, Vol. 29(Januar), Universität Linz.

Schneider, F. and Enste, D.H. (2000a), 'Shadow Economies: Size, Causes, and Consequences', *Journal of Economic Literature*, Vol. 38, pp. 77-114.

Schneider, F. and Enste, D.H. (2000b), *Schattenwirtschaft und Schwarzarbeit – Umfang, Ursachen*, Wirkungen und wirtschaftspolitische Empfehlungen, München.

Schneider, F. and Enste, D.H. (2002), *The Shadow Economy – An International Survey*, Cambridge.

Tanzi, V. (1998), 'Corruption around the world: Causes, consequences, scope, and cures', *IMF-Working Papers*, Vol. 98(63), pp. 1-39.

Tanzi, V. (1999), 'Uses and abuses of estimates of the underground economy', *Economic Journal*, Vol. 109, pp. 338-47.

Thomas, J.J. (1992), *Informal Economic Activity*, Harvester/Weatsheaf, New York, London.

The Fraser Institute (2003), Economic Freedom of the World: 2003 Annual Report, www.fraserinstitute.ca.

The Heritage Foundation (2003), Index of Economic Freedom, www.heritage.org.

Transparency International (2003), Transparency International Corruption Perceptions Index 2002, www.transparency.org.

Worldbank (2003), Governance Indicators for 1996-2002, www.worldbank.org/wbi/governance/govdata2002/.

Chapter 8

The Shadow Economy in Norway 1980-2003: Some Empirical Evidences from Voluntary Sample Surveys

Kari Due Andresen, Tone Ognedal and Steinar Strøm

Introduction

Shadow economy activity with a focus on tax evasion has attracted the attention of economist for a long time, starting with Cagan (1958) who studied the correlation between currency demand and tax pressure on US data. Later, this currency demand approach to measure the size of the shadow economy has been extended by various researchers in the field and applied on data from many countries. Recently, the currency demand approach, as well as other approaches, has been discussed at length in a survey, see Schneider and Enste (2000). The literature also abounds with theoretical studies of the microeconomics of tax evasion. To our knowledge, Allingham and Sandmo (1972) initiated this vein of research. Examples of later theoretical microeconomic studies, which have focused on labour supply in the irregular part of the economy, are Andersen (1977), Baldry (1979), Isachsen and Strøm (1980), Sandmo (1981) and Cowell (1985). However, to be able to provide the tax authorities with more information than what theoretical studies can achieve, empirical evidence is needed. For obvious reasons it is difficult to observe activities that generates income, which is not reported to any authorities. Yet, there exists some in-depth surveys that have provided researchers with micro-data, which have been employed to analyse empirically the possible causes of working in the shadow economy and also to estimate tax evasion related activities like labour supply in the shadow economy, see CENSIS (1976), Isachsen, Klovland and Strøm (1982), Isachsen and Strøm (1985), Isachsen, Samuelson and Strøm (1985), Isachsen and Strøm (1989), Lacroix and Fortin (1992), Lemieux, Fortin and Frechette (1994) and Jørgensen, Ognedal and Strøm (2005).

In this study we use survey data from Norway. With a few minor changes, the survey has been repeated five times: in 1980, 1983, 1989, 2001 and 2003. We use data from all of them except the 1983 survey, where the data is lost. The questionnaire has about 35 questions. In addition to questions about individual characteristics such as sex, age and education, there are questions about both registered and unregistered work (reported and unreported). The individuals are also asked about their beliefs about other peoples' unregistered labour income and their opinion about such tax evasion.

One argument against survey data has been that individuals may hesitate to reveal their illegal activities in a survey, since they may fear that the tax authorities may identify them. It is therefore important that the survey is carried out in a way that guarantees anonymity to the respondents. In the survey we use, each person asked to participate in the survey is given a letter where they are assured of anonymity, and they are instructed to return the questionnaire in an anonymous envelope. The high response rates indicate that people have trusted the guarantee of anonymity. The 1980 survey is well documented in Sporastøyl (1982) and in Isachsen, Klovland and Strøm (1982).

According to the definition given by Feige (1989) activities in the shadow economy consist of all activities that contribute to the gross national product but are currently not registered. Here, we only study activities related to non-reported wage income. Thus capital income and profit that are not reported to the tax authorities are not included. The survey method that we apply has the advantage of being able to provide detailed information about the causes of working in the shadow economy, and of the composition of the work force in the shadow economy. Moreover, with surveys covering a period of 23 years, we should be able to estimate the long run trends in the shadow labour market participation.

It can be questioned whether we are able to estimate, with sufficient accuracy, the size of the total shadow economy in terms of income. Most likely, data from the survey method may give an estimate of the lower bound on the size of total income evaded, while the currency demand approach may give an upper bound. In that respect the two approaches supplement each other. The actual size of the shadow economy is hard to estimate with accuracy in any of the approaches applied so far.

The main findings in our study can be summarized as follows:

1.   The propensity to participate in the shadow labour market has decreased from around 20 percent of the population in 1980 to 10 percent in 2003.
2.   This finding seems contrary to the results reported for Norway in Schneider and Enste (2000) and in Schneider (2001). It should be noted, however, that Schneider et al. estimate the size of the shadow economy in terms of money evaded, while we estimate the fraction that participates in the shadow labour market. We have also estimated the unreported wage income and find no significant reduction over time in these incomes. The explanation might be that productivity and hence real wages are growing in the shadow economy as it has done in the regular economy.

The reason for the decline in shadow labour market participation rates may be many.

1.   First, the tax systems have been reformed in Norway, as in many other countries. As seen from Appendix 2 the marginal tax rates have been drastically reduced from 1980 to 2003, with most of the reforms taking place in the early 1990s.

2. Second, also evident from Appendix 2, the tax system has been simplified.

3. Third, income has been growing. Since the income effects in labour supply may first affect the individuals' side jobs, the incentive to take on work in the shadow economy have been weakened. At present, as an oil and gas producing country, Norway is ranked as the richest country in the world. Most of the increase in income, rather evenly distributed in the Norwegian welfare state, took place from 1980 till to day.

4. Forth, the labour market participation rate of women in the regular economy has risen drastically since 1980. At present, the labour market participation rate among married females is higher in Norway than in any other OECD country. Long maternity leaves with high compensation, expansion of childcare facilities and better-paid jobs with lower tax burden are some of the explanation behind this development. Thus, and as argued by Contini (1981), a rise in the participation rate in the regular labour market may reduce the participation in the shadow labour markets.

5. Fifth, the industrial structure has changed, away from primary and secondary industries toward tertiary sectors producing a variety of services. Norway, like the other Scandinavian welfare states, has a long tradition of having a relative large public sector. This sector is responsible for providing a lot of services like health care, education and even banking. As more people work in the public sector, the opportunity for unregistered work at the workplace has been reduced. Moreover, there have also been changes in the sizes and the management of firms. These changes are most easily observed in the retail sectors, where big supermarkets have replaced small shops at street corners or small groceries spread around in the country. Thus the opportunity to evade taxes at the workplace may have been reduced also in the private service sector over the last two decades. The decline in the opportunity to do unregistered work is evident both from the surveys and from the microeconometric studies reported below. The willingness to take part in tax evading activities, given that the respondents had the opportunity to participate, has not been reduced as much at the actual participation. This also means that the potential participation in the shadow economy is much higher than the actual.

6. Judged by the answers to the questionnaire, tax morale seems to have improved over the years. However, with weaker incentives to take part in the shadow economy and with lesser opportunities, it may be easier to convey a message of a better tax morale.

7. One important finding is that the participation rate in the shadow labour markets increases in periods of recessions. Even though the fraction that is willing to do unreported work has fallen over the years, it is still high enough to make tax evasion a serious problem if people get more opportunities to do unreported work. A period of high unemployment may be enough to reverse the reduction in shadow labour market participation.

The chapter is organized as follows. In the following section we describe the data. In the next section we present some trends in shadow labour market activities during the period from 1980 to 2003 and this is followed by a discussion of some econometric evidence based on estimation of logit models on the survey data. The final section concludes. In Appendix 1 we list the questions asked in the surveys and in Appendix 2 we give the tax functions for1980 and 2001.

Data

The data we have used are taken from four similar surveys done by a private Norwegian polling institute MMI in the years 1980, 1989, 2001 and 2003. The questions asked in these surveys are, with only a few exceptions, the same questions each year, giving us the opportunity of comparing results.

In the three first surveys participants were recruited by MMI's personal omnibus in the month of October and questions on tax evasion were distributed in anonymous envelopes. In 2003 the recruiting of participants was done by MMI over the telephone asking the person in the household, above 15 years of age and who most recently celebrated his or her birthday if he/she wanted to participate in a research study. The recruitment was conducted randomly in the Norwegian population, again in October. That the recruitment method is different for the 2003 survey might imply that the results cannot be directly compared with the other survey results. However, the procedure of filling out the questionnaire is the same every year and should reduce the concerns regarding non-comparability.

The surveys gather information regarding relevant personal characteristics of the respondents, such as age and employment, economic variables such as income and taxes, and people's engagement in as well as attitudes towards non-reported income activities. The questions asked in the last survey are given in Appendix 1.

As Table 1 shows the answer percentage is fairly high in all years. The lowest percentage of 58 percent occurred in 2001 despite the fact that as many as 81 percent of the people asked that year agreed to participate. In 2003 as many as 73 percent of the people asked filled out the questionnaire, implying that 62 percent of the persons initially contacted ended up participating in the survey. Final response rates fluctuating around 60 percent in the period 1980 to 2003, with the exception of 2001, is very good compared to response rates in other surveys, for instance in the consumer expenditure surveys of Statistics Norway.

A relevant question regarding the results is the one of possible systematic bias. A common experience with surveys is that people agreeing to participate might have better knowledge of and a higher interest in the subject in questions than the people refusing to participate. The participants might also have 'an agenda' when answering. However, the 2-staged process of recruiting and filling out of questionnaires allows for some control of the possible bias. In addition to drawing the recruiting areas randomly the results have afterwards been weighted as if everyone agreed to participate and filled out the questionnaire. Thus the final sample is rather representative for the whole population, with a minor exception for 2001.

Table 1   Response rates in the surveys

	1980	1989	2001	2003
Asked to participate	1198	1130	1690	1742
Agreed to participate (%)	80	87	81	86
Of which answered (%)	73	73	58	72
Respondents, percentage of asked (%)	58	63	47	62

Tax Evasion 1980-2003, Some Trends

Reduction in Shadow Labour Market Participation

One of the most robust results from our surveys is that the fraction of the labour force who participate in the Norwegian shadow labour market has gone down over the last twenty years: The fraction who admit they have had unreported labour income in the last 12 months has gone down from 20 percent in 1980 to 10 percent in 2003. There has also been a significant decrease in the fraction who admit they have ever had unreported income, and in the fraction who would like to leave some income unreported if they had the opportunity. The percentages are shown in Table 2, 3 and 4.

Table 2   During the last 12 months, have you had labour income that was not reported to the tax authorities? Percent

	1980	1989	2001	2003
Yes	20	22	13	10
No	76	75	87	90
No answer	4	3	0	0
Sum	100	100	100	100

Table 3   Have you ever had income that you did not report to the tax authorities? Percent

	1980	1989	2001	2003
Yes	39	44	33	34
No	60	53	67	65
No answer	1	3	0	1
Sum	100	100	100	100

Table 4   If you had the opportunity to receive income without having to report it to the tax authorities, would you accept such an income? Percent

	1980	1989	2001	2003
Yes	64	59	44	35
No	18	20	26	29
Uncertain	Not an alternative	20	26	35
No answer	18	1	3	1
Sum	100	100	100	100

A Peak during the Recession

In 1989, the fraction of the population that did unreported work peaked. Also, in 1989, the total unreported labour income peaked (see Table 5). This year, 1989, differs from the other survey years in that unemployment was high by Norwegian standards, and rising. Moreover, both the real interest rates and housing prices were increasing. Together this caused a debt crisis. Many households had serious and acute payment problems, especially those who lost their jobs. Paradoxically, there is no peak in the fraction that is willing to do unreported work (Table 4), or in the fraction that thinks tax evasion is socially acceptable (Table 6).

Table 5   Estimates of non-reported income in Billion NOK 2001

	1980	1989	2001	2003
Females	2.8	4.6	1.7	0.8
Males	5.1	8.6	5.1	3.0
Total	7.9	13.2	6.8	4.8
95% confidence intervals	[5-10.8]	[8-18.8]	[2.9-10.9]	[1.6-6.0]

Tax Evasion Less Accepted

The change in people's attitudes towards unreported income is consistent with this reduction in unreported work, as shown in Table 6. For example, the percentage that finds tax evasion 'acceptable' has gone down. Thus, it may seem that the 'tax morale' has been improving over the years. However, at the same time, as discussed below, opportunities and incentives for engaging in tax evading activities have also changed and may have contributed to a lower level of tax evading activities in Norway. It may be easier to demonstrate a better morale when tax evasion activities have lost some of its attractiveness.

Table 6 **What do you believe is the general attitude towards doing work that is not reported for taxation? Percent**

	1980	1989	2001	2003
Acceptable	76	54	49	48
Acceptable under doubt	Not an alternative	29	30	33
Not acceptable	6	5	6	6
Uncertain	16	11	13	11
No answer	2	1	2	1
Sum	100	100	100	100

No Significant Reduction in Total Unreported Income

Although the fraction that does unreported work has gone down since 1980, there is no significant reduction in the total unreported income. The estimates for 1980, 1989, and 2001 are shown in Table 5 (for details concerning the method of calculation see Goldstein et al. (2002)). As indicated by the large confidence intervals in the parenthesises, the estimates are uncertain. The confidence intervals imply that the estimated non-reported income from work ranges around 1 percent of GDP in all years, with an increase towards 2 percent in 1989. Although there appear to be a slight reduction in the total unreported income from 1980 to 2003, the reduction is not significant. The reduction from 1989 to 2003 is significant, however. Shima (2004) found a similar development based on a macro-econometric currency demand approach proposed by Schneider (2001) who extended a model suggested by Klovland (1984). Her estimates for the total non-reported incomes relative to GDP peaked when the unemployment was at its highest (1995) in the period 1990 to 2002, with an estimate of 10.2 percent of GDP in 1995, and thereafter declining to a level of 5.6 percent of GDP in 2002. For 2002 she reports an uncertainty that gives a range of the estimates from 2.4 percent to 7.8 percent. The lower bound is not that much different from the estimate than can be derived from the direct survey approach, keeping in mind that in our approach we are only estimating non-reported wage income related to otherwise legal work. Of course, there is an order of magnitude difference between the point estimates based on the indirect currency demand approaches and our direct survey approach. Both are uncertain, but it is of interest to note that the trends are similar. In both studies, Shima's and ours, we predict declining tax evading activities over the recent years, with the exception during recession periods in which there is an increase in the shadow market activities. It should also be noted that even if the number of people participating in shadow economy activities is predicted to decline, with the exception of during recessions periods, the non-reported income may not decline that much. The reason why is that even in the shadow economy there is an productivity growth going on like in the regular part of the economy.

Women have Left the Black Labour Market?

One striking result from Table 5 is the difference between the changes in unreported income for men and women. While the estimated total unreported income for men is unchanged, it is significantly reduced for women. The average unreported income for men has gone up, and the women's average unreported income has gone down with approximately 40 percent.

How can we Explain the Changes in Unreported Income and in People's Attitudes toward Unreported Income during the Period 1980 to 2003?

Tax reductions   One obvious candidate for explaining the reduction in both the willingness to do unreported work and the fraction who actually does it, is the reduction in marginal taxes over the last twenty years. In Appendix 2 we show the tax functions in 1980 and 2001. Clearly, the marginal tax has been drastically reduced. For example, while more than 15 percent of the respondents had a marginal tax rate above 60 percent in 1980, in 2001 only 5 percent had such high marginal tax rate. Jørgensen et al. (2004) find that the reduced marginal tax rates reduce significantly the hours of unreported work chosen by an individual, although the effect is not large. The reduction in tax rates can only explain part of the reduction in unreported work over the last twenty years. For example, if the respondents of 2001 were given the higher tax rates of 1980, other things held equal, they would still work fewer hours of unreported work than the respondents of 1980. More importantly, the tax rate has almost no effect on the fraction that chose to do unreported work. Because the reduction in this fraction is the most profound change in the Norwegian shadow labour market, we must search for other factors than the tax rate to explain the changes.

Fewer opportunities   One interesting observation from Tables 2 and 3 is that the fraction that does unreported work is much lower than the fraction that is willing to do such work, with some exceptions for 2003. The big gap between the fraction that is willing to do unreported work and the fraction that actually does it suggests that many people may be constrained by the opportunities for such work. Barth and Ognedal (2004) find more support for this hypothesis. They show that while the use of unreported labour varies a lot, both between industries and within industries, the willingness to do unreported work varies only little. Moreover, the fraction that does unreported work varies with the size of the firm and with firm productivity in a way that cannot be explained by wage differentials alone. Jørgensen et al. (2004) finds that industrial affiliation is important in explaining the individuals' choice between doing unreported work or not. Table 7 shows that the fraction that does unreported work varies a lot between sectors. Unsurprising, it is highest in construction and lowest in public administration. Hence, fewer opportunities for unreported work may be an important reason why the fraction that does unreported work has gone down. Opportunities may be fewer because sectors with fewer opportunities for unreported work employs a higher fraction of the labour force, or because of changes within sectors. Over the last 20 years or so there has been considerable changes in the industry sector in almost all industrialised countries, and even more so in Norway. When an economy becomes richer, the service sector expands at the expense of other sectors of the economy. Norway is a gas and oil producing country and has thus benefited from increasing production of petroleum at rather high prices in some of the years in the considered period. At present Norway is considered to be the richest country in the world according to GDP per capita. Moreover, Norway belongs to the Scandinavian welfare states with a rather sizeable public sector relative to other countries. Because the opportunity to evade taxes in the main job differs considerably across sectors, with lesser opportunities in some service sector and especially in public sectors, one should expect that tax evasion has gone down in an economy which has gone through periods with sharp increases in incomes and hence with a considerable change in the industry structure. Moreover, the increase in income, distributed rather evenly across households, has reduced the incentives to take on side jobs in the regular as well as in the irregular part of the economy.

Table 7   Employed by sectors that has engaged in non-reported income activities during the last 12 months. Individuals are below 60 years of age. Percent

	1980	2001	2003
Primary sectors	20	18	17
Construction	65	48	27
Manufacturing	26	23	14
Consumer goods	18	10	12
Transportation	36	13	11
Health services	7	9	7
Public administration	13	4	3
Service sectors, other	22	21	13
Education	15	11	8

Women entered the regular labour market   One of the most important reductions in the opportunities for unreported work are caused by the trend that women are leaving informal jobs such as unreported child care and enter the regular labour market. A large fraction of women in 1980 had no job or only a part-time job in the regular labour market. This gave them more opportunities than men to do unreported work in the informal labour market, for example with child care. In 1980, the average women who had unreported labour income worked many hours unreported. The average number of unreported work hours was 166 for women and only 87 for men. From 1980 to 2003 there has been a large increase in women's participation in the regular labour market, in 2003 the female participation rate in the labour market is the highest in the world. This development, from low participation rates towards the higher participation rates among males, has reduced the incentives and opportunities to do unreported work in the informal labour market. At the same time, the demand for private, unreported childcare may have gone down since the paid maternity leave is longer, schooling starts one year earlier and the supply of subsidized public kindergartens is much higher.

Peak during recession   While the fraction that does unreported work has fallen over the period, Tables 2 and 3 show that it had a peak in 1989, when unemployment rose sharply. This year, the total unreported labour income also peaked (see Table 5 and Goldstein et al. (2002)). Both the fraction that is willing to do unreported work and the fraction that thinks tax evasion is acceptable, goes down during the entire period, as shown in Tables 3 and 4. These observations are consistent with the hypothesis that unreported work is constrained by limited opportunities for such work in the regular labour market. When people become unemployed, however, they face more opportunities for unreported work in informal jobs and self-employment.

We will now turn to an econometric analysis of the possible causes for the willingness to participate in the shadow economy.

Tax Evasion: An Econometric Analysis of Participation Probabilities

We will first start with the discussion of the probability of being engaged in tax evasion activities during the last 12 months. Let $P_{12,n}$ denote the probability that individual n has taken part in tax evading activities through wage work in the last 12 months. Let X_n denote a vector of observed individual characteristics and let $Y_{12,n}^*$ denote a latent variable that reflects the value for individual n to evade taxes through wage work.

$$Y_{12,n}^* = X_n \alpha_{12} + \varepsilon_{12,n}; \quad n = 1,2,..,N \tag{1}$$

where α_{12} is a vector of unknown coefficients that relate the observed variable in the vector X_n to the value for individual n to evade taxes during the last 12 months. N is the total number of individuals and $\varepsilon_{12,n}$ is a random variable assumed to be iid standard logistic distributed. $\varepsilon_{12,n}$ is assumed to represent the unobserved variables affecting the choice of evading taxes. We now let $Y_{12,n}$ be a variable that equals 1 if the individual n is observed to have been engaged in tax evading activities and 0 otherwise.

Thus $P_{12,n}$ is given by:

$$P_{12,n} = Pr(Y_{12,n} = 1) = Pr(Y_{12,n}^* \geq 0) = Pr(X_n \alpha_{12} + \varepsilon_{12,n} \geq 0)$$
$$= Pr(\varepsilon_{12,n} \geq -X_n \alpha_{12}) \tag{2}$$

The probability of not being engaged in tax evading activities, $\Pr(Y_{12,n}=0)$ equals $1-P_{12,n}$. With the assumption of logistic distribution we get the following logit probability for taking part in tax evading activities:

$$P_{12,n} = \frac{\exp(X_n\alpha_{12})}{1+\exp(X_n\alpha_{12})} \tag{3}$$

The joint a priori probability of what we observe is then given by the following likelihood, L:

$$L = \prod_{n=1}^{N} P_{12,n}^{Y_{12,n}} \left(1-P_{12,n}\right)^{1-Y_{12,n}} \tag{4}$$

The unknown coefficients are determined so that this likelihood is maximized. We note that if none of our assumed observed variables have any impact on the choice of evading taxes, then L equals $(0.5)^N$. In that case the individuals make their choice at random as if by tossing a coin. This random alternative is the benchmark of our model, and how well our model explains data is measured relative to this pure random alternative. Our goodness of fit simply says by how many percentages we explain data better than a pure random model.

The variables appearing in X_n is given in Table 8 together with the estimates of the coefficients. We show the results for 1980 and 2003 only. The variables are:

1. Gender, and our hypothesis is that males are more likely to take part in tax evading activities.
2. Age, and the younger the individual is the more likely it is that he or she takes part in tax evading activities.
3. Education in years, the more educated the individual is, the less likely it is that the individual will take part in tax evading activities.
4. 'Norm', defined as to what degree the individual says that tax evasion is acceptable in the society, the more he or she thinks that tax evasion is socially acceptable, the more likely it is that the individual will take part in tax evasion. (We should add that those engaged in tax evasion activities report more than the others that tax evasion is socially acceptable in their environment, but it is important to note that also a high number of those not engaged in these activities say the same.)
5. Subjective detection probability, the higher the individual thinks that the chance of being caught is, the less likely it is that he or she participates in tax evasion.

Table 8   **Estimates of the probability of being engaged in non-reported income activities during the last 12 months. t-values in parentheses. Respondents are below 60 years of age**

Variables	1980	2003
Constant	-0.8184	-0.8639
	(-2.0)	(-1.9)
Gender (M=1)	1.2546	0.5045
	(5.9)	(2.1)
Age in years	-0.0411	-0.0212
	(-4.5)	(-2.3)
Education in years	-0.9194	-0.8093
	(-3.5)	(-3.3)
Norm	0.5449	1.2477
	(2.1)	(5.2)
Detection probability	-1.2910	-0.7457
	(-2.1)	(-2,6)
No of observations	729	859
Goodness of fit	0.49	0.53

From Table 8 we note that the coefficients are sharply determined and that our model explains data around 50 percent better than a pure random choice model. We note that our conjectures with respect to the signs of the impact of observed variables on the probability are all met, but we also note that there have been some changes over time:

1. The difference in the propensity to participate in tax evasion activities across gender has declined.
2. Tax moral judged by how socially acceptable the agents think that tax evasion is play a more important role in 2003 than in 1980.
3. The subjective probability of being caught is of lesser importance in 2003 than in 1980.

To illustrate the results further we have used the estimated model to characterize the probability of taking part in tax evasion the last 12 months across different individuals. The results are set out in Table 9.

The reference person in Table 9 is a 25 years old male with low education and who thinks that tax evasion is common and socially acceptable. He also thinks that the probability of being caught, given that income is evaded, is less than 0.5. We observe that for this individual the model predicts that there is a 49 percent probability that he will participate in tax evasion activities in 1980, while the probability is predicted to 59 percent in 2003. Thus, the reported decline in observed fractions, which are equal to aggregate probabilities, may occur together with an increase in participation probabilities of some particular individuals. If the agent were a female, the participation probabilities drop, but more so in 1980 than in 2003 (from 0.49 to 0.21 in 1980 compared to from 0.59 to 0.46 in 2003). If we consider an older individual, 40 years old compared to 25, we observe that the probability of tax evasion participation drops, and again more so in 1980 than in 2003. If we consider a higher educated individual, the participation probabilities drop for both years, but now the strongest relative decline takes place in 2003 rather than in 1980. The same is true with respect to the subjective beliefs about the tax morale in the society. If we consider an individual who thinks that tax evasion is not socially acceptable at all, the tax evasion probabilities drop considerably, in particular in 2003. If the agent thinks that the probability of being detected is higher than 0.5 rather than lower, the propensity to take part in tax evasion activities declines, and relatively more in 1980 than in 2003.

We have also tried with occupation by sector as one of the covariates. We then get that working in the construction sector increases the probability of taking part in tax evading activities, while working for the government has the opposite impact. The other coefficients do not change much.

Table 9   The probability of participation in non-reported income activities during the last 12 months

Reference person	Gender		Age	Education	Norm	Detection
Constant	√	√	√	√	√	√
Gender	Male	Female	√	√	√	√
Age	25	√	40	√	√	√
Education	Low	√	√	High	√	√
Norm	Yes	√	√	√	No	√
Detection	<0.5	√	√	√	√	≥0.5
Participation prob. 1980	0.49	0.21	0.34	0.28	0.36	0.21
Participation prob. 2003	0.59	0.46	0.51	0.39	0.29	0.40

The next question we will address is the probability of taking part in tax evasion activities, if one had the opportunity to do so. The model is formally equivalent to the preceding one, with the same explanatory variables included.

From Table 10 we observe that the sign of the estimated coefficients are all as expected and that they are all sharply determined. We observe that in modelling the probability of tax evasion, given that the agent had the opportunity to evade taxes, we get lower goodness of fit than in the preceding case. Obviously, unobserved heterogeneity or random aspects, has a more important impact on the choices here than in the case above. It is also interesting to note that the estimates of the coefficients have changed less over the years in the model of tax evasion, given opportunities, than in the preceding model of tax evasion the last 12 months.

This result gives some support to the hypothesis that opportunity matters and that these opportunities have changed towards making it less likely to find a job in 2003 that can be combined with tax evading activities than in 1980.

Table 10 **If you had the opportunity to receive an income without having to report it to the tax authorities, would you accept such an income? Estimates of the probability of accepting. t-values in parentheses. Respondents are below 60 years of age**

Variables	1980	2003
Constant	1.1064	0.5625
	(5.3)	(1.5)
Gender (M=1)	0.8770	0.4408
	(8.3)	(2.8)
Age in years	-0.0223	-0.0144
	(-4.7)	(-2.2)
Education in years	-0.9775	-0.6215
	(-7.7)	(-3.8)
Norm	1.8108	2.0073
	(17.3)	(9.0)
Detection probability	-1.3305	-0.9085
	(-8.6)	(-3.5)
No of observations	729	859
Goodness of fit	0.21	0.18

Table 11 **The probability of accepting non-reported income**

Reference person	Gender		Age	Education	Norm	Detection
Constant	√	√	√	√	√	√
Gender	Male	Female	√	√	√	√
Age	25	√	40	√	√	√
Education	Low	√	√	'High'	√	√
Norm	'Yes'	√	√	√	'No'	√
Detection	<0.5	√	√	√	√	≥0.5
Participation prob. 1980	0.96	0.91	0.95	0.91	0.81	0.87
Participation prob. 2003	0.93	0.90	0.92	0.88	0.66	0.85

Again, to illustrate the estimated model further we predict the probability of participation in tax evasion activities, given the opportunities to do so. From Table 11 we note three things. First the predicted probabilities are very high, which indicates that there is a large potential for evading taxes. Second, the probabilities are almost the same in the two years (1980, 2003). Third, changes in the covariates have a minor impact on the probability of tax evasion, with one important exception. If one considers individuals who think that tax evasion is not socially acceptable compared to if they think the opposite, the probability of being willing to participate in tax evasion activities is reduced, and very much so in 2003.

Conclusions

There has been a reduced participation in the shadow labour market over the last 23 years as well as lower acceptance for tax evasion. In the population there is a lower fraction that does unreported work and a lower fraction that thinks it is acceptable and willing to do such work. Total number of unreported hours has gone down, but there is no significant reduction in total income from unreported work.

Reduced tax rates can only explain a small part of these changes. Reduced opportunities for doing unreported work may play an important role. In 2003 compared to in 1980 there are more jobs in sectors where the opportunities for unreported work are few, such as in the public sector. An overall higher education level in the population has lead to different type of jobs in which the chances to combine the main job with tax evading activities have become reduced. In 2003 a higher fraction of women work in the regular labour market than in 1980, and consequently there are less woman working in the informal sector where the opportunity for unreported work is better.

It also seems that norms against tax evasion has improved, but this may partly be explained by lower tax rates and lesser opportunities for combining regular work with tax evading activities.

Even though the fraction that is willing to do unreported work has fallen over the years, it is still high enough to make tax evasion a serious problem if people get more opportunities to do unreported work. A period of high unemployment may be enough to reverse the reduction in black labour market participation.

References

Allingham, M. and Sandmo, A. (1972), 'Income Tax Evasion: A Theoretical Analysis', *Journal of Public Economics*, Vol. 1, pp. 323-38.

Andersen, P. (1977), 'Tax Evasion and Labor Supply', *Scandinavian Journal of Economics*, Vol. 79, pp. 375-83.

Baldry, J.G. (1979), 'Tax Evasion and Labor Supply', *Economics Letters*, Vol. 3, pp. 53-6.

Barth, E. and Ognedal, T. (2004), 'Unreported income from work across industries and firms', Manuscript.

Cagan, P. (1958), 'The Demand for Currency Relative to Total Money Supply', *Journal of Political Economy*, Vol. 66(3), pp. 302-28.

CENSIS (1976), 'L'Occupazione Occulta – Caratteristiche della Partecipazione al Lavoro in Italia', Fondazione CENSIS, Roma.

Contini, B. (1981), 'Labor Market Segmentation and the Development of the Parallel Economy – the Italian Experience', *Oxford Economic Papers*, Vol. 33(4), pp. 401-12.

Cowell, F.A. (1981), 'Taxation and Labour Supply with Risky Activities', *Economica*, Vol. 3, pp. 365-79.

Cowell, F.A. (1985), 'Tax Evasion with Labour Income', *Journal of Public Economics*, Vol. 26, pp. 19-35.

Feige, E.L (ed.) (1989), *The Underground Economies. Tax Evasion and Information Distortion*, Cambridge University Press.

Goldstein, H., Hansen, W.G., Ognedal, T. and Strøm, S. (2002), 'Svart Arbeid fra 1980 til 2001' (in Norwegian), Rapport nr 3, Ragnar Frisch Centre for Economic Research, Oslo.

Isachsen, A.J. and Strøm, S. (1980), 'The Hidden Economy: The Labor Market and Tax Evasion', *Scandinavian Journal of Economics*, Vol. 82, pp. 304-11.

Isachsen, A.J. and Strøm, S. (1985), 'The Size and Growth of the Hidden Economy in Norway', *Review of Income and Wealth*, Vol. 31(1), pp. 21-38.

Isachsen, A.J. and Strøm, S. (1989), 'The Hidden Economy in Norway with Special Emphasis on the Hidden Labour Market', in E.L. Feige (ed.), *The Underground Economies: Tax Evasion and Information Distortion*, Cambridge University Press.

Isachsen, A.J., Klovland, J. and Strøm, S. (1982), 'The Hidden Economy in Norway', in V. Tanzi (ed.), *The Underground Economy in the United States and Abroad*, Lexington, D.C. Heath, pp. 209-31.

Isachsen, A.J., Samuelson, S.O. and Strøm, S. (1985), 'The Behavior of Tax Evaders', in W. Gartner and A. Wenig (eds), *The Economics of the Shadow Economy*, Springer Verlag, Berlin.

Jørgensen, Ø., Ognedal, T. and Strøm, S. (2005), Labor Supply When Tax Evasion is an Option, Memorandum from Department of Economics, University of Oslo.

Klovland, J. (1984), 'Tax Evasion and the Demand for Currency in Norway and Sweden: Is There a Hidden Relationship?', *Scandinavian Journal of Economics*, Vol. 86, pp. 423-439.

Lacroix, G. and Fortin, B. (1992), 'Utility-Based Estimation of Labour Supply Functions in the Regular and Irregular Sectors', *Economic Journal*, Vol. 102, pp. 1407-22.

Lemieux, T., Fortin, B. and Frechette, P. (1994), 'The Effect of Taxes on Labor Supply in the Underground Economy', *American Economic Review*, Vol. 84, pp. 231-54.

Sandmo, A. (1981), 'Income Tax Evasion, Labor Supply and the Equity-Efficiency Trade Off', *Journal of Public Economics*, Vol. 16, pp. 265-88.

Schneider, F. (2001), 'Increasing Shadow Economies in OECD Countries: Some Further Explanations', Annual Choice Meeting, March, Charleston.

Schneider, F. and Enste, D.H. (2000), 'Shadow Economies: Sizes, Causes and Consequences', *Journal of Economic Literature*, Vol. 38, pp. 77-114.

Shima, I. (2004), The Shadow Economy in Norway: Demand for Currency Approach, Memorandum from Department of Economics, University of Oslo.

Sporastøyl, J.O. (1982), 'Svart arbeid – en utvalgsundersøkelse' (in Norwegain), Master Thesis, Department of Economics, Univeristy of Oslo.

Appendix 1: The Questions Asked in the Questionnaire

The respondents were asked to cross out answer-alternatives that vary across the questions. These alternatives are not shown here, but are available upon request.

Q.1. Gender
Q.2. Age
Q.3. No of children living in the house
Q.4. Marital status

Q.5. Does your spouse have income generating work, and if so, how many hours?

Q.6. Education in years

Q.7. Occupational status (wage worker, self-employed, unemployed, retired, etc)

Q.8. Hours of work last week in the regular economy

Q.9. Hours of work last 12 months in the regular economy

Q.10. Hourly pre-tax wage rate in main occupation

Q.11. Annual net income (after tax) in main occupation

Q.12. Annual pre-tax income in main occupation

Q.13 Occupation by industry

Q.14. Years of work at current workplace

Q.15. Number of employees at current workplace

Q.16. How easy is it for your superior to evaluate the quality of your work?

Q.17. Would other employees at your current workplace have difficulties in replacing you if you skipped a couple of days without notifying them in advance?

Q.18. Imagine a person with a similar education as yours, but with no working experience. How long will it take to train that person to do your job?

Q.19. Do you receive other income than wage income such as social security benefits/unemployment benefits/capital income?

Q.20. What is your tax rate for overtime work, the marginal tax rate in percent?

Q.21. How much tax do you in percent of your total annual gross income?

Q.22. What do you believe is the general attitude towards engaging in non-reported income activities?

Q.23. Which of the following statements do you agree with?
1) Breaking the law is never acceptable
2) Income differentials in the society should be as low as possible
3) Income differentials that are due to social background and intelligence should be eliminated
4) Income differentials that are due to individual choices such as choice of education level, occupation and working hours should be eliminated
5) Equal pay for equal work
6) Income should be distributed according to everyone's needs

Q.24. Can tax evasion be justified?

Q.25. Which of the following conditions, if true, would make tax evasion more acceptable?
1) Tax evasion is common
2) Hard working individuals are taxed too much
3) The tax system has loopholes that only the rich can benefit from
4) Tax evasion is accepted in your social environment
5) Tax revenue is unwisely used by the politicians
6) Tax revenues are redistributed to undeserved receivers

Q.26. Have you ever been engaged in non-reported income activities?

Q.27. If so, what kind of activities was it?

Q.28. If you had the opportunity to receive income without having to report it to the tax authorities, would you then accepted such income?

Q.29. If you don't report income to the tax authorities, how large do you think the chance (percent) is that you would be caught?

Q.30. If you not report income to the tax authorities, say NOK 20 000, and you are caught, you have to pay a penalty tax in addition to the regular tax on the non-reported income. How large do you think this penalty tax rate is (percent)?

Q.31. Have you evaded taxes by reporting false tax exemptions?

Q.32. During the last 12 months, have you received compensation for work that has not been reported or will not be reported to the tax authorities?

Q.33. Approximately how many hours of non-reported income activity have you worked during the last 12 months?

Q.34. What was your hourly pay for these activities?

Q.35. At the last tax declaration what was the total annual income, including capital income that you did not report?

Appendix 2: Tax Functions, 1980 and 2001

Table A.2.1 Tax function for wage earners in 1980. NOK 2001 values

Income brackets (gross income=Y)	Tax T
Y≤33300	0
33300≤Y≤37000	0.524Y-17316
37000≤Y≤41625	0.513Y-17279
41625≤Y≤59200	0.313Y-8720
59200≤Y≤64750	0.285Y-7096
64750≤Y≤114700	0.296Y-7807
114700≤Y≤132460	0.324Y-10948
132460≤Y≤165760	0.384Y-18895
165760≤Y≤224960	0.434Y-27184
224960≤Y≤261960	0.484Y-38431
261960≤Y≤298960	0.544Y-54149
298960≤Y≤335960	0.604Y-72087
335960≤Y≤398860	0.654Y-88885
398860≤Y≤509860	0.704Y-117375
509860≤Y≤674880	0.744Y-137769
674880≤Y≤694860	0.694Y-171513
694860≤Y≤1064860	0.734Y-199307
1064860≤Y	0.754Y-220531

Table A.2.2 Tax function for wage earners in 2001. NOK 2001 values

Income brackets (gross income =Y)	Tax T
Y≤47491	0
47491≤Y≤186956	0.2936Y-20468
186956≤Y≤320000	0.358Y-17358
320000≤Y≤830000	0.493Y-58958
830000≤Y	0.553Y-108758

Chapter 9

The Underground Economy in Canada[*]

Lindsay M. Tedds

Introduction

The Bougons are a French-Canadian family that has recently achieved notoriety not only in their home province of Quebec but also across Canada. The father, Paul Bougon, bribed a Canada Post letter carrier to deliver fraudulent welfare cheques to the Bougon house. His wife, Rita, is a self-employed phone sex operator. Their eldest son, Paul Jr., engages in car theft, among other illegal activities, and their daughter, Dolorès, is an exotic dancer/prostitute. The family also adopted a Chinese child, Mao, to help the family with computer scams. Not a penny of the income earned through any of these activities is reported to the appropriate tax collecting agency.

The family, however, has not attained their infamy as a result of a tax audit. Rather, the Bougon are a fictional family that is the subject of a sitcom (*Les Bougons*) that airs weekly on Radio-Canada, the French-language service of the Canadian Broadcasting Corporation (CBC), a public broadcaster. In an article entitled 'Boozing scam artists steal hearts of viewers', published in the *Globe and Mail*, 16 February 2004, Ingrid Peritz reported that the show has quickly become popular, 34 percent of the French-speaking population in Canada tune in, and viewers seem to admire the enterprising Bougon family, describing them as contemporary Robin Hoods.

The Bougon family is participating in what is commonly called the underground economy. With the apparent wide-scale acceptance of the lifestyle of the Bougon family, it appears timely to reexamine the phenomenon of the underground economy in Canada and provide an update to the empirical evaluation conducted by Giles and Tedds (2002). In particular, this study extends Giles and Tedds' study by: lengthening the period under examination to 2001; including a number of new variables that the theoretical literature purport to have a sizeable impact on the underground economy; and making important modifications to the empirical techniques. The results reported in this paper are more robust than those reported in Giles and Tedds (2002) and responds to many of the comments contained in the discussion of Hill (2002) and Smith (2002).

Overall, the results indicate that, in general, the underground economy in Canada grew steadily relative to measured GDP over the period 1976 to 2001. The value of the broadly defined underground economy grew from about 7.5 percent of GDP in 1976 to about 15.3 percent in 2001. In real (1997) dollar terms, it increased from about \$38 billion to \$159 billion *per annum*. The paper begins with a discussion of the definition of the underground economy, followed by a description of the six key methodologies that have been used to obtain estimates of the underground economy. A discussion of the causes and previous estimates of the Canadian underground economy is then provided. This is followed by a brief description of the modeling methodology employed in this study and a discussion of the results. The paper ends with some concluding remarks.

Defining the Underground Economy

Which activities are included in the definition of the underground economy affects the interpretation of any estimate of the extent of this phenomenon. For example, a very narrow definition would include only legal, market transactions that are not included in measured GDP. A somewhat broader definition would include both legal and illegal market transactions that are not included in measured GDP. One can also approach the above definitions by considering activity that is not detected by the tax authorities, rather than that omitted from GDP. Finally a very broad definition of the underground economy would be one that included all transactions, legal and illegal, market and non-market that are either intentionally excluded from GDP or omitted from the tax base. These definitions are summarized in Table 1. The one employed in this study is the fourth.

Table 1   Definitions of the underground economy[a]

1.   Legal market based transactions missing from measured GDP.
2.   Legal market based transactions not reported to the revenue-gathering agency.
3.   Legal and illegal market based transactions missing from measured GDP.
4.   Legal and illegal market based transactions not reported to the revenue-gathering agency.[b]
5.   Legal and illegal market and non-market based transactions that escape detection or are intentionally excluded from measured GDP.

Source: Taken from Giles and Tedds (2002, p. 89)

Notes: (a) Following from the discussion above, the relationship between the resulting estimates from these definitions can be portrayed as follows: $1 < 2 < 3 < 4 < 5$; (b) Definition employed in this study.

Whichever definition is used, it has become common practice to report the size of the underground economy as a percentage of GDP. This practice is simply a way of facilitating international and intertemporal comparisons by avoiding units of currency. The authors of these studies are not suggesting that reported GDP is mis-measured by this percentage amount. This is largely for two reasons: GDP is a value-added measure rather than a measure of total economic activity, whereas many measures of the hidden economy report total hidden activity; and, depending on the definition employed, the measure of the underground economy usually includes both legal and illegal activities, the latter of which are often excluded in the definition of GDP.

Measuring the Underground Economy

There are essentially six key methodologies that have been used to obtain estimates of the underground economy and they will be summarized briefly here. A more detailed account can be found in Giles and Tedds (2002).

The first three approaches base their measure on the amount of currency in circulation in the economy. Gutmann's (1977) Method or the *Currency Ratio Method* dates back to Cagan (1958) and studies the ratio of currency to demand deposits. It postulates that increases in the ratio over some base year are the result of the need to hold cash for underground transactions. *Tanzi's (1980) Method* relaxes the assumption of a constant ratio of cash to the money supply by making this ratio a function of the rate of interest, per capita income, various tax variables, and the share of wages in national income. Feige's (1979) *Transaction Method* examines the relationship between the total value of transactions (measured by adding currency transactions to cheque-based transactions, except purely financial ones) and measured GDP.

The fourth approach, the *National Accounts/Judgmental Method*, involves no formal 'modeling' of the underground economy, but instead rests on a detailed breakdown of either the expenditure or income side of the national accounts into its component parts, and the application of subjective judgments as to the maximum likely levels of unrecorded incomes or expenditures.

Fifth is the *Latent variable or MIMIC model*, which involves the use of is a structural econometric model. The application treats the size of the underground economy as an unobservable 'latent' variable that is linked on the one hand to a collection of (observable) indicators which 'reflect' changes in the size of the underground economy and on the other hand to a set of (observed) causal variables which are believed to be important driving forces behind underground economic activity. It is this method of estimating the size of the underground economy that is employed in this paper.

These macroeconomic measures, however, have been criticized for not being based on consumer theory and for employing flawed econometric techniques (Thomas, 1999). A technique developed by Dilnot and Morris (1981) and modified by Pissarides and Weber (1989) and Lyssiotou et al. (2004) responds to these criticisms. This *Expenditure-based method* uses estimates of the relationship between food consumption and income (i.e., an Engel curve) to measure the size of the underground economy.[1]

The Canadian Underground Economy: Determinants and Previous Estimates

There is considerable agreement internationally, on both theoretical and empirical grounds, about the factors that determine the relative size of the underground economy. These factors include the tax burden, regulation, enforcement, labour force characteristics, confidence in government, and morality. The relationship of these factors to the Canadian underground economy will be briefly discussed here.

Tax Burden

Perhaps the single most commonly cited 'driving force' of the underground economy is the tax burden. Since the 1970s Canada has been subject to: a rise in personal income taxes net of transfers; a rise in these taxes as a share of personal income; an increase in total tax revenue as a share of GDP; and, the replacement of the narrowly-based federal manufacturing sales tax in 1991 with the more broadly-based Goods and Services Tax (GST). This trend has only recently been halted, with reductions in the federal marginal personal income tax rate, and decreased tax rates in many of the provinces, with the majority of the tax changes taking place in the 2000 and 2001 tax year.

The implementation of the GST in 1991 has probably received the most 'credit' for increasing the size and growth of the Canadian underground economy in recent times. It is often argued that the switch from the more narrowly based federal manufacturers' sales tax to this broadly based consumption tax may have increased the incentives and opportunities for tax evasion (Spiro, 1993; Hill and Kabir, 1996; and Giles and Tedds, 2002). This is interesting because, when the GST was first proposed (and throughout its implementation), the federal government argued that the GST would reduce the scope for tax evasion. This was based, in part, on evidence at that time from New Zealand. In fact, until the advent of the Canada Customs and Revenue Agency's 'Underground Economy Initiative' in November 1993, the Canadian government has dismissed the notion that the underground economy was of any significance, in contrast with the position of the IRS in the United States.

The 'stacking' of taxes in Canada, is also a likely driver of underground activity. In Canada, both the federal and the provincial governments have the ability to utilize methods of direct and indirect taxation to raise revenue. As a rule, Canadians are taxed on the same base – whether it is income or consumption of goods and services – by both levels of government. Provincial personal taxes, for the most part, are based on a set percentage of federal personal tax collected.[2] In 1998, the maximum values for these ranged from a low of 42.75 percent in Ontario to a high of almost 70 percent in Newfoundland. As a result, any increase in the federal marginal tax rate automatically increased the amount of provincial tax paid, even if the provincial tax rate remained unchanged. The provinces, with the sole exception of Alberta, also charge provincial sales taxes (PST).[3] The PST's are applied primarily on retail goods, are paid solely by the consumer, and, now with the existence of the GST, are paid in addition to the latter tax. While the PST rates vary from province to province, the average sales tax rate paid (including GST and PST) by consumers is 15 percent.

Excise taxes are also a popular revenue generating tax for both levels of government. Goods that are susceptible to high levels of excise taxation at the federal and/or provincial level (other than those mentioned above) are alcohol, tobacco, and gasoline. For example, the Federal Excise Tax on gasoline adds 15 cents to the price of a litre of gasoline and the average provincial tax is 14.9 cents a litre. The GST is also collected, adding approximately another 3-4 cents a litre (depending upon the actual pump price), and some provinces also collect municipal gas surtaxes. Combined, these taxes amount to about half of what Canadians pay for a litre of regular gas. While these taxes have received little attention in the past, in the face of rising gas prices and government surpluses, Canadians are now questioning their existence.

It is sometimes argued that due to this stacking effect Canadians may suffer from 'tax fatigue'. That is, it is the number of different taxes that Canadians pay that drives them into the underground economy, and not necessarily a particular tax. According to this argument, simply lowering one tax, such as the federal marginal tax rates, would likely do little to curb underground activity, whereas eliminating a tax, such as the GST or PST, would likely have a substantial impact on curbing underground activity.

Canadians are, for the most part, extremely proud of their social safety net, but it too provides incentive to hide income and to work 'off the books'. Small businesses in Canada often find it difficult to pay their portion of payroll taxes, notably workers' compensation, employment insurance and pension premiums in the Canadian context. Employees can also find these so-called payroll taxes a burden. In addition, people receiving welfare or disability payments find that their payments are reduced if they earn any other income and an additional tax is imposed on those receiving Employment Insurance benefits if their total annual income exceeds about $35,000. Put these together and you have a segment of employers and employees who prefer to hire and work off the books to avoid these costs. In fact, Lemieux et al. (1994) present evidence that taxes and social welfare payments do in fact distort labour-market activities away from the regular sector, and into the underground sector.

Regulation

The degree of regulation is often cited as a factor that influences people to engage in underground activity as regulations reduce an individual's freedom of choice. Canada underwent significant deregulation with the implementation of the Regulatory Reform Strategy in 1986, one of the first comprehensive regulatory policies developed in the OECD (OECD, 2002). Since 1986, Canada has shown a declining trend in the growth rate of new legislation and regulation.

Enforcement

Greater effort put into the repression of crime and tax evasion by governments results in a greater probability of offenders being caught, thus lowering the rewards of participating in underground activity. The first important enforcement action taken by the Government of Canada was the implementation of the 'Underground Economy Initiative' (UEI) by Canada Customs and Revenue Agency (CCRA) in November 1993.[4] The UEI was introduced in response to a widespread perception that the underground economy in Canada was growing rapidly. The initiative, which was directed at the narrowly-defined underground economy, brought significant additional resources to the CCRA's enforcement and collection programs, a redirection of the CCRA's field-audit resources into specific areas in which the probability of underground activity is high, and it led the CCRA to work more closely with tax accountants and with community and industry groups.

A key program under the UEI is the Voluntary Disclosure program (VDP) which allows people to come forward and correct inaccurate or incomplete information or disclose material they did not report during previous dealing with CCRA, without penalty or prosecution. The program appears to be popular, with over 2,000 individuals using the VDP in 2000, up from 557 in 1993-94 (CCRA, 2000).

The UEI, however, may not be as successful in reducing underground activity as first thought. The initiative was scrutinized by the Auditor General of Canada (Canada, 1999) in 1999. The auditor general found that the reported gains in compliance were by no means all attributable to the UEI. According to CCRA, its activities to combat the underground economy had resulted in $2.5 billion in additional tax revenue over a five-year period. However, according to the auditor general, this amount included the results of regular ongoing enforcement programs. The actual amount of additional tax revenue that could be attributed to the UEI's audit activities over the period was actually less than $500 million.

Labour Force Characteristics

Many studies have found that the average worker in the underground economy also holds a regular job in the official economy (Dallago, 1990 and Mogensen, 1995). Further, Lemieux et al. (1994), using micro data from a survey conducted in Quebec City, found that the substitution between labour market activities in the observed and underground sector was quite high and that there was high mobility between the sectors. This relationship seems to imply that there will be a strong positive causal relationship between labour force participation rates and the underground economy. Participation in the Canadian labour force steadily increased until 1990, when the Canadian economy entered into a recession from which it was slow to recover. Participation rates did not begin to improve until 1996.

The self-employed generally have greater opportunity to evade taxes than do regular employees, if they so choose. In Canada, the self-employment rate has increased dramatically over the last 25 years: from about 12 percent in 1976 to almost 18 percent in 1998, although it has decreased in recent years to just over 15 percent in 2001. As such, this feature of the Canadian workforce raises some interesting questions about tax evasion in this country in recent years. For example, Pissarides and Weber (1989), Apel (1994), and Mirus and Smith (1997) note that in the U.S., U.K., Sweden, and Canada respectively, only 60 percent to 80 percent of income in the self-employment sector is actually reported to the tax authorities.[5]

Confidence and Morality

Lack of confidence in the performance of government may also be a factor in the decision to participate in the underground economy. Some tax payers may have concerns about the way in which tax dollars are being spent or are perceived as being spent. Closely related to this issue is morality. Individuals may choose their level of compliance with laws and regulations to match their perception of the extent to which others comply. Recent survey evidence shows that 'some 86 percent of Canadians believe that governments squander a lot of the money they collect in taxes. Less than one quarter of Canadians could be categorized as "model citizens". Half of our respondents were categorized as "upset and envious" or "tax anarchists".' (Flexman, 1997, p. 72).

Previous Canadian Estimates

Table 3 summarizes the estimates for Canada, obtained by various researchers using one of the six methods described in the previous section. The estimates are reported in terms of a percentage of nominal Canadian GDP, unless otherwise noted. The studies that used the same definition of the underground economy that is employed in this study are noted in bold type and they estimate the value of the underground economy to be approximately 11 percent of GDP in 1993 and about 15 percent of GDP in 1995.[6]

MIMIC Model Approach

The MIMIC model is a structural econometric model that treats the size of the underground economy as an unobservable 'latent' variable.[7] The MIMIC model was first applied to the problem of measuring the underground economy by Frey and Weck-Hannemann (1984). The application treats the size of the underground economy as an unobservable 'latent' variable that is linked on the one hand to a collection of (observable) indicators which 'reflect' changes in the size of the underground economy; and on the other hand to a set of (observed) causal variables which are believed to be important driving forces behind underground economic activity. Given data for the causes and the indicators, one estimates the model by applying fairly standard econometric procedures. The MIMIC model methodology has become generally accepted as the most comprehensive approach to this problem, with a small but growing number applications. In fact, it has been described as a 'meaningful and intellectually fascinating' approach (Helberger and Knepel, 1988). Details of the model will not be provided here and readers are urged to consult Giles and Tedds (2002) for a comprehensive discussion of the model and its estimation, and a technical appendix detailing the estimation of the particular model described in this paper is available from the author upon request.

One of the benefits of working with the MIMIC model is that it produces a time-series of the underground economy. Unfortunately, it can only generate an index for a time-series: it can tell us about changes in the ratio from year to year, but not about the actual values of the ratio in individual years. To convert the index series into a time series of values, a reliable estimate of the underground economy ratio for the sample period under consideration is required. Giles and Tedds (2002) formulated a non-linear currency demand model for Canada based on that adopted by Giles (1999) for New Zealand and by Bhattacharyya (1990) for the U.K., in each case also developed in the context of trying to measure the size of the underground economy. Essentially, the method utilizes a conventional demand for cash model that is extended to allow for two sectors – one measured and one underground. This model, however, has subsequently been found to be extremely unstable.[8] An alternative way to incorporate the underground economy into a demand for money equation is to treat underground output as an unobserved component and then estimate the resulting state space model by Maximum Likelihood using the Kalman (1960) filter.[9] This was the approach taken in this paper and the author found that the results using this method were quite robust.[10] The index series is then calibrated using the mean value of the underground economy obtained using the Kalman filter. The calibration process followed preserves the proportional relationships found in the original index series.[11]

Table 2   Empirical measures of the Canadian underground economy

Study	Definition (see Table 1)	Year	UE (% of GDP)* *Unless otherwise noted
GUTTMAN			
Mirus and Smith (1981)	3	1976	15.7%
Haas (1978)	3	1977	11.1% (of GNP)
Barthelemy (1988)	3	1978	13%
Mirus (1984)	3	1980	11%
Mirus et al. (1994)	3	1980	13.5%
Mirus et al. (1994)	3	1985	25.9%
Karoleff et al. (1993)	3	1990	21.6%
Mirus et al. (1994)	3	1990	27.6%
Schnieder and Enste (2000)		1996, 1997	14.9%
Schnieder (2000)		1997, 1998	15%-16.2%
TANZI			
Barthelemy (1988)	3	1976	2.5%-12.4%
Mirus and Smith (1981)	3	1976	4.9%-7.5%
Éthier (1982)	**4**	**1980**	**8.8% (tax rev.)**
Ethier (1985)	3	1981	5.7% (of GNP)
Ng and Karolyi (1984)	3	1982	12%-16%
Mirus et al. (1994)	3	1990	5.1%
Pouftis (1993)	3	1990	7.4%-13%

Hill and Kabir (2000)	4	Increase attributable to GST	0.02%-0.3%
Spiro (1993)	**4**	**1992**	**0.8% growth**
Spiro (1994)	**4**	**1993**	**8%-11%**
Hill and Kabir (1996)	3	Growth from 1964-1995	3%-11%
TRANSACTION METHOD			
Mirus and Smith (1981)	3	1976	27.5%
Mirus (1984)	3	1976	10%
Barthelemy (1988)	3	1979	22%
Mirus (1984)	3	1980	13.5%
Mirus and Smith (1989)	3	1982	10.96%-12.36%
Karoleff et al. (1993)	3	1984	19.3%
Mirus et al. (1994)	3	1984	23.9%
NATIONAL ACCOUNTS/JUDGEMENT/SURVEY			
Berger (1986)	1	1981	2.8%-3.3%
Gervais (1994) and	1	1992	2.7%
Philip Smith (1997)	3	1992	3.7%
	4	1992	5.2%
	5	1992	47.1%
Paquet (1989)	5	1989	33%-100%
Drummond et al. (1993)	3	1993	4.5%
Lemieux, Fortin and Frechette (1994)	**4**	**1986**	**1.4% (Quebec)**
LATENT VARIABLE			
Frey and Weck Hannemann (1984)	**4**	**1978**	**8.7%**
Schneider (1997)	**4**	**1994**	**15%**
Tedds (1998)	**4**	**1976-1995**	**4.2%-14.7%**
Giles and Tedds (2002)	**4**	**1976-1995**	**3.5%-15.7%**
EXPENDITURE BASED			
Mirus and Smith (1997)	2	1990	1% (Self-Employed)
Schuetze (2002)	2	1969	20% (Degree of
		1974	12% income
		1984	15% concealing by
		1986	17% Self-Employed)
		1990	18%
		1992	21.5%

Source: Table is modified from Giles and Tedds (2002, pp. 90-91)

Notes: Bold type indicates studies that used the definition of the underground economy that is employed in this study.

In order to ensure that the various time-series are stationary, and to avoid the consequences of estimating spurious regressions, the data are tested for unit roots.[12] The variables in the demand for money equation were found to be a mixture of $I(1)$ and $I(2)$ series. The series were then tested for cointegration using Haldrup's (1994) procedure and the results suggest that there is cointegration between the series. As a result, the demand for money equation is estimated using the levels of series. The variables for the MIMIC model were found to be a mixture of $I(0)$, $I(1)$ and $I(2)$ variables. Unfortunately there is no established literature to act as a guide for testing for cointegration in the context of the MIMIC model. Instead, the MIMIC model is estimated using the differenced data.

Results

The Canadian underground economy is estimated for the sample period 1976-2001. A number of different models based on different combinations of causal and indicator variables were estimated and it was found that the model was robust to alternative specifications and normalizing choices.[13] The models were also subjected to various econometric tests to determine the statistical 'quality' of the estimates and to assist in the choice of a final, 'preferred' model.[14]

The preferred model incorporates three indicator variables and eleven key causal variables.[15] The indicator variables are:

1.   Growth rate of gross domestic product (GDP);
2.   Real currency per capita (RCURR); and
3.   Ratio of expenditures on goods and services to disposable income (CONSUMP).

It is argued that a change in the size of the underground economy may be mirrored in the growth rate of measured real GDP, although the directional impact that this variable has on the underground economy is debatable and may vary from country to country. Those that find a positive relationship between GDP and the underground economy using the MIMIC method include Tedds (1998), Giles (1999), Giles and Tedds (2002), and Schneider and Bajada (2003).[16] It is expected that there exists a positive relationship between GDP and the underground economy in Canada.

Another key indicator is some type of monetary aggregate, as suggested by the monetary approaches to measuring the underground economy, briefly discussed above. Most of the monetary methods advocate a ratio approach to examining this issue, which would measure changes in currency relative to a broader monetary aggregate such as M1 or M3. In Canada, however, these monetary aggregates have been distorted seriously over the sample period due to interest rate effects and banking innovations, and this makes the inclusion of a ratio of currency to a broader monetary aggregate in our model undesirable here. Instead, real currency per capita is used as an indicator variable.

The third indicator variable is the ratio of personal expenditures on goods and services to personal measured disposable income. It is designed to measure changes in spending behaviour, based on the assumption that income earned through underground activities will be used to bolster consumption patterns rather than being used for savings (which leaves a paper trail for the authorities).

The causal variables,[17] the relationship to the underground economy were discussed above, are:

1.   Labour force participation rate (LFPR);
2.   Average direct tax rate (ADTR);[18]
3.   Average indirect tax rate (AITR);[19]
4.   Average marginal tax rate (AMTR);[20]
5.   Average payroll tax rate (APTR);[21]
6.   Dummy variable for the Voluntary Disclosure program (VDP) that equals the marginal tax rate (AMTR) for 1994 and onwards;
7.   Crime rate (CRIME);
8.   Dummy variable for the implementation of the GST (GST) that equals 1 in 1991 and onwards;
9.   Dummy variable for the implementation of the Underground Economy Initiative (UEI) that equals 1 in 1994 and onwards;
10.   Logarithm of real self-employment income; and
11.   Flow of federal regulatory transactions by the Governor in Council and individual Ministers[22] (REGS).

Figure 1 displays the results of the estimation of the MIMIC model. The indicator variables enter positively and significantly, implying that the Canadian underground economy has a positive relationship with currency holdings, personal consumption, and the growth rate of GDP.

Most of the causal variables are statistically significant and of the appropriate sign. Marginal tax rates are an important contributor to the underground economy whereas the average direct and average payroll tax rates, while positive, are not statistically significant. Indirect tax rates have a negative relationship with the underground economy, however, the implementation of the GST caused an increase in the Canadian underground economy. Generally, the Underground Economy Initiative (UEI) did not help combat underground activity, however, the specific initiative, the Voluntary Disclosure program, has had the anticipated negative effect. The fact that the MIMIC model produces an estimate that indicates that the UEI had a positive and significant impact on the underground economy in Canada is, on the surface, counter intuitive. While enforcement was increased, many of the policies enacted under the UEI, however, increased the regulatory burden on businesses and individuals. This increased burden increased, rather than decreased, the incentive to participate in the underground economy. Finally, as anticipated, regulations, the crime rate (acting as a proxy for morality), the amount of self-employment income earned and labour force participation are all positive and significant. The author believes that this is the most richly specified model of the underground economy using the MIMIC model.

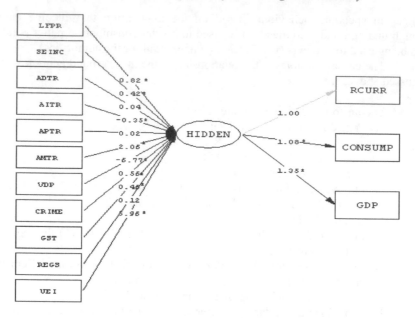

Figure 1 MIMIC model of the Canadian underground economy

Note: * Indicates coefficient is statistically significant.

        The index series is converted into a time-series of values using the results from the demand for money equation. A long-run value of the Canadian underground economy of 11.35 percent was obtained, with an associated 95 percent confidence interval of [9.98 percent, 12.76 percent]. Figure 2 presents the resulting time-series values for the size of the Canadian underground economy (expressed as a percentage of GDP), given the preferred specification of the model shown in Figure 1. The results indicate that, in general, the underground economy in Canada grew steadily relative to measured GDP over the period 1976 to 2001. The value of the broadly defined underground economy grew from about 7.5 percent of GDP in 1976 to about 15.3 percent in 2001. In real (1997) dollar terms, it increased from about $38 billion to $159 billion. Figure 2 also shows the uncertainty that these results are subject to, via a 95 percent confidence interval.[23]

        The time-series depicted in Figure 2 shows that the growth of the Canadian underground economy contracted in 1977, 1991 and 1995 and experienced no change in 1982, all periods of slow or negative GDP growth. The introduction of the GST in 1991 apparently halted the contraction of the underground economy. The Canadian underground economy also contracted in 1987, likely a temporary reaction to regulatory reform. Figure 2 shows that the underground economy experienced a very high growth rate during the mid- to late-1980s, despite the fact that there were a number of tax reforms during the 1970s and 1980s. These reforms included base broadening and lower rates, the intent of which was to address issues of fairness, complexity and distortions.[24] A complex and inequitable tax system, however, allows for more legal tax avoidance by providing various tax exemptions and reductions (Schneider and Neck, 1993). Broadening the income tax base and removing tax exemptions, therefore, caused an increase in the size of the Canadian underground economy.

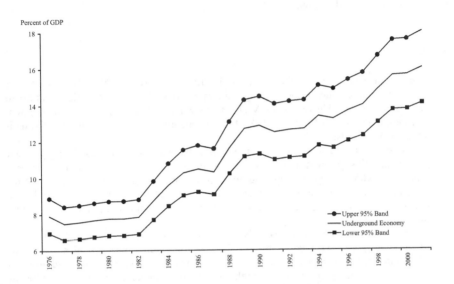

Figure 2   The Canadian underground economy and approximate 95 percent confidence internal

Conclusion

According to the estimates of this study, the underground economy in Canada is sizable and continues to grow, despite the increased enforcement efforts of CCRA. The results show that, not surprisingly, the underground economy responds positively to marginal tax rates, the GST, the amount of self-employment income, labour force participation, the overall crime rate and regulatory reform. Additionally, while CCRA's enforcement activities under the UEI may have been unsuccessful, the Voluntary Disclosure program appears to play an important role in encouraging less underground activity. The findings indicate that the underground economy in Canada grew from about 7.5 percent of GDP in 1976 to about 15.3 percent in 2001. These figures are consistent with previous studies employing the same definition as this study.

The results are different from those reported by Giles and Tedds (2002), who report that the underground economy grew from about 3.5 percent of GDP in 1976 to about 15.7 percent of GDP in 1995. There are three main reasons why the results differ. First, the MIMIC model presented here is more richly specified than that of Giles and Tedds (2002) and includes more of the variables that the theoretical literature purports to cause the underground economy. Second, the calibration process followed in this study preserves the proportional relationships found in the original index series. Third, this study estimated a demand for money equation using the Kalman filter, which resulted in a larger long-run value of the Canadian underground economy (11.35 percent compared to the 9.46 percent obtained by Giles and Tedds, 2002).

Notes

*   The author would like to thank Roderick Hill, University of New Brunswick, for providing data on the various average tax rate series. The author is also grateful to David E.A. Giles, University of Victoria, David Perry, Canadian Tax Foundation, Toronto, Ontario, and Mike Veall, McMaster University, Hamilton, Ontario, for their valuable comments.

1.   To do so, it is assumed that wage and salary earners always accurately report their income and this group is used as a baseline measure, which is compared to the self-employed, who have greater opportunities to hide income from tax authorities. If the self-employed are concealing income, then it is expected that their household food consumption will be high relative to wage/salary earners with similar reported incomes and characteristics.

2.   The provinces, however, have recently moved towards a tax-on-income system. Under this system, provincial income tax is calculated on taxable income and not on basic federal tax. Ontario moved to this system starting with the 2000 tax year and all other provinces (excluding Quebec) and the three territories, implemented this system for the 2001 tax year. The province of Quebec has had an independent tax system since the change over from the Income War Tax Act.

3.   In 1997, the provinces of New Brunswick, Nova Scotia, and Newfoundland signed comprehensive integrated tax co-ordination agreements (CITCAs) with the federal government to harmonize their provincial sales taxes with the goods and services tax (GST), creating the harmonized sales tax (HST). Additionally, Quebec introduced a modified form of VAT which it collected itself, along with the GST.

4.   An additional enforcement program is the 'Anti-Smuggling Initiative' (ASI) which is a joint Canada Customs and Revenue Agency/RCMP program introduced in 1994 to crack-down on tobacco smuggling.

5.   Schuetze (1999), in a comprehensive study on self-employment in Canada, found that increases in average income tax rates have a large and positive effect on the self-employment rate which he indicates '... suggests that under-reporting of self-employment income may be a key motivating factor for becoming self employed'. (Schuetze, 1999, p. 3) This evidence allows some researchers to conclude that self-employment income should be considered as an indicator variable. There are many other factors, however, that have contributed to the increase in self-employment and self-employment income in Canada. For example, Canada has many special programs in place to assist self-employment and small businesses, financial institutions have created numerous financing options to support self-employment and small businesses, and the increasing use of contracting-out by governments and business. This leads the author to conclude that self-employment is a causal variable of the underground economy.

6. The exception is the estimate obtained by both Gervais (1994) and Smith (1997) of 5.2 percent of GDP for 1992. There are three key reasons for the difference: first, they measure the underground economy from a value-added perspective; second, they exclude such items as capital gains and inheritances from underground economy; and third, they assumed illegal activity amounted to no more than 1 percent of measured GDP. With respect to this latter point, Giles and Tedds (2002, p. 89-92) conduct some 'back of the envelope' calculations of the size of illegal activity in Canada and obtain a minimum estimate of 5 percent of GDP for the same year.

7. The technique of modeling with an observable variable is not confined to the study of the underground economy or to economics itself. The archetypal example of an unobservable variable is intelligence. The estimation of supply and demand equations and the well known permanent-income hypothesis are probably two of the earliest examples in the field of economics of models based on unobservable variables.

8. In particular, the highly nonlinear model that was used in the previous work proved to be sensitive to small data changes.

9. There are two equations in a state space model. The first equation is called the 'measurement equation' or 'signal equation', and it describes the stochastic relationship between the dependent variable and a vector of 'state variables'. The second equation is called the 'state equation' or 'transition equation' and contains the unobservable components. In the demand for money equation (1), the logarithm of the money stock (m_t) is the dependent variable in the measurement equation, which, in the preferred version of the model, has been modeled as a function of last periods values of the logarithms of interest rate (r_{t-1}), money (m_{t-1}), prices (p_{t-1}), and the current period's unobserved value of the logarithm of underground output (u_t). The single state variable is the logarithm of underground output (u_t), which is modeled as a function of last period's value of the logarithm of underground output (u_{t-1}), the logarithm of output from two previous period ago (y_{t-2}), the compounding annual rate of inflation, lagged one period $(p_{t-1} - p_{t-2})$, and a random shock (η_t).

$$m_t = \alpha_{1t} y_t + \alpha_{2t} r_{t-1} + \alpha_{3t} p_{t-1} + \alpha_{4t} m_{t-1} + u_t \tag{1}$$

$$u_t = c_1 u_{t-1} + c_2 y_{t-2} + c_3 (p_{t-1} - p_{t-2}) + \eta_t \tag{2}$$

The coefficients in equation (1) are estimated recursively.

10. Notably, the estimates were insensitive to small changes to the sample of data.

11. Tedds (1998) and Giles and Tedds (2002) calibrated their resulting index series from the MIMIC model by finding the mean year of the sample, dividing each observation in the index series by the value the index series took in that mean year, and then multiplying those values by the average value of the underground economy obtained using the currency demand model. If, however, one wants to preserve the content of the original index, then the values of the time series must retain the same proportional relationships present in the index values. Suppose that I_t denotes the index for the ratio of the underground economy to the measured economy in period t,

$$I_t = a_t I_1$$

Then to preserve the proportional relationships in I_t, one requires

$$\text{Ratio}_t = a_t \text{Ratio}_1$$

Making use of the estimated average ratio (Ratio*=11.35 percent) from the money demand equation, one has the additional relationship

$$\text{Ratio*} = \frac{1}{T}\sum_{t=1}^{T}\text{Ratio}_t = \frac{1}{T}\left(\text{Ratio}_1 + \sum_{t=2}^{T}a_t\text{Ratio}_1\right) = \frac{\text{Ratio}_1}{T}\left(1 + \sum_{t=2}^{T}a_t\right)$$

These relationships yield T equations to be solved for the T unknown ratio values.

12. This is a commonly ignored step in the study of the underground economy, not only in the application of the MIMIC model. It has, in fact, been applied previously only by Giles (1999), Tedds (1998), Giles and Tedds (2002) and Dell'Anno (2003) in this context. To be conservative, both the Augmented Dickey-Fuller test (Said and Dickey, 1984) for non-stationarity, and the KPSS test (Kwiatkowski, Phillips, Schmidt and Shin, 1992) for stationarity are used. Several of the series used in modeling appear to exhibit structural breaks. As the ADF and KPSS tests, as well as tests for cointegration, are adversely sensitive to the presence of breaks in the data, special attention was paid to this issue. Perron's (1989) modified ADF test and well as Kurozumi's (2002) modified KPSS test were applied to allow for exogenous structural breaks. All of these tests were employed by testing downwards (Dickey and Pantula, 1987), assuming that the highest possible order of integration was I(3). Mackinnon's (1991) critical values were used in the ADF tests, Perron's (1989) critical values were used in the modified ADF test, Kwiatkowski, Phillips, Schmidt and Shinn's (1992) asymptotic critical values were employed when applying the KPSS tests, and Kurozumi's (2002) critical values were used for the modified KPSS test. In the case of conflicting conclusions, the results of the KPSS test were chosen over the results of the ADF test because of the test's standard set up of the null hypothesis, and the fact that the ADF test has notoriously low power.

13. As with all structural models, normalization must be imposed in order for it to be estimated. The choice among the endogenous variables is arbitrary as the normalization does not identify the dependent variable in any formal or causal sense. The relative impacts of the underground economy on the other 'indicator' variables are then measured relative to this pre-assigned value.

14. Rather than focus just on statistical significance of the resulting parameter estimates, attention has also been paid to various goodness-of-fit measures, charts of the 'Q-plots' of the standardized 'residuals' (in LISREL terminology, a 'residual' is the difference between an observed and fitted covariance), and tests for normality of the conventional residuals.

15. The series used were obtained from Statistics Canada's CANSIM database, the *National Economic and Financial Accounts*, Canada Customs and Revenue Agency's *Taxation Statistics/Statistics on Individuals*, the Canadian Tax Foundation's *The National Finances/Finances of the Nation*, and the *Canada Gazette, Part II*. A data summary is available from the author upon request.

16. Other authors argue that '[a]n increase in the underground economy means that inputs move out of the official economy ...' (Frey and Weck-Hannemann, 1984, p. 38) This would, therefore, have a depressing effect on the officially measured growth rate of the economy. Frey and Weck-Hannemann (1984), Helberger and Knepel (1988), Loyaza (1996), Kaufmann and Kaliberda (1996), Schneider and Enste (2000), and Dell'Anno (2003) all find a negative relationship between GDP and the underground economy using the MIMIC model, though these studies primarily focus on developing/transition economies (with the exception of Frey and Weck-Hannemann (1984) and Helberger and Knepel (1988) who examine 17 OECD countries).

17. A dummy variable for the tax changes which began in 1998, which equaled the marginal tax rate for 1998 and onwards, was also considered as a causal variable. In the models in which it appeared, the coefficient was positive but insignificant. This latter results could be due to the limited amount of data available after the tax changes (only four years) or because there is a lag effect in behavioral changes. Alternatively, once a person becomes active in the underground, there is little incentive to transfer back to the observed economy. As a result, tax reform would simply act to stabilize the underground economy, rather than reduce its size.

18. A broad average tax rate was found by dividing annual Personal Direct Tax Revenue by Personal Income.

19. An average indirect tax rate was calculated using general provincial sales tax revenue. Annual GST revenues are included for the years 1991-2001.

20. This measure combines federal and provincial marginal personal income tax rates. Average assessed income was determined by dividing total assessed income by the number of tax returns. The average taxable income of taxpayers with this average assessed income was calculated from detailed data by income group. For each income bracket, taxable income in that income bracket was divided by the number of tax returns. The combined federal and provincial marginal tax rates applicable to a single tax payer with that level of taxable income was then determined from the various annual editions of *The National Finances* (Toronto: Canadian Tax Foundation, various years). Where provincial tax rates differed, the Ontario provincial tax rate was used.

21. An average payroll tax rate was calculated using total contributions to social insurance plans (both federal and provincial) divided by the total payroll tax base.

22. Includes new federal regulations as well as items that amended, repealed or revised an existing regulation. Data regarding provincial regulations over the sample period were not included because similarly defined data was not available for every province. In addition, it was not clear how to weight the provincial observations.

23. The reported confidence interval only accounts for the randomness associated with the 'benchmark' estimate of 11.35 percent. There is, however, also the randomness associated with estimated coefficients of the 'causal' variables in the MIMIC model, and these in turn translate into randomness for the year-by-year predictions of the underground economy ratio, conditional on the average benchmark figure. It is, however, unclear as to how to combine these two sources of randomness, and hence only the randomness associated with the benchmark value is reported.

24. The tax reforms also had the effect of raising the effective marginal rate for average income workers and the top rate came down for high income earners, in part to compensate them for lost deductions.

References

Apel, M. (1994), 'An Expenditure-Based Estimate of Tax Evasion in Sweden', Working Paper 1994:1, Department of Economics, Uppsala University.

Barthelemy, P. (1988), 'The Macroeconomic Estimates of the Hidden Economy: A Critical Analysis', *Review of Income and Wealth*, Vol. 34, pp. 183-208.

Berger, S. (1986), 'The Unrecorded Economy: Concepts, Approach and Preliminary Estimates for Canada, 1981', *Canadian Statistical Review*, Vol. 22, pp. vi-xxvi.

Bhattacharyya, D.K. (1990), 'An Econometric Method of Estimating the "Hidden Economy", United Kingdom (1960-1984): Estimates and Tests', *Economic Journal*, Vol. 100, pp. 703-17.

Cagan, P. (1958), 'The Demand for Currency Relative for the Total Money Supply', *Journal of Political Economy*, Vol. 66, pp. 302-28.

Canada (1999), *Report of the Auditor General of Canada to the House of Commons*, Ottawa: Public Works and Government Services, Chapter 2.

Canada Customs and Revenue Agency (2000), *News Releases*, 12 June.

Dellago, B. (1990), *The Irregular Economy: The 'Underground Economy' and the 'Black Labour Market'*, Dartmouth: Publishing Company.

Dell'Anno, R. (2003), 'Estimating the Shadow Economy in Italy: A Structural Equation Approach', Working Paper 2003-07, Institut for Økonomi, Aarhus University.

Dickey, D.A. and Pantula, S.G. (1987), 'Determining the Order of Differencing in Autoregressive Processes', *Journal of Business and Economic Statistics*, Vol. 15, pp. 455-61.

Dilnot, A.W. and Morris, C.N. (1981), 'What do we Know About the Black Economy', *Fiscal Studies*, Vol. 2, pp. 58-73.

Drummond, D., Éthier, M., Fougère, M., Girard, B. and Rudin, J. (1994), 'The Underground Economy: Moving the Myth Closer to Reality', *Canadian Business Economics*, Vol. 2, pp. 3-17.

Éthier, M. (1982), 'L'Economie Souteraine: Revue de la Litterature et Nouvelles Estimation pour le Canada', Mimeograph, Department of Finance, Ottawa.

Éthier, M. (1985), 'The Underground Economy: A Review of the Economic Literature and New Estimates for Canada', in F. Vaillancourt (ed.), *Income Distribution and Economic Security in Canada*, pp. 77-109, Toronto: University of Toronto Press.

Feige, E.L. (1979), 'How Big is the Irregular Economy?', *Challenge*, Vol. 22, pp. 5-13.

Flexman, B. (1997), 'Canadian Attitudes Towards Taxation', in O. Lippert and M. Walker (eds), *The Underground Economy: Global Evidence of its Size and Impact*, pp. 53-74, Vancouver: The Fraser Institute.

Frey, B.S. and Weck-Hannemann, H. (1984), 'The Hidden Economy as an Unobserved Variable', *European Economic Review*, Vol. 26, pp. 33-53.

Gervais, G. (1994), *The Size of the Underground Economy: A Statistics Canada View*, Statistics Canada, Catalogue No. 13-603.

Giles, D.E.A. (1999), 'The Hidden Economy and the Tax-Gap in New Zealand: A Latent Variable Analysis', *Empirical Economics*, Vol. 24, pp. 621-40.

Giles, D.E.A. and Tedds, L.M. (2002), *Taxes and the Canadian Hidden Economy*, Toronto: Canada Tax Foundation.

Gutmann, P.M. (1977), 'The Subterranean Economy', *Financial Analysts Journal*, Vol. 34, pp. 24-7.

Haas, R.D. (1979), 'Short Note on the Recent Behaviour of Currency', Mimeograph, Bank of Canada, Ottawa.

Haldrup, N. (1994), 'The asymptotics of single-equation cointegration regressions with $I(1)$ and $I(2)$ variables', *Journal of Econometrics*, Vol. 63, pp. 53-181.

Helberger, C. and Knepel, H. (1988), 'How Big is the Shadow Economy? A Re-Analysis of the Unobserved-Variable Approach', in B.S. Frey and H. Weck-Hannemann, *European Economic Review*, Vol. 32, pp. 965-76.

Hill, R. (2002), 'The Underground Economy in Canada: Boom or Bust?', *The Canadian Tax Journal*, Vol. 50, pp. 1641-54.

Hill, R. and Kabir, M. (1996), 'Tax Rates, the Tax Mix, and the Growth of the Underground Economy in Canada: What Can We Infer', *Canadian Tax Journal*, Vol. 44, pp. 1552-83.

Hill, R. (2000), 'Currency Demand and the Growth of the Underground Economy in Canada', *Applied Economics*, Vol. 32, pp. 183-92.

Kalman, R.E. (1960), 'A New Approach to Linear Filtering and Prediction Problems', *Journal of Basic Engineering*, pp. 35-45.

Karoleff, V., Mirus, R. and Smith, R.S. (1993), 'Canada's Underground Economy Revisited: Update and Critique Paper', presented at the 49th Congress of the International Institute of Public Finance, Berlin.

Kaufmann, D. and Kaliberda, A. (1996), 'Integrating the Unofficial Economy into the Dynamics of Post Socialist Economies: A Framework for Analyses and Evidence', Working Paper 1691, World Bank, Washington.

Kurozumi, E. (2002), 'Testing for Stationarity with a Break', *Journal of Econometrics*, Vol. 108, pp. 63-99.

Kurozumi, E. and Enste, D. (2000), 'Increasing Shadow Economies All Over the World – Fiction or Reality? A Survey of the Global Evidence of Their Size and Their Impact From 1970 to 1995', *Journal of Economic Literature*, Vol. 38, pp. 77-114.

Kwiatkowski, D., Phillips, P.C.B., Schmidt, P. and Shin, Y. (1992), 'Testing the null hypothesis of stationarity against the alternative of a unit root', *Journal of Econometrics*, Vol. 54, pp. 159-78.

Lemieux, T., Fortin, B. and Fréchette, P. (1994), 'The Effect of Taxes on Labor Supply in the Underground Economy', *American Economic Review*, Vol. 84, pp. 231-54.

Loayza, N.V. (1996), 'The Economics of the Informal Sector: A Simple Model and Some Empirical Evidence from Latin America', *Carnegie-Rochester Conference Series on Public Policy*, Vol. 45, pp. 129-62.

Lyssiotou, P., Pashardes, P. and Stengos, T. (2004), 'Estimates of the Black Economy Based on Consumer Demand Approaches', *Economic Journal* (forthcoming).

MacKinnon, J.G. (1991), 'Critical Values for Co-Integration Tests', in R.F. Engle and C.W.J. Granger (eds), *Long-Run Economic Relationships*, pp. 267-76, Oxford: Oxford University Press.

Mirus, R. (1984), 'The Invisible Economy: Its Dimensions and Implications', in G. Lermer (ed.), *Probing Leviathan, An Investigation of Government in the Economy*, pp. 113-126, Vancouver: The Fraser Institute.

Mirus, R. (1997), 'Self-Employment, Tax Evasion, and the Underground Economy: Micro-Based Estimates for Canada', Working Paper 1002, International Tax Program, Harvard Law School.

Mirus, R. and Karoleff, V. (1994), 'Canada's Underground Economy Revisited: Update and Critique', *Canadian Public Policy*, Vol. XX, pp. 235-51.

Mirus, R. and Smith, R.S. (1981), 'Canada's Irregular Economy', *Canadian Public Policy 7*, pp. 444-53.

Mogensen, G.V., Kvist, H.K., Kömendi, E. and Pedersen, S. (1995), 'The Shadow Economy in Denmark 1994: Measurement and Results', The Rockwool Foundation Research Unit, Copenhagen.

Ng, S. and Karoyli, A. (1984), 'The Underground Economy in Canada: Preliminary Estimates', Mimeograph, Bank of Canada, Ottawa.

OECD (2002), 'Canada: Maintaining Leadership Through Innovation', OECD Review of Regulatory Reform series.

Paquet, G. (1989), 'The Underground Economy', *Policy Options*, Vol. 10, pp. 3-6.

Peritz, I. (2004), 'Boozing scam artists steal hearts of viewers', *Globe and Mail*, Monday February 16.

Perron, P. (1989), 'The Great Crash, the Oil Price Shock and the Unit Root Hypothesis', *Econometric*, Vol. 57, pp. 1361-1401.

Pissarides, C.A. and Weber, G. (1989), 'An Expenditure-based Estimate of Britain's Black Economy', *Journal of Public Economics*, Vol. 39, pp. 17-32.

Pouftis, A. (1993), 'Estimating the Size of the Underground Economy in Canada', M.A. Dissertation Essay, Department of Economics, Queen's University.

Said, S.E. and Dickey, D.A. (1984), 'Testing for Unit Roots in Autoregressive-Moving Average Models of Unknown Order', *Econometrica*, Vol. 71, pp. 599-607.

Schneider, F. (1997), 'Empirical Results for the Size of the Shadow Economy of Western European Countries Over Time', Working Paper 9710, Institut Für Volkswirtschaftslehre, Linz University.

Schneider, F. (2000), 'The Increase of the Size of the Shadow Economy in 18 OECD Countries: Some Preliminary Explanations', Mimeograph, Department of Economics, Johannes Kepler University of Linz, Austria.

Schneider, F. and Bajada, C. (2003), 'The Size and Development of the Shadow Economies in the Asia-Pacific', Working Paper 0301, Department of Economics, Linz University.

Schneider, F. and Enste, D. (2000), 'Increasing Shadow Economies All Over the World – Fiction or Reality? A Survey of the Global Evidence of Their Size and Their Impact From 1970 to 1995', *Journal of Economic Literature*, Vol. 38, pp. 77-114.

Schnieder, F. and Neck, R. (1993), 'The Development of the Shadow Economy under Changing Tax System and Structure', *Finanzarchiv NF*, Vol. 50, pp. 344-369.

Schuetze, H.J. (2002), 'Profiles of Tax Noncompliance Among the Self-Employed in Canada, 1969-1992', *Canadian Public Policy*, Vol. XXVIII.

Smith, P.M. (1994), 'Assessing the Size of the Underground Economy: The Statistics Canada Perspective', *Canadian Economic Observer*, Vol. 7, pp. 3.16-3.33.

Smith, R.S. (2002), 'The Underground Economy: Guidance for Policy Makers?', *The Canadian Tax Journal*, Vol. 50, pp. 1655-61.

Spiro, P.S. (1993), 'Evidence of a Post-GST Increase in the Underground Economy', *Canadian Tax Journal*, Vol. 41, pp. 247-58.

Spiro, P.S. (1994), 'Estimating the Underground Economy: A Critical Evaluation of the Monetary Approach', *Canadian Tax Journal*, Vol. 42, pp. 1059-81.

Tanzi, V. (1980), 'The Underground Economy in the United States: Estimates and Implications', *Banco Nazionale del Lavoro*, Vol. 135, pp. 427-53.

Tedds, L.M. (1998), 'Measuring the Size of the Hidden Economy in Canada', M.A. Extended Essay, Department of Economics, University of Victoria.

Thomas, J. (1999), 'Quantifying the Black Economy: Measurement without Theory Yet Again', *Economic Journal*, Vol. 109, pp. F381-F337.

PART 3

DETECTION, PREVENTION AND PROGRESS

Chapter 10

Tax Policy and the Underground Economy[*]

Peter S. Spiro

The purpose of taxation is to raise revenue to pay for public goods, but along the way it has impacts on economic growth and income distribution. These impacts are often undesirable, and sometimes difficult to predict.

Tax policy is the most complex area of economic policy, because each tax change has so many ramifications. One can say very little about the impacts of taxation based simply on economic theory and deductive logic. Only empirical estimates of the elasticity of response to specific taxes can enable us to choose which is the least bad alternative. This empirical analysis is inherently difficult, and it is made even more difficult by the existence of an unmeasured underground economy.

One of the considerations that is all too often ignored in discussions of tax policy is the way it affects the underground economy. Theoretical tax models almost always assume that everybody follows the rules. In reality, the behavioral response to tax changes has a wider range of variation than the choice between labour and leisure. Many otherwise honest citizens are prepared to break the law in order to evade taxes.

Once the underground economy is taken into account – in effect, the proposition that individuals may decide to 'opt out' of the tax system – there is a whole new layer of complexity to tax policy. Taxes that may seem to be optimal without the underground economy may no longer be optimal once it is taken into consideration.

There are a number of serious policy issues that may result from the growth of the underground economy:

1. Tax evasion caused by higher tax rates will siphon off revenue, forcing even higher tax rates in the areas where evasion is difficult. Tax evasion is affected both by tax rates and enforcement, and therefore the choice of tax policy must also depend on the type of enforcement that accompanies it.

2. The opportunity to participate in the underground economy represents a 'subsidy' to certain types of economic activity where evasion is easier. These are often relatively low productivity areas of the economy.

3.   The underground economy makes official statistics on economic growth less reliable, and this faulty information may lead to incorrect economic policy decisions.

The above three items are all negative consequences of the underground economy. However, it should be pointed out that the underground economy also has its supporters. Some economists argue the following positive points:

1.   Governments sometimes undertake excessive and wasteful spending, and the electoral system is too blunt an instrument to rein them in. The underground economy is a form of tax protest that forces governments to realize that there is a limit to how much they can raise their spending.[1]

2.   Governments sometimes establish unnecessary and inefficient regulation of economic activity, and the underground economy is the result of a situation where there is a willing seller and a willing buyer who cannot make a legal exchange. In such an instance, the underground economy is a useful outlet that increases economic welfare. However, it should be noted that this is a situation in which the activity has gone underground not in order to evade tax. Where an activity has gone underground mainly to evade tax, it is usually carried out in a less efficient manner than it would be in the legal economy, and there are welfare costs.

There is no simple universal answer to what is good tax policy that takes into account the underground economy. The answer will be different for different countries, depending on their pre-existing tax policies and institutions. This paper will attempt to survey the types of issues that need to be considered in setting tax policy in a world where 'opting out' of the tax system is an ever-present reality.

How Should the Underground Economy Influence Tax Policy?

The underground economy is just one of many concerns that affect tax policy. Taxes are a necessary evil for raising tax revenue, to pay for what are considered by society to be public goods. Tax policy is concerned about the impacts of taxes on economic efficiency, aggregate demand and income distribution.

Whenever there are taxes, there will be tax evasion. Tax policy cannot be concerned solely or even primarily with minimizing evasion. However, the fact of evasion, and its consequences, alters the way in which taxes impact on economic efficiency and income distribution. Therefore, the underground economy needs to be taken into account in predicting the impacts of tax changes.

In particular, it can reasonably be argued, following Palda (1998), that the underground economy suffers from diseconomies of small scale and other inefficiencies. Anything which drives more activity into the underground economy reduces productivity. In a benefit-cost calculation, this is the main cost of any tax move that increases the incentive to engage in underground economic activity.

There has been an increasing tendency for fiscal analysts to think in terms of the marginal cost of public funds. This concept takes into account the disincentives to economic activity from taxation, and implies that each dollar raised through taxation has a larger cost in terms of lost economic output. This can occur due to effects such as disincentives to work from higher marginal tax rates even in the absence of evasion. The implication is that the optimal level of public expenditure in a country occurs where the marginal cost of public funds equals the marginal utility of public services.

The marginal cost of public funds can only be measured with a considerable margin of error, and measuring the marginal utility of public services is even more problematic. It is questionable whether this concept can be put into practice with much precision, but it has nevertheless been influential. It has focussed attention on the need to limit the growth in government expenditure as a share of the economy. The study that comes closest to applying this concept empirically at a macroeconomic level is Tanzi and Schuknecht (1995).

Studies that attempt to estimate the marginal cost of public funds focus on empirical estimates of the elasticity of supply of labour with respect to the after tax wage rate. The existence of the underground economy leads to an interesting empirical anomaly. The existence of the underground economy implies that empirical estimates probably overstate the elasticity of supply and thus overstate the marginal cost of public funds.[2]

Suppose that a higher marginal tax rate discourages people from spending more hours working legally and paying tax. For example, somebody in a building trade may refuse to work overtime for his regular employer because taxes take too large a share of his marginal income. He will, instead, take on private jobs in his spare time on which he does not pay tax. Assuming that this underground work is not reported for statistical purposes, the decline in working hours due to the higher tax rate will be exaggerated.

It is ironic that the underground economy appears to reduce the true marginal cost of public funds in this example. There is a good chance that this worker will be less productive in this extra underground work, since he will not benefit from the economies of scale and the equipment that he has access to in his regular work. Therefore, there is an economic cost to this underground economy participation. However, the economic cost is not as great as if the work had not been done at all.

Public policy may be influenced toward reducing tax rates if concerns about the underground economy loom large. However, if this is the case, it is also reasonable to consider whether there is a greater benefit to improved enforcement as opposed to reduced taxation. In most advanced countries, especially the ones following the British legal system, the collection of taxes from the self-employed sector has been left on a voluntary basis to a remarkable degree. There has been a sense that greater government surveillance would intrude on personal liberty.

In any country, there are going to be a significant number of people working who are not registered with the authorities at all. The greater the degree of personal liberty, the more of these people there are likely to be. Often, they are illegal immigrants. However, at any point in time there are also going to be some legal residents who choose to work entirely underground, filing no tax return at all. This may well be the most effective form of tax evasion. Somebody who files a tax return, and under-reports income, is at some risk of being audited. By contrast, somebody who never files a return is likely to be safer, and under present arrangements may completely escape the notice of the authorities.

If there are concerns about the erosion of revenue due to the underground economy, it ought to be possible to improve enforcement. The remarkable growth in computer processing power and databases would make possible much greater economic surveillance without significant intrusions on the liberty or privacy of honest taxpayers. All that would be required is that anybody who accesses a government service would be required to supply his taxpayer identification number – every time a real estate transaction is registered, a new car is registered, a driver's license is issued, a child is enrolled in school, or a government health card is issued. This would greatly reduce the scope for these 'ghosts' to live comfortably by working entirely in the underground economy without filing any tax returns at all.

Taxation of Income versus Consumption

The existence of an underground economy can have a number of significant impacts on conventional views of what is optimal tax policy. One of the most important choices regards the 'tax mix' between consumption versus income taxes. There has been a considerable groundswell of enthusiasm among economists, especially in the United States, for the idea that income taxes should be abolished or at least minimized, and replaced with a tax on consumption instead.[3]

This view is often supported by politicians who misunderstand how narrow the economic justification for it is. A common logical error is to suppose that a 'tax on work' discourages work more than a 'tax on spending'. This is a fallacy, since the purpose of work is to earn money to spend. The supply of labour is affected by the real after-tax wage rate. That wage rate will fall if the income tax is raised. It will also fall if the sales tax is raised, which affects the price index used in calculating the real wage rate.[4]

The actual economic argument for the superiority of a consumption tax is that it avoids the taxation of the income earned from the return to saving. The after-tax rate of return to savings theoretically determines the allocation of consumption over time. If you earn a dollar today, and spend it, you will not pay any more income tax on it. If you put that dollar away for a few years, you may have $1.50 to spend before tax, but perhaps only $1.25 after tax. Therefore, an income tax tends to reduce the savings rate and biases consumption toward the present.

It might be asked, if the concern is about saving, why not just exempt income from savings? The main reason is that income from savings is not always easy to identify. It is obvious when it is income on a deposit in a bank account, or dividends from a widely held stock. However, a significant proportion of the population works in situations where the division of income from their labour versus their capital is ambiguous, and subject to manipulation. This applies both to self-employed entrepreneurs and to the management of widely owned corporations, who can often choose to forego salary in exchange for stock options.

The argument in favour of savings is sometimes presented in a quasi-mercantilist way, as if to say that measures to boost national saving are vital to a country's long-term strength. Such an argument is a mis-use of the economic analysis, which is simply an issue of allowing each individual to make his utility maximizing decision, without taxation distorting his choices.

There is considerable doubt about whether this is as important an issue as its proponents claim. Economic theory is ambiguous about whether taxing the return to savings leads to reduced saving. There is both a substitution and an income effect. The substitution effect predicts that a higher reward for waiting to consume will shift consumption into the future. On the other hand, if people save because they have a specific income target that they want to achieve in the future, they will not need to save as much if the rate of return has risen, and the saving rate would go down. Empirical evidence about the effect of the real rate of return on the savings rate is mixed. Some studies have found an elasticity close to zero.

Even if there is a significant elasticity of savings with respect to the rate of return, the argument in favour of consumption taxes versus income taxes is significantly impacted by the scope for tax evasion and the underground economy. As already noted, the underground economy has lower productivity, and therefore a tax move that encourages underground activity is undesirable. If consumption taxes do not encourage underground activity any more than income taxes, then this is not a problem. However, if it turns out that some kinds of consumption taxes increase underground activity, that may seriously undermine the claim that they are desirable because of their neutrality toward saving.

Cross-Section Studies on Tax Structure and Economic Growth

A number of economists have conducted cross-section studies that compare growth rates (usually of per capita real GDP) in different countries, and some appear to have found that a higher growth rate occurs in countries which rely more on consumption taxes than income taxes. However, these studies are fraught with difficulties that render their results unreliable.

A recent study by Widmalm is probably the most rigorous of these cross-section studies. She found that a higher share of taxes from income is associated with lower growth. However, she is honest enough to admit (p. 209) that 'if richer countries rely more on the taxation of individuals' income than do poorer countries, the effect on economic growth of personal income taxation is difficult to distinguish from the catching-up effect'.[5]

There is good reason to suppose that rich countries do have a greater ability to rely more on income taxation simply because they are rich, as it takes a high level of economic development (and factors that come with it, such as literacy and a well organized government) to be able to successfully levy an income tax. By contrast, consumer taxes are generally easier to organize, and less developed countries inevitably have to rely much more on them.[6]

This creates a bias in the cross-section econometric estimation. Countries that are already at a high level of development at the beginning of the sample period have less scope for higher growth, since they are already using the best available technology, whereas countries that start out poorer can catch up by borrowing technology from the leaders. Therefore, the observation that a higher share of tax revenues being from income is followed by lower economic growth, may be a case where *post hoc, ergo propter hoc* is the wrong conclusion.

The Effects of Different Types of Taxation on the Underground Economy

The question of how the tax mix affects the size of the underground economy is one of the most important issues for its application to tax policy. However, the empirical evidence on this subject is limited and also somewhat ambiguous. As with most other aspects of the underground economy, there is no firm rule as to what will apply. The outcome will probably vary with circumstances, and the best tax policy will be the one that is sensitive to these differences.

People who earn income in the underground economy receive this income in the form of cash, and will want to spend it in that form as well to avoid leaving a record of spending that is in excess of their declared income.[7] However, there is no stigma to using cash for purchases in most above-ground transactions, so they are not forced to spend their income in the underground economy just because they earned it there.

There is a major asymmetry between the spending and income sides of the underground economy. Anybody can participate in the underground economy as a consumer, and many may do so without even knowing it, since they cannot know if the businesses they deal with report all their sales to the tax authorities. However, the vast majority of the population will not participate in the underground economy as a worker. The underground economy is not a closed system. It can only survive if those who work in it can capture the business of the vast majority of the population that works in the legal economy.

Most people in an industrial economy work for a large company or the government, and have no opportunity to participate in the underground economy unless they quit their employment and set up an underground business (or set up a part-time business to supplement their salary income). Participation in the underground economy is rarely feasible for any business that is too large to be privately owned and run by family members.

A higher income tax rate therefore increases underground activity through a relatively narrow channel. It encourages more people to become self-employed, in the realization that higher after-tax incomes (facilitated by evasion) are available through self-employment. As well, for those who are already self-employed, it increases the reward for evasion, and is likely to encourage more of it.[8]

The main body of research on this subject has consisted of general equilibrium models, whose data was to a considerable extent judgemental rather than based on direct statistical inference. Kesselman (1993) responded to previous suggestions that shifting toward greater reliance on indirect taxes would reduce evasion. He found that a shift to more indirect taxation would just lead to more evasion of indirect taxes, if less evasion of direct taxes, with little or no net effect on the total amount of evasion.

Considering the types of activities in which evasion is concentrated, Kesselman's observation appears to be intuitively plausible. From the viewpoint of the after-tax income of a producer in the underground economy, either the income tax or the sales tax will have approximately the same impact. Suppose that somebody is interested in having home renovation work done, and has a budget of $1000 to spend on it. From the viewpoint of the consumer, it does not matter whether the seller accommodates this by not charging sales tax, or by accepting a lower wage rate since he plans not to pay income tax on it.

From another viewpoint, however, one could argue that sales taxes create a greater likelihood of underground activity. The existence of a sales tax facilitates the bargaining process regarding the division of the spoils from tax evasion. Let us take the example of a home repair service provider who operates partly in the underground economy and partly legally. He will offer an alternative to the customer: 'if you need a receipt, you will pay sales tax; if you pay in cash and need no receipt, you don't have to pay the sales tax'.

In a frictionless model where bargaining costs do not exist, it would make no difference here if all taxation was on purchases or all taxation was on income. Even if there is no sales tax, the service provider can still give a price discount for cash transactions, since it facilitates his evasion of income tax. In the real world, such negotiations are more awkward, and having a sales tax in place creates an easy definition of a 'fair' discount. It makes the customer more willing to collude in the evasion, particularly if the sales tax is perceived in some ways as objectionable and unfair (Spiro, 1997).

An alternative view, coming from Caragata and Giles (1998, 9-10) argues that direct taxes are more likely to promote evasion:

> Income is easier to disguise than a sales transaction because individuals have more control over opportunities to disguise income than over opportunities to disguise business ... while purchases are generally made in stores owned and managed by people with whom the taxpayer has no personal contact.

This point is valid for certain types of purchases from mass merchandisers. However, it is less likely to be the case for taxes applied to services such as home renovation activities. Moreover, it does not take into account the limited ability of those who are not self-employed, and who have income tax deducted by their employer, to disguise income.

Maurizio Bovi (2002) has done perhaps the most comprehensive cross-country empirical analysis of the role of taxation versus other factors in determining the size of the underground economy. He took estimates of the size of the underground economy from previously published studies, and then he ran cross-section econometric analysis for the OECD countries. The dependent variable is the underground economy as a percentage of GDP (estimated by two alternative methodologies by other researchers). For independent variables, he uses measures of corruption, the quality of the legal system, restrictions in the labour market, along with the size of different types of taxes as a percentage of GDP.

By including such a diverse range of variables, Bovi is able to account for a considerable diversity in the character of different countries. Indeed, his starting motivation is the observation that the four southern European countries of Spain, Portugal, Italy and Greece are considered to have the largest underground economies in Europe, even though their tax rates are well below the European average. By contrast, the Scandinavian countries are believed to have moderate sized underground economies in spite of having much higher tax rates. In Bovi's model, this is explained by the fact that the Scandinavian countries rank much better on the indicators of corruption.[9]

Regarding the impact of tax variables, the results from Bovi's analysis are mixed. In his analysis of the share of the underground economy in GDP (his Table 1), taxes on consumption appear to dominate, with a much higher degree of significance. Indeed, when tax on consumption and tax on labour income are included in the same regression, the latter has a coefficient not significantly different from zero. However, for this kind of levels regression, correlation does not prove causation.

In a second set of regressions, looking at the change in the size of the underground economy over the period from 1990 to 1998, it is income taxes which were the more significant determinant. However, given the small sample size, the result may just reflect the fact that consumption taxes did not vary much over this period.

As Bovi (2002) noted, the correlations between the underground economy and its determinants 'seem to be different not only over time, but also across countries'. To that, one might add that it is likely to be different for different sectors of the economy. There are some types of consumption where the scope for evasion is relatively limited, and in those areas a consumption tax may not have much impact. By contrast, there are certain types of services where consumers have an easy alternative in the underground economy to evade the tax.

There are two Canadian time series studies which use econometric analysis of different types of taxation on the growth of the economy which also comment on this issue. On casual inspection, the two studies appear to come to opposite conclusions. Hill and Kabir (1996) find that indirect tax increases have a much greater impact on the underground economy than direct tax increases. They conclude (p. 1576) that 'a decrease in average direct tax revenues ... and its replacement by an increase in indirect tax revenues of the same amount ... would lead to an increase in currency holdings and presumably a corresponding increase in the underground economy'. They note that 'the sum of the estimated coefficients for the average indirect tax rate greatly exceeds the sum of the coefficients of the average direct tax rate'.[10]

By contrast, Giles and Tedds (2001, 203) state that 'if one wishes to reduce the hidden economy as a share of measured GDP, then one way in which to do it is to shift the tax mix away from direct personal taxes and toward indirect taxes'. However, in the very next paragraph, they qualify this by noting that, for 1992, their estimated indirect tax elasticity was 'roughly double our estimated indirect personal tax elasticity ... Given these figures, it is only reasonable that the introduction of the GST should have led to an increase in the underground economy'.

Another perspective on this is given by Hill and Kabir's Figure 1, which shows the different tax rates historically from 1947 to 1995. There was much less variance in the indirect tax rate than in other tax rates, until 1991 when it doubled with the introduction of the GST. This factor in the data should remind us of one of the pitfalls of time series analysis. If there is very little variance in an explanatory variable during the sample period, econometric analysis may find that it has a coefficient near zero even if its true elasticity is quite high.

Another point to keep in mind is that categories such as 'direct tax' and 'indirect tax' are very broad. It stands to reason that an indirect tax on manufactured goods (collected mainly from a few thousand large businesses) will induce much less underground activity than an indirect tax on hundreds of thousands of small service providers.

It is misleading to categorically state that direct or indirect taxes will have particular impacts on the underground economy. What matters is the specific tax change that is in question. Some kinds of direct taxes will encourage certain kinds of underground activity, while others will not. For example, income tax rates in the range that affect manual workers will likely encourage the growth of underground home repair services. By contrast, the marginal tax rate for people earning over $200,000 per year is unlikely to cause any surgeons or lawyers to abandon their licenses and go underground, but it might encourage some owners of profitable medium sized businesses to under-report revenue in order to evade income tax, even though the business operates 'above ground'. That is why intelligent tax policy needs to be based on a detailed knowledge of the structure of the economy, as will be discussed below.

VAT versus Retail Sales Tax

It is often suggested that a value added tax (VAT), because it is a multi-stage tax, is less likely to be fully evaded than a retail sales tax. Most of the OECD countries now have a VAT, in contrast to a single-stage retail sales tax. The United States (along with the majority of the Canadian provinces) remains the major exception. In the United States, there is no national consumption tax, but most of the states and some city governments impose a retail sales tax.

One can certainly think of instances where a VAT will be less prone to evasion. In spite of that, a broad based tax reform which imposes a new VAT on a wide variety of goods and services may still lead to an increase in overall evasion.

The argument for a VAT reducing evasion is that members of the underground economy are often forced to purchase inputs from the legal economy, on which they pay VAT. If they do not charge VAT on their own sales, they will not receive input tax credits for their purchases. Thus, it is argued, the government only loses the tax on the value added by the underground producer, rather than on the total sale.

For example, if a retail sales tax is charged on the final sale price, an underground dealer will submit no tax. However, if the dealer bought the goods from a wholesaler who charged tax, only the tax on the markup will be lost.

Insofar as the retail sale of goods is concerned, it is quite likely that the VAT does a better job of collecting taxes than a pure retail tax.[11] However, the consequence of introducing a VAT is usually to spread the consumption tax over a much wider range of goods and especially services. Retail sales taxes tend to be levied mainly on goods, while VATs encompass most services as well. In the case of services, the value of inputs purchased by the service supplier is often only a small portion of the cost of the service. The bulk of the value added is at the point of final sale, in the form of the service provider's own work. In this case, a VAT recaptures relatively little revenue when the service provider goes underground.

At the same time, the existence of VAT on the service makes the consumer more aware of the potential saving from dealing with an underground provider, and thus increases the demand for underground services.

There is an important related issue which is on the borderline of the underground economy, although it is not usually defined as part of it. This is the choice between purchasing a service or doing it yourself.

In the theory of income taxation, one usually talks about a choice between work versus 'leisure'. In reality, the range of choice is wider than that. One can choose among three main categories: leisure, work in the market, and work at home. The latter is clearly part of production, but is not counted in GDP and it is generally considered to be outside the pale for taxation.

Let us consider the example of a teacher. Teachers often have the opportunity to earn extra income by teaching evening or summer classes outside the regular curriculum. However, if the teacher does take on this extra work, he will pay income tax, possibly at a rising marginal rate. He will have less time around the home to do chores such as gardening, painting and repairs. If he hires a professional painter to paint his home, the painter (if he is honest) will have to pay income tax on that work.[12] If there is a VAT on the service as well, that further tilts the balance toward the teacher painting the house himself, instead of spending more hours teaching.

From an economic efficiency point of view, this choice is clearly inefficient. Adam Smith long ago pointed out that the source of increasing wealth in economic development is specialization. The teacher is better at teaching than at painting, and if it were properly measured, national welfare would be higher if he stuck to teaching and let someone else paint his house. Instead, the tax system encourages teachers to become part-time painters.

As often as not, if the teacher does not do the painting himself, he will hire an underground provider to do it, saving much of the tax. This is likely to be more efficient than the teacher doing it himself. However, the underground provider is still likely to be less specialized and operate at a less efficient scale than would be the case in the absence of this taxation.

However, the existence of these inefficiencies does not mean that these activities should not be taxed in this way. In tax policy, there are tradeoffs everywhere. If house painters are not required to charge VAT, the government will have to seek that revenue elsewhere, and the burden of taxation from that other source may cause an even greater efficiency loss. What we are trying to do is arrange the tax system so as to minimize the total efficiency loss to the economy.

Ideally, the way to analyze these choices is through a general equilibrium model that describes the whole economy in considerable detail, looking at the effect of each kind of tax on each sector of the economy. An attempt at such a model was described by Piggott and Whalley (2001), and they applied their analysis to the introduction of the Canadian Goods and Services Tax (GST) in 1991. As they note (p. 1084), their analysis:

> builds on the observation that, in a typical base-broadening exercise, newly taxed commodities (services such as haircuts, garden care and house repair) are easier to provide within the household ... As a result, tax-induced substitution into relatively inefficient household production occurs ... a further effect is to stimulate underground activities that avoid the tax but that are again inefficient (at the margin) because of the tax.

The elasticities of substitution between purchased services and home produced or underground services cannot be known with precision, so Piggott and Whalley experimented with a range of estimates. They found that, with the most plausible values of the elasticities, there was a net loss in economic welfare due to base broadening. Not surprisingly, they found that the effect is exacerbated by the existence of a relatively high income tax rate.

The Underground Economy and the Scope for Commodity Substitution

It might be thought that there are certain types of goods and services in which there is no scope for underground economic activity. These would be sectors where, for reasons of economies of scale, essentially all output is provided by large companies. In that case, it might be argued that these are preferred targets for taxation. However, a careful analysis may call for some qualifications to this conclusion.

One example is electricity generation. Consumers have no choice but to buy their electricity from a large (and, in many countries, government owned) electric utility. There is no scope to pay cash under the table for electricity or to buy it from small independent producers. However, that does not mean that an increase in the taxation of electricity cannot have any underground economy impacts. There is an elasticity of demand for electricity, which is low in the short-run but rises with the passage of time as consumers have an opportunity to adjust.

Consumers can reduce their electricity consumption in a variety of ways. For example, they can improve the attic insulation in their homes to reduce the energy needed for heating in winter and cooling in summer. They can have electronic devices installed to automatically turn off lights and equipment that are not being used. They can ensure better and more frequent maintenance of their equipment so that it uses less power. All of these renovations and services have the potential for being provided by participants in the underground economy.

Another example might be the taxation of airline tickets. Apart from small charter operators, it can be assumed that there are no airlines in the underground economy. However, more expensive airline tickets cause people to look for more affordable alternatives. At the margin, some people will choose to take land transportation, increasing the demand for automobile maintenance and intercity buses, which do have underground economy components.

These examples show why a comprehensive tax policy analysis can only be done through general equilibrium modelling. A model of that kind would need to have several hundred or even thousands of equations that properly represent the scope for substitution among different goods and services. Needless to say, these models are only as good as the data that goes into them. The parameters have to be based on careful empirical studies rather than *ad hoc* assumptions about elasticities.[13]

The Importance of Microeconomic Estimates of the Underground Economy for Tax Policy

If there is a major risk that a tax change being contemplated will push people into the underground economy, then this should be a factor in setting tax policy. However, we have to step back, and take note of another layer of complexity. The size and importance of the underground economy is itself a controversial and unresolved issue. There is an immense literature on the subject, some of it covered in other parts of this volume. However, much of the empirical estimation regarding the underground economy is at a very general macroeconomic level. In order to be useful for formulating tax policy, more detailed information is needed about the nature and composition of the underground economy.

There are few areas of economic policy analysis where the key empirical fact is so elusive as in the case of the underground economy. There is a burgeoning literature arguing that the underground economy has grown, and linking this to high rates of tax.

Not to impugn the integrity of any researcher in this area, but we have to be particularly wary of the possibility that preconceived ideas about the desirability of tax cuts may influence researchers' views on this subject. It is not too hard to find examples of researchers who think the underground economy is large, and who think that may be a good thing. For example, Roger Smith (2002, p. 1660) writes in praise of the underground economy:

> In a world of minimum wages, high payroll taxes, immigration and employment controls, limits on hours worked, and clawbacks of social transfers, the underground economy may enable some individuals to be employed who would otherwise not be employed, enable other individuals to increase their incomes by holding second jobs, and provide services that would otherwise be unavailable. Activity of this kind may add a dynamic element to an economy and increase competition in some sectors. These potentially positive aspects of underground activity deserved more attention ...

In the case of Canada, estimates of the underground economy range from about 5 to 20 percent of GDP. The upper end is based on econometric estimates, while the lower end comes from analysts at Statistics Canada, the national statistical agency, as exemplified in the study by Philip Smith (1994).

The Statistics Canada methodology is a microeconomic one, and thus very different from the macroeconomic approach embodied in the econometric studies, which are much more common. In effect, Statistics Canada shows a detailed structural breakdown of output in the economy. They apply a judgmental factor regarding the potential size of the underground economy in that sector – e.g., moderately large percentages among small service providers, and near-zero in areas such as electric and gas utilities and financial services.

One of the pitfalls in this approach, as noted by Spiro (1994a, 20) is that it starts out with the assumption that the official statistics of output by sector are correct:

> As these sectors [susceptible to evasion] total only 11 per cent of GDP, they conclude that the underground economy cannot be large. Unfortunately, this is a circular argument. It is only if one believes in Statistics Canada's ability to capture the underground economy that one can conclude that these sectors really do total only 11 per cent of the economy. In fact, if the underground economy is considerably larger than Statistics Canada believes, there will be considerable spending in the 'susceptible sectors' that is already missing from their chart.

This 'bottom-up' or microeconomic methodology is clearly susceptible to incorrect assumptions, as is the macroeconomic methodology. Nevertheless, I would argue that it is a valuable adjunct to the macroeconometric approach, and more work needs to be done in this area. Having an understanding of the microeconomic sectors where the underground economy is most important is vital to the intelligent design of tax policy.

First of all, estimates of the overall size of the underground economy will have more credibility if they have a microeconomic counterpart. If we tell policymakers that the underground economy is 15 percent of GDP, based on econometric analysis of the money supply, they are likely to be skeptical, because they will not understand the analysis behind the estimate. If we can fill in the blanks by telling them where, on the ground, the underground economy is located, they are likely to take it more seriously as a factor in designing tax policy.

The reality is that the macroeconometric approach has a very large margin of error. Any econometric methodology is sensitive to the specification of the model, although this can be accounted for if the modeller is sufficiently careful. Bajada (2002) suggests a methodology for evaluation this aspect of the uncertainty. However, even if these concerns are accounted for, there are issues such as not knowing the value of the underground economy in a base year, and not knowing the velocity of circulation of cash in the underground economy.[14] The macroeconometric analyses gain credibility when they are grounded in microeconomic studies that give reference points.

Perhaps the ideal form of such a study is the Taxpayer Compliance Measurement Studies that used to be undertaken by the Internal Revenue Service (IRS) in the United States. In these studies, the IRS picked a scientifically chosen random sample of businesses and individuals to audit. (This is different from the normal practice, where audits are directed to areas where the largest revenue gains are expected relative to the effort.) The results of one such study are described in the Schoepfle (1992). Among the remarkable findings of this study is that sole proprietors as a group reported only about 40 percent of their true income (including those that did not file a return at all). Looking at the whole population, the study estimated that tax returns under-reported actual personal income by about 11 percent.

Of course, the IRS studies are not perfect either. On the one hand, there are forms of evasion that even the most persistent auditors cannot detect. On the other hand, the estimates of evasion in these cases are the opinions of the auditors, and there is a risk that auditors may occasionally exaggerate malfeasance to justify their own value. Nevertheless, this kind of detailed information greatly enriches our knowledge of the underground economy. As it happens, the IRS has discontinued these large random studies, both because of their cost and their unpopularity with the auditees. They are, instead, investigating the feasibility of adjusting the data from regular audits so that the results can be extrapolated to the general population.

A variety of methodologies is available for microeconomic analysis, not all of them as expensive as the IRS randomized audits. Inevitably, public opinion surveys would be one of the tools for deriving this information. These surveys have many potential pitfalls, as noted by Schneider and Bajada (2003). People are reluctant to admit to doing something illegal, and therefore the more anonymous the survey, the more accurate it will be. A Norwegian study (Isachsen and Strom, 1989) found that almost twice as many people admitted to underground activity when they responded to an anonymous mail-in written questionnaire as when they participated in a face to face interview.

A recent study that is a very good model for this approach was done for Australia by Schneider et al. (2001), using a written questionnaire. It provides quite a lot of detail about the underground economy in Australia, including income earned per individual and the types of services offered. Interestingly, the result implies that income earned in the underground economy was up to about 8.8 percent of national income, a considerably lower figure than Schneider's econometric estimate for that country.

The empirical research needs to try to answer questions such as the following: What kinds of goods or services are provided in the underground economy? What is the predominant income distribution in the underground economy? Knowledge about these issues can make a very large difference concerning the best tax policy. For example, marginal income tax rates in the middle range of income may become a more important concern if it is found that those are the people who are most susceptible to moving into the underground economy. Likewise, it is best to avoid sales tax increases on those services that are most prone to evasion.

Understanding the Business Structure of the Underground Economy

To know how tax policy affects the underground economy, the policymaker must learn who the participants are. This is something that can vary considerably from country to country, depending on its customary institutions and forms of regulation and business organization. To understand it does require a certain effort at investigation.

Inevitably, a large part of the focus of microeconomic studies has to be on the structure of the business population. There are three main types of participants in the underground economy: small to medium-sized family run firms; self-employed individuals, usually in service occupations, and criminal enterprises (including some larger units in the form of organized crime mobs).

Under-reporting of sales can be carried out with a tolerable risk only when the firm is small enough that the accounting is done by an owner or a member of the family rather than an employee. An employee in a large organization can only be relied on when the business is part of organized crime, which can then use the threat of violence to discourage employees from revealing embarrassing secrets.

The self-employed population has different definitions in different countries. In the classic sense, a self-employed person works alone, without employees. However, this definition can be quite fluid. A person who owns a small corporation, and may have dozens of employees, can still be considered self-employed.

There is a tendency to think of the underground economy as mainly consisting of self-employed individuals, such as babysitters or home repair people, who ask their customers to pay in cash without a receipt. The self-employed with no employees are no doubt an important component of the underground economy. There are some self-employed individuals with substantial income who never file a tax return. In most democratic countries, a citizen is able to go through life without being called on by anybody to explain his source of income to the government. However, the demand for such services is largely restricted to the household sector, and it is unlikely that these 'ghosts' make up a large part of the labour force. If it were restricted to such individuals, the underground economy would have to be much smaller than it is usually estimated to be by economists.

However, a considerable part of the underground economy consists of fully legal and registered business, who are only underground in the sense that they hide part of their income. This is not as difficult as it may appear. It should be realized that the profits in a business are always a residual after expenses are deducted from receipts. A small understatement of sales can lead to a large percentage understatement of income.[15] For example, suppose a business has sales of $1 million and expenses of $800,000, for a true net income of $200,000. Suppose that the proprietor understates his sales by just 10 percent, and reports the total as $900,000. As a result, net income is understated by 50 percent.

The underground economy needs cash transactions in order to avoid leaving an audit trail. However, a business does not have to go out of its way to ask its customers for cash in order to participate. In the normal course of events, a substantial portion of receipts will be in cash, in a retail business, for example.[16] Of course, some businesses encourage cash transactions more than others. For example, some retailers offer a cash discount of 2 or 3 percent (on the grounds that this allows them to avoid the service charge that credit card companies charge).

As long as a family member is in charge of keeping the books (and altering the computerized cash register database, if necessary) it is easy enough to substantially understate sales, and hence net income. Family firms with several millions of dollars of annual turnover can easily be substantial participants in the underground economy, without their employees or customers knowing anything about it. The owners of the company merely have to take a substantial portion of their income in cash, and be a little bit discrete in how they spend it.

The greatest scope for the understatement of sales through cash transactions is for businesses that deal directly with the public. However, these businesses in turn can use cash to pay their suppliers, thus understating both their sales and their expenses. The latter is not directly beneficial to them, but by enabling their suppliers to evade tax, they can purchase goods and services more cheaply. This can even apply to small local manufacturers supplying retailers with merchandise, although the scope for this has diminished through the globalization of manufacturing. Where a small business has trusted employees, they can be paid partly in cash as well. In this case, they too are evading tax, and as a result of this complicity there is less risk that they will report the underground cash to the authorities.

In analyzing the underground economy, the investigator needs to look at these key aspects of the structure of the business population. In each segment of business, how many firms are there that are small enough to be family run? What proportion of total employment do they account for in that sector? It is particularly important to establish the 'susceptible population' according to approximate income categories, in order to discover how important marginal tax rates in a particular range are for influencing underground economic activity.

In the extreme case where businesses employ unregistered workers paid entirely in cash, even the total employment may not be accurately reported to the statistical authorities. However, in these cases it can reasonably be assumed that the pay rates are relatively low, and the employees in question are mainly illegal immigrants. The evasion of taxes is a secondary motivation in those cases, and therefore less of a concern for the design of the income tax rate schedule.

The Impact of the Self-Employed and the Underground Economy on Productivity

The self-employed population is of particular interest for studying the underground economy, as people in these occupations have the greatest scope for participating in the underground economy. There is also evidence from Schuetze (2000) that higher tax rates encourage greater participation in self-employment.

There is evidence that in some countries the productivity of the self-employed is significantly lower than that of workers in the regular economy. This was emphasized by Stabile (2004), who studied the consequences of higher payroll taxation, and found that it significantly encourages participation in self-employment.

Palda (1998) emphasizes the welfare loss that results because taxation gives a competitive advantage to smaller scale firms, which means especially the self-employed. He notes that 'in the presence of differing abilities to evade taxes, markets select producers for their evasive skills and their abilities to keep costs of production low. Inefficient firms crowd out efficient firms. If the least efficient firms are the best tax evaders, adverse selection is severe and output comes entirely from the high cost end of the supply curve'.

It is very hard to assess empirically just how much less productive the self-employed sector is. The income in this sector is under-reported due to evasion, and statistical agencies rarely attempt to correct for this under-reporting. A particularly impressive example of the importance of this question, not just for tax policy but for broader economic policy, can be found in Baldwin and Chowhan (2003).

Since the mid-1990s, one of the most persistent sources of concern in Canadian economic policy literature (and the news media) has been the belief that Canada has fallen behind the US in productivity growth. Quite remarkably, Baldwin and Chowhan found that, when both the GDP contribution and the hours worked of the self-employed are excluded, there was virtually no difference between Canadian and US productivity growth in the 1990s.

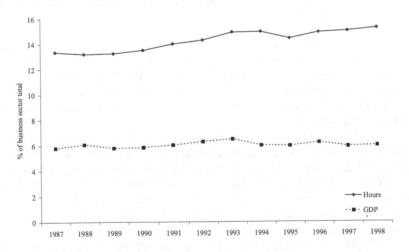

Figure 1 Self-employed in Canada: hours worked vs. income reported

Source: Data from Baldwin and Chowhan (2003), Table A2

The reason for this is two-fold. In Canada, the self-employed share of employment grew, while in the US it fell. In Canada, productivity growth among the self-employed was essentially zero, while in the US it was greater than for the rest of the economy. The growth rate of productivity of the self-employed was relatively high in the US in the 1990s, but in both countries the output per hour worked in the self-employed sector was considerably less than the economy's average.

In the late 1990s, the self-employed represented about 15 percent of hours[17] worked in Canada, but only about 6 percent of GDP.[18] In the US, the self-employed represented about 11 percent of employment, and 8 percent of GDP.

Baldwin and Chowhan provide what appears to be a plausible macroeconomic explanation of the productivity problem in Canada, so it is useful to quote some key sections of it directly:

> It is tempting to conclude that it was our entrepreneurs who were the cause of the productivity slowdown in the early 1990s. But that is probably too simplistic an interpretation. It is more likely that in comparing total business sector productivity growth in the two countries in the 1990s, we are making the mistake of comparing two quite different ratios – even though we are calling them by the same name (output per worker), they are capturing different phenomena (page V).

> Restructuring led to substantial layoffs of many individuals who did not find regular work and it is possible that these individuals chose not to call themselves unemployed, but to classify themselves as self-employed ... The income earned by those choosing, or those being forced into self-employment, was not zero; but it was considerably below the income of those who normally classified themselves as self-employed.

However, one remarkable point of omission in this paper is the complete absence of any mention of the underground economy. Most analysts believe that the underground economy is larger in Canada than in the United States, and that it grew more in Canada during the 1990s. That is an obvious alternative explanation for at least part of the divergence in productivity growth that ties in neatly with Baldwin and Chowhan's findings.

Baldwin and Chowhan's study is an important piece of the puzzle, even though it so completely ignores the underground economy. It is likely that Baldwin and Chowhan's data understates the true output of the self-employed sector. If that is the main explanation for the low level of productivity in the self-employed sector, their analysis is still very useful for showing how the underground economy can obscure the macroeconomic data, possibly leading to serious macroeconomic policy errors.

To the extent that productivity in the self-employed sector really is much lower than in the rest of the economy, that takes us back to our tax policy concerns. The main force through which higher tax rates increase the size of the underground economy is by increasing self-employment. The tax wedge between legal businesses and underground businesses 'subsidizes' inefficient production, as argued by Palda, and it is one of the main economic costs of the underground economy.

Conclusions

Tax policy debates, more than most other areas of economics, have been driven by ideology rather than evidence. The level of taxation is at the core of the debate between those who want more versus less government participation in the economy, between collectivists versus individualists. Not too far behind the ideological debate is the battle over income shares and economic rents, and the reality that some of the most profound impacts of tax policy are on the distribution of income among different factors of production and different income groups.

However, for those who are interested in positive tax policy, it is possible to penetrate this fog. A great deal of good empirical research about the effects of specific kinds of taxation already exists, and this body of knowledge will grow as increased computer processing power gives researchers access to immense new databases.

This survey of the issues only scratches the surface of a very complex subject. This complexity, most of all, is what I want the reader to take away from what I have written. There are no easy, cut and dried axioms that can be used for setting good tax policy. The correct answer varies with circumstances, and specific choices need to be subjected to detailed empirical analysis. A change in taxation may appear to increase economic welfare when viewed in isolation, but could actually lead to a decline in welfare due to distortions elsewhere in the economy.

In the end, good tax policy analysis has to be empirical, and based on a very well articulated general equilibrium model of the economy. Along with all the other information going into this model about the response to tax changes, the modelers have to pay due regard to how each kind of tax change influences participation in the underground economy. As I have noted, this can only be done through a very detailed microeconomic analysis. The underground economy is not a monolith that exists at a distance from the rest of the economy. Tax evasion is always a potential part of individuals' economic responses. How it plays out varies greatly from sector to sector, based the opportunities for tax evasion that arise due to the character of that sector.

Notes

* The views expressed in this article are his personal opinions and should not be attributed to any organisation with which he may be affiliated.
1. On this view, it is possible that the underground economy causes tax rates to be lower than they would otherwise have been, contrary to the common view (expressed above) that the underground economy forces legal activities to bear a larger tax burden. An economist who believes that government spending would otherwise go beyond the point where its marginal cost exceeds its utility could argue that the underground economy increases fiscal efficiency.
2. A useful new study by Davis and Henreksen (2004) properly takes this into account, estimating both the decline in hours worked in the market sector and increased informal sector activity due to higher tax rates.

3.   The Congressional Budget Office (1997) provides an extensive survey and analysis. This 90 page paper is also a good example of the short shrift that has been given to the underground economy in tax policy analysis. The paper devotes a total of three paragraphs to the question of whether a consumption tax would be less prone to evasion than an income tax, and concludes in the negative.

4.   The only instance in which there would be a different impact is when workers who earn their income in one country plan to move later to another country to spend it. In that case, raising the sales tax would have (for the same amount of revenue raised) a smaller impact on the supply of work than raising the income tax.

5.   Widmalm (2001, p. 209). She also note that 'when the share of personal income tax is included in the growth regressions the coefficient on the proxy for initial GDP becomes insignificant in many specifications'.

6.   North America provides a dramatic example of this, in the contrast between the United States (15 percent of tax revenue from consumption) and its neighbour Mexico (48 percent of tax revenue from consumption taxes). Among other recent OECD member countries, one finds consumption taxes accounting for 38 percent of the total in Korea, 37 percent in Poland and Hungary, and 45 percent in Turkey. These are well above the average for the more developed OECD countries. (Data from the OECD's *Revenue Statistics, 1965-2003*, Table 27.)

7.   It is not necessary for tax auditors to be able to find proof of underground business income to secure a conviction for tax evasion. In Canada, at least, the tax authorities have successfully prosecuted tax evaders based on the evidence of a high level of spending, without an adequate explanation for it in the form of legally declared income. Therefore, a careful evader would not buy a house that is much more expensive than his declared income could support, as this would be fairly obvious evidence of evasion.

8.   It should be noted that economic theory is somewhat ambiguous about whether higher income tax rates inevitably lead to evasion. Allingham and Sandmo (1972) pointed out that this is not necessarily the case where individuals are risk averse. Therefore, this becomes an empirical issue. Probably the best empirical study is Clotfelter (1983). He used the results of IRS audits of tax evasion in different states, taking into account the fact that tax rates vary from state to state. Clotfelter's study did find that evasion rises with tax rates, but interestingly he concluded (p. 372-3) that 'whether it should become an explicit consideration in formulating tax policy depends, of course, on its magnitude, and the estimates in this paper suggest that it is probably not large compared to other objectives'.

9.   To some extent, this is a circular argument. The index of corruption comes from an international agency which does surveys of the extent to which public officials are bribe-takers in different countries. However, as bribes to government officials often come from members of the underground economy, it might be questioned whether this is really an independent variable in these regressions.

10. Brou and Collins (2001) update Hill and Kabir's estimates and concur (p. 1555) that 'a government interested in reducing informal economic activity will find it better to raise revenue through direct rather than indirect taxation. Higher indirect taxes will increase price distortions between the formal and informal sectors and encourage consumption of informal production'.

11. It should be noted, however, that in this sense it is no different than a wholesale goods or manufacturer's sales tax. A tax of this kind existed in Canada prior to 1991, when a VAT (Goods and Services Tax, or GST) replaced it. The GST was spread over a much larger range of goods and services. Spiro (1993) argues that the larger evasion potential on the services portion led to an increase in the underground economy.

12. Services are more labour intensive than goods, and therefore the personal income tax imposes a larger burden on the cost of providing services. The analysis by Kleven et al. (2000) suggests that services which are a close substitute for home production should bear a lower rate of tax than other consumer goods.

13. The study by Chirinko et al. (2004) includes some interesting examples of the dramatic differences in policy implied by relatively small variations in key elasticities.

14. These problems are discussed by Spiro (1994b and 1996).

15. In addition to understating sales, income can be understated by overstating expenses. A self-employed entrepreneur has a lot of scope to make purchases in the name of his company which are actually for personal consumption purposes. For example, a dentist who renovates his office may ask a contractor to do work on his home as well, and charge it to the same bill. This would represent an illegal understatement of income, and is an aspect of the underground economy.

16. Robert Shiller (2003) envisions a future in which electronic means of payment become so pervasive that 'paying in cash may become regarded as a suspicious activity', and he predicts that this will restrict the underground economy. However, it is possible to envision anonymous forms of electronic payment as well. If privacy laws remain sufficiently strong that they prevent pervasive monitoring of private transactions by the state, the underground economy could continue to thrive even with electronic payments.

17. It should be noted that some participants in the underground economy would be reluctant to divulge the fact that they are working at all to statistical agencies. Both the amount of work and the income in self-employment are understated, but income data (which comes from income tax returns) would be even more understated.

18. The percentage of GDP produced by the self-employed is remarkably low when one considers that most of the highest earning professions in the economy (physicians, lawyers, dentists, and professional accountants) are found primarily in the self-employed category.

References

Allingham, M.G. and Sandmo, A. (1972), 'Income Tax Evasion: A Theoretical Analysis', *Journal of Public Economics*, Vol. 1, pp. 323-38.

Bajada, C. (2002), 'How Reliable are the Estimates of the Underground Economy?', *Economics Bulletin*, Vol. 3(14).

Baldwin, J. and Chowhan, J. (2003), 'The impact of self-employment on labour-productivity growth: A Canada and United States comparison' (Statistics Canada Research Paper 11F0027MIE No. 016).

Bovi, M. (2002), 'The Nature of the Underground Economy. Some Evidence from OECD Countries', Istituto di Studi e Analisi Economica Rome, June, http://www.isae.it/Working_Papers/wpbovi26.pdf.

Brou, D. and Collins, K.A. (2001), 'Winning at Hide and Seek: The Tax Mix and the Informal Economy', *Canadian Tax Journal*, Vol. 49(6), pp. 1539-62.

Caragata, P. and Giles, D.A.E. (1998), 'Simulating the Relationship Between the Hidden Economy and the Tax level and Tax Mix in New Zealand', Mimeo.

Chirinko, R.S., Fazzari, S.M. and Meyer, A.P. (2004), 'That Elusive Elasticity: A Long-Panel Approach to Estimating the Capital-Labor Substitution Elasticity', CESifo Working Paper Series, No. 1240.

Clotfelter, C.T. (1983), 'Tax evasion and tax rates: An analysis of individual returns', *Review of Economics and Statistics*, Vol. 65(30), pp. 63-373.

Congressional Budget Office (1997), *The Economic Effects of Comprehensive Tax Reform*, ftp://ftp.cbo.gov/0xx/doc36/taxrefor.pdf.

Davis, S.J. and Henrekson, M. (2004), 'Tax Effects on Work Activity, Industry Mix and Shadow Economy Size: Evidence from Rich-Country Comparisons', National Bureau of Economic Research, Working Paper no. 10509.

Giles, D.A.E. and Tedds, L.M. (2002), *Taxes and the Canadian Underground Economy*, Canadian Tax Foundation, Toronto.

Hill, R. and Kabir, M. (1996), 'Tax Rates, the Tax Mix, and the Growth of the Underground Economy in Canada: What Can We Infer?', *Canadian Tax Journal*, Vol. 44(6), pp. 1552-83.

Isachsen, A.J. and Strom, S. (1989), 'The Underground Economy in Norway with Special Emphasis on the Hidden Labor Market', in E.L. Feige (ed.), *The Underground Economies: Tax Evasion and Information Distortion*, Cambridge University Press, New York.

Kleven, H.J., Richter, W.F. and Sørensen, P.B. (2000), 'Optimal taxation with household production', *Oxford Economic Papers*, Vol. 52, pp. 584-94.

Palda, F. (1998), 'Evasive Ability and the Efficiency Cost of the Underground Economy', *Canadian Journal of Economics*, Vol. 31, pp. 1118-38.

Piggott, J. and Whalley, J. (2001), 'VAT Base Broadening, Self Supply, and the Informal Sector', *American Economic Review*, Vol. 91(4), September, pp. 1084-94.

Schneider, F., Braithwaite, V. and Reinhart, M. (2001), 'Individual Behaviour in Australia's Shadow Economy: Facts, Empirical Findings and Some Mysteries', Centre for Tax System Integrity, Research School of Social Sciences, Australian National University, Working Paper no. 19.

Schneider, F. and Bajada, C. (2003), 'The Size and Development of the Shadow Economies in the Asia-Pacific', Johannes Kepler Universität Linz, Institut für Volkswirtschaftslehre, Working Paper No. 0301.

Schoepfle, G.K. et al. (1992), *The Underground Economy in the United States*, US Department of Labor, Occasional Paper No. 2.

Schuetze, H.J. (2000), 'Taxes, economic conditions and recent trends in male self-employment: A Canada-US comparison', *Labour Economics*, Vol. 7, pp. 507-44.

Schuetze, H.J. (2002), 'Profiles of Tax Noncompliance Among the Self-Employed in Canada, 1969-1992', *Canadian Public Policy*, Vol. XXVIII, No. 2.

Shiller, R.J. (2003), *The New Financial Order: Risk in the 21st Century*, Princeton University Press, Princeton.

Smith, P.M. (1994), 'Assessing the Size of the Underground Economy: The Statistics Canada Perspective', *Canadian Economic Observer*, April. Statistics Canada catalogue 11-010.

Smith, R.S, (2002), 'The Underground Economy: Guidance for Policy Makers?', *Canadian Tax Journal*, Vol. 50(5), pp. 1655-61.

Spiro, P.S. (1993), 'Evidence of a Post-GST Increase in the Underground Economy', *Canadian Tax Journal*, Vol. 41, pp. 247-58.

Spiro, P.S. (1994a), 'The Underground Economy: Toward a More Balanced View of Alternative Methodologies', *Canadian Business Economics*, summer issue.

Spiro, P.S. (1994b), 'Estimating the Underground Economy: A Critical Evaluation of the Monetary Approach', *Canadian Tax Journal*, Vol. 42(4), pp. 1059-81.

Spiro, P.S. (1996), 'Monetary Estimates of the Underground Economy: A Critical Evaluation', *Canadian Journal of Economics*, Vol. 29, pp. 171-75.

Spiro, P.S. (1997), 'Taxes, Deficits and the Underground Economy', in *The Underground Economy: Global Evidence of its Size and Impact*, O. Lippert and M. Walker (eds), The Fraser Institute, Vancouver.

Stabile, M. (2004), 'Payroll Taxes and the Decision to be Self-Employed', *International Tax and Public Finance*, Vol. 11(1) January, pp. 31-53.

Tanzi, V. and Schuknecht, L. (1995), 'The Growth of Government and the Reform of the State in Industrial Countries', International Monetary Fund Working Paper no. 95/130.

Widmalm, F. (2001), 'Tax Structure and Growth: Are some taxes better than others?', *Public Choice*, Vol. 107, pp. 199-219.

Chapter 11

Tax Noncompliance in the United States: Measurement and Recent Enforcement Initiatives[*]

Kim M. Bloomquist, Alan H. Plumley and Eric J. Toder

Introduction

For more than four decades, the US Internal Revenue Service (IRS) has conducted research into the causes and major sources of tax noncompliance. Beginning in Tax Year (TY) 1963, the IRS launched a series of random taxpayer audits known as the Taxpayer Compliance Measurement Program (TCMP). The TCMP had two purposes: to provide the necessary data to develop the discriminant function (DIF) formulas, which use a mathematical technique to identify tax returns likely to have significant understatement of tax, and to provide estimates of what became known as the 'tax gap'; i.e., the difference between taxpayers' true tax liability and the amount that is paid voluntarily and timely.[1]

Over the next 25 years, IRS conducted studies approximately every three years.[2] IRS shelved the TCMP in 1991 due to concerns that the intense line-by-line audits of randomly selected tax returns (sometimes referred to as 'audits from hell') posed an unacceptable burden, both in terms of time and money, on many otherwise compliant taxpayers. A few years later the IRS reversed course and proposed an expanded version of the TCMP sample from 50,000 to 150,000 audits, combining the previous surveys of both individuals and corporations. A larger sample would facilitate identification of unique taxpayer 'market segments' and enable compliance treatment programs to be designed for each group. However, when the plan was unveiled in 1994, a new Congress decided to eliminate all funding for the program.

But this was only the beginning of challenging times for the IRS. A series of highly publicized Congressional hearings on the alleged abuses of taxpayers by collection agents was held in 1997-98. Although many of the cases presented in these hearings were later discredited, both Congress and President Clinton agreed to a massive agency-wide restructuring that emphasized improved delivery of customer services and imposed new restrictions on traditional enforcement actions (e.g., placing liens on taxpayers' primary residences). Tight budgetary restraints on annual agency appropriations precluded hiring of new staff. Therefore, expansion of the customer service units was accomplished mainly by reassigning employees from existing enforcement-related positions. This caused the number of Field Compliance personnel to decline significantly from 29,730 full-time positions in fiscal year (FY) 1992 to 21,421 in FY 2002, a drop of 28 percent (Rossotti, 2002, pg. 13). During this same time, the number of individual tax returns filed grew from 113.8 million to 129.4 million, an increase of nearly 14 percent.[3]

The combination of a growing IRS workload and shrinking enforcement staff led to a dramatic drop in enforcement activity in the late 1990s. Seizures of assets dropped 97 percent from 11,000 in 1995 to just 364 in 2002. Between 1998 and 2002, the number of liens fell 38 percent, levies plunged 75 percent, and the audit rate declined from 1.67 percent in FY 1996 to 0.50 percent in FY 2000, though this rate has remained approximately steady since 2000.[4] In his final report to the new IRS Oversight Board, outgoing Commissioner Rossotti cited the improvements in providing taxpayer services made during his five years in office, but remarked that the declining trend in enforcement activity meant that the IRS was 'winning the battle, but losing the war'. Specifically, Rossotti outlined the following critical compliance problems at the end of 2002:

- 60 percent of identified tax debts are not pursued
- 75 percent of taxpayers who do not file a tax return are not pursued
- 79 percent of identified taxpayers who use abusive devices (e.g., offshore accounts and abusive tax shelters) to evade tax are not pursued
- 56 percent of identified taxpayers with incomes of $100,000 or more and underreported tax are not pursued
- 78 percent of cases identified through document matching (10.4 million taxpayers) with estimated underreported tax of $6.960 billion are not pursued.[5]

In order to reduce these enforcement gaps by FY 2010, Rossotti recommended hiring an additional 17,000 full-time IRS staff (a 17.4 percent increase) and raising overall productivity by three percent a year, primarily through the modernization of obsolete data processing systems. However, the Rossotti report hinted even this might fall short of the resources needed to address the growing compliance workload because it assumed IRS productivity would significantly exceed private financial sector productivity, which in its best decade (the 1990s) rose only 2.3 percent per year.

Some observers have suggested that the steep decline in the level of tax enforcement, along with news stories about a resurgence of overt tax protester activity[6] and widespread use of corporate tax avoidance schemes,[7] has encouraged more evasion. Public opinion polls conducted by RoperASW for the IRS Oversight Board show an increase in the number of Americans who say it is acceptable to cheat on their taxes, from 11 percent in 1999 to 17 percent in 2003. Mark W. Everson, who succeeded Charles O. Rossotti as IRS Commissioner in May 2003, has linked the deterioration in taxpayer attitudes to the agency's 'single-minded' focus on customer service in the late 1990s and the diversion of resources from exam and collection activities. Commissioner Everson has indicated one of his main goals is to 're-center' the IRS to ensure a more balanced approach to carrying out the agency's dual missions of taxpayer service and enforcement.[8] Recently, the IRS has launched several new measurement and enforcement programs in order to meet the challenge of growing tax noncompliance. This chapter reviews past and present efforts to measure the size and scope of US tax noncompliance and describes the latest IRS initiatives aimed at improving compliance.

In the next section, we examine the subject of noncompliance measurement. First, we begin by introducing some basic terms and concepts. This is followed by a brief review of factors contributing to individual taxpayer noncompliance, including both intentional and unintentional forms of behavior. Next, we present historical TCMP data on individual compliance trends. We then discuss our current state of knowledge of the size and scope of noncompliance activity in the US To aid this discussion we present the Tax Gap Map, a visual tool for conveying detailed compliance data in a format accessible to a non-technical audience. Finally, we give a brief overview of the National Research Program (NRP), the IRS's latest initiative for measuring noncompliance with the Federal income tax.

Following the discussion of measurement issues, we provide a summary of several recent IRS initiatives undertaken to reduce noncompliance in specific areas, such as questionable tax shelters that are aggressively marketed to wealthy individuals and the growing use of off-shore tax havens by US corporations to reduce or eliminate taxable domestic profits. Other programs include: (1) the Off-Shore Voluntary Compliance Initiative (OVCI), an investigation into the use by individuals of credit cards issued by banks in off-shore tax havens, (2) pre-certification of claimants of the Earned Income Tax Credit (EITC), which has a known high level of noncompliance and (3) development of an automated process for matching tax returns of so-called pass-through entities, such as partnerships and small corporations. The final section summarizes the chapter and indicates several topics, such as modernization of information systems and commitment to staff enforcement functions adequately, the IRS believes are key elements of a strategy to meet the growing challenge of tax noncompliance.

The Size and Scope of Tax Noncompliance in the US

Concepts and Definitions

The federal income tax operates on a self-assessment basis. That is, taxpayers are responsible for determining their own tax liabilities, rather than have the government tell them how much tax they owe (although taxpayers do have the option of allowing the IRS to calculate their tax liability for them). The success of such a system, obviously, depends on the willingness of taxpayers to file tax returns when required to do so, and to report their tax liability accurately and to pay on time. Although the Internal Revenue Code includes many provisions intended to make sure that most people comply with their tax obligations (e.g., information reporting and withholding, as well as various penalties and enforcement powers), it is still certain that government revenues would be significantly lower if the majority of people and businesses did not fulfill their obligations voluntarily.

The Internal Revenue Code places three basic obligations on taxpayers. Generally, taxpayers are required to: (1) *file* annual tax returns, on which they (2) *report* the correct amount of tax that they owe, and (3) *pay* their tax on a timely, pay-as-you-go, basis. Tax noncompliance can therefore be categorized into three corresponding categories: *nonfiling*, *underreporting*, and *underpayment*. The total dollar value of noncompliance (for a given tax year) is called the *gross tax gap*; this is the amount of tax that is owed but is not paid voluntarily and timely. Although a taxpayer can be noncompliant in just one of these categories, some noncompliance could involve more than one category (e.g., someone who does not file a required return could have a tax liability that should have been reported, and might not have been fully prepaid). For expositional simplicity, however, we generally classify the tax consequences of noncompliance according to the first of the three basic obligations that was unmet. The three components of the tax gap can therefore be defined as follows:

- The *nonfiling gap* is the tax that is owed but is not paid voluntarily and timely by those who fail to file required returns by their due date (e.g., April 15th for most individual taxpayers). Note that by this definition, the nonfiling gap is net of any tax paid by or on behalf of these taxpayers before the due date of the return (e.g., through withholding);
- The *underreporting gap* is the amount of tax that is owed but not paid voluntarily and timely by those who file their returns timely, but do not fully report their tax obligations – whether intentionally or unintentionally; and
- The *underpayment gap* is the amount of tax that is reported on timely-filed returns, but is not paid voluntarily and timely.

Most of the gross tax gap is not detected by IRS (due to limited enforcement resources), and is therefore never assessed or paid. However, some of it is paid late – either through IRS enforcement efforts, or through late payments that precede an IRS inquiry. The portion of the gross tax gap that is not eventually collected is called the *net tax gap*.

Several important compliance measures are expressed as percentages. These can be defined as measures of voluntary compliance or as the complement – measures of noncompliance. Like the tax gap, these measures cannot be observed; they must be estimated. The *Noncompliance Rate (NCR)* is the gross tax gap expressed as a percentage of the corresponding true tax liability. It is the percentage of the overall tax obligation that is not paid voluntarily and timely, and reflects nonfiling, underreporting, and underpayment. The *Voluntary Compliance Rate (VCR)* is just 100 minus the NCR. These measures can be defined algebraically as:

L $=$ Total true tax liability; the tax burden imposed by the tax laws

V $=$ The amount of tax that is paid voluntarily and timely

G $=$ The gross tax gap $= L - V$

NCR $=$ $\dfrac{G}{L} \times 100$

VCR $=$ $\dfrac{V}{L} \times 100 = \dfrac{L - G}{L} \times 100 = 100 - NCR$

Our best estimates of noncompliance relate to the individual income tax. This tax represents the largest share of all federal tax receipts, is the most visible, and accounts for the largest share of the $80.9 billion gross tax gap in TY 1988. Figure 1 below displays the components of the individual income tax gap for TY 1988, the most recent survey-based measure available.

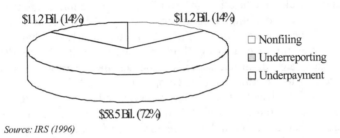

$11.2 Bil. (14%) $11.2 Bil. (14%)

☐ Nonfiling
☐ Underreporting
☐ Underpayment

$58.5 Bil. (72%)

Source: IRS (1996)

Figure 1   Components of the gross tax gap in TY1988 (billions of 1988 US dollars)

Figure 1 shows that underreporting noncompliance accounts for the largest share (72 percent) of the gross tax gap. Of the $58.5 billion in underreported tax, an estimated $47.1 billion was due to underreported income and $11.3 billion is from overstated offsets, such as deductions to income and tax credits. The remaining $200 million is the amount related to net 'math errors' taxpayers made on their returns.

Enforcement programs including taxpayer audits, automated document matching, the Substitute for Return (SFR) program[9] and field collection activities reduced the gross tax gap by another $16.7 billion in TY 1988 bringing the net tax gap to $64.2 billion (IRS, 1996). Thus, only about 20 percent of the individual tax gap is eventually collected.

Determinants of Tax Noncompliance

While much of the theoretical literature on tax evasion focuses on intentional behavior, the term tax noncompliance as used in this chapter includes behavior that is both intentional and unintentional. As regards the former, a review article by Andreoni, Erard and Feinstein (1998) unambiguously concludes that 'noncompliance is discouraged by a high risk of detection'. They cite numerous studies that support the conclusion that taxpayers' willingness to report income (and tax) is greater when faced with a high audit rate or when the source of income is subject to information reporting and withholding. On the other hand, the same authors find little agreement in the literature for a correlation (either positive or negative) between the propensity to evade and either marginal tax rates or income.[10]

The causes of inadvertent or unintentional noncompliance are even less clear. However, the following factors have been cited as contributing to the frequency of taxpayer errors: growing tax law complexity, the burden of obtaining required documentation or filing supporting worksheets, carelessness, language barriers and a lack of education. Although only anecdotal evidence links these factors to observed noncompliance, a recent study of low-income taxpayers who claimed the Earned Income Tax Credit (EITC) found nearly one-half of overclaims were due to claiming a qualifying child improperly. In 2002, the IRS' National Taxpayer Advocate identified seven of the 22 most serious problems facing taxpayers related to the administrative complexity of the EITC (see IRS, 2002a).

In the last decade, the US has experienced a 'perfect storm' of falling audit rates, reduced transaction visibility and increasing complexity, all of which would suggest that tax noncompliance generally, and tax evasion specifically, may be on the rise. Unfortunately, the combined impact of these trends is not known due to the absence, until recently, of an active program of random taxpayer audits (more on this later). While operational audit rates have stopped falling, they remain at historically low levels. The share of taxpayer adjusted gross income (AGI) subject to matching against third-party information reports has also declined in recent years from 88 percent in TY 1990 and to about 82 percent in TY 2000 (Bloomquist, 2003). TCMP studies have consistently found lower reporting compliance for less visible sources of income (IRS, 1988; IRS, 1996).

Perhaps a more immediate concern to millions of taxpayers is a significant increase in complexity that is about to occur due to the Alternative Minimum Tax (AMT). In 1970, in response to a Treasury study that showed that 155 taxpayers with income over $200,000 paid no income tax, Congress imposed a minimum tax on preference income. The minimum tax was in addition to the regular income tax paid by taxpayers. Congress first imposed an AMT in the 1978 Revenue Act in order to prevent certain high-income individuals with capital gains income from paying little or no income tax. The AMT was expanded significantly in the 1986 Tax Reform Act, with many additional preference items added to the base.

The AMT is a parallel tax system that requires taxpayers to calculate their income tax liability two ways if their income and deductions exceed certain thresholds. For most of its existence the AMT has applied only to a small number of households. However, because the AMT is not indexed for inflation, it is projected that 33 million taxpayers – about one-fourth of all taxpayers – will be subject to the AMT by the year 2010. In fact, several experts have noted that by TY 2008, under current law, it would be less costly (in terms of revenue) to repeal the regular income tax than to repeal the AMT (Burman, Gale and Rohaly, 2003).

The IRS' National Taxpayer Advocate has repeatedly flagged the AMT as one of the most difficult and complex tax provisions to comply with and administer. Not only does the AMT require taxpayers to calculate their tax liability two ways, but many must also keep two separate sets of books because of the deferral preferences – the AMT rules on the timing of income recognition and deductions that differ from regular income tax rules. Moreover, the AMT applies to many taxpayers because of two AMT preference items – exemptions for dependents and the deduction of state and local income taxes. These provisions are widely used by middle-income taxpayers and are not the types of 'tax loopholes' that the minimum tax was originally meant to capture. For the 33 million taxpayers for whom it soon will become a reality under current law, the AMT likely will create unwanted confusion and complexity that could further erode the public's sense of fairness in the tax system and produce more noncompliance.

Tax Noncompliance Trends

Noncompliance rates (NCRs) for US individual taxpayers exhibited little apparent improvement or deterioration based on TCMP surveys conducted between 1973 and 1988. Table 1 shows that the overall NCR exhibited very little change from TY 1973 to TY 1988, although it did rise and fall somewhat in the intervening years. The gross tax gap[11] increased by an amount roughly in line with the growth in number of aggregate tax receipts during this period, from $22.7 billion in 1973 to $80.9 billion in 1988.

The gross tax gap estimate for all Federal taxes including individual and corporation income, employment, estate and excise taxes was estimated to be $147.8 billion in TY 1988, resulting in an NCR of 15.4 percent. The IRS recently projected these gross tax gap estimates to TY 2001, yielding a combined gross tax gap estimate of $310.6 billion and an NCR of 14.9 percent. Except for a few items, this projection of the tax gap assumes constant compliance percentages for each major component of the tax gap since the most recent compliance data were compiled in the 1980s.

The US Tax Gap: What We Know and Don't Know

Since the last broad-based compliance study was completed for TY1988, the IRS has had little new data at its disposal to determine recent noncompliance trends. As mentioned previously, the latest tax gap estimate for TY 2001 is projected mainly using noncompliance percentages from the 1988 (or earlier) TCMP surveys. Recently, in an effort to inform policy makers and others interested in the status of tax compliance research, the IRS Office of Research developed the Tax Gap Map shown in Figure 2. The Tax Gap Map is a useful visual aid for conveying the structural composition of the tax gap, the relative contribution of different components and the IRS' level of confidence in the various estimates. A brief explanation of the major features of the Tax Gap Map is given below.

Table 1   Individual income tax gap and noncompliance rates, selected tax years (US dollars in billions)

Tax Year	Gross Tax Gap	Noncompliance Rate (%)
1973	$22.7	17.4
1976	$33.7	19.3
1979	$53.2	20.2
1982	$59.1	18.2
1985	$70.4	18.8
1988	$80.9	17.5

Source: IRS (1990) for the years 1973, 1986, 1979 and 1982; IRS (1996) for the years 1985 and 1988

Figure 2 shows total tax liability in TY 2001 was estimated to be $2,078.0 billion and tax paid voluntarily and timely was $1,767.4 billion, which represents a gross tax gap of $310.6 billion and a NCR of 14.9 percent. Enforced and other late payments of TY 2001 tax liabilities already received and likely to be collected in future years were estimated at $55.4 billion, leaving a net tax gap of $255.2 billion. The gross tax gap amount is divided into the three primary categories of nonfiling, underreporting, and underpayment, with underreporting accounting for the largest share of the gross tax gap at $248.8 billion (80.1 percent).

As Figure 2 shows, not all components of the tax gap are estimated with the same level of confidence. Payment noncompliance has the highest accuracy because it is based on actual amounts reported and paid by taxpayers. The amount of payment noncompliance is simply the difference between what taxpayers say they owe and what they remit by the due date. This amount was $31.7 billion in TY 2001, of which 61 percent was due to the individual income tax.

Nonfiling projections for individual taxpayers are based on the TY 1988 Nonfiler TCMP study (see IRS, 1996). This study had two segments: (1) a sample of apparent nonfilers who were attempted to be located, and from whom delinquent returns were attempted to be secured, if applicable; and (2) a sub-sample of the secured delinquent returns that was subjected to the same line-by-line audits as the timely-filed returns examined in the TY 1988 Filer TCMP. These two segments account for the probability that an individual with particular observed characteristics would be located, so that the examined returns could be made to represent all nonfilers – whether locatable or not. Projections for nonfiling by individual taxpayers in TY 2001 assume a growth rate based on the increase in reported tax liability and a constant relationship between the TY 1988 nonfiling and underreporting gaps.

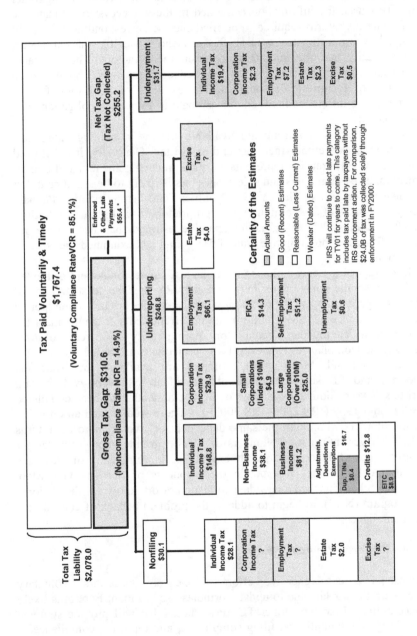

Figure 2 Tax gap map for tax year 2001 (in $billions)

Estate tax[12] nonfiling is based on two external surveys administered by the Institute for Social Research at the University of Michigan designed to gather data on the health status, retirement behavior and changes in wealth among older Americans. IRS used the information contained in these surveys to estimate the number of estate tax returns required to be filed and the corresponding amount of tax liability.[13] These estimates control for household wealth, marital status, individual mortality and the interaction between these factors. The estimated number of estate tax returns and the tax reported on them were obtained from IRS's Statistics of Income (SOI) samples. The estimate of $2 billion for the nonfiling gap is the difference between our estimate of estate tax obligations and the actual behavior.

No estimates of nonfiling are available for the remaining categories: corporation income tax, employment tax and excise tax. Generally, it is believed that nonfiling by corporations represents a small understatement. Nonfiling of employment taxes by employers and sole proprietors is likely to be significant, but no comprehensive data exist. The TY 1988 Nonfiler TCMP study estimated unpaid self-employment taxes of $2.8 billion by sole proprietors ($4.2 billion in inflation-adjusted 2001 dollars). However, no comparable estimate has been made for employer nonfiling and no definitive study of any kind has examined the issue of excise tax[14] nonfiling.

Underreporting noncompliance is the largest single component of the tax gap and it is also the category about which the IRS has the least amount of confidence as Figure 2 shows. The two largest sub-categories are tax on unreported individual business income ($81.2 billion) and underreported self-employment tax ($51.2 billion), which together account for approximately 53 percent of total underreporting noncompliance. However, these projections are based on data that are over 15 years old. More recent estimates are available for estate tax underreporting and for sub-populations of individual taxpayers with certain characteristics. Two random audit surveys of EITC claimants have been completed for TYs 1997 and 1999 (IRS 2000; IRS 2002b).[15] These studies, and an on-going investigation of filers who claim the same dependent on two or more tax returns (Duplicate Taxpayer Information Numbers or TINs), provide good estimates for these specific types of noncompliance although those more recent estimates have not allowed updates to the corresponding components of the Tax Gap Map. Recently, the IRS has launched a new data collection effort, known as the National Research Program (NRP), to begin to address the problem of lack of current data on tax noncompliance.

The National Research Program (NRP)

NRP represents a comprehensive effort to measure taxpayers' voluntary compliance with the tax law and to update formulas used to identify returns likely to be noncompliant. Like the former TCMP studies, NRP will provide strategic measures of payment compliance, filing compliance, and reporting compliance. It will aid IRS in its pursuit of fairness and efficiency in tax compliance administration. The first phase of the reporting compliance portion of NRP is data collection and compliance measurement for the individual income tax. It involves an analysis of a random sample of about 49,000 income tax returns, comparable in size to past TCMP surveys. Unlike the TCMP, which required a line-by-line audit of selected taxpayers, the IRS classified the NRP sample of returns into different groups to receive varying levels of attention. While a small number of taxpayers (under 3,000) will be subject to a line-by-line examination (the so-called 'calibration audits'), many more taxpayers in the NRP sample will have their income validated entirely through the use of information reporting documents and will not be aware they were part of the NRP sample. Others will be handled through a correspondence audit of selected issues. However, NRP also oversamples on sole proprietors in order to better understand nonreporting behavior among this group of taxpayers. The examinations began in fiscal year (FY) 2003, and continued through FY 2004. It is anticipated that findings from NRP will be incorporated into Examination return selection criteria by FY 2006.

NRP has the following four major objectives:

1. Improve IRS's ability to detect noncompliance and to develop appropriate cost-effective treatments for prevention and early intervention.

2. Update deteriorating workload selection formulas (e.g., DIF score technology). In recent years, the percentage of individual return audits closed with no tax change rose from 13 percent in FY 1997, to nearly 19 percent in FY 2002.[16] The increased 'no change' rate means the IRS now devotes more resources to unproductive examinations and that compliant taxpayers are being burdened unnecessarily.

3. Provide IRS with results to develop customer-focused programs. The study will collect data to provide insight into the causes of reporting errors and how to improve customer service. If examinations turn up systemic compliance errors on particular items for otherwise compliant taxpayers, the IRS may be able to address the source of these errors through redesigned forms, better communications, improved taxpayer education, or perhaps through recommendations for legislative change.

4. Measure compliance. The study will provide data to update IRS estimates of the tax gap. Reporting noncompliance among individuals is the largest contributor to the tax gap. Misreporting of individual income tax is believed to account for over 45 percent of the total estimated $310.6 billion tax gap for TY 2001.

The total cost related to the first phase of NRP, from planning and design through implementation of examinations, is an estimated $120 million. The largest single cost component is Examination staff resources. For FYs 2003 and 2004, the IRS used about 1,200 full-time equivalents (FTEs) from its Small Business/Self Employed operating division to perform the face-to-face NRP examinations. These resources cost an estimated $90.1 million.

While these costs are not insignificant, the bulk of them would have been spent in a similar way regardless of whether the IRS implemented the NRP study. The largest costs – those associated with examining returns – would remain, as IRS examiners simply would have focused on other returns. The marginal costs of this study – those that the IRS incurred by implementing the NRP – include those associated with the NRP program office, IRS's Detroit Computing Center, and special field training for NRP examinations. These costs total an estimated $24.5 million.

A final, but equally important, aspect of the NRP program costs are the opportunity costs associated with the study. The IRS is forgoing revenues that would have been collected as a result of operational examinations by diverting resources to NRP examinations. In previous reporting compliance studies, the opportunity costs vastly outweighed the direct costs of the study. Approximately half of the cases in previous studies resulted in no change to the reported tax due to the random nature of the research sample. NRP has tried to reduce the lost revenue associated with the study. While the NRP sample is a random one, case-building (which provides extra taxpayer information that might allow the IRS to determine compliance) and classification processes eliminated some of the cases from face-to-face audits. Approximately 3,000 returns in the sample were 'accepted as filed', and required no work on the part of IRS examiners. The long interval between the current NRP study and the last TCMP reporting compliance study (and the resultant increase in the no-change rate) will mitigate the opportunity costs of NRP to some extent. To be sure, the benefits of the reporting compliance information this study will produce should more than offset its costs.

Planning for the next NRP study began, even as the IRS is conducted the individual income tax return reporting compliance study. There are several other areas where the IRS needs to be concerned about reporting compliance. It has been nearly 20 years since the IRS examined reporting compliance for most businesses, and the populations of business returns have grown dramatically in these years. The next NRP study will therefore focus on flow-through entities (partnerships and Subchapter S corporations). Current research on flow-through entities has revealed some extremely intricate relationships among partnership returns, corporate returns, and individual returns. Some of these linkages can be associated with tax evasion strategies. Examining partnership returns alone, therefore, may not yield sufficient data to address the compliance questions at hand. In fact, the best approach may be to combine all related returns as a single economic entity and consider the accuracy of all returns within the economic entity. Future studies may focus on employment taxes, which raise equally vexing questions, such as distinguishing between employees and independent contractors. As the Tax Gap Map in Figure 2 illustrates, underreporting of employment taxes is the second largest single source of noncompliance and merits renewed research attention.

Although the next NRP study is still in the planning stage, IRS is also focusing its attention on developing strategies to deal with emerging noncompliance issues. It is to this topic we turn next.

Recent IRS Initiatives to Reduce Noncompliance

In this section, we describe several recent IRS programs aimed at combating emerging trends in tax noncompliance. These efforts form part of an overall strategy under Commissioner Mark Everson to strengthen the enforcement side of the IRS and to stem a growing perception among taxpayers that tax evasion has few consequences. Many of these programs target higher-income individuals whose number has increased approximately 220 percent between FY 1991 and FY 2001.[17] In FY 2002, IRS increased audits of taxpayers who made more than $100,000 per year more than 22 percent over the previous year. Readers interested in following developments on IRS compliance programs should check the IRS Newsroom website.[18] The site is updated daily.

Abusive Offshore Financial Transactions

Abusive offshore financial transactions include various arrangements designed to circumvent tax laws or evade taxes. Two recent IRS programs aimed at curbing specific types of abusive transactions are the Off-Shore Voluntary Compliance Initiative (OVCI) and Offshore Credit Card Program (OCCP).

The OVCI began in January 2003 and taxpayers were given until April 15, 2003 to respond. Under the OVCI, taxpayers who engaged in illegal offshore financial arrangements to hide their income could come forward and avoid civil fraud and information return penalties, but would still be required to pay back taxes, interest and applicable penalties. The goal of the program was to identify taxpayers engaged in abusive offshore activities and understand how various schemes were carried out. In particular, the IRS is focusing on four areas: who introduced the taxpayer to offshore schemes, how assets are sent offshore, how assets are controlled and how assets are repatriated. In the request to participate, the taxpayer had to provide full details on those who promoted or solicited the offshore financial arrangement.

By early 2004, the IRS had received more than 1,300 taxpayer applicants to OVCI and the initiative yielded more than $170 million in taxes, interest and penalties. Preliminary analysis of reported schemes indicates that a wide variety of financial arrangements were used to avoid US taxes, including foreign entities, foreign bank accounts, foreign trusts, and credit cards. Most transactions were very complex and involved professional individuals with high incomes and a high net worth. Perhaps the most promising result of OVCI was the identification of nearly 500 scheme promoters, nearly half of whom were previously unknown to IRS. Investigation of these promoters has identified 20,000 individuals, in addition to the 1,300 self-reported taxpayers, who may have engaged in illegal offshore tax avoidance schemes. The IRS recently has shared the names of these individuals with state tax agencies as part of a coordinated multi-governmental effort to curb tax evasion.[19]

A related, but separate component of the offshore compliance effort is the OCCP. Since October 2000, the IRS has issued a series of summonses to a variety of financial and commercial businesses to obtain information on residents who held credit, debit or other payment cards issued by offshore banks. Investigators have been using records from these so-called 'John Doe' summonses to trace the identities of people whose use of these payment cards may be related to hiding taxable income.

The results of OCCP have also been promising. As of July 2003, OCCP had produced the following results:

- About 2,800 tax returns were either under audit or had been completed. That number is expected to grow.
- More than $3 million in taxes had been assessed. But, taxes had not yet been assessed on the vast majority of taxpayers under investigation. Therefore, the amount assessed is also expected to increase.
- Dozens of cases have already been referred to Criminal Investigation for possible action.

The IRS will continue to work the new information provided by the OVCI and OCCP programs. A key part of this process is the pursuit of those individuals who engage in promoting these illegal tax avoidance schemes.

Promoters of Abusive Tax Shelters

The IRS is engaged in a broad effort to understand and combat the recent proliferation of abusive tax sheltering activity. It is doing so at a variety of levels. For example, the IRS's Large and Mid-Size Business Division (LMSB) recently reported having 118 promoter cases open for investigation. In addition, the Small Business/Self Employed Division (SB/SE) had 41 technical tax shelter promoter investigations open.[20]

Within LMSB, the IRS established the Office of Tax Shelter Analysis (OTSA) in February 2000. OTSA plans, centralizes and coordinates LMSB's tax shelter operations and collects, analyzes and distributes within the IRS information about potentially abusive tax shelter activity involving corporations. OTSA also maintains a Tax Shelter Hotline to which interested persons can submit information on abusive transactions by phone, e-mail, letter or fax.

The SB/SE Division also established a Lead Development Center (LDC) in order to identify promoters of illegal tax shelters at the 'retail' level. The LDC has three purposes:

- Centralize the receipt and development of leads on promoters of abusive tax schemes.
- Authorize and monitor on a national level abusive tax promoter investigations assigned to field personnel.
- Promote and coordinate parallel investigations with the IRS Criminal Investigation Division.

Focusing on tax scheme promoters has several advantages. Promoters are required to maintain investor lists that identify taxpayers who participate in or purchase tax shelters that are 'reportable' or 'listed' transactions under IRS rules. Such shelters can be and sometimes are abusive. By auditing the promoters and obtaining investor lists and following up with audits of those investors, IRS can deter the promotion of as well as demand for such products.

More information about abusive tax shelters and related transactions can be found on the IRS website.[21]

Flow-Through Entity Document Matching Program[22]

Partnerships, S corporations, trusts, and estates are collectively known as flow-through entities because they do not pay income tax directly, but instead pass net income or loss through to their partners, shareholders, and beneficiaries. Flow-through entities are required to report their net income or loss to the IRS and to provide IRS and each partner, shareholder, or beneficiary with a Schedule K-1 stating the individual share of net income or loss to be reported. These taxpayers are then responsible for reporting this income or loss on their individual or corporation income tax returns and paying any applicable tax. In TY 2001, over 5 million flow-through entities (not including trusts) reported passing through almost $550 billion in taxable net income to partnerships, shareholders and other beneficiaries. IRS research efforts suggest that 6 to 15 percent of the K-1s attached to flow-through returns are currently being omitted from beneficiary, partner, and shareholder returns. To detect such noncompliance better, IRS began transcribing paper Schedule K-1s for TY 2000.

In 2001, IRS added Schedule K-1 document matching to its Automated Underreporter (AUR) program.[23] It began matching Schedule K-1 data to individual tax returns to identify taxpayers who had underreported flow-through income and had consequently underpaid their taxes. In the first year of the program, IRS issued about 69,000 notices to taxpayers and assessed about $29 million in additional taxes directly attributable to Schedule K-1 underreporting. IRS began notifying taxpayers of potential discrepancies between income reported on the K-1 and individual tax returns in April 2002. However, after receiving complaints that too many notices were being sent to compliant taxpayers, IRS stopped issuing notices in August 2002.

For 2003, IRS adopted a revised set of standards for screening Schedule K-1 cases for review, with the intent of minimizing the number of no-change notices sent. In particular, IRS issues a notice to the taxpayer if K-1 income information is completely missing from a return. IRS is also trying to educate taxpayers and practitioners via news releases and webcasts about the proper way of reporting flow-through income, carryover losses, and deductions in order to reduce the need to send notices to compliant taxpayers about apparent mismatches. Finally, IRS is changing certain forms and schedules in order to make reporting compliance easier as well as studying ways to simplify the Schedule K-1 and its instructions for different tax situations.

IRS has used Schedule K-1 data to determine characteristics of potentially noncompliant taxpayer populations. Its preliminary profiling efforts identified over 227,000 business entities with almost $64 billion in Schedule K-1 income for TY

2000 that potentially did not file tax returns. IRS has begun to analyze whether these businesses were required, but failed, to file returns, or whether inaccuracies in Schedule K-1 data produced false nonfiler leads. In addition, IRS has begun to research the effectiveness of using information returns, such as the K-1, to identify business nonfilers.

Unreported Income Discriminant Function (UI-DIF)

As previously indicated, unreported income represents the largest component of the tax gap. IRS has developed a new tool for identifying returns with a high probability of unreported income. The new tool is known as Unreported Income Discriminant Function (UI-DIF).

All individual tax returns are assigned a DIF score the rates the probability of inaccurate information on the return. Under the traditional DIF approach, the dependent variable is predicted tax change. In contrast, the new UI-DIF score rates the likelihood of income being omitted from the return. The IRS has customarily used indirect examination methods to identify unreported income but until now has had no systemic method for selecting the returns at highest risk for unreported income.

UI-DIF gives the IRS the ability to identify returns at high risk for unreported income. Beginning in FY 2003 all returns now receive a UI-DIF score in addition to the traditional DIF score. More information on the development and testing of the UI-DIF methodology can be found in Cyr, Eckhardt, Sandoval and Haldorson (2002) and Asner (2002).

Earned Income Tax Credit (EITC) Certification Program

The EITC is a refundable credit for low-wage taxpayers. Approximately 21.6 million taxpayers claimed more than $37.8 billion in EITC for TY 2002. It is intended as an offset for Social Security taxes and as a means of lifting low-income working families out of poverty. Families with children receive a larger EITC credit than childless individuals or couples and received 98 percent of EITC payments in TY 2000. However, studies consistently have shown a high rate of erroneous payments. A recent study (IRS 2002b) indicated the error rate was between 27 percent and 31.7 percent for TY 1999, resulting in an aggregate overpayment of $8.5 billion to $9.9 billion. The largest single source of error is the determination of eligibility of qualifying children.

In an effort to reduce the rate of overclaims, the IRS launched a new program to certify individuals who claim the EITC starting in the 2004 filing season. The new pilot program will allow the IRS to use an integrated approach to address potential erroneous claims by identifying cases that have the highest likelihood of error before they are accepted for processing and before any EITC benefits are paid. The General Accounting Office (now the Government Accountability Office) has identified EITC as a 'high risk' area for the government because of the high rate of erroneous payments.

For the 2004 filing season, the IRS asked 25,000 EITC claimants to certify when they file that the child(ren) claimed for EITC purposes resided with them for more than half of the year as required by law. In addition, the IRS will expand efforts to reduce erroneous payments to taxpayers who underreport their income or who file using an incorrect filing status. In TY 2004, the IRS will investigate at least 300,000 taxpayers who claim the EITC but failed in the past to report all of their income. These taxpayers may not be eligible because the EITC has an income cap. In addition, approximately 46,000 taxpayers who appear to misrepresent their filing status also will be investigated.

Following the 2004 certification pilot, the IRS will carefully assess the pilot results and performance before deciding on how to proceed with the program. The goal of the certification pilot is to evaluate high-risk EITC claims before they are paid, using a process that is less burdensome on taxpayers and less costly to the government than an audit. In addition, the certification program will enable eligible taxpayers to receive their refunds faster than if their refunds were to be held pending an examination.

Summary and Future Directions

The IRS recently underwent its most significant reorganization in the last half century. The driving motive behind this effort was to improve the agency's ability to deliver reliable and prompt services to the taxpaying public. A related goal was to give taxpayers additional rights and protections when subject to IRS enforcement actions. While these actions did result in improved delivery of customer services and an enhanced public perception of the IRS, they also involved shifting personnel from enforcement-related activities to customer service functions, eroding the agency's ability to enforce the law at a time of growing concern about increasing tax evasion.

Realizing the need to balance customer service with a credible deterrence capacity, the IRS recently has begun rebuilding its enforcement functions. The IRS has initiated a number of related enforcement actions focusing on offshore tax avoidance schemes and high-income individuals. Several innovative programs aimed at improving information on taxpayers' financial transactions (e.g., flow-through entities document matching, UI-DIF) are being incorporated into return selection strategies. On the operational side, IRS Commissioner Mark W. Everson unveiled a plan in January 2004 to close or consolidate a number of back-office functions and use the savings to hire more auditors and collection officers.

Some 16 years have passed since the last TCMP study of taxpayer compliance was performed. The tax gap map (Figure 2) illustrates both the structural outlines of the tax gap and the level of confidence in available estimates. The NRP study will give the IRS information on individual reporting noncompliance to fill in some of the questionable boxes on the tax gap map and enable the agency to modernize its workload selection formulas and improve operational audit efficiency. Future NRP studies of small business taxpayers are now in the planning stages.

These efforts represent only the beginning stages of a long-term effort to prepare the IRS to meet the tax administration challenges in the years ahead. In his final report to the IRS Oversight Board, former Commissioner Charles O. Rossotti emphasized the vital importance of modernizing the Service's information processing systems to improve overall productivity. However, even with these technology-based enhancements, the projected growth in enforcement workload and the rising demand for IRS services also will require a long-term commitment to staff enforcement activities adequately.

Notes

*   The authors would like to thank Lance Asner, Fred Cox, Ed Emblom and Mary-Helen Risler for their review and comments on portions of this chapter.

1.   The tax gap, however, is not synonymous with the 'underground economy' – not even with the tax forgone due to the underground economy. The term 'underground economy' is defined in a variety of ways. Although most definitions would overlap somewhat with the tax gap, some components generally included in the underground economy are not included in IRS tax gap estimates (e.g., tax on income derived from illegal activities), while other components (e.g., erroneously claimed dependent exemptions or filing status) are a part of the tax gap, but do not arise from the underground economy.

2.   Results of the most recent TCMP study were published in 1994 for individuals filing tax returns in tax year 1988. See Christian (1994). The corresponding tax gap estimates were published in 1996. See Internal Revenue Service (1996).

3.   IRS Databook, various issues. See http://www.irs.gov/taxstats/article/0,,id= 102174,00.html for most recent issues.

4.   See Internal Revenue Service (2003a), Table 2, 'Summary of IRS Compliance Activity Individual Income Taxpayers Fiscal Years 1996-2002'.

5.   Rossotti (2002, p. 16).

6.   The New York Times, '400 Anti-Tax Leaders Meet to Plan Campaign', February 19, 2001.

7.   The New York Times, 'Treasury Chief: Tax Evasion Is on the Rise', July 19, 2001.

8.   Washington Post, 'GAO Finds Increase in Tax Evasion', December 19, 2003.

9.   In the SFR program the IRS prepares a tax return for individuals who fail to file a required return using income information from available third-party documents.

10.   However, theory does predict high-income taxpayers evade more (in absolute terms) than middle- or low-income taxpayers.

11.   The gross tax gap figures shown in Table 1 include nonfiling, underreporting and underpayment noncompliance.

12.   Estate tax is levied on the portion of an estate valued in excess of the minimum filing threshold ($675,000 in 2001). Of the 108,112 estate tax returns filed in tax year 2001, 51,841 returns owed net estate taxes of $23.5 billion (unpublished SOI data).

13.   The two surveys are the Asset and Health Dynamics among the Oldest Old (AHEAD) dataset and the Health and Retirement Study (HRS). They provide extensive economic, financial, demographic, and health information about older Americans.

14.   Federal excise taxes encompass many different categories, the largest of which include taxes on sales of motor fuels, cigarettes and other tobacco products and telephone usage.

15. It should be noted, however, that overclaims identified in both the 1997 and 1999 random audit studies of EITC claimants represent only a portion of total EITC noncompliance. Other contributing factors include, among other factors, net 'math errors' and income underreporting.
16. IRS Data Book, various issues.
17. From approximately 3.4 million filers in FY 1991 to 10.9 million filers in FY 2001. See SOI Publication 1304, various issues.
18. See http://www.irs.gov/newsroom/index.html.
19. See The Associated Press, 'IRS Collects $170 Million Hidden Offshore', February 10, 2004.
20. See prepared testimony of IRS Commissioner Mark W. Everson before the Permanent Subcommittee on Investigations, United States Senate, November 20, 2003.
21. See http://www.irs.gov/businesses/corporations/article/0,,id=97384,00.html.
22. This section based on material in US GAO (2003), Appendix I.
23. The AUR program matches information return data, such as Forms W-2 and 1099 and Schedule K-1, with individual tax return data to verify that all income is reported.

References

Andreoni, J., Erard, B. and Feinstein, J. (1998), 'Tax Compliance', *Journal of Economic Literature*, Vol. 36, pp. 818-60.

Asner, L. (2002), 'Testing the UI-DIF Formulas', The IRS Research Bulletin, Publication 1500, pp. 173-185, http://www.irs.gov/pub/irs-soi/uidiffor.pdf.

Bloomquist, K.M. (2003), 'Trends as Changes in Variance: The Case of Tax Noncompliance', The IRS Research Bulletin, Publication 1500, pp. 59-66. http://www.irs.gov/pub/irs-soi/bloomquist.pdf.

Burman, L.E., Gale, W.G. and Rohaly, J. (2003), 'The AMT: Projections and Problems', Tax Notes, July, http://www.brookings.edu/views/articles/gale/20030707.htm.

Christian, C.W. (1994), 'Voluntary Compliance With The Individual Income Tax: Results From the 1988 TCMP Study', *The IRS Research Bulletin*, IRS Publication 1500 (Rev.9-94) (1993/1994), pp. 35-42.

Cyr, D., Eckhardt, T., Sandoval, L.A. and Halldorson, M. (2002), 'Predictors of Unreported Income: Test of Unreported Income (UI) DIF Scores', The IRS Research Bulletin, Publication 1500, pp. 187-219. http://www.irs.gov/pub/irs-soi/puidif2.pdf.

Internal Revenue Service (1990), *Income Tax Compliance Research: Net Tax Gap and Remittance Gap Estimates (Supplement to Publication 7285)*, IRS Publication 1415 (4-90), Washington, D.C.

Internal Revenue Service (1996), *Federal Tax Compliance Research: Individual Income Tax Gap Estimates for 1985, 1988 and 1992*. IRS Publication 1415 (Rev. 4-96), Washington, D.C.

Internal Revenue Service (2000), *Compliance Estimates for Earned Income Tax Credit Claimed on 1997 Returns*, Washington, D.C. September.

Internal Revenue Service (2002a), National Taxpayer Advocate FY 2002 Annual Report to Congress, Washington, D.C. December 31, http://advocate.no.irs.gov/Library/Reports/2002_TAS_report_to_congress.pdf.

Internal Revenue Service (2002b), *Compliance Estimates for Earned Income Tax Credit Claimed on 1999 Returns*, Washington, D.C. February 28, http://www.irs.gov/pub/irs-soi/compeitc.pdf.

Internal Revenue Service (2003a), *Report to Congress: IRS Tax Compliance Activities*, Washington, D.C. July 15, http://www.irs.gov/pub/irs-soi/03congressrpt.pdf.

Internal Revenue Service (2003b), *Data Book 2002*, Publication 55B, Washington, D.C. http://www.irs.gov/pub/irs-soi/02databk.pdf.

Internal Revenue Service (various years), Statistics of Income, Individual Income Tax Returns, Publication 1304, http://www.irs.gov/taxstats/article/0,,id=96586,00.html.

Rossotti, C.O. (2002), *Report to the IRS Oversight Board and Assessment of the IRS and the Tax System*, September, http://www.irsoversightboard.treas.gov/documents/commissioner_report.pdf.

US General Accounting Office (2003), *Internal Revenue Service: Challenges Remain in Combating Abusive Tax Schemes*, GAO-04-104T, Washington, D.C. October, http://www.gao.gov/new.items/d04104t.pdf.

Chapter 12

Tackling the Underground Economy in the UK: A Government's Response[*]

Christopher Bajada

Introduction

When an individual participates in the underground economy and does not pay their fair share of tax, the rest of the community must bear the burden of higher taxes that are needed to fund ongoing government expenditure on public works and services. When there are only a small number of participants engaged in such clandestine activities, the burden of tax collections may be spread thinly on the compliant community. If on the other hand, the number of participants are large and the extent of evasion is significant, the compliant community suffers by having to shoulder a greater burden for funding public goods and services, from which ultimately both the honest and dishonest individuals derive a benefit.

The extent of participation and the range of activities taking place in the underground economy vary considerably. At one end of the spectrum, participation includes illegal immigration, drug trafficking, money laundering and welfare benefit fraud. At the other end, participation includes non-disclosure of part-time work and the failure to report all or part-of any cash payments received by businesses. Although both ends of the spectrum are undesirable from an economic and social point of view, the severity of each is notably different and thus the distribution of resources that go towards tackling these activities should also be correspondingly different. However, although there is some agreement on this, it is far from being a consensus view. For some people, the underground economy allows for the provision of goods and services that may not otherwise be available in the legitimate economy, or provides for the purchase of cheaper products, which for those on low income is a significant benefit. For these people such activities may be acceptable. It is the more serious offences however that they reject.

Although the underground economy needs to be addressed across the board spectrum of activities, community support for tackling this problem is often strengthened by tackling first the more serious crimes and demonstrating success. Ultimately the direct benefits from these enforcement activities may not only change community perceptions about the benefits from these activities, but also on the chances of being detected.

No doubt the underground economy in the United Kingdom shares many similar characteristics to the underground economies of the other developed nations. It poses a threat not only to tax revenue and funding of public works and services but also to tax morale in general. In 1999 the Chancellor of the Exchequer commissioned Lord Grabiner QC to investigate and recommend ways to deal with illicit economic activities in the United Kingdom. This chapter provides an overview of these recommendations and how the government has since responded to each of these. This chapter begins with a brief overview of the consequences of an underground economy, highlighting in particular some examples pertaining to the UK case. This discussion is followed by a review of each of the recommendations in the Grabiner Report, followed by a discussion of the government's response and the outcomes achieved to date. We will see from this discussion that much effort has been made to reduce these activities and the preliminary evidence seems to suggest that some positive progress on tackling the UK underground economy is being made.

The Underground Economy and its Consequences

There are many consequences from a large and growing underground economy. These include: loss of opportunities and protection that can come from legitimate employment; limited job security; the absence of bargaining rights; no employer references and thus limited future legitimate job opportunities; the absence of protection with regards to the minimum wage guarantee and other industrial awards; an inability to build up rights to the State pension; difficulties in obtaining a credit card, mortgage, personal loans, etc; difficulty with raising business finance for investment projects when a substantial component of business income is undeclared; the unfair tax burden shouldered by honest tax payers; and the unfair price competition that often results from underground economic activities.

From this list alone it is clear that the underground economy often serves as the vehicle by which economic agents escape the inspections and regulations of government. There are also a number of adverse social consequences from the presence of these activities that also need careful consideration. Very often it is the economic consequences that are at the forefront of discussion and the social consequences are left by the wayside. The following three examples highlight just a few cases of the adverse social implications that come with underground economic activity.

Tobacco Smuggling

It is estimated that in the UK alone, nearly 120,000 people die of smoking each year (see HMCE, 2001). Whenever there is significant smuggling and sale of smuggled tobacco, the government's policy of increasing excise duty and expenditure on education campaigns to encourage fewer people to smoke, becomes significantly less effective. Smuggling of tobacco also competitively disadvantages legitimate business because they have to compete with cheaper (smuggled) tobacco products. There is also concern that the funds from such activities could support more dangerous criminal activities. So there are many reasons why tackling (say, tobacco) fraud is so important.

Welfare Benefit Fraud

Welfare benefit fraud has been estimated by the Department of Social Security to be anywhere from £2-£4 billion as much as £7 billion in 1999. This fraudulent activity takes on many forms, some less organised than others. The following example demonstrates some of the problems in action faced by the Department of Social Security, in its attempt to stamp out social security fraud.[1]

Case 1 The Department of Social Security suspected a young person of claiming welfare benefits while in full-time employment at a restaurant in the West End of London. This person worked alongside another 30 staff employed in one of a half a dozen establishments owned by a restaurateur. In a cooperative agreement between staff and employer, staff were released at set times of the day to collect their benefit pay, while the employer paid them cash on the understanding that the employees would also receive benefit payments in addition to their income. No tax (PAYE) was paid on their behalf. Cash paid by restaurant customers included an element of VAT but this was never paid to Customs and Excise, which collects this tax. The investigators from the Department of Social Security met up with the restaurateur and challenged him. He presented them some modified bookkeeping software which was specifically designed to satisfy superficial investigation that his books were genuine and that his employees were legal. In the event he was charged only with giving a dishonest answer. He pleaded guilty at the Magistrates Court and was fined only £250.

   In this case all the benefits associated with honest employment were lost to those working at these restaurants, including their redundancy and minimum pay rights, unfair dismissal and sex discrimination rights, etc. In addition, the employees lived in daily fear of being spotted and prosecuted or deported if they were found to be illegal immigrants.

   As we will discuss later in this chapter, this case is a good example of how fraudulent activity may affect a number of government departments – Inland Revenue, Customs and Excise, Department of Social Security, Treasury and the Home Office.

Illegal Immigration

The tragedy of the illegal Chinese cockle pickers at Morecambe Bay is yet another example of some of the consequences an underground economy may bring. On February 5th 2004, 33 illegal Chinese workers headed down the shore of Morecambe Bay, passing signs in English warning them of rising tides and quicksand. After walking for roughly two miles through salt marshes to Warton Sands, the tide rushed in behind them and 19 of the 33 Chinese cockle pickers drowned in the dark as a result. Their deaths generated a sympathetic view from the media. These illegal Chinese workers, presumed taken from their Chinese villages to work in the underground economy for little money, died as a consequence of the exploitation by those engaged in the underground economy.[2] This is another example of those engaged in underground economic activity exploiting other people's misery and offering little respect to workers rights and conditions. A number of these issues will be taken up again later in this chapter.

An Action Plan for Tackling Taxpayer Non-compliance

The United Kingdom introduced a 10 percent VAT in 1973 to replace the Purchase Tax and the Selective Employment Tax. By January 1993 the VAT rate climbed to 15 percent and has since increased again to 17.5 percent.[3] In the early days of its introduction the government collected about 10 percent of its revenue from this tax but since 2000 it has returned the government approximately 21 percent of its total tax revenue.

Has the Change in the Tax Mix Affected the Size of the Underground Economy in the UK?

The various estimates of the underground economy have suggested that illicit economic activities have grown over time. Bhattacharyya (1990) and in Chapter 6 of this book, Bhattacharyya finds that the introduction of the VAT had no long-run effect on reducing participation in the underground economy in the UK. In fact the year after the VAT's introduction the underground economy was estimated at 9.5 percent of GNP, up from an average of 5 percent of GNP during the 1960s. Feige (1981) also reported the underground economy to have grown since the introduction of the VAT. Although subterranean activities declined somewhat after 1974, illicit transactions exceeded those estimated to be taking place prior 1973.

In response to growing concerns of such fraudulent activity, the Chancellor of the Exchequer in 1999 commissioned Lord Grabiner QC to investigate and make recommendations on ways to address the underground economy. The terms of reference required a focus on high risk areas including unregistered businesses, those engaged in self-employed activities and those claiming social security payments while also working surreptitiously in the underground economy. Defining the underground economy to include not only unreported legitimate transactions but also criminal activities, the taskforce headed by Lord Grabiner QC reported the underground economy in the UK to be a major problem worth billion of pounds a year. The remainder of this section provides a summary of the findings of the Grabiner Report (*Report* hereforth).

Incentives to go Legitimate

To promote legitimate work practices, particularly to assist those on low income, the government supports a number of initiatives: (1) the minimum wage; (2) the raised starting point for employees' National Insurance Contributions (NIC) and (3) the Working Families Tax Credit scheme. There is also the New Deal Program and the ONE service giving benefit claimants a personal adviser to help them get back into work sooner. For legitimate businesses the government also offers a range of support that is not available to businesses operating in the underground economy. Assistance is available in the form of Business Links, Small Business Service, local enterprise agencies and other small business support initiatives.

Although the government has in place a number of initiatives to assist low-income earners and those starting up new businesses, the challenge in encouraging people to become legitimate is as much about raising awareness of current opportunities as devising new incentives. Consequently the *Report* recommended that there should be more publicity about people's entitlements. For example, a self-employed person earning low profits needs to only make a £2 payment per week to the NIC rather than the £6.55 per week in the usual circumstances. This self employed person may contemplate participating in the underground economy to raise their disposable income in order to pay their weekly contribution to the NIC scheme so as to be entitled to benefit payments should they have to draw upon them in future.

To assist those who have not been compliant in the past and wish to become so, the *Report* recommended that a confidential telephone advice line be provided to assist in the smooth transition to legitimacy. However the *Report* was against offering a general amnesty. There are clearly a number of problems with implementing a general amnesty: (1) how to treat various degrees of tax evasion. Should they be treated in the same way? Is claiming welfare benefits while working in the underground economy a greater crime than just actively participating in the underground economy? And by how much?; (2) for businesses that have not declared their VAT collection, should they be allowed to keep this given that consumers have paid this tax with the understanding that the government would receive this? and (3) evidence abroad of general amnesties (France, US, Italy and Ireland) appear not to have worked well. These amnesties were perceived as being grossly unfair – a free lunch for those who have not met their tax paying obligations. A general amnesty may also be perceived as one of many to come, encouraging some individuals to continue participating in such illicit activities in anticipation of future amnesties.

On the welfare benefits system, the *Report* found its structure to be outdated. The rules as they stood made it unattractive for anyone receiving welfare assistance to declare that they have found employment. The Housing Benefit scheme for example, would cease to be paid once a claimant finds works. If this person is still able to legitimately claim assistance under the Housing Benefit scheme, they would have to reapply as a low-income earner, in which case they may have to wait several weeks for the payments to recommence. There is no incentive therefore for such individuals to declare employment if they are disadvantaged by the system in this way. Consequently the *Report* made two recommendations not only to increase the flexibility of the benefits system, but to increase the uptake of claimants finding legitimate work: (1) those long-term claimants of Jobseeker's Allowance and Income Support should be given automatic extensions on their payments when they report to have found work; (2) to suspend rather than close the file of claimants receiving welfare assistance so that if the job (which may have been insecure in the first place) falls through, that person is able to resume receipt of welfare assistance without having to start a whole new claim again. This would reduce the uncertainty with taking a new job offer and potentially reduce the incentive to go underground to accommodate such rigidities.

Prevention

Although everyone who works or claims a benefit must have a National Insurance Number, the number itself does not constitute sufficient proof of identity. In fact there are many ways by which the use of the National Insurance number may be abused. The widespread and sophisticated uses of forged documents, particularly birth certificates, are a constant problem for authorities. The *Report* made a recommendation that the issue of birth certificates come under stricter controls. In many instances those seeking a National Insurance Number to claim benefits may work temporarily to obtain this number and then subsequently leave legitimate employment and claim benefits while working in the underground economy. It is the fact that less effort is given to employment-driven applications for National Insurance Numbers that has contributed to a fraudulent use of such numbers. However recently there have been attempts to counteract fraud by forgery. In Balham (south west-London) 'centres of excellence' have been set up to issue National Insurance Numbers. Using appropriate equipment, trained staff assume the necessary security procedures to identify forged documents. Since its inception, these centres have identified a significant number of cases of fraudulent claims by use of forged documents.

Detection

The case for data sharing is an obvious one. An individual or business involved in fraudulent activity is likely to give inconsistent information to various government departments and other relevant private sector institutions. If data sharing is easily available to Inland Revenue or the Department of Social Security, cross-checks can be undertaken to uncover these inconsistencies. However there is a major obstacle to data sharing which could facilitate effective cross-checking of individual or business information. This obstacle is the data protection laws governed by the Data Protection Act 1998 which came into force on 1 March 2000, incorporating the European Directive on data protection. There are also data sharing problems within government departments. Although data is usually shared between departments on a case-by-case basis, where there is suspicion of fraud, Inland Revenue is limited by the Data Protection Act to providing information only when the law specifically allows it to.

Data sharing would be most effective in detecting underground economic activity when data is shared amongst Inland Revenue, HM Excise and Customs and the Department of Social Security. Data sharing is most beneficial when it is carried out routinely and the complete databases are available for each department to scrutinise. The following table identifies the powers to disclose information from each of these three departments.

Table 1   Powers to disclose information

To: From:	Customs and Excise	Inland Revenue	Department of Social Security
Customs and Excise	No (but not needed)	Voluntary (but may be for any relevant purpose)[a]	Voluntary (but may be for any relevant purpose)[e]
Inland Revenue	Voluntary (but may be for any relevant purpose)[a]	A series of measures allowing 'pooling' of data within the Department (but no comprehensive power	Mandatory for NICs[c] and tax credits,[d] otherwise voluntary (fraud and accuracy)[b]
Department of Social Security	Voluntary (fraud and accuracy)[b]	Mandatory for NICs[c] and tax credits;[d] otherwise voluntary (fraud and accuracy)[b]	Yes[f]

Source: Grabiner (2000); (a) Finance Act 1972, s127; (b) Finance Act 1997, s110; (c) Social Security Administration Act 1992, ss121E-121F, and other amendments by Social Security Contributions (Transfer of Functions, etc) Act 1999, s6, Sch 6; (d) Tax Credits Act 1999, s12, Sch 5; (e) Social Security Administration Act 1992, s122; (f) Social Security Act 1998, s3.

From Table 1 it is clear that: (1) information relating to tax credits must be shared with other departments if needed; (2) there are similar provisions for information relating to the administration of National Insurance Numbers and related matters (since these Inland Revenue functions were formally carried out by the Department of Social Security); and (3) each department may, but is not obliged, to disclose tax or benefit information for the purposes of checking the accuracy of records and for investigating fraud.

At the time the *Report* was published, a number of data sharing exercises had been taking place. These included: (1) matching benefit contribution records against details of people starting new work. This is intended to detect people who commence legitimate work while at the same time are in receipt of welfare benefits; (2) checking Department of Social Security benefits data against details from Inland Revenue of people receiving Working Families Tax Credit; (3) a pilot scheme for Inland Revenue to give Department of Social Security information it collects on interest paid on bank/non-bank accounts; and (4) checking the details of sub-contractors registered with Inland Revenue under the construction industry scheme.

On data sharing the *Report* made a number of recommendations including:

i) Examine how to make use of information held by the private sector. Although there is a huge volume of data held by the private sector, current government legislation prevents it being easily tapped to investigate a benefit claimant. For example, a person claiming a means-tested benefit may admit to holding a bank account, which the Department of Social Security may check for any evidence of regular deposits that would suggest that person is in receipt of an income from either legitimate or underground economy work. However if that person does not reveal any bank account history, it is difficult for the department to know whether that person is entitled to claim benefits from Social Security. Only if the department has access to private sector records could it search to uncover whether that person does in fact receive an income from an undisclosed source. The *Report* suggested the use of software that communicates with say, bank account records held within the banking/finance sector, which could be used to cross-check claimants details before making benefit payments. Similar searches could be used for uncovering unregistered businesses and self-employed individuals who are at most risk of participating in the underground economy. Of course, to ensure the integrity of the existing data protection legislation, appropriate legislation backed up by a code-of-practice, needs to be written and implemented.

Of all the government departments, Inland Revenue has the widest of powers to obtain external information. It can obtain information from statutory registers on say motor vehicle registrations from DVLA and interest paid on accounts held by banks and non-banks alike.

ii) Inland Revenue should have powers to make reverse searches of the telephone directory as a tool for investigating the underground economy, that is, those advertising and selling goods and/or services and offering only a telephone number as their contact. Once this personal information from the reverse search is available, it is possible to determine whether that person is registered for tax or in receipt of a benefit claim. A match of data should not presume evidence of fraud or tax evasion but rather as a starting point for a more detailed investigation. However, legislation prevents this from happening. Unless the individual has given prior consent that the information they have supplied when applying for a telephone number can be used for other purposes, that individual is protected from reverse searches. There are exemptions to the restriction on reverse searching limited by legislation, which Customs and Excise have been undertaking for many years. If, on the grounds of public interest (say) to protect government funds, reverse searches may be undertaken (Data Protection Act 1988). However investigating an individual who has listed a telephone number in the local paper may not, on its own, constitute sufficient grounds for a reverse search.

iii) Departments to work together to establish clear and practical guidelines for data sharing.[4] One of the main obstacles in data sharing across departments is tied to government funding relative to the outcome achievements. Where it may be the case that data sharing produces a significantly larger benefit relative to cost of providing data to one department and not the other, there may be little incentive to cooperate in data sharing arrangements particularly by the department that benefits little by this arrangement. The *Report* recommended that organised data sharing arrangements be funded by the government and incentives be given to departments for helping other departments limit the extent of fraud or tax evasion. The following table presents some idea of the various possibilities for joint investigation.

Table 2   Sources of fraud and joint investigations

Source of fraud/tax evasion	Department with most interest
Legitimate employee fraudulently claiming welfare benefits	Department of Social Security
Employee colluding with employer so as to obtain welfare benefit payments	Inland Revenue Department of Social Security Customs and Excise
Self employed individuals working in the underground economy	Inland Revenue
Unregistered businesses (employing workers that are not recorded on the books, evading VAT, etc)	Inland Revenue Department of Social Security Customs and Excise

Sanctions

The Inland Revenue tends, wherever possible, to make settlements or use civil proceedings against offenders rather than initiate criminal prosecution. It has the power to recover the tax owed, together with interest, plus a civil penalty up to the value of the evaded tax. Alternatively it has discretion to mitigate or remit any penalty applied, or in cases where penalty proceedings would otherwise be appropriate, draw up a 'contract settlement' with the taxpayer. This is an agreement not to take formal proceedings in exchange for an appropriate payment, to reflect the tax loss, interest and abated penalties. In instances where the person found evading taxes has no means to make monetary reparation for their fraudulent behaviour, the tax debt is treated as a tax loss and not recoverable.

The Department of Social Security has a policy to recover all amounts overpaid to individuals as long as the cost of doing so does not exceed the overpayment. Typically this is often recovered as small weekly reductions in on-going payment and so a large sum of money may take some time to repay back. In any case, only a certain amount of benefit can be deducted for repayment of an overpayment. The law requires priority to be given to other monetary obligations of those receiving benefits, that is, electricity and water bills, etc. In cases where there is serious fraud, the Department of Social Security has the power to seize assets to recover money that has been paid after a fraudulent claim. Typically, in cases where the benefit fraud exceeds £5,000 the matter is taken to the Crown Court and prosecutions are followed up under the Theft Act 1968. In these cases the court proceedings are much slower and far more expensive. For smaller amounts, which are more often the case, it is the social security legislation that is used to prosecute the offending individual.

When an individual applies for welfare assistance (Jobseeker's Allowance) while searching for legitimate employment, the claimant is expected to attend a regular appointment at the Jobcentre every two weeks. This appointment is set up on the first day and meets fortnightly thereafter. Because of the regularity and certainty of the appointment time, this allows those who are participating in the underground economy to arrange their working schedule around this time. The *Report* recommended that for those suspected of fraudulently receiving welfare assistance, the arrangement is altered so that additional appointments be scheduled at unpredictable times. Another, but more costly suggestion, is to make those suspected of fraudulently claiming welfare benefits to attend daily interviews to ensure that their work routines are severely disrupted. The costs in this instance would have to include travel reimbursement as well as the costs of having to employ additional staff to facilitate such an arrangement.

There are also the other benefit schemes (Income Support) that do not receive as much attention by Department of Social Security staff as does Jobseekers Allowance. In this instance, those that are receiving welfare assistance have very infrequent contact with the Department and thus there exists a greater opportunity for regular employment in the underground economy. Recently however a number of schemes are in operation to increase the contact with these welfare recipients (e.g. New Deals for lone parents and for disabled people and the ONE service, giving a claimant a personal adviser).

For persistent offenders, the *Report* recommended a policy of barring entitlements to welfare benefits for a given time period to any offender convicted of concealing work while claiming benefits. Similar type sanctions exist for the Jobseekers Allowance. If a person is found to be prolonging their unemployment, benefit payments can be withheld for a period of 1 to 26 weeks, with the appropriate safeguards put into place to protect the innocent and vulnerable affected by this.

Deterrence

One effective form of deterrence is publicity of the costs and consequences of the underground economy. The *Report* made two recommendations regarding publicity:

i) *publicising both the incentives available for people to join the legitimate economy and the risks for staying in the underground economy.* An important issue that needs to be kept in mind is that unless sanctions are a real threat, advertising will only undermine the objective of a publicity campaign. However publicity in its self can be a sanction (for example, when names of those convicted of benefit fraud are published in local newspapers and to a limited extent, those that are found guilty of tax offences). The *Report* also suggested a joint campaign by the various government departments affected by underground economic activity might prove to be more effective than a separate campaign by each of the individual departments. On the other hand, another strategy would be to publicise the alternatives to the underground economy (eg. The New Deals, the Working Families Tax Credit, etc).

ii) *testing the use of advertising as a tool for changing public attitudes, insofar as they currently regard the underground economy as socially acceptable.* The importance of the publicity campaign is to demonstrate the link between the underground activity and the adverse consequences that it can lead to (tax cheats are burdening their fellow citizens, legitimate businesses face the threat of closure from illegitimate operations, etc). The *Report* raises a very important issue about the prospect of a successful advertising campaign. Unlike the drink-driving campaign in which victims are easily identifiable, a publicity campaign to tackle the underground economy may not be as successful because victims are not easily identifiable. In fact the underground economy does not appear to cause any visible harm to either party in the transaction. Claiming that benefit fraud contributes to hospital bed shortages or under-funded schools may be true, but is a difficult message to get across. To determine the benefits of a publicity campaign, much more research needs to be undertaken. An unsuccessful campaign can have a much more damaging effect than no campaign at all.

The UK Government's Response to the Report Recommendations

In response to the Grabiner Report on the underground economy, the Inland Revenue, the Department of Social Security and HM Customs and Excise committed themselves to implementing each of the relevant recommendations. In each of the three sections that follow, we examine the responses made by each of these government departments. These responses are sourced from the various reports published by these agencies.

The Inland Revenue: Response to Recommendations[5]

The Inland Revenue responded positively to a number of recommendations, many of which are now in operation. For example:

1.   In response to the recommendation that investigators should have power to conduct routine reverse searches of the telephone directory, the Inland Revenue is now permitted to do so under the Regulation of Investigatory Powers Act (2000).

2.   In response to the recommendation that suggested a common set of guidelines be given to staff about what is legally permissible in relation to data sharing, the Inland Revenue responded with a Quick Guide on disclosure of customer information which was circulated to all its staff.

3.   In response to the recommendation for a greater working relation with other government departments in order to tackle the underground economy, the Inland Revenue set up 64 Risk Intelligence and Analysis teams as well as 20 Joint Shadow Economy teams with HM Customs and Excise and the Department for Works and Pensions.

4.   In response to the recommendation for establishing a new statutory offence for fraudulently evading income tax, the Finance Act 2000 was passed by parliament allowing the fraudulent offence to be tried in a magistrate's court (s144 Finance Act 2000 – enforceable from January 1, 2001). The Finance Act 2000 has facilitated tax information agreements with some countries whereby UK authorities are now able to obtain financial transaction information of UK taxpayers outside of the UK.[6] Civil investigations by the Inland Revenue provide the individual in question the opportunity to fully disclose any irregularities in their tax affairs. This is known as the Hansard procedure. The threat of the Hansard procedure being withdrawn (and criminal prosecutions to follow), is a means to encourage those who have unpaid tax liabilities to completely disclose this information. As of November 2002, any individual that fully discloses any irregularities in their tax affairs will not be subject to criminal prosecution as long as it is made under the Hansard procedure.

5.   In dealing with tax credit fraud, the Inland Revenue has: (i) has used a score card approach to assessing the risk of fraud by individual applicants, from which internal Inland Revenue data is cross-checked with data from other departments; and (ii) set up a Tax Credit Office Compliance Team responsible for dealing with identity fraud and employer arrangements. There has been some success in this area. For example, between 2000-01 and 2001-02 the proportion of non-compliance cases and yields have doubled – 17 percent of claimants in 2000-01 vs. 36 percent in 2001-02 (see NAO, 2003). However unless we know the extent of total benefit fraud, these numbers, although positive, do not tell us with certainty that that problem is subsiding.

The Inland Revenue has also taken a number of approaches to prevent fraud through legislative changes and education programs systems designs.

6.   In response to the recommendation that a confidential help line be established to advise people how to put their affairs in order, Inland Revenue responded by introducing this help line in July 2000. As of March 2002, approximately 11 percent of calls made to the hotline were by those who were operating in the underground economy.

7.   In response to the recommendation that Inland Revenue provide assistance to those individuals planning to go into self-employment, Inland Revenue responded by (a) setting up a new help-line for those newly self employed; and (b) a business starter pack, titled 'Starting Up in Business'.

8.   In response to the recommendation that those going into self-employment are required to notify the Inland Revenue as soon as they have commenced their business, has resulted in a new offence for failing to comply with National Insurance Contributions scheme.

9.   In response to the recommendations for publicising the incentives available to join the legitimate economy, the Inland Revenue now publicises these incentives in its Tax Bulletins and on its Web-site. The Inland Revenue has not yet launched its own publicity campaign, as has the HM Customs and Excise and the Department of Works and Pensions. The Inland Revenue continues to evaluate the benefits from such a costly campaign from lessons that might be drawn elsewhere.

Department of Social Security: Response to Recommendations[7]

Fraud is believed to be greatest in the means-tested benefits category (e.g. Income Support and Job Seeker's Allowance) (see Grabiner, 2000; para 1.10). That is, fraud is quite high in these areas when compared with say the simple age entitlement benefits where determination of payments is less complicated (e.g. Retirement Pension, and Child Benefits) (refer to the Social Security Fraud Act 2001). Fraud includes undeclared cohabitation, undeclared income, giving false addresses or failing to notify of an address change, falsifying rent payable, misleading statements on capital assets and falsifying identities.

One of the major problems of welfare benefit fraud is that is reduces the confidence in, and the integrity of, the social security program particularly when welfare benefit fraud is perceived to be a widespread problem. Of the estimated £2 billion, the department hopes its activities in this area will help recover some 50 percent of fraud and error on Income Support and Job Seeker's Allowance, and 25 percent on Housing Benefits by 2006 (see DWP, 2003). One of the major difficulties faced by the Department of Social Security is that the complexity of the benefit payments system allows fraudsters to claim ignorance or unintentional errors to cover up their fraudulent intentions.

In a series of Green Papers: (1) *New Ambitions for Our Country: A New Contract for Welfare* (March, 1998); (2) *Beating Benefit Fraud is Everyone's Business: Securing the Future* (July, 1998); and (3) *A New Contract for Welfare: Safeguarding Social Security*, the government shifted the emphasis in dealing with social security fraud from detection to prevention, although detection still remains an important objective. The Grabiner Report made a number of recommendations to deal with social security fraud. These recommendations (discussed previously) were embodied in the document: *Safeguarding Social Security: Getting the Information we Need*. This document sought views on Lord Grabiner's recommendations. The result of this process culminated in the Social Security Fraud Bill giving legislative effect to the social security fraud recommendations outlined in the Grabiner Report.

Prior to these more recent initiatives, the Social Security Administration (Fraud) Act 1997 contained a number of provisions including the sharing of information between relevant government departments and the tax authorities; the authorisation of the Post Office to share information regarding redirection of mail; the creating of new criminal offences in relation to providing misleading information and power to authorise authorities to inspect business premises for documents proving the suspicion of fraud (see The Social Security Fraud Act 2001).

a. The Social Security Fraud Act 2001   The recommendations on welfare benefit fraud made in the Grabiner Report were instrumental in the implementation of the Social Security Fraud Act (2001). The Department of Social Security in 1999 estimated social security fraud to be somewhere in the order of £2-£4 billion and as much as £7 billion.[8] In July 2000 at a Committee of Public Accounts, the Department of Social Security gave their best estimates to be some where in the order of £3 billion annually.[9]

It expected that as a result of the Social Security Fraud Act 2001, some 10 percent of current fraudulent activities would be detected (refer to the Social Security Fraud Act 2001 for further details). The principle objective of the Act is as follows:

1.   to grant authorised public officers access to selected private and public sector records of individuals suspected of social security fraud;
2.   to allow reciprocal exchange of information between the various benefit administrations;
3.   to cease or reduce benefit payments from individuals connected with benefit fraud;
4.   to prosecute and subject employers to financial penalties if found to be colluding with the benefit recipients;
5.   to make third-parties liable for failing to notify changes of circumstances applying directly to a benefit recipient.

One of the recommendations of the Grabiner Report was to consider the option of punishing persistent fraudsters by removing, or heavily reducing, their right to benefits for a specified period of time. In March 2000 the Secretary of State for Social Security announced that legislation would be introduced to withdraw benefits from those convicted twice of benefit fraud. (see DSS Press Notice 00/079). Clause 7(6) of the Social Security Act 2001 states that if within three years a person is convicted twice of benefit fraud, a sanction of restricted payments for 13 weeks will apply. The reader is referred to the Social Security Fraud Act 2001 for further details.

b. Income Support and Jobseeker's Allowance   The Department of Social Security has focused heavily on Income Support and Jobseeker's Allowance. Since 1997-98 to 2001-02, the department estimates that the level of benefit fraud has declined from an estimated 9 percent of its total expenditure to 6.8 percent. This is a decline in expenditure by £400 million and is well above the Department's 10 percent reduction target.

The Department of Social Security since 1997 has carried out additional checks known as interventions on those applying for welfare assistance or those already receiving payment and who are suspected of posing an integrity risk to the social security system. The Department has ongoing plans to continually improve interventions to increase their overall success rate. Of all the investigations carried out by the department, 41 percent have resulted in an adjustment to the benefit payment. Of all the cases investigated, the Department of Social Security imposed sanctions on only 15 percent of cases. The sanctions included warnings, fines or prosecution. Fines or penalties are typically applied to fraudulent cases below £1,500. Approximately half of those cases involving sanctions were followed through by prosecution. The success rate of those going to prosecution is 98 percent (see DWP, 2003).

The Department of Social Security has also implemented a number of publicity campaigns aimed at changing people's attitude towards benefit fraud. The advertisements are clearly designed to highlight the greater risk of getting caught and the long-term adverse consequences of such fraudulent behaviour. Since 2001 the Department of Social Security has been working with HM Customs and Excise as well as Inland Revenue to ensure that those who participate in the underground economy are not also participating in welfare benefit fraud.

c. Housing Benefit Fraud   The Department of Social Security has estimated the extent of Housing Benefit fraud to be roughly £500 million. One suspected motive of this fraudulent behaviour is the complexity of the Housing Benefit Scheme. Reform of the Housing Benefit Scheme will clearly reduce not only the complexity but will also simplify its administration. By 2006 the Department hopes to have a Verification Framework implemented in all local authorities. The objectives of the Verification Framework are to set out minimum standards for the verification of customer information before the benefit payment is made. To help achieve a desirable outcome the Department is committed to provide funding to local authorities to help improve controls in preventing fraud.

HM Customs and Excise: Response to Recommendations[10]

Adams and Webley (2001) found that the majority of small businesses surveyed in the UK felt the VAT system was particularly unfair towards small business because of the costs associated with the administration of the tax collection. Cowell (1992) and Adams (1996) have shown for individuals and small businesses respectively, that even perceptions of inequity in the tax system is sufficient to encourage taxpayers to withdraw partially or completely from the legitimate economy. Shefrin and Thaler (1988) have also suggested that VAT non-compliance may be due to a lack of mental counting. Mental counting is described by Winnet and Lewis (1995) as a psychological mechanism whereby income is compartmentalised into (say) that which belongs to the business and that which belongs to the tax office. Shefrin and Thaler (1988) suggest that the absence of this mental counting makes an individual more likely to regard all income earned as their own and find difficulty parting with it.

In response to this serious problem, HM Customs and Excise implemented a number of strategies to deal with such fraudulent behaviour. What follows is an account of some of the most common frauds HM Customs and Excise have in recent times pursued quite extensively.

a. Tackling Tobacco Smuggling   HM Customs and Excise in November 2001 (see HMCE, 2001) estimated that approximately one quarter of the cigarette market was made up of smuggled cigarettes. At that time, it forecasted that by 2003 this would grow to one-third of the market if sufficient steps are not taken to reduce it. The Chancellor of the Exchequer commissioned Martin Taylor to provide an independent evaluation of the problem. The government launched a strategy that included a number of new measures such as: (i) recruitment of 955 new staff and investigators, (ii) a national network of x-ray scanners to detect smuggled goods in freight containers, (iii) the introduction of 'UK duty paid' marks on tobacco products (with penalties for those dealing in unmarked products), and (iv) £3 million on a publicity campaign.

By 2000-01 HM Excise and Customs had reached its market penetration target of 21 percent (down from 25 percent previously) and had broken up 56 smuggling gangs seizing 10,200 vehicles from the so-called 'white van trade' and almost 2.8 billion cigarettes. From the use of the x-ray scanners, they uncovered in the first 6 months of operation approximately 80 million cigarettes and 4.5 tonnes of tobacco (see HMCE, 2002b). By 2001-02 HM Excise and Customs had broken up another 60 smuggling gangs and almost 2.6 billion cigarettes. From the use of the x-ray scanners alone, they uncovered approximately 325 million cigarettes and 13 tonnes of hand-rolled tobacco (see HMCE, 2002a).[11]

By 2002-03 HM Customs and Excise estimated that cigarette smuggling has been reduced to 18 percent of the total market, down from 20 percent the year earlier. This is significantly lower than the projected 34 percent of the market that smuggled tobacco would have accounted for had these new strategies not been implemented. Smuggling nevertheless continues. In that same year, HM Customs and Excise uncovered some 2 million cigarettes in a furniture consignment and a further 4 million cigarettes in a shoe consignment headed for the UK. It is estimated however that the Exchequer has been able to safeguard some £3 billion in revenue with these on-going initiatives (see HMCE, 2003).

b. Alcohol Fraud in 2001   HM Customs and Excise proposed the introduction of stamps for spirits, much like those for cigarettes, in an attempt to deal with its illicit trade. Following consultation with the business community, it was decided that these would not be introduced because of the compliance costs involved for those in the industry. As the government has been unable to determine an alternative means to stamps that would help in reducing this illicit trade in alcohol, the Chancellor announced that in 2006 such stamps will be introduced. The estimated market share of illicit spirits in the UK has been increasing since 1997-98 from approximately 7 percent to 16 percent in 2001-02 (see HMCE, 2003).

c. Oil Fraud   HM Customs and Excise had estimated during 2000, approximately £380 million was lost in cross-border petrol and diesel fraud. Although Customs has had some initial success in dealing with these illegal activities, the problem was still perceived to be significantly high, warranting more resources and intelligence to curb such activities. The misuse of rebates or low tax fuels for non-road use was also a growing problem. These frauds have been estimated to cost the Exchequer some £450 million (see HMCE, 2001).

During 2001-02 HM Customs and Excise broke up 30 oil laundering plants, seized 2.2 million litres of fuel and convicted twice as many individuals with oil fraud than the previous year. The 2002 budget added further measures to continue the governments' process of significantly detecting ongoing oil frauds. These included: (i) an EU-wide 'Euromarker' added to fuel to make it easier to detect rebated fuel purchased abroad, (ii) tighter controls on the supply of duty free oils for use in specified industrial processes and (iii) the establishment of approved distributors supplying rebated gas oil and kerosene supplies (see HMCE, 2002a).

d. VAT Missing Trader Fraud In the HM Customs and Excise Report of November 2002, estimates of VAT revenue losses are believed to be accounted for mostly by 'abusive tax avoidance' and 'thousands of ordinary businesses looking to gain relatively small financial advantages by delaying or reducing their VAT payments' (see HMCE, 2001). As part of the new VAT strategy, the government has targeted 'Missing Trader Fraud, abusive tax avoidance, non-compliance and the failure of businesses to register for VAT'. Part of this strategy is to employ additional staff to monitor and action suspicions of non-compliance.

Missing trader fraud occurs when a fraudster registers for VAT in order to acquire VAT free goods from other member states, but sell the goods inclusive of VAT in the UK. The fraudster then disappears, paying neither the VAT collected nor the income tax obligation from the sale of these goods. It was estimated that during 2000-01 somewhere between £1.7 and £2.6 billion was lost due to missing trader fraud (see HMCE, 2001). For 2003, Missing Trader Fraud has been estimated to be between £1.65 and £2.64 billion. This decline has been the result of numerous initiatives including: 5,700 pre-registration visits to new traders, refusing 900 suspect registrations, and the cancellation of 1,200 existing missing trader registrations.

In the 2003 Budget, a number of anti-fraud measures were announced. These involved (i) 'imposing liability on any business that knows or has reasonable grounds for believing that VAT will go unpaid in a supply chain'; (ii) 'denying recovery of VAT in circumstances were an individual holds an invalid invoice and is unable to demonstrate that they took reasonable steps to ensure the supply and their supplier were bona fide'; and (iii) requiring 'security from any business repeatedly involved in a supply chain where there is evidence of actual or potential fraud or evasion' (see HMCE, 2003).

Concluding Remarks

In this chapter we reviewed the recommendations of the Grabiner Report into the underground economy in the United Kingdom. To date the majority of the recommendations have been implemented and the results reported here suggest that the strategies are having an impact on reducing the growth in the underground economy in a number of areas (for example, welfare and housing benefit fraud, tobacco and alcohol fraud and VAT missing trader fraud). However the nature of the underground economy is such that the various government departments affected need to continually work together and focus on improving their strategies for tackling these activities. As we made clear at the outset, this is very important not only from an economic but also from a social point of view. With that said, the recommendations of the Grabiner Report and the government's response serves as a great example for other tax administrations around the world, yet to embark on a more active campaign, with a reference by which to address their own underground economic activities at home.

Notes

*   I would like to thank Lord Anthony Grabiner for helpful comments and suggestions during the course of writing this paper, particularly for permission to discuss extensively the recommendations in his Report. Naturally an errors and omission are my own.
1. I am thankful to Anthony Grabiner for providing this example.
2. *The Economist*, 14th February 2004, p. 11.
3. There are however a number of goods that are still taxed between 4 percent and 7 percent while others are 'zero rated' (a zero tax rate applies). For example, domestic fuel is taxed at 5 percent while postal services, lotteries, trade unions, professional bodies, fund-raising and cultural services are 'zero rated'.
4. This process had already started at the time of the Report. Customs and Excise and the Inland Revenue published a 'Closer Working Guide' for staff in 1999. The service statement between the Department of Social Security and the Inland Revenue covers both the principles and procedures for data sharing, and is supplemented by a written guidance for staff.
5. The reader is referred to the National Audit Office report for a detailed review of Inland Revenue's strategies to tackling fraudulent activities (see NAO, 2003).
6. The UK is also a supporter of the EU Mutual Assistance Directive that has been in operation since 1979 and which facilitates the exchange of information between members in an effort to tackle international tax fraud.
7. The reader is referred to the report by the Comptroller and Auditor General 'Tackling Benefit Fraud', for a detailed review of the Department of Work and Pensions strategies to tackle fraudulent activities (see DWP, 2003).
8. DSS, A New Contract for Welfare: Safegaurding Social Security, Cm 4276, March 1999, para 1.4.
9. National Insurance Fund 1998-99 and the Wider Issues of Fraud and Error in Benefits Paid by the Department of Social Security, HC 350 of 1999-2000, 19 July 2000, Evidence, Q112.
10. The reader is referred to a number of reports published by HM Customs and Excise for further details, namely, HMCE (2001), HMCE (2002a); HMCE (2002b) and HMCE (2003).
11. However in 2002 HM Customs and Excise had found a large proportion of cigarettes to be counterfeit. In fact 41 percent of all those cigarettes seized were counterfeit. The major problem with these counterfeit cigarettes is that they are untaxed and unregulated, meaning that they would potentially form a greater health hazard to the public than ordinary regulated cigarette production.

References

Adams, C.J. (1996), *Satisfaction with the Tax Authorities and Propensity to Avoid Taxes*, unpublished MSc dissertation, University of Exeter, in Webley, Adams and Elffers (2002).

Adams, C.J. and Webley, P. (2001), '"Small Business Owners" Attitude on VAT Compliance in the UK', *Journal of Economic Psychology*, Vol. 22(2), pp. 195-217.

Bhattacharyya, D.K. (1990), 'An Econometric Method of Estimating the Hidden Economy, United Kingdom (1960-1984): Estimates and Tests', *The Economic Journal*, Vol. 100, September, pp. 703-17.

Cowell, F. (1992), 'Tax Evasion and Inequity', *Journal of Economic Psychology*, Vol. 22, pp. 521-43.

DWP (2003), *Tackling Benefit Fraud: A Report by the Comptroller and Auditor General*, Department of Works and Pensions, HC 393 Session 2002-2003, UK.

Feige, E.L. (1981), 'The UK's Unobserved Economy: A Preliminary Assessment', *Journal of Economic Affairs*, Vol. 1(4), July.

Grabiner, A. (2000), *The Informal Economy – A Report by Lord Grabiner QC*, March, HM Treasury UK.

HMCE (2001), *Tackling Indirect Tax Fraud*, HM Customs and Excise, November, UK.

HMCE (2002a), *Protecting Indirect Tax Revenues*, HM Customs and Excise, November, UK.

HMCE (2002b), *Measuring Indirect Tax Losses*, HM Customs and Excise, November, UK.

HMCE (2003), *Measuring and Tackling Indirect Tax Losses: An Update on the Government's Strategic Approach*, HM Customs and Excise, December, UK.

NAO (2003), *Tackling Fraud Against the Inland Revenue: Report by the Comptroller and Auditor General*, National Audit Office, HC 429 Session 2002-2003, UK.

Priest, G. (1994), 'The Ambiguous Moral Foundations of the Underground Economy', *Yale Law Journal*, Vol. 103(80), pp. 2259-88.

Shefrin, H.M. and Thaler, R.M. (1988), 'The Behavioural life-cycle Hypothesis', *Economic Enquiry*, Vol. 26, pp. 237-41.

Webley, P. Adams, C. and Elffers, H. (2002), 'VAT Compliance in the United Kingdom', *The Centre for Tax System Integrity Working Papers*, Australian National University, WP.41.

Winnett, A. and Lewis, A. (1995), 'Household accounts, mental accounts and Savings Behaviour: Some Old Economics Rediscovered?', *Journal of Economic Psychology*, Vol. 16, pp. 431-48.

Chapter 13

Recent Government Initiatives in Tackling the Underground Economy in Australia[*]

Christopher Bajada

Introduction

In July 2000, Australia undertook a major step in reforming its tax system by introducing a Goods and Services Tax (GST). This tax replaced part of the government's revenue from its indirect tax with an across the board tax on most goods and services. The GST is a broad based tax set at 10 percent of sales or supplies and borne by the end consumer. So although the GST is paid at each step of the supply chain, each business registered for the GST is able to claim an input tax credit, implying that the GST flows along this supply chain until it reaches the end consumer who is not entitled to claim an input tax credit on purchases.

There was considerable debate at the time of the introduction of the GST whether such tax reform would contribute to either an improvement or deterioration in underground economic activities. The government at the time, particularly prior to the changes in the tax system, argued fervently that the new reporting requirement of the GST would ensure that much of the underground economy would be detected and taxed. The government argued that as a result of reform, the GST would increase the tax base and the revenue raised would be used to fund the growing demand for public goods and services. In countries such as Canada, Britain and New Zealand, where similar attempts to reform the tax system have been made, the outcomes have been less than favourable. Not long after each country's tax reform package was introduced, the evidence pointed to a growing underground economy. Although the Australian tax system shares similar features with those of Canada, New Zealand, and Britain, the Australian government expected that the few differences, namely the Australian Business Number (ABN), would ultimately succeed in curbing the underground economy. As we will argue in the next section, this conclusion very much depends upon the nature of activities occurring in the underground economy. Public perception in Australia on the effectiveness of the GST in meeting the government's underground economy objectives have been largely influenced by such overwhelming international evidence described in the media. In fact, public opinion prior to the tax changes was generally unanimous in concluding that the underground economy would increase as a result of the tax change (see BRW, 2000).

In response to these and earlier concerns (especially from the ATO's community perception surveys – *to be discussed below*),[1] the ATO engaged extensively with the Cash Economy Task Force (CETF) as a way of seeking advice from the community on how to tackle the underground economy problem in Australia. The CETF was initially set up in 1996 and its membership comprised of a cross-section of the community, including individuals from academia, small business, representatives of industry peak bodies, the tax profession and staff from various government departments directly affected by the underground economy (for example, the Department of Family and Community Services, formerly the Department of Social Security). Since its first meeting in 1996, the Cash Economy Task Force has produced three reports. The government, in conjunction with the ATO, has actively pursued the various recommendations made in each of these reports, and without doubt, the enactment of numerous recommendations have had a positive impact on reducing underground economic activities in Australia.

The objective of this chapter is to provide a review of the progress made by the government and the Australian Taxation Office in response to the recommendations from the Cash Economy Task Force. The chapter begins with a brief overview of the distinctive feature of the New Tax System – the Australian Business Number, and a brief discussion on a general classification of economic activities, which to a varying degree, create problems for the government when devising strategies to reduce the size of the underground economy. These classifications, as we will discuss, are important for devising appropriate strategies to tackle such activities. In the remainder of the chapter we provide a summary account of the recommendations contained in the three Cash Economy Task Force reports and this is followed up with a discussion on the governments' progress in pursuing these recommendations.

The New Tax System in Australia[2]

The Federal government expected to make a substantial windfall gain from the introduction of the Goods and Services Tax (GST) which came into force on July 1, 2000. However much of this tax net depended on successully taxing clandestine activities. The experiences abroad have proven that tax reform on its own has had little impact on reducing underground economic activities. After the introduction of the GST in Canada in 1991, the size of the underground economy grew dramatically (see for example Giles and Tedds, 2002), and similarly for the United Kingdom, which introduced a Value-Added Tax (VAT) in 1973 (see for example Smith and Weid-Nebbeling, 1986 and Bhattacharyya, 1990). Although the underground economy in New Zealand declined following the introduction of the GST, by 1994 the underground economy had grown beyond the levels in 1986, suggesting the GST has had little impact in reducing illicit activities there also (Giles, 1999).

The Australian Business Number

As part of the tax reform package, the Australian government introduced an Australian Business Number (ABN) to make it easier for businesses to deal with government departments, while at the same time helping improve the ATO's tax auditing process. Of course this assumes that much of the underground economy is being generated by legitimately registered businesses. If on the contrary, consumers (or employees) are participating to a greater extent in these illicit activities by trading as 'sole traders' in the underground economy, the ABN and tax reform will prove ineffective in culling the growth in this participation.

In principle the ABN should make it harder for businesses to operate in the underground economy. As part of the new Pay-As-You-Go (PAYG) system, any business-to-business transactions must quote an ABN on invoices. In the event that an ABN is not provided, the supplier of the good or service is required to withhold the top marginal rate of tax plus the Medicare levy (or 48.5 percent) from the business that receives the goods or services. If the business intends to claim an input tax credit on creditable purchases to offset the GST component, it must report an income received from the sale of those inputs. To help identify unreported income, the ATO has compiled a series of financial ratios for various industries as benchmarks to compare incomes and expenditures reported by individual businesses in their Business Activity Statements (BAS).[3] The BAS is a single form used by businesses to report their tax entitlements (GST paid on inputs) and obligations (GST collected from the sale of goods and services) typically on a quarterly basis.[4] This is expected to increase the efficiencies in the ATO's auditing processes by reducing the ATO's costs of constructing the financial information provided by each business for auditing purposes.

To accelerate ABN registrations, the government made it explicit early on that any business that trades without any ABN would be regarded as operating in the underground economy. However much of the ABN's success depends heavily on the nature of these clandestine activities. The underground economy typically supports two types of activities, namely business and household transactions, the latter the government concedes as the difficult component to tackle. Business transactions include business-to-business and business-to-consumer transactions while household transactions make up the remaining consumer-to-consumer transactions. Which of these dominates the activities of the underground economy will determine how successful tax reform and the ABN will be in curbing such activities. If household transactions make up the majority of the transactions taking place in the underground economy, it is unlikely that Australia's tax reform package will have a significant impact on eliminating illicit activities.

As part of the new tax system the government set up a public register (Australian Business Register – ABR) of business ABN and GST registration information. This register can be used to verify whether a business is correctly reporting its ABN and GST registration details. To register for the GST a business must first apply for an ABN, which will then uniquely identify that business and provide a paper trail for auditing for the possibility of tax evasion (at least in a business-to-business environment). The ABR can allow consumers to check businesses that are charging them the GST but are not registered for the GST. In this case there is the possibility that that business is withholding an amount equal to the GST and not reporting that income. A number of small and large businesses have an automatic process of checking the GST status of a new supplier using the ABR to ensure that they are entitled to claim an input tax credit. This automatic verification process can catch out those businesses attempting to claim a GST component in their pricing when in fact they are not entitled to charge the GST.

Another design feature of the new tax system is the Pay-As-You-Go (PAYG) withholding (PAYGW) and instalments (PAYGI). PAYGW is a collection system for those businesses who hire employees or labour-hire workers whereas PAYGI is a collection system for individuals and businesses not registered for the GST to report their revenue and instalment payment they are obliged to make to the ATO on a regular (quarterly) basis.

Business Transactions

The ATO has unveiled numerous attempts by businesses to conceal income earned in the underground economy in a variety of business-to-business and business-to-consumer transactions. In most of these cases the offenders have been made to meet their tax obligations and fined in principle for the tax evasion. Some of the methods businesses have used to avoid detection in the past have been to explicitly request cash payment in return for significantly discounted prices for their services; keeping two sets of books – one for cash receipts and the other for non-cash receipts; failing to declare interest income; paying cash to employees in order to report lower levels of expenditures to justify the lower reported earnings; arranging for clients to purchase materials while the business provides the labour services; inflating expenditures; and invoice splitting, where labour and materials are recorded separately.

However with the introduction of the ABN, some businesses participating in the underground economy are at risk of being detected. If previously these businesses simply disclosed only some of their income and expenditure, the introduction of the ABN will make it much more difficult to continue this practice particularly for those concealing income from business-to-business transactions. For example, when Couriers Pty Ltd contracts with Mechanical Repairs Pty Ltd to service its fleet of vehicles both businesses are expected to disclose an ABN – Couriers to claim an input tax credit on the GST component of the contracted price and Mechanical Repairs to avoid Couriers withholding 48.5 percent and to ensure it can claim an input tax credit on the parts used to service the vehicles. So for most transactions, records of incomes and expenditures will be referenced by an ABN, thereby discouraging (but certainly not eliminating) inter-business misreporting of income and expenditure.

However some businesses may remain undetected if they deal directly with the consumer (business-to-consumer transactions) and are willing to forego the input tax credits on their expenditures, particularly if they believe that the returns from tax evasion are greater. The businesses in question may purchase inputs as 'consumers' absorbing the 10 percent GST, offer their services at subsidised prices, and conceal this income from the tax department. This is most likely to occur in occupations where the cost of labour services relative to the cost of physical inputs is very large. For example, computer service occupations are generally labour intensive and consequently much of total earnings is from labour service not from the sale of computer hardware (the physical inputs). In such circumstances the input tax credits, which the business is entitled to claim, would be much less than the tax savings if the business decided not to declare that income. However for occupations where the cost of labour services relative to the cost of physical inputs are small, participation in the underground economy may shrink. For those business transactions where the cost of labour services relative to the cost of physical inputs is large, an input tax credit is unlikely to have any significant impact on the size of clandestine activities, the tax-gap and therefore tax revenue.

Household Transactions

The ATO's track record in detecting illicit consumer-to-consumer transactions has not been as successful as for illicit business-to-business transactions. We use the term household transactions to identify individuals who are employees in the legitimate economy, but who outside of their official working hours, participate in the underground economy by offering the sale of goods and services to other consumers. For example, an employee of Mechanical Repairs Pty Ltd who accepts to repair a neighbour's car after work in return for payment is an example of a consumer-to-consumer transaction. Most often these payments are made in cash and never declared as income. Typically many of these consumer transactions are labour intensive, which suggests that the introduction of the ABN has limited impact on these activities. As the customer is not entitled to claim an input tax credit on any purchase, an individual contemplating participating in the underground economy could easily profit by absorbing the GST on an input purchase and not disclose income received from the transaction. Alternatively the individual could ask the consumer to purchase the physical inputs and the labour services would be provided at a discounted rate. Only the value added from the labour services would constitute part of the underground economy. The greater the volume of these household transactions to the overall number of transaction taking place in the underground economy, the less likely will tax reform impact on the size of the underground economy.

The Cash Economy Task Force

During the course of the last 10 years, the Australian Taxation Office (ATO) has collected information from surveys about community perceptions of the ATO and its role in tackling underground economic activity. In part these surveys have been a significant motivator for the ATO in initiating an active agenda in trying to improve its self image and in the process earn a reputation for successfully tackling underground economic activity. In the three tables that follow (Tables 1, 2 and 3) we report the results from a number of surveys conducted by an independent consultant on behalf of the ATO on community perception (on the ATO in general and on the ATO's response to underground economic activities). The Centre for Tax System Integrity has also undertaken similar surveys (see Chapter 3 for more details).

Table 1   Community perceptions I: percentage of respondents who agree with the statements (1996-97 to 1999-2000)

Perception	1996-1997	1997-1998	1998-1999	1999-2000
ATO people are really helpful	48	52	51	49
I always get my return back quickly	74	77	71	75
The ATO responds promptly to queries	42	47	48	47
I usually support the decisions the ATO makes	54	52	52	51
ATO staff have too much power over taxpayers	48	46	43	43
The ATO is doing a good job overall	60	59	59	58
People who don't pay tax on their cash earnings are almost certain to be caught by the Tax Office	-	37	46	47
I've heard a lot lately about what the ATO is doing to stop people evading tax on their cash earnings	-	37	36	40

Source: ATO (2003)

        In columns 2-5 of Table 1 are the percentage of respondents who agreed with the statements given in column 1. Over the period from 1996-97 to 1999-00 there has been relatively little movement in perceptions with the exception of a few questions: 'people who don't pay tax on their cash earnings are almost certain to be caught by the Tax Office' and 'I've heard a lot lately about what the ATO is doing to stop people evading their tax on their cash earnings'. For the first statement, the percentage of respondents agreeing to it rose from 37 percent in 1997-98 (when this question was first added to the survey) to 47 percent by 1999-00. The jump no doubt can be attributed in part to the publicity of the first CEFT report and the government's response to its recommendations. This is confirmed by the second statement 'I've heard a lot lately about what the ATO is doing to stop people evading tax on their cash earnings', rising from 37 percent of respondents that agreed in 1997-98 to 40 percent that agreed with it by 1999-00. Although, as we will discuss below, the ATO had in place processes to deal with the underground economy before the establishment of the CETF but it was the publicity generated from the first report that appears to have produced this marked swing in community perceptions.

However on the image of the ATO, the results over this period were not so favourable. For example, people's perceptions that the 'ATO people were really helpful' declined marginally from 51 percent during the period 1996-98 to 49 percent during 1999-00. In response to the statement 'I usually support the decision the ATO makes', the percentage of respondents agreeing to it fell from 54 percent to 51 percent over this time period.

In columns 2-4 of Tables 2 and 3 are the percentage of respondents who agreed with the statements given in column 1. This question set is somewhat different from the question set in Table 1. The responses to these questions were collected over the period 2000-01 to 2002-03. In Table 2 an improvement would require the percentage of respondents agreeing with each statement given in column 1 to increase over time, while an improvement would require the percentage of respondents agreeing with each statement given in column 1 of Table 3 to decline over time. The shaded statements in each of Tables 2 and 3 are similar in interpretation to the shaded statements in Table 1. In this way we can refer to these questions to make a preliminary conclusion as to how perceptions towards the Tax Office have changed since the implementation of the new tax system.

Table 2   Community perceptions II: percentage of respondents who agree with the statements (2000-01 to 2002-03)

Questions requiring an upward trend to show improvement	2000-2001	2001-2002	2002-2003
I think the Tax Office people are really helpful	69	48	53
The Tax Office has improved a lot lately	40	35	37
The effort involved in completing my tax return is less now than in previous years	26	36	37
The effort involved to maintain records to support claims in my tax return is less now than in previous years.	24	31	33
The Tax Office looks for new ways of doing things to help taxpayers[a]	49	44	43
The Tax Office responds promptly to any queries I have[a]	65	50	50
Overall I think the Tax Office is doing a good job	61	60	62

Source: ATO (2003)

Notes: (a) In June 2001, these questions were asked only of those respondents who had had contact with the Tax Office in the last 12 months.

Comparing the (shaded) statements from each of the Tables 2 and 3, with their corresponding ones in Table 1, it appears that the Tax Office has marginally improved its image in the public arena (50 percent of respondents agreed with the statement 'I think the Tax Office people are really helpful' for the period 1996-97 to 1999-00, compared with 56.7 percent over the period 2000-01 to 2002-03). The overall perception of the ATO has also improved particularly from the number of respondents agreeing with the statement 'The ATO is doing a good job overall'. Prior to the introduction of the GST, 59 percent of respondents agreed with this statement while 61 percent of respondents agreed post-GST. In fact prior to July 2000, the percentage of respondents agreeing with this statement declined consistently from 1996 to 2000, while post-GST the percentage of responses agreeing with the statement rose consistently every year.

Unfortunately the wordings of the questions relating to the underground economy are different, making a direct comparison of the responses somewhat difficult. However there does appear to be an upward trend in the general community perception that the probability of getting caught evading taxes is increasing and that the ATO is slowly gaining an upper hand in tackling these clandestine activities.

Table 3   Community perceptions III: percentage of respondents who agree with the statements (1999-00 to 2002-03)

Questions requiring a downward trend to show improvement	2000-2001	2001-2002	2002-2003
Tax Office staff have too much power over taxpayers	37	41	35
The Tax Office spends too much time clamping down on ordinary people and lets the real tax cheats get away	78	79	73
I feel very confused about tax matters	53	51	54
Most people try and avoid paying their fair share of tax	51	53	48

Source: ATO (2003)

Prior to the establishment of the Cash Economy Task Force, the ATO had in place a number of programs to try to deal with tax evasion and the underground economy in Australia. These included:[5]

•   *Record Keeping Programs*: the objective of this program was to educate taxpayers in ways to improve their record keeping skills with the intention that better record keeping will help improve taxpayer compliance. The components of this program included ATO sponsored publications and information to tax agents as well as record keeping reviews of small businesses. Targeted audit activities ensured that record keeping requirements were being kept.

- *Serious evasion program*: using information from the Australian Transaction Reports and Analysis Centre (AUSTRAC) and ATO intelligence, the ATO audits those suspected of being involved in serious tax evasion. The ATO undertakes its risk analysis based on a number of indirect income measurement techniques as well as information reporting requirements specified by the Financial Transactions Reports Act, 1988. The major financial transaction information available under the Act are: (i) Suspect Transactions Reports; (ii) Significant Transactions Reports; (iii) Significant Betting Transactions Reports; (iv) International Currency Transfer Reports; and (v) International Funds Transfer Instructions.

- *Prescribed and Reportable Payments System (PPS, RPS)*: The PPS, introduced in 1983, was a system of collecting income tax at the source from industries prone to significant tax evasion. The industries included building and construction, road transport, motor vehicle repairs, joinery and cabinet making and cleaning. The payers under this system were required to withhold tax from payments made to the payee, unless the payee had a certificate from the ATO that withholding was not required. In 1994 the RPS system was introduced to prevent tax evasion in other high risk industries, including clothing and fishing industries (1994), smash repairers (1995) and fresh fruit and vegetable suppliers (1997). This system required the payee to quote their tax file number and failure to do so would mean the payer is required to withhold the tax from the payment. These two systems are no longer in operation under the new tax system.

- *Compliance Improvement Projects*: Based on risk assessment information, the ATO undertook a number of compliance improvement initiatives in various industries by working with industry associations and community groups to develop strategic solutions to non-compliance. The industries included clothing, taxi, restaurant, and flower growing.

- *Lodgement Enforcement Program*: The objective of this program is to identify those that have failed to lodge by the due date and that processes are in place to ensure that they continue to lodge on time in future. The other involves the use of external information to help identify those that have never lodged an income tax return.

The Cash Economy Taskforce Force (CETF) was established in 1996 to understand taxpayer compliance in Australia and to recommended strategies to curb growing community perceptions that the underground economy in Australia was growing. In May 1997 the CETF presented its first report to the tax commissioner identifying a number of important aspects found to be influencing participation. In particular the CETF recommended that the ATO better understands these influences in order to develop a systematic approach to tackling taxpayer non-compliance. In the process, the ATO would also need to become more involved with tax practitioners, industry associations and community groups to develop effective industry and community specific strategies to minimise the shrinking tax base.

In what follows is an overview of the reports published by the CETF and the government's response to the various recommendations made in these reports. Although what follows is a summary of what is contained in the various Cash Economy Task Force reports, the reader is referred to each of these for further details.

The First CETF Report (1997)[6]

The first meeting of the Cash Economy Task Force was guided by a number of important terms of references, namely, that it should investigate the nature and compliance issues surrounding underground economy activities with the objective of making recommendations to the ATO with how it could proceed to deal with these. A summary of these recommendations included:

Compliance Improvement Initiatives:
- Undertake a significant shift in ATO resources to deal with the underground economy;
- Undertake industry-based and community-group-specific compliance improvement initiatives in major risk areas. Focus should be given to research, publicity, consultation and audit activity;
- Improve systematic use of all available data;
- Undertake a skills assessment of ATO compliance improvement staff;
- Develop and implement a staff communication strategy to support underground economy activities.

Policy Proposals:
- Develop proposals for extending Financial Transaction Reporting (FTR) requirements based on research into third parties with significant cash handling;
- Review the effectiveness of sanctions for non-compliance, in particular the current administrative and judicial penalty regime;
- Evaluate the possibility of an amnesty for business taxpayers who have unreported cash receipts and kept false records;
- Introduce on-the-spot fines for record keeping offences;
- The re-introduction of naming tax offenders in the Commissioner's Annual Report;
- The possibility of one common tax file number and or business registration number across all Federal or State agencies.

Community Communication Program:
- Develop and implement a communication program based on an understanding of community attitudes and taxpayer motivations;
- Ensure that ATO school programs includes an emphasis on the cost of tax evasion;

- Develop and implement a communication strategy to promote to industry associations that there are benefits for their industry being seen as good compliers.

Tax Practitioners:
- Seek tax agent participation in the implementation of industry and community compliance initiatives;
- Provide assistance to agents whose practice includes a significant proportion of high risk areas.

Research Program:
- Increase understanding of the underground economy by undertaking community and taxpayer research that includes individual motivations, the effects of the welfare system and the relevant industry practices.

Agency Coordination:
- Liaise with the Department of Immigration and Multicultural Affairs;
- Establish effective networks across ATO Business Lines and with other agencies on underground economy issues (e.g. Department of Social Security, AUSTRAC).

The Second CETF Report (1998)[7]

One of the major terms of reference for the CETF in its second round of meetings was to understand what contributes to a decline in taxpayer morality, particularly how the ATO may engage the community to reverse what appears to be a trend in voluntary non-compliance. The CETF was requested to examine the existing enforcement techniques in the current environment and their likely effectiveness in the future.

The Task Force made 34 recommendations that were grouped under various headings. Below we discuss each of the various classes of recommendations.

a) Understanding Compliance By the time of the publication of the second CETF report, the ATO had tripled its field presence in the community becoming involved in a number of national and regional projects. The focus of the fieldwork centred on cash industries following a decision by the taskforce to deal specifically with these activities.

From a number of commissioned studies, the ATO uncovered a number of taxpayer attitudes that are worth noting here:

- Small businesses perceived the tax system was too complex;
- Some businesses had little respect of the ATO while others demonstrated a lack of trust of the ATO;
- Certain ATO staff were not helpful and lacked communication skills;
- It was felt that there was always a presumption of guilt by ATO officials.

Some of the common factors influencing tax payer compliance include a combination of drivers such as economic, sociological, psychological, business profile and industry factors. Some of the sociological factors include age, the level of education and ethnicity background, while the psychological factors include an individual's perception of risk and fear of detection as well as the opportunities that may arise to evade. Business profile factors include issues such as the structure of business (sole trader, partnership, etc) while the industry factors include the nature of the industry the individuals work within (competition, the degree of infrastructure, etc). It is the combination of these factors that may motivate individuals to engage in underground economic activity. One industry identified by the ATO demonstrated a number of characteristics consistent with the factors influencing taxpayer compliance we have just discussed. In particular the clothing industry in Australia was characterised as having a small capital base, a large number of home operations, a concentration within a certain cultural or ethnic background, poor compliance with government regulations, high levels of unemployment and a large degree of social security fraud.

The Compliance Model

The Task Force adapted the work of Ayres and Braithwaite (1992) on strategies for regulation and Braithwaite (1998) on trust norms to develop a compliance model to complement the ATO's Taxpayer's charter. The compliance model represented in Figure 1 advocates that the ATO should adopt a hierarchical or escalating approach to compliance initiatives, that is, to promote and encourage voluntary compliance and to follow this through with tough sanctions if necessary.

The compliance pyramid has three aspects that are worth noting. The right-hand side of the pyramid represents regulatory strategies as a process of encouraging compliance (see Ayres and Braithwaite, 1992). The preferred system by the tax office is one which encourages self regulation because this is least costly to society, however avenues exist for the tax office to escalate punishment to those found to be abusing the voluntary compliance arrangement. The left hand side of the pyramid represents the motivational postures and trust norms discussed by Braithwaite et al. (1994). There are various degrees of attitudes that affect taxpayer behaviour. The more compliant individuals are classified in the managerial accommodation or capture classifications in the compliance pyramid. The top two classifications are resistance and disengagement and they respectively define those that are least cooperative with the voluntary tax compliance system. The front of the pyramid then maps the possible enforcement strategies that would correspond to the relevant right- and left-hand sides of the pyramid. For example, at the base of the pyramid self-regulation is dominant and individuals are most compliant. The appropriate enforcement strategy in such an environment is for the tax office to further promote education on matters such as good record keeping skills. At the top end of the compliance pyramid however, there is a strong degree of absence in voluntary compliance which requires a significant escalation in punishment. The relevant enforcement strategy in this case is prosecution (seen in the top panel in the compliance pyramid).

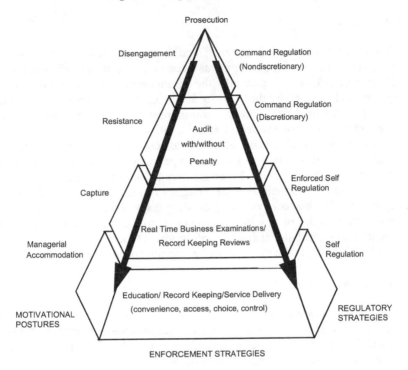

Figure 1 The compliance model

Source: ATO (1998)

The Task Force suggested that a way to maximise voluntary compliance is to promote this escalating approach to regulation. To achieve this it is important that the ATO better understand taxpayer behaviour, engage in more community partnerships and become more flexible in its tax compliance operations.

b) Building Community Partnerships Building industry partnerships and changing community attitudes was presented by the Task Force as a major objective. Meetings with industry associations proved very positive, many offering to work with the ATO to encourage comprehensive reporting of income, particularly cash income. This took the form of an educational campaign of members on reporting and record keeping practices through industry or community newsletters and similar modes of communication.

The Task Force proposed two strategies: (i) a communication strategy intended to make the community aware of the costs associated with underground economic activity; and (ii) fostering industry partnership so that industry specific strategies may be put into place to limit these clandestine activities.

Communication

The Task Force recommended that an effective communication strategy would be one that targets specific market segments because a one-strategy-fits-all approach is unlikely to be effective. In particular the communication strategy should identify the key approaches taken by the ATO to deal with the underground economy, the necessity and the importance to the community of the underground economy initiative and the results of any compliance initiative.

Given some academic literature on the neutralisation strategies adopted by certain individuals in reaction to market campaigns on the adverse effects of the underground economy, the Task Force encouraged the use of market research to follow up on the communication campaigns. An example of a neutralisation strategy by an individual contemplating evading taxes is the rationalisation that the government wastes the money that is collected from tax revenue so why should they continue to contribute, at least in full anyway. Therefore it is important that the ATO is able to deal with these issues before embarking on such a strategy.

Building Partnerships

Establishing cooperative partnerships with industry groups and the wider community is essential to maximise voluntary compliance. The ATO could benefit significantly from such a strategy particularly since the community or industry groups can identify specific areas of non-compliance that may not be known to the ATO. An example is the system of financial transactions reporting, for example, the banks identify to the ATO and other government agencies financial transactions that exceed a specified threshold level.

c) Encouraging and Supporting Compliance   Although the ATO had consulted with various industry groups (for example, the construction, restaurants and the taxi industries), the Task Force suggested that much more work needs to be done to promote better tax compliance. This work may begin with simple strategies such as contacting those visited by the ATO in field reviews, thanking them for their participation and offering help if the need arises. Such engagement with the community not only helps improve the ATO's image but may potentially motivate greater compliance within the community.

The Task Force sees that unintrusive educational support to businesses is an effective way to promote taxpayer compliance. The ATO has promoted a number of educational support schemes to encourage better record keeping and business practices. These have included business seminars, publications and technical advice, all of which are provided free of charge.

Record keeping is an essential part of running a business. It provides valuable information that may assist in strategically targeting future opportunities for business growth. The same records also provide a prospective buyer with information on the real value of the business. On a number of occasions the ATO has uncovered non-complying businesses often keep two sets of books – one for cash and the other for non-cash payments. It is when both sets of books are produced during the sale of a business that the non-compliance activities are discovered. The objective of the ATO's real time reviews is not only to ensure that such practices are not followed, but to assist the taxpayer keep an adequate and efficient system of business records. On this issue the Task Force strongly recommended the ATO to work with industry groups or associations to ensure that record keeping requirements do not adversely affect the daily operations of the business.

In 1998 the ATO released a set of preliminary financial ratios intended not only to assist businesses and their advisors to identify areas (for example, high cost items) where the business could improve upon, but to also identify those 'suspected' underground economy businesses reporting financial data that is markedly different from these benchmarks. These ratios are used as one of the identifying strategies to detect suspected underground economy operations.

The Task Force reviewed the possibility of amnesties offered to those who have evaded their tax paying obligations. However it is necessary, the Task Force believes, that the success of such a program depends on the ATO's ability to follow up those taxpayers whom are suspected of evading taxes and that have not taken up the amnesty offer. Its success also depends on the ATO's ability to follow up those claming amnesties to ensure that these individuals or businesses are not using this opportunity to distract the ATO from other serious non-compliance activities that they are involved in. On the implementation of such a strategy, the Task Force recommended that the amnesties be applied on an industry basis, particularly for those that have demonstrated a high risk of non-compliance.

The Task Force also recommended that the ATO encourage business regulatory practices that they could implement to help limit the opportunities for undertaking clandestine activities. Help from the community and industry associations, the CETF believed is the most effective way to deal with non-compliance.

d) Enforcing Compliance The Task Force recognised that there is no simple solution to the underground economy, however strategic policies need to be in place to help reduce underground economic activity. On *enforcing compliance*, the CETF made the following recommendations.

- The CETF recommended the widening of the scope of the financial transaction reporting requirements as defined by the Financial Transactions Reporting Act (1988). In particular the Task Force made a number of important suggestions, namely, (i) to extend the definition of cash dealers (to include businesses such as car dealers, travel agents, etc) and to require them to report cash transactions that exceed $10,000; (ii) to broaden the reporting requirements for a number of negotiable instruments such as bank drafts, bearer bonds and traveller cheques; (iii) the identification of all those individuals involved in International Funds Transfer Instructions to the Australian Transactions Reports and Analysis Centre (AUSTRAC); and (iv) solicitors to report large cash transactions ($10,000 or more) as well as suspicious transactions;

- The Task Force recommended that the ATO publicise it enforcement activities in industry and community publications;
- The Task Force recommended that the ATO work with the judiciary to highlight the costs of tax evasion so that more seriousness is given to the penalties handed out by the judicial system;
- The Task Force also made suggestions for on-the-spot fines with the condition that there would be clear guidelines for the fines, the offence and the obligations on the taxpayer. These guidelines would need to be drafted in consultation with industry associations and representatives;
- The Task Force also considered a number of other possible strategies to encourage compliance. These included: (i) compulsory education for first and minor offenders who would be required to attend an ATO compliance workshop; (ii) the naming of very serious offenders; and (iii) introducing reintegrative shaming. This last point stresses that public shaming may be undesirable and that it may be better to use a 'combination of disapproval of a wrong act combined with affirmation of the person as a worthy citizen', to improve future compliance.

Some Selected Results

The following industries have been targeted by the ATO: building and construction; cafes and restaurants; hairdressing; smash repairs; taxi service; road freight; cleaning services; fishing; fruit and vegetables; computing; clothing and textiles; scrap metals; security services; vehicle retailing; pubs, clubs and taverns and liquor wholesaling and manufacturing. The ATO had proposed at the time that the following industries become the next target for cash economy field work: tourism and hospitality; agricultural services; financial services and antique and art dealing.

The results from a number of selected industries include:

- Cleaning: of the sample of businesses in this industry that were investigated, 20 percent required upward adjustments in income by roughly $55,000 per case;
- Building and construction: of the sample of businesses in this industry that were investigated, 30 percent required upward adjustments in income by roughly $20,000 per case;
- Clothing: From a sample of roughly 300 businesses investigated, the ATO collected approximately $2.4m in unpaid tax and penalties;
- Scrap metal: Of 55 cases investigated by the ATO almost $1.2 million in unpaid taxes and penalties have been collected;
- Pubs, clubs and taverns: From a sample of roughly 620 businesses investigated, the ATO collected approximately $2.6m in unpaid tax and penalties;
- Community tip-offs: From approximately one-third of tip-offs received by the ATO have resulted in $70 million in unpaid taxes and penalty collections.

The Third CETF Report (2003)[8]

There were two major issues the Tax Commissioner asked of the Cash Economy Task Force when it met for its third sitting: (i) how the new tax system and the progress from the 1998 report has impacted on the underground economy and (ii) how the ATO may be better able to tackle non-compliance in the business-to-consumer sector. This last point is important because the new tax system has little in place to identify or limit these forms of clandestine activities.

Before the introduction of the GST, the ATO undertook a number of field activities in relation to the underground economy that were partially suspended when the new tax system was being introduced. The reason for this was the enormous pressure on resources required for the implementation of the new tax system. Nevertheless the more serious non-compliance issues were investigated and followed up by prosecutions.

During the introduction of the new tax system, the tax office made every effort to help individuals and businesses comply with the new tax regulations. In the process of doing so, it learnt a substantial amount about business practices which contributed immensely to implementing more effective tax compliance initiatives.

The Task Force in its third report made a total of 38 recommendations, 10 of which are worth noting here. The reader is referred to CETF (2003) for a detailed discussion on these and the other recommendations (which are summarised briefly below).

Summary of 10 Key Recommendations from the Third CETF Report (CETF, 2003, pp. xi-xiv)

1.	To continue to promote the benefits of the Australian Business Register (ABR) both to businesses and consumers.
2.	To continue promoting and sustaining compliance checks on businesses to ensure that they are withholding the right amount of tax from suppliers that do supply them with an Australian Business Number (ABN). To then follow up those businesses that do not report their ABN to encourage them to meet their compliance obligations.
3.	The Australian Taxation Office (ATO) to provide educational assistance to industry and small businesses to help meet their tax compliance obligations. This can be achieved through various products including industry codes of conduct and possibly promotion of self-regulating industries.
4.	To extensively promote and widen the scope of information on industry ratios obtained from income tax return data.
5.	To work with industry groups to help make the payments.
6.	The ATO to publicise how it will deal with poor record keeping, reporting and business registration and in particular to work with high risk industry groups to implement better compliance outcomes.

7.   The ATO to publicise cases of tax evasion involving either a jail sentence or significant monetary penalty.

8.   The ATO to evaluate the benefits and the costs associated with a broad advertising campaign designed to influence consumer attitudes towards tax compliance. This may involve a 'Get it in Writing' campaign similar to the one implemented in Canada.

9.   The ATO to provide information about the cash economy by providing feedback to the community on the information provided to them.

10.   The ATO work with other government agencies to examine data matching opportunities.

The ATO needs continue focusing on its relationship with industry and community groups and promote more effectively the various initiatives and products that the ATO has available to small business. In regards to compliance, the Task Force supported the use of escalating penalties for serious offences and the dissemination of information about ATO successes from its auditing and compliance strategies.

The risks of tax evasion from business-to-consumer transactions saw the Task Force recommend a strategy of 'get it in writing', much like the Canadian campaign to deal with these activities. The campaign in Canada was specifically targeted at consumers to educate them of the benefits of getting 'it in writing' (for example, having warranties).

The Task Force also make a further two recommendations: (i) a greater use of third party data (e.g. from local councils on building approvals, etc) for better data matching strategies; and (ii) the possibility of making it compulsory for businesses to report an ABN through requirements, say by insurance companies, to insure an extension to a home, etc.

How effective has this new tax system been? The Task Force made the assessment on the basis on the following criteria: (i) the effectiveness of the new tax system to encourage businesses in the underground economy to comply with the new regulatory requirements; (ii) whether the system is simple and fair; and (iii) whether there has been a growth in revenue from underground economy activities as expected by the government.

Details provided by the ATO to Task Force members included: (i) a greater number of ABN registrations than had been expected; (ii) a number of past non-lodgers appear now to be engaged in the legitimate economy; (iii) the new tax system is increasingly becoming perceived as more simple, evident from an AC Nielsen Businesses experiences survey in 2002 (see CETF, 2003). An expected $2.6 billion in additional revenue was believed would be collected from the underground economy over a three year period. The ATO reported to the Task Force that, at the time of the writing of the report, the expected target was likely to be reached.

In the three years since the introduction of the GST the amount of tax withholdings for not reporting an ABN has increased steadily, $21 million in 2000-01, $42 million in 2001-02 and $72 million in 2002-03 (see CETF, 2003). From those that have had income withheld, about 25 percent have not applied for an input tax credit. The ATO is researching this to determine whether (i) the entity is operating in the underground economy and has other income which it is not reporting; or (ii) whether some taxpayers are unaware of their entitlements. The Task Force encourages this research as well as research into why businesses do not report their ABN in the first place.

a) Encouraging and Enforcing Compliance The Task Force recommended that the ATO become involved at the early stages of business formation to provide advice and assistance. This could take the form of 'information starter packs' detailing bookkeeping information, and adequate cash flow management strategies, information on tax invoices and the use of the ABN and withholding obligations. The ATO currently offers free Bizstart seminars which focus on setting up a business, reporting and bookkeeping obligations, income tax and deductions and the GST.

The Task Force also highly recommended the continuing and strengthening of the relationship with industry and business associations and in particular to possibly undertake the following initiatives: (i) the development of a tax best practice code for various industry classifications to include information on record keeping, GST and income tax obligations, cash flow management, invoicing, etc; (ii) industry codes of conduct that might detail specific consequences if a business fails to meet these obligations; (iii) industry regulation by peer review whereby the industry self-monitors non-compliance with best practice or industry codes. The industry panel overseeing this regulation may provide a non-compliant member with solutions to follow or refer them to the tax office if appropriate.

The Task Force also made a number of recommendations in relation to enforcing compliance: (i) those business participating in the underground economy need to know the consequences of non-compliance; (ii) there should be transparency in the compliance program so that agents may advice their clients on the right choice of action following an ATO enforcement action; and (iii) there needs to be transparency and community acknowledgement that the compliance program is being targeted across all types of businesses.

The ATO has conducted a number of visits to businesses in high risk industries to monitor record keeping and compliance. ATO data suggests that during 2002-03, 660 ATO officers visited 16,500 businesses which was projected to increase to 30,000 visits during 2003-04. Field staff are currently using a variety of compliance products to deal with underground economy activities. These include: (i) the use of customised letters to businesses that have reported income/expenses that fall outside the industry norm. The ATO then requests that these businesses provide an explanation for this outcome; (ii) review of the firm's books to ensure that there are adequate record keeping strategies in place; (iii) unannounced visits intended to offer assistance with tax related matters; (iv) comprehensive audits that provide an in-depth examination of the business's financial affairs; and (v) the use of inter-agency data for cross-checking information.

In response to the Task Force recommendation on record keeping, the ATO is expecting to put into place on-the-spot fines for poor record keeping. The penalties will apply to those who do not improve their record keeping behaviour after being advised to do so.

The Task Force also recommended increasing the visibility of enforcement activities by the use of either media messages or industry publications.

b) Business-to-Consumer Dealings   The major focus of the third Cash Economy Task Report was on business-to-consumer dealings. Typically these transactions are high-volume small-value transactions. Acknowledging that this area of non-compliance is a difficult one to monitor and stamp out, the Task Force made a number of important recommendations. We briefly look at each of these.

The Cash Economy Task Force recommended influencing community attitudes (say through media campaigns) in the fight against non-compliance. Other channels that may be used could include mail outs either from the ATO or large employers through the industry partnerships they may have with the ATO. The Task Force (and the ATO) have reviewed some of the media campaigns used abroad (e.g. Canada and Sweden) to measure their effectiveness. The Task Force believes that more research needs to be undertaken on the cost-benefits of a communication strategy.

The Task Force observed that the process of reporting of tax evasion by the community to the ATO is not well understood. The recommendation is that the public needs to be further educated about this. At the same time the ATO is obligated to ensure that timely information is provided on the outcomes based on the information provided by the community.

The Task Force also suggested further examination of third party requirements to demand an ABN prior to offering a service. For example, the Yellow Pages require that a business provides an ABN before they can advertise with them.

Government's Response to the CETF Reports

a) First CETF Report[9]   In June 1997 the Commissioner of Taxation responded to the first CETF report announcing the implementation of a number of key recommendations. At the time there was a significant deployment of staff in a number of national and regional cash orientated industries. The ATO significantly increased its engagement with tax practitioners, industry and community groups in an attempt to influence community attitudes towards paying taxes while improving its communication with a number of government agencies including the Department of Social Security.

There remained a number of other issues however that would take some time for the ATO to completely achieve. Although progress on these has been ongoing, at the time these included:

- developing a stronger relationship with the community to help reduce tax payer non-compliance;
- developing a more coherent and structured approach to existing compliance programs; and
- developing a better understanding of the dynamics influencing underground economy behaviour.

b) Second CETF Report[10] By the time of the second report, the ATO's approach to dealing with the tax evasion and underground economy activities included real time reviews of high-risk industries (fieldwork), collaboration with the Cash Economy Team and advice given by the members of the Cash Economy Task Force. The Cash Economy Team is responsible for designing compliance approaches to deal with specific underground economy issues, to measure the compliance dividend and to make suggestions and refinements to the strategies used by the ATO in dealing with tax evasion. The Cash Economy Team has a number of objectives, some of which are summarised in the table below.

Table 4   Strategies and activities of the ATO's cash economy teams

Strategies	Activities
To address those who omit income	
Tax Return and BAS Verification and Analysis	- BAS Outliers - Field Visits - Random Sampling
Responding to community and other information	- Community Information Storage - Communication and Observation - Other referrals - AUSTRAC - Barter Pilot
Matching	- Comparing BAS to Income Tax Returns - Large Payer/s project - BAS Withholding/ABN checks
Client Education	- Advisory visits - Record keeping reviews - Media and publications
Mandatory Reporting	- Research and analysis in high risk industries - Develop and submit case for legislative changes
To address those not in the system	
Matching	- New entrant and new registrants - Internal and external data re ABR - BAS withholding and ABN checks - Large Payer/s project - Community Information Storage Communication and Observation (CISCO) - AUSTRAC

Source: ANAO (2002)

As part of the Cash Economy initiative the ATO introduced real time reviews in a number of industries including the building/construction and the restaurant/cafe industries. The ATO would frequently, but irregularly, visit these businesses to ensure that good records are being kept. During the review process the ATO would collect information to establish its benchmark ratios. These ratios are used by the ATO to give a first impression as to whether the business is likely to be non-compliant. Depending on whether there is a large discrepancy between the ratio constructed from the business's records and these industry wide benchmarks, the ATO would recommend follow up visits and extend the review period. Below we provide the findings for each of the Cash Economy Initiatives for the various industries targeted.

b.1) Building and Construction   The ATO undertook field visits to building sites with the objective to increasing its direct contact with the major payers and payees in order to help establish an external database that could be used to cross check particular tax returns. This initiative helped uncover a number of undesirable practices in the building and construction industry (see ATO, 1998):

- A number of workers in the industry did not have tax file numbers;
- There was a substantial number of tax returns that had not been lodged. The ATO detected one sub-contractor who had not lodged their tax return for eight years;
- Cash transactions were not properly recorded;
- There was a number of failures by those in the building industry who did not remit or deduct withholdings under the old Prescribed Payments System (PPS);
- There was evidence of cheques being cashed in licensed pubs to avoid them appearing in business records.

b.2) Clothing Industry   Before the introduction of the Reportable Payments System (RPS) in the clothing industry, a number of audits revealed that tax evasion was happening on a wide scale. With the introduction of the RPS, the ATO had uncovered a number of tax evasion schemes including false invoicing. The clothing industry in Australia was characterised as having multi-stages of production involving both formal and informal occupational practices. Many of these stages of production appeared tied together with loose contractual agreements particularly with the more informal sector of the economy. The informal sector was characterized by a large number of home based production typically paid in cash. The clothing industry was found to exhibit the following characteristics (ATO, 1998):

- that much of the work undertaken is performed at home (home-based production);
- the production process is very labour intensive and very little capital equipment is required;
- there is typically exploitation of outworkers that generally have low employment opportunities elsewhere;

- there are often a large number of fraudulent Social Security claims amongst outworkers;
- very low levels of cooperation with government regulation; and
- cultural factors which may include poor language skills.

Although these characteristics varied widely, they clearly highlight the fact that underground economy drivers are many and complex. The findings suggest that sector specific policies targeted at the underground economy are likely to be most efficient in reducing tax evasion than a broad and singular reform.

b.3) Restaurants and Cafes and Fruit and Vegetables   The Prescribed Payments System (no longer in place) was introduced in the Fruit and Vegetable industry in 1997. The ATO had since undertaken over 1,000 visits to businesses in the industry including green grocers, wholesales and growers. The ATO was happy with the improvement in record keeping but there was still some concern about the volume of cash payments that were taking place.

In the Restaurant and Cafe industry the ATO implemented a three month trial of real time interviews. The owner/operators were required to keep records which the ATO would assess using the financial ratios they had constructed for that industry. The piloted study produced some good results. It increased reported sales by 14.85 percent or an equivalent of $45,000 per taxpayer per year. Of the sample that was under investigation, 44 percent had shown improvements in their sales, possibly due to the fact their records were being constantly monitored, and where appropriate, cash counts would be made to match records with till tape records.

b.4) Prescribed Computer Goods   In response to a large number of complaints by businesses that there was widespread sales tax evasion in the personal computer industry, the ATO increased its field presence and fined offenders quickly so that the message gets out that sales tax evaders will be detected and prosecuted. When it became clear that sales tax evasion in the computer industry was extensive, the project was given a high priority. The federal government in 1997 allocated additional funding for the ATO to help eliminate sales tax evasion in the industry. After extensive audits had been undertaken many income tax returns were adjusted upwards, refunds were withheld and penalties imposed that reaped the ATO approximately $20 million.

b.5) Taxis   The ATO undertook a Taxi Industry Project in 1994 with an objective of developing a tax collection system for taxi drivers, decreasing non-disclosure of taxi income and to increase the lodgement of tax returns. The ATO has increased its presence in the industry by offering a number of educational strategies that have included seminars, articles in relevant magazines, and distribution of flyers. The Taxi Industry Project delivered some benefits, namely, (i) a $53.2 million increase in taxable income; (ii) a $9.06 million increase in tax being assessed; and (iii) a $2.67 million increase in penalties and interest. Almost 7,000 taxi operators and taxi drivers were reviewed and a number of annual benchmarks were established (takings per kilometre). When a taxi driver had not kept adequate records these benchmarks could be used to determine the tax liability of the taxi driver.

The recommendations made by the CETF in its second report (CETF, 1998) required the ATO to pursue a more active and multi-dimensional strategy to dealing with the underground economy. In particular the ATO was recommended to: (i) develop and sustain a partnership with the community; (ii) implement appropriate educational strategies designed to improve record keeping and general compliance with the tax system, (ii) adopt a hands on approach to compliance either through more intensive audits or field work presence; and (iv) undertake or encourage research to better understand issues driving non-compliance in the community.

In the following table we briefly summarize the ATO's response to the various recommendations made by the CETF in its second report. These recommendations are divided according to the headings discussed previously in the chapter. A more detailed discussion of these recommendations can be found in the Australian National Audit Office (ANAO) report (2001-02), The ANAO's task was to report to Parliament on the ATO's progress on the underground economy. The summary of the results given in Table 5 is drawn from this report.

Table 5   An analysis of the CETF recommendations – Second Report

Recommend-ations on:	Status of the CETF Recommend-ations	Comments
Understanding Compliance	Implemented	- The ATO has implemented the use of the compliance model into the ATO's compliance strategy.
	Partially implemented	- The ATO continues to pursue a research agenda into underground economy activities. - The ATO to engage more actively in undertaking market research to identify areas of high risk and to put this to strategic use. Since the ANAO report the ATO has engaged more actively in this area.
Building Community Partnerships	Implemented	- The ATO has engaged effectively with the various state revenue authorities and has undertaken a community strategy to produce brochures targeted to specific industries, while engaging in community and industry discussion involving tax reform.

Table 5   (continued)

	Partially implement	- The ANAO found that although the ATO has engaged with the business community, stakeholders reported to the ANAO that discussion on the underground economy were limited. The ATO is now more actively engaging with the community and business on matters relating to the underground economy specifically.
Encouraging and Supporting Compliance	Implemented	- The ATO has worked on improving its image by reviewing its correspondence with the community. It has also worked on giving taxpayers timely feedback and providing public education programs on good record keeping. - The ATO has also worked with industry and community groups to maximise the benefits from the use of industry benchmarks as well as on producing innovative industry specific regulatory solutions to dealing with under-reporting of income.
	Partially implemented	- Although the ATO has worked to promote good record keeping for reasons other than taxation, the ANAO found that there was little understanding in the micro-community of the need to keep better records.
	Not Implemented	- The CETF recommended targeted amnesties as part of an integrated approach to reducing non-compliance. The Tax Commissioner did not agree to this recommendation, as there are already concessions in place for voluntary disclosure.
Enforcing Compliance	Implemented	- The ATO has undertaken research to test the reliability of using industry benchmarks to raise default assessment. The ATO have found these benchmarks to be credible and uses these to make adjustments on default assessments.
	Partially Implemented	- At the time of the ANAO report, the ATO was found not effectively using AUSTRAC data, however since this ANAO report a more active engagement between the ATO and AUSTRAC senior staff have occurred.

Table 5   (continued)

	- The ANAO also found the ATO lacking in its publication of media releases that publicise its enforcement activities, which are necessary for increasing public awareness of the ATO's engagement in deterring underground economic activities. Work in this area continues.
	- The CETF recommended on-the-spot fines for poor record keeping. The Act has been amended to allow for an administrative penalty when a tax law is not adhered to in relation to record keeping, but on-the-spot fines have not be introduced.
Not Implemented	As compulsory education to complement current enforcement strategies may require legislative backing, this has not be undertaken by the ATO.

Source: ANAO (2002)

In addition to reviewing the ATO's response to the CETF recommendations, the ANAO made five (5) of its own recommendations to the ATO (see ANAO, 2002). The reader is referred to this report for further details on these five recommendations.

• *The Cash Economy Team needs to review its management framework to ensure that its initiatives are supported effectively with clear planning, communication, priorities, monitoring processes and project deliverables.* The ATO agreed with this and has actively engaged in ensuring staff are aware not only of the management structure and project responsibilities relating to the underground economy, but also on the more important project initiation briefs as well as evaluation techniques to monitor the progress of existing underground economy projects.

• *The Cash Economy Team take appropriate action to improve its knowledge sharing by maintaining a formal system of records that is nationally accessible and regularly updated.* The ATO agreed with this recommendation and in conjunction with the CEFT and other government departments are exploring ways to expand this electronic data-sharing requirement.

• *The ATO pursue further its engagement with industry and the community by more regular meetings to discuss their concerns relating to the cash economy and to promote these meetings not only as an intelligence forum but to gain industry based support for the ATO's cash economy projects.* The ATO has agreed with this and has already expanded its engagement with its industry partners beyond that which had already been established.

- *The ATO take action to implement a coordinated education campaign to address community attitudes to the cash economy.* The ANAO found that more effort by the ATO is required if an education campaign is to raise an awareness of the underground economy and change community attitudes on participating in this sector. It is important however that more research be undertaken before any communication campaign is pursued given the considerable expense and time it may take to effectively execute this strategy.
- *The ATO enhance its cash economy intelligence and to take steps to use AUSTRAC data more strategically in its cash economy project.* The ANAO found that while the ATO exhibited declining demand for AUSTRAC data, there was still a number of staff inadequately trained to use this data even if the desire arose. The ANAO made a strong recommendation that ATO better integrate AUSTRAC data in its underground economy planning and better train their staff in the use of AUSTRAC data. Since this recommendation a number of senior staff at the ATO has been working with staff at AUSTRAC to help identify areas of AUSTRAC data that may be of significance for ATO cash economy compliance programs.

c) Third CETF Report[11] The ATO responded positively to the recommendations made by the CETF in its third report, agreeing to the majority of the recommendations, while also agreeing in principle to the other recommendations that the ATO felt required feasibility testing before implementing. In the following table we provide the Tax Commissioner's response to the recommendations. For further details the reader is referred to ATO (2003a).

Table 6   The ATO's response to the cash economy task force recommendations – Third Report

Recommend-ations on:	ATO's Response	Comments
The Current Environment	Agreed (to 8 of 8 recommend-ations)	- The ATO has a number of tools to promote the ABR namely staff information kits, brochures, e-mail feedback channels, an agency web-site and privacy kits for agencies. The ATO however is committed to promote further the benefits of the ABR to get the message across to the wider community. - The ATO to continue with integrity checks to make sure that businesses are withholding from suppliers that don't provide an ABN. The ATO currently undertakes invoice checks during its field visits. In addition to providing integrity checks, real time interviews allow for on-the-spot education for those failing to meet obligations.

Table 6   (continued)

		- The ATO to place a greater emphasis on educating those in high risk industries on their obligations with regards to reporting their ABN. The ABN registration Guide is being reviewed to ensure that individuals are given clear instructions on its use. - The ATO will undertake research to determine why new businesses end up accumulating substantial debts in their start up period when they are not obliged to make PAYGI. This research will involve a range of focus groups and discussions with industry partners.
Encouraging Compliance	Agreed (to 9 of 10 recommend-ations)	- The ATO agreed to continue working with industry groups to improve with the current range of products offered to new business (e.g. *Tax Basics* booklet and the *Activity Statement Updater* publication). - The ATO agreed to work more extensively with industry partners to identify appropriate communication channels to get across key cash economy messages. The ATO will develop a cash economy website that is linked to its current tax evasion referral centre site as well as providing seminars to tax practitioners on specific cash economy industries. - The ATO is working to develop codes of conduct addressing tax issues for those industries where its members may be know to be operating outside the tax system. - The ATO will review its information products in conjunction with the relevant industry groups to ensure that they cover the usual problem areas such as poor record keeping, inappropriate invoices, poor cash flow management and inadequate use of the ABN. - The ATO to market voluntary payments and voluntary agreements to small business so that they are aware of the opportunities available to better manager their cash flow. The ATO however acknowledges that for this to be successful the support of industry groups is required.

Table 6   (continued)

	Agreed subject to testing (1 of 10 recommend-ations)	- The ATO is working to find ways to ensure making payments is a lot easier and cheaper. One option is the adoption of the easy-pay card that is being used in the taxi industry. If the card is a success, the ATO intends to take this approach across other industries. - The CETF recommended calls for expression of interest to develop a best practice tax curriculum for small business, which the ATO could then record such accreditation against the business's ABN. The ATO agreed to a trial period for testing this recommendation because it realises that the approach has to be a cost effective one that delivers the desired benefits.
Enforcing Compliance	Agreed (to 7 of 9 recommend-ations)	- The ATO to continue to disseminate outcomes of successful and significant cases that have resulted in conviction of individual(s) for tax evasion. - The ATO to examine more efficient and effective ways to collect data for matching purposes without infringing on the rights of businesses and individuals. - The ATO to continue to evaluate the effectiveness of all cash economy projects, in particular through an analysis of costs and benefits for businesses following stakeholder consultations. - The ATO to explore ways of furthering their current communication strategies for publishing their enforcement initiatives.
	Agreed subject to testing (to 2 of 9 recommend-ations)	- The ATO to consider, subject to testing, a case management system to monitor and assist in reintegrating non-compilers guilty of serious offences from 1 July 2003.
Business-to-consumer dealings	Agreed (to 7 of 11 recommend-ations)	- The ATO undertake a risk assessment of industries with significant business-to-consumer dealings. The ATO from its current projects acknowledges that there may be some difficulties in the assessment of specific business-to-consumer dealings as many businesses in the high-risk areas have a mix of business and consumer dealings.

Table 6   (continued)

	- The ATO to continue its research on consumer attitudes towards tax compliance.
	- The ATO to undertake a broad scale advertising campaign to influence community attitudes to tax compliance. The ATO acknowledges that such a campaign will have significant cost because of the long-term nature that such campaigns will need to be run in order that they become effective.
	- The ATO to continue to encourage the community in general to report suspected tax evasion by contacting the ATO anonymously either by internet (tax evasion web-site), phone or mail.
Agreed subject to testing (to 4 of 11 recommend-ations)	- The ATO to consider a 'get it in writing' campaign similar to the one implemented in Canada. The ATO is considering a pilot in the building and construction sector depending on industry support. The objective is to have industry promote the benefits of getting it in writing as a way of protecting consumer rights.
	- The ATO to develop and distribute jointly branded brochures setting tax responsibilities in the various industries, particularly those dealing heavily with the consumer.
	- The ATO to consider the possibility of providing tax compliance messages in addition to other mail outs sent by businesses to their employees and clients. In addition, following business support, the material will need to be reviewed to ensure that the most effective format for delivery is undertaken.

Source: ATO (2003a)

Conclusion

There is no quick fix strategy for reducing the size of the underground economy. The CETF was set up to assist the ATO to come to terms with the motives, consequences and possible strategies to deal with the underground economy in Australia. The Task Force stressed the importance of the Taxpayer's Charter in facilitating a better 'relationship with the community based on mutual respect and trust' as a good starting point to tackle non-compliant behaviour.

The Cash Economy Task Force adapted the work of Ayres and Braithwaite (1992) on strategies for regulation and Braithwaite (1998) on trust norms to develop a compliance model to complement the ATO's Taxpayer's charter. The model has multiple tiers each designed to reduce tax evasion by dishonest taxpayers. In the first instance the ATO' strategy is to encourage self-compliance through means such as education and ATO support. If this approach does not to work then various escalating enforcement strategies are pursued in order to produce the compliant behaviour required. The main principles of the compliance model are: (i) to develop an understanding of taxpayer behaviour; (ii) to establish strong community partnerships which will be on-going; (iii) to give the ATO the necessary flexibility to not only support compliant behaviour but also to encourage a strong compliant attitude among the taxpaying community; and (iv) to develop more options to enforce tax compliance on those who consistently choose not to comply.

The ATO's engagement with the CETF proved to be a fundamental stepping-stone for rapid changes in the ATO's internal policy towards effectively tackling the underground economy in Australia. Each of the three reports produced by the CETF provided a number of recommendations, which have essentially been adopted by the ATO. As in the case of Canada, the US and the UK discussed in earlier chapters of this book, their active engagement by their respective tax administration highlights the benefits being reaped in the form of better tax compliance. The results overall set a great example for other countries to follow, which have yet to embark on a dedicated program aimed at tackling underground economic activities adversely affecting their economies.

Notes

*   I would like to thank the Australian Taxation Office for providing copies of the Cash Economy Task Force Reports. Any views expressed in this article are the author's personal opinion and should not be attributed to either the Australian Taxation Office or the Cash Economy Task Force.

1. The surveys are conducted by an independent consultant for the ATO. The survey is nationwide and the sample size is approximately 2000 individuals aged 18 years and over. Age and sex quotas were used for each state and the survey was conducted by telephone (for more details see ATO, 2003).

2. The reader may wish to consult CETF (2003) for a more detailed discussion on the current tax environment.

3. For example, a painter with a gross income of $60,000 would typically report a net profit somewhere between $21,000 and $24,000. This implies a net profit to gross income ratio between 35 percent and 40 percent. At the same time if the painter is paying wages of say $10,000, that painter would typically have an income between $40,000 and $50,000, which implies a wage to turnover ratio between 20 percent and 25 percent (see Media Release – 'Benchmarks established to assist cash industries', 7 January 1998, Nat 98/01, Australian Taxation Office, Canberra).

4. All businesses that have an annual turnover of $50,000 or more must register for the GST. Only businesses registered for the GST can issue a valid tax invoice that another business, if also registered for the GST, can use to claim an input tax credit. For those businesses registered for the GST they need to report their activities in a Business

Activity Statement (BAS) whereas those businesses not registered for the GST are required to complete an Instalment Activity Statement (IAS) to make their regular tax payments to the tax office throughout the year.

5. See CETF (1997).
6. The reader is referrred to CETF (1997) for more details.
7. The reader is referrred to CETF (1998) for more details.
8. The reader is referrred to CETF (2003) for more details.
9. See CETF (1998).
10. Various sources including ATO(1998), CETF (1998) and ANAO (2002).
11. The reader is referred to ATO(2003a) for more details.

References

Australian National Audit Office (ANAO) (2002), *ATO Progress in Addressing the Cash Economy*, Audit Report No.35 (2001-2002), ANAO Publication, Canberra.

Australian Taxation Office (ATO) (1998), *Benchmarks Established to Assist Cash Industries*, Cash Economy Media Release, ATO Publication, Canberra.

Australian Taxation Office (ATO) (2003), *The Commissioner of Taxation – Annual Report (2002-2003)*, ATO Publication, Canberra.

Australian Taxation Office (ATO) (2003a), 'Commissioner's Response to the Cash Economy Task Force Recommendations', Response to the *Cash Economy Under the New Tax System*, ATO Publication, Canverra.

Ayres, I. and Braithwaite, J. (1992), *Responsive Regulation, Transcending the Deregulation Debate*, Oxford University Press, New York, pp. 3-53.

Bhattacharyya, D.K. (1990), 'An Econometric Method of Estimating the Hidden Economy, United Kingdom (1960-1984): Estimates and Tests', *The Economic Journal*, Vol. 100, September, pp. 703-17.

Braithwaite, V. (1998), 'Communal and Exchange Trust Norms, Their Value and Relevance to Institutional Trust', in V. Braithwaite and M. Levi (1998), pp. 46-74.

Braithwaite, V. and Levi, M. (1998), *Trust and Governance*, Russel Sage, New York.

Braithwaite, V., Braithwaite, J., Gibson, D and Makkai, T. (1994), 'Regulatory Styles, Motivational Postures and Nursing Home Compliance', *Law and Policy*, Vol. 16(4), pp. 363-94.

Business Review Weekly (BRW) (2000), 'Why the GST is Good news for the Black Economy', June 2000, pp. 10, 68-76.

Cash Economy Task Force (CETF) (1997), *Imporving Tax Compliance in the Cash Economy*, Report to the Tax Commissioner (No. 1), ATO Publication, Canberra.

Cash Economy Task Force (CETF) (1998), *Imporving Tax Compliance in the Cash Economy*, Report to the Tax Commissioner (No. 2), ATO Publication, Canberra.

Cash Economy Task Force (CETF) (2003), *The Cash Economy under the New Tax System*, Report to the Tax Commissioner (No. 3), ATO Publication, Canberra.

Giles, D.E.A. (1999), 'Modeling the Hidden Economy and the Tax-Gap in New Zealand', *Empirical Economics*, Vol. 24. pp. 621-40.

Giles, D.E.A. and Tedds, L.M. (2002), *Taxes and the Canadian Hidden Economy*, Canada Tax Foundation, Toronto.

Smith, S. and Weid-Nebbeling, S. (1986), *The Shadow Economy in Britain and Germany*, Anglo-German Foundation, London.

Chapter 14

Tax Compliance Strategies to Tackle the Underground Economy*

Simon James

Introduction

When 'Public Enemy No. 1' Al Capone was convicted for income tax evasion he apparently exclaimed 'This is preposterous. You can't tax illegal money!' He was sentenced to eleven years in prison. In many countries revenue authorities continue to respond not only to tax evasion as conventionally understood but also to financial crimes associated with organised crime, money laundering, public corruption, smuggling and other aspects of the 'underground economy'. Much of this work, of course, is less dramatic than the jailing of famous gangsters but no less important for that.

Although by its very nature it is impossible to measure the level of tax evasion accurately, in the USA the Commissioner of the Internal Revenue Service (Everson, 2004) estimated that quarter of a trillion dollars were lost each year because taxpayers do not pay their tax voluntarily or in a timely fashion. Furthermore the problem could be getting worse – again taking the USA as an example, Everson (2004) reported that over the period 1999 to 2003 the number of Americans saying that it was acceptable to evade taxation rose from 11 to 17 percent.

Furthermore strategies designed to tackle the underground economy should be revised as necessary to take account of changing times and circumstances. For example, in the UK the House of Commons Committee of Public Accounts (2004) stated that the tax compliance strategy set out by the Inland Revenue in the 1980s was no longer adequate. The Committee stated that the Inland Revenue should set a date for completing and publishing their revised compliance strategy, which should include 'an explicit strategy for preventing, detecting investigating and deterring fraud, and the performance measures by which they will assess achievement'.

The issue affects everyone because, of course, tax evasion necessarily means that the tax burden on honest taxpayers is higher or the levels of public expenditure are lower than they would otherwise be, or both. However, action to enforce compliance should be taken with care since it may not only increase public expenditure but also adversely affect the legitimate sector in other ways, such as greater regulation and more extensive auditing. Furthermore, a harsh and overzealous policy of enforcing tax compliance may produce undesirable and unnecessary side effects such as taxpayer resistance. It might generate an unwillingness to undertake legitimate commercial activities if there is a risk of heavy handed treatment from the tax authorities. It might also make a country less competitive in all sorts of ways – an increasingly important consideration in a global economy. The process of developing sophisticated tax compliance strategies is not a simple or easy one but necessary if tax evasion is to be tackled without excessive economic and political collateral damage.

A distinction is often made between tax avoidance and evasion. Tax avoidance refers to behaviour of individuals or businesses designed to reduce tax liability by legal means, for example by taking advantage of tax concessions for particular activities. Tax evasion refers to action to reduce tax paid by illegal means, for example by failing to disclose taxable income. Tax evasion is the primary concern relating to the underground economy though some strategies designed to reduce tax evasion might also help contain undesirable forms of tax avoidance.

To examine the process of developing tax compliance strategies the next section turns to academic literature in management for guidance in the process of developing strategy. The following section then examines this process with respect to tax compliance. The main themes in developing optimal tax compliance strategies are to take wider considerations into account – such as the purposes of the tax system, individuals' motivations regarding compliance and the different ways in which tax authorities can both encourage compliance and discourage evasion. The final section provides a summary and offers some conclusions.

Developing Strategies

Management is the academic discipline that has paid most attention to the subject of developing strategy. An essential input in the development of successful strategies is the systematic analysis and understanding of the factors involved. This includes the wider environment in which the activity is being conducted as well as the areas of immediate concern. Furthermore a key part in the development of strategy is implementation. Henry Mintzberg (2004, p. 55) is one of the most prominent management scholars in the area and believes that strategy is an interactive process requiring constant feedback between thought and action and that successful strategies evolve from experience. He also stresses the importance of strategists having expertise in the area and that they should not simply pontificate at a high level of abstraction and leave it to others to implement the strategies (and certainly not blame them for any shortcomings in the strategy). Other commentators, such as Grant (2002, p. 25), are also clear that the formulation and implementation of strategy go together. A well-designed strategy should take account of the process of implementation and it is through the implementation that a strategy can be refined and reformulated.

A strategic approach to tax policy has been explored before – for example with respect to tax simplification by James and Wallschutzky (1997), Here it was stressed that even tax simplification was a complicated process – and needed not just *ad hoc* responses but a strategy that took account of the different factors generating complexity and the best ways of responding to them in the context of the tax system as a whole.

More generally, all aspects of policy should be consistent not only with other activities within a particular government department or agency but also with other government policies. For example, because they frequently have a large proportion of their receipts in the form of cash, small businesses may have more scope than other taxpayers to evade tax. However, government policy is often designed to encourage small business activity for a range of reasons (see for instance Channon et al., 2002; Holz-Eakin, 1995). If small businesses are to be a particular target then care should be taken that the effect of the action will deter tax evasion without also discouraging small business enterprise. The failure to take account of wider effects of enforcement action may result in a particular action appearing successful but only at a cost elsewhere that might be overlooked. Klepper and Nagin (1989), for example, point out that a policy change designed to reduce one form of non-compliance might result in taxpayers transferring their non-compliance activities to take advantage of a now superior alternative opportunity.

Developing Tax Compliance Strategies

The OECD (2004) has laid out a process, which it refers to as compliance risk management, for the identification, assessment, ranking and treatment of tax compliance risks systematically. This general approach is also followed in this paper but with a number of differences including an analysis of non-compliance earlier in the process. The process developed here consists of the following stages:

1. Establish clearly the aims of the tax system. A major function of taxation is, of course, to raise revenue but tax systems are also used for other purposes.
2. Specify the administrative constraints under which the tax system must operate.
3. Identify different risks of non-compliance.
4. Assess the importance of the risks.
5. Analyse compliance behaviour.
6. Develop tax compliance strategies, taking account of the aims and objectives of the tax system and broader government economic and social policies. The strategies should take account of both the areas of highest priority and those where there is the highest probability of success. These strategies should also take account of the work of other government enforcement agencies and wherever possible be developed in conjunction with them.
7. Plan and implement compliance strategies including intended outcomes.
8. Monitor and evaluate the performance of the strategies against the plan.

These stages will now be examined further.

The Aims of the Tax System

As indicated above the main objective of a tax system is usually to raise revenue for public expenditure. However, in some cases taxes are used to pursue other policy objectives such as discouraging some activities and encouraging others (see, for example, James and Nobes, 2004). If the tax structure is designed to promote particular economic and social policies then these considerations should also be reflected in the compliance strategy. For example, if the aim of higher taxes on tobacco is designed to reduce tobacco consumption then a different strategy regarding tax compliance might be appropriate than in an area where the government wishes to encourage a particular activity or sector, such as small businesses mentioned above.

Public opinion is also important and it should not be forgotten that the overall aim of the tax system and the public expenditure it supports is an overall increase in economic welfare. Compliance is not an end in itself but a means to an end. Excessive or inappropriate compliance activity will reduce the point of the whole process. Unfortunately sometimes this is lost in the process of implementation as illustrated by the following quotation from an Internal Revenue Service [IRS] collection officer's statement before a Senate Committee in the USA:

> To exhibit any sensitivity to and understanding of the taxpayer's current individual circumstances is anathema ... When the question of priorities comes up, [IRS] management replies that: 'The maximizing of revenue is not a priority. The priorities are compliance and making an example of delinquent taxpayers through seizure'. This statement was actually made by two branch chiefs.
>
> This attitude of punishing citizens permeates the entire management cadre. The manager in Ann Arbor has stated that he does not care if he has to close up half the businesses in Ann Arbor in order to get compliance ...
>
> This same manager has also referred to some business taxpayers as 'dens of thieves'. The management's guiding principle seems to be that if we apply very heavy-handed enforcement, we will dissuade other potential tax delinquents. (Quoted in Payne, 1993, p. 72)

Fortunately such extreme views are not commonly expressed but even unduly intrusive compliance activity may be counter-productive even in terms of very narrow objectives. For example, both Schmölders (1970) and Strümpel (1969, p. 29) reported that the German system was very rigid in its assessment procedures, which led to an effective but expensive and confrontational system. The result 'of the relatively coercive tax-enforcement techniques is the high degree of alienation from the state ... [which] negatively influences the willingness to cooperate'.

Such matters make it very clear that optimal policy is something less than total compliance at all costs.

Administrative Constraints

Furthermore, there are often other constraints on some forms of action. For instance some compliance strategies may be politically sensitive. There may be legal aspects, including obligations under international arrangements, which should be taken into account. Also, all strategies are subject to the overall resource limitations including staff resources and skills of the revenue agency and it may have changing priorities with respect to the use of these scarce resources.

Identify Different Risks of Non-Compliance

To establish the areas of significant risk a multilevel approach is needed. At the top level, an assessment is needed of the tax environment and the aspects that might be relevant to tax compliance. James and Sawyer (2004) examined globalisation and international tax trends and such an approach can be used to establish areas of risk and changes to risk. For example, globalisation poses particular difficulties for national tax authorities in ensuring compliance. Bhagwati's (2004) definition of globalisation is:

> Economic globalisation constitutes integration of national economies into the international economy through trade, direct foreign investment (by corporations and multinationals) short-term capital flows, international flows of workers and humanity generally and flows of technology.

The more internationally mobile money and people become the more scope there may be to evade taxation imposed at national level.

Such difficulties are magnified by technological changes, in particular the development of the internet and the World Wide Web. As we know, the internet consists of computer networks that enable users to share services and communicate with each other in ways that transcend national boundaries. The world wide web is the graphical hypertext part of the internet that incorporates images, video and audio elements as well as text. The internet was originally designed to reduce the damage to communications by nuclear attack since there is no central computer which can be targeted. In the same way the internet poses enforcement problems for revenue agencies as services and funds can flow in ways that are very difficult for revenue authorities to track (Sawyer, 1999).

Electronic commerce (e-commerce) – the ability to undertake transactions involving the exchange of goods and services electronically – is a rapidly growing phenomenon. Many commercial items are suitable for trading over the internet, for example computer software and recorded entertainment. On-line information, including research databases, periodicals and some encyclopaedias are available, as are consulting and similar services. Financial transactions and stock trading now take place electronically around the world and there are apparently even internet casinos located outside restrictive jurisdictions. Some of the problems of compliance facing revenue authorities as a result of the growth of e-commerce are outlined by Hickey (2000) and it is clear that international co-operation in these matters is very important for any successful compliance strategy (see, for example, Sawyer, 2003 and 2004).

As in other areas, however, the problem is not one simply of compliance. The benefits from the development of global electronic commerce in the form of increased wealth in all countries are very large. Therefore it is important to take care to avoid the creation of unnecessary barriers to its development, including taxation. At least part of the solution is international co-operation – a process that has been encouraged by international bodies such as the OECD.

Market Segmentation   One particular approach to developing compliance strategy is 'market segmentation'. This is a concept borrowed from the study of marketing but it also has an application in terms of public administration since it permits policy to be developed with respect to different client groups according to their particular circumstances. In the present context it helps to identify areas of above average risk of non-compliance. Furthermore it allows the revenue officials dealing with particular segments to develop their expertise in these areas. Categories often used by revenue services include the type of business – for example, farming, retail enterprises and professional taxpayers. Taxpayers might also be classified by size of business – such as 'small', 'medium' and 'large' businesses. Some of these categories may have more opportunity for non-compliance, for instance where a large proportion of revenue is received in cash.

Assess the Importance of the Risks

Since no tax authority is ever likely to have the resources to eliminate all non-compliance some assessment needs to be made of the importance of different risks of non-compliance.

Quantitative Estimates of Non-compliance   One method is the analysis of audit results and this is usually based on the frequency or magnitude or both of resulting adjustments to taxpayers' liability. Both dimensions are important since small tax losses over a large number of taxpayers can mean a large overall loss. It might also be possible to address such a widespread aspect of non-compliance through a change in the tax system itself.

Feinstein (1999) has outlined three ways of measuring non-compliance:

1.   Intensive data collection for a focused sub-sample of the population.
2.   Detection controlled estimation.
3.   Comparison of estimates produced by distinct datasets and models.

The first method may be based on audits of a sample of possible offenders. In the USA, the Internal Revenue Service's Taxpayers Compliance Measurement Program (TCMP) provided a good example, though it is now defunct.

The second method – detection controlled estimation – is designed to produce estimates of non-compliance that remain undetected even by auditing. Its main disadvantage, of course, is that it is not based on precise information about non-detection in specific cases. The third method involves the comparison of compliance data with data that measure a closely related activity or by taking the existing observable behaviour into account and then estimating the 'residual' effect of unobserved behaviour – see, for instance, Feige (1989) and a recent is example is provided by Lyssiotou et al. (2004).

Effects on Other Taxpayers   As indicated below, taxpayers are motivated by a wide range of factors and a belief in the integrity of a tax system is an important factor in encouraging compliance. If evasion is perceived to be widespread, acceptable and easy to undertake without detection or penalty then the more likely it is that others will also be tempted to evade tax themselves. Non-compliance practices that fall into such categories might therefore be considered a more important part of tax compliance strategy than other less obvious non-compliance risks.

The fairness of a tax system is important and a non-compliance policy that is perceived as bearing heavily on otherwise 'deserving' cases might have negative effects elsewhere. For instance where elderly, sick, poor taxpayers are perceived as being treated harshly, or where there were mitigating circumstances, then this might reduce the willingness of other taxpayers to co-operate with the tax authorities.

Analysis of Compliance Behaviour

One general point that has been suggested is that, in the past, most of the attention in this area has been devoted to why some taxpayers do not comply rather than why others do (Wallschutzky, 1993). Yet these are clearly two sides of the same coin and since the aim to is encourage the former group of taxpayers to behave like the latter group, it is necessary to understand the behaviour of both.

Compliance can be analysed further as, for example, along the lines laid out by the OECD (2004) into four broad categories of taxpayer obligation:

1.   Registering with the system.
2.   Submitting tax returns on time, also known as filing, furnishing or lodging tax returns.
3.   Reporting complete and accurate information, which includes good record keeping which might be required in case of further enquiry.
4.   Paying the taxation due on time.

In addition, of course, there are different degrees of non-compliance. As indicated above, lawful tax avoidance is not an issue here. However, even where a taxpayer does not meet his or her legal obligations in full there are different degrees of non-compliance and some of these are more serious than others. Indeed overpayment of tax might be regarded as a form of non-compliance and may be a matter of concern where it occurs as result of poor administration. Nevertheless it is true that many taxpayers do not seek out every possible method of reducing their tax liability. For example, in one Australian study McCrae and Reinhart (2003) had one respondent who stated 'I pay too much tax, I'm just too lazy to claim it! [a tax rebate] But I'd rather have a decent health system and pay more'.

Non-compliance may also arise from unintentional mistakes on the part of taxpayers, their advisers and even the tax authorities. The appropriate response to this sort of non-compliance is likely to be different from the failure to meet deadlines – in the submission of tax returns or payment of tax – and, even more seriously, deliberate fraud. Here again there are some areas of non-compliance that might merit a different level or type of response depending on the precise nature of the non-compliance. Furthermore all tax authorities have finite resources and decisions have to be made about how best to use them in combating non-compliance.

In developing a tax compliance strategy it is also important to analyse compliance behaviour with respect to taxation and an enormous amount of work has been done. Jackson and Milliron (1986) undertook a comprehensive review of tax compliance research prior to 1986 and Richardson and Sawyer (2001) repeated this exercise for subsequent tax compliance research. These studies looked at methodological issues and theoretical areas with potential relevance. They also focused on the relationship between compliance and fourteen variables, namely age, gender, education, income level, income source, occupation, peer influence, ethics, fairness, complexity, revenue authority contact, sanctions, the probability of detection and tax rates. In terms of these variables the evidence was often mixed, for instance even the overall impact of the severity of sanctions on tax compliance seems unclear. The existence of sanctions has a positive effect on compliance but increased severity of sanctions may or may not produce further increases in compliance.

One way of classifying the huge amount of research results in this area is to divide it into two categories – that which is concerned with purely economic motivation and that which is concerned with wider 'behavioural' motivation on the part of taxpayers and tax evaders. Such a distinction has been made before, for example by James and Alley (1999), and is particularly relevant in the present context.

Purely Economic Factors and Compliance   Even if something like tax evasion is illegal, if there is a financial gain there must be a temptation. Compliance strategies based on this type of motivation are therefore concerned with affecting the possible financial gain to evasion including the risks and costs of punishment if caught. Allingham and Sandmo (1972) published a seminal and extensively quoted paper developing this approach and there have been many refinements and developments of their model since. A particularly clear exposition of mainstream economic analysis of tax evasion was presented by Cowell (1985). This approach indicates a number of variables that are likely to be important in such a technical analysis of compliance. An important one is the tax structure – that is the set of tax rates – which may have a direct influence on compliance (Alm et al., 1990; Clotfelter, 1983). There has been work on regressive taxes (for example by Nayak, 1978) and non-linear tax schedules (Pencavel, 1979). Other aspects that might affect the expected rate of return to non-compliance, such as uncertainty, have also been examined (see, for example, Alm et al., 1992).

The chances of getting caught are important so the probability of tax evasion being detected is relevant, (Fischer et al., 1992). So are the deterrent effects of auditing for non-compliance (Dubin and Wilde, 1988) and the relative effects of different audit schemes (Alm et al., 1993; Collins and Plumlee, 1991). The analysis can, of course, be extended to other players in this game. Tax agents are important so the whole approach can also be applied to them – for instance with respect to the penalties that might be imposed on them (Cuccia, 1994). This economic approach can also be extended to the possibility that compliance might be improved with pecuniary rewards to taxpayers (Falkinger and Walther, 1991) as well as pecuniary punishments for non-compliance. After all they are just two aspects of money incentives to conform.

However, although there are clear financial rewards for those who evade taxation successfully, many taxpayers are honest and disclose their financial affairs accurately (see for example Erard and Feinstein, 1994a; Gordon, 1989). Furthermore there has been an increasing amount of evidence to the effect that taxpayers are often motivated by many factors other than simple financial ones.

Other Behavioural Factors and Compliance There are many contributions from different disciplines suggesting other factors that might influence taxpayers' behaviour. For instance, work in sociology has focused on a number of relevant variables such as social support, social influence, attitudes and certain background factors such as age, gender, race and culture. Psychology reinforces this approach and has even created its own branch of 'fiscal psychology' (Schmölders, 1959; Lewis, 1982). The contribution of psychology includes the finding that attitudes towards the State and revenue authorities are important factors as well as perceptions of equity in determining compliance decisions. The main theme of this approach is that individuals are not simply independent selfish utility maximisers (though this might be partly true) but that they also interact with other human beings in ways that depend on different attitudes, beliefs, norms and rules.

There are many specific contributions to this approach. The importance of perceptions of equity and fairness in encouraging compliance has been a frequent theme (for example, Bordignon, 1993; Cowell, 1992). Background factors such as cultural influence have been examined (Coleman and Freeman, 1997), so too have the implications of different political systems (Pommerehne et al., 1994).

More direct contributions to policy in this area have come from a number of authors. For example, one is an appeal to taxpayers' conscience (Hasseldine and Kaplan, 1992) and also to feelings of guilt and shame (Erard and Feinstein, 1994b). Others have suggested more positive help for taxpayers (Hite, 1989) and different methods of achieving this – such as the use of television to change taxpayers' attitudes towards fairness and compliance (Roberts, 1994). All of these aspects should be included in the process of developing tax compliance strategies.

Develop Tax Compliance Strategies

Given the different aspects of the subject, strategies for encouraging compliance should be both comprehensive to address the position of taxpayers in general and sufficiently flexible to focus on areas of particular concern.

A framework for promoting compliance can be developed using a variety of general strategies. For example, measures can be taken to promote taxpayers' confidence in the fairness and integrity of the tax system and its administration. This can be done in many ways. The OECD Committee of Fiscal Affairs (1990) published the results of a survey of its member countries and found that a range of basic taxpayers' rights were generally present, such as the right to be informed, assisted and heard, the right of appeal and the right to privacy. A particular manifestation of this approach is a taxpayers' charter such as that introduced in Australia in 1997 and described as:

> the document that defines the kind of relationship the Australian Tax Office aspires to have with the Australian public. The *Charter* provides the basis for establishing a cooperative, respectful and trusting relationship with the public. (Braithwaite and Reinhart, 2000, p. 1)

A more general examination of taxpayers' charters as part of a general review of taxpayers' rights and obligations has been undertaken by the OECD Committee of Fiscal Affairs Forum on Tax Administration (2003).

Other strategies include simplifying the tax system which has been examined by James and Wallschutzky (1997) and which might make it easier for taxpayers to comply. A programme of taxpayer education may increase their motivation to comply as well as assisting them to do so. This can be reinforced by further resources devoted to helping taxpayers such as written explanatory material, advice centres, help lines and so forth.

There are also administrative arrangements that promote compliance. Withholding tax at source is a well-tried method. Indeed, Soos (1997) found that the principle of withholding tax at source was established in England as early as the sixteenth century and the first instance appears to have been the lay subsidy of 1512. In its modern version withholding at source is sufficiently extensive in the UK that it is not necessary for most British income taxpayers to be asked to complete a tax return every year (James and Nobes, 2004). Another arrangement is ensuring that information reporting is such that revenue agencies are aware of the existence of most income that might be taxable.

In the USA the Internal Revenue Service has recognised the importance of voluntary compliance – for example as outlined in its document *Compliance 2000* (Internal Revenue Service, 1991). The views of those with an interest in tax administration, both inside and outside the IRS, were sought with respect to the organisational goals of the IRS and compliance strategies to achieve those goals. The IRS document states (p. 17):

These efforts should be viewed as 'doing the job right on the front end'. Correcting problems and unintentional non-compliant behaviour through enforcement sanctions should be viewed as 'rework'. Quality principles demonstrate that 'rework' is more costly than 'doing the job right on the front-end' ... Increasing citizen participation and ownership of the tax system is an integral part of this direction. Such techniques as taxpayers accessing their own account data; identifying and removing organisational barriers to compliance; and positive incentives for compliance should be pursued.

However, such general strategies are unlikely to ensure the compliance of all taxpayers. The task of deterring evasion without also alienating honest taxpayers is not an easy one and requires a compliance strategy that provides an appropriate response to different forms of taxpayer behaviour. For example, both Australia (Australian Tax Office, 2002) and New Zealand (2003) have developed a 'Compliance Model' that links different motivating factors in taxpayers' compliance behaviour and the appropriate tax department response. The model shows a continuum of taxpayer attitudes towards compliance at four levels together with the appropriate compliance strategy as follows:

Attitude to Compliance	**Compliance Strategy**
Have decided not to comply	Use full force of the law
Don't want to comply	Deter by detection
Try to, but don't always succeed	Help to comply
Willing to do the right thing	Make it easy.

In the academic version of this model the style of enforcement emphasised is to begin by taking account the problems, motivations and conditions behind non-compliance (see, for example, Braithwaite and Braithwaite, 2001). Taxpayers are initially given the benefit of the doubt and the revenue service's trust in their honesty is an important part of an initial regulatory encounter. Strong emphasis is placed on educating taxpayers regarding their tax obligations and assisting them to comply, while those aspects of administration that rely principally on threats and the automatic imposition of penalties are not emphasised. It is only when taxpayers continue to be unco-operative that more interventionist measures (for example sanctions) are considered. In this way the compliance strategy is related to the taxpayers' particular approach and hopefully avoids alienating co-operative taxpayers.

Planning and Implementing Strategies

There are several general considerations involved in planning and implementing strategies. As indicated before, one is to ensure that the planning in this area is consistent with the overall activities of the revenue agency and that resources are used in an efficient and effective way. It is important to gain the support of stakeholders and this can be done in a number of ways such as involving them in the planning stage and providing explanations with respect to the intended strategy. For example the Australian Tax Office has been successful in involving stakeholders including its own staff in the development of its Taxpayers' Charter (James et al., 2004). Appropriate staff training is also necessary for the successful implementation.

The plan should also include intended outcomes and a mechanism for monitoring and evaluating the strategies. Where possible the relevant variables should be quantifiable but not everything in this area can be measured so qualitative feedback should also be sought. Finally there must be provision for modifying the strategies in the light of their performance in practice as well as to take account of changing circumstances.

Monitor and Evaluate Performance

Monitoring and evaluating performance, of course, is not always an easy task particularly with regard to activities that are necessarily hidden from official view. However a number of issues are worth mentioning. Given the complexity of the tax administration process, one single indicator is unlikely to be sufficient to monitor the whole situation. As pointed out above, success in decreasing tax evasion in one area may be offset if it leads to increased compliance problems elsewhere. Observing the trends in particular outcomes is a useful exercise but care should be taken also to continue to monitor the changing situation with regard to the tax environment and practice, particularly taxpayer behaviour. Over time different compliance issues may well change in their importance with respect to the overall strategy and new ones might emerge.

The final stage in this process is to use the results of the monitoring and evaluation of performance to feed back into the continuous development of the most appropriate tax compliance strategies.

Summary and Conclusions

Tax compliance strategies are clearly important, not only in terms of the very large amounts of tax that are evaded but also the implications for the community as a whole. Furthermore tax compliance strategies should be developed carefully as crude and inappropriate strategies might alienate taxpayers and have undesirable results with respect to other important concerns of public policy.

The management literature on strategy gives clear guidance on the development of strategy. Successful strategies incorporate a systematic analysis of the factors involved and of the wider context. Furthermore to ensure success strategy must be refined and reformulated in the light of experience.

To develop tax compliance strategies to tackle the underground economy, the aims of the tax system and enforcement generally should be considered. The importance of different risks of non-compliance should be assessed and compliance behaviour analysed. Compliance strategies should be developed taking account of the wider roles of the tax system and the position of other government enforcement agencies. Finally it is important that the performance of these strategies is monitored and that they are modified as appropriate.

Note

* The author is very grateful to the British Academy for funding his research in this area, Ali Edwards for helping collect the relevant material and Ian Hipkin for discussion regarding management strategy.

References

Allingham, M.G. and Sandmo, A. (1972), 'Income Tax Evasion: A Theoretical Analysis', *Journal of Public Economics*, Vol. 1, pp. 323-38.

Alm, J., Bahl, R. and Murray, M.N. (1990), 'Tax Structure and Tax Compliance', *Review of Economics and Statistics*, Vol. 62, pp. 603-13.

Alm, J., Jackson, B. and McKee, M. (1992), 'Institutional uncertainty and taxpayer compliance', *American Economic Review*, Vol. 82, pp. 1018-26.

Alm, J., Cronshaw, M.B. and McKee, M. (1993), 'Tax Compliance with Endogenous Audit Selection Rules', *Kyklos*, Vol. 46, pp. 27-45.

Australian Taxation Office (2002), *Compliance Program 2002-03*, Canberra: Australian Taxation Office.

Bhagwati, J. (2004), *In Defence of Globilization*, Oxford University Press.

Bordignon, M. (1993), 'A Fairness Approach to Income Tax Evasion', *Journal of Public Economics*, Vol. 52, pp. 345-62.

Braithwaite, V. and Braithwaite, J. (2001), 'An Evolving Compliance Model for Tax Enforcement', in N. Shover and J.P. Wright (eds), *Crimes of Privilege*, Oxford University Press, New York, pp. 405-19.

Braithwaite, V. and Reinhart, M. (2000), *The Taxpayers' Charter: Does the Tax Office comply and who benefits?*, Centre for Tax System Integrity Working Paper No. 1, Canberra: Australian National University.

Channon, G., Edwards, A. and James, S. (2002), *Disincorporation, Taxation and Small Business Behaviour*, London, Centre for Business Performance, Institute of Chartered Accountants in England and Wales.

Clotfelter, C.T. (1983), 'Tax Evasion and Tax Rates: An Analysis of Individual Tax Returns', *Review of Economics and Statistics*, Vol. 65, pp. 363-73.

Coleman, C. and Freeman, L. (1997), 'Cultural Foundations of Taxpayer Attitudes to Voluntary Compliance', *Australian Tax Forum*, Vol. 13, pp. 313-36.

Collins, J.H. and Plumlee, R.D. (1991), 'The Taxpayer's Labour and Reporting Decision: the Effect of Audit Schemes', *The Accounting Review*, Vol. 66, pp. 559-76.

Cowell, F.A. (1985), 'The Economic Analysis of Tax Evasion', *Bulletin of Economic Research*, Vol. 37, pp. 163-93.

Cowell, F.A. (1992), 'Tax Evasion and Equity', *Journal of Economic Psychology*, Vol. 13, pp. 521-43.

Cuccia, A.D. (1994), 'The Effects of Increased Sanctions on Paid Tax Preparers; Integrating Economic and Psychological Factors', *Journal of the American Taxation Association*, Vol. 16, pp. 41-66.

Dubin, J.A. and Wilde, L.L. (1988), 'An Empirical Analysis of Federal Income Tax Auditing and Compliance', *National Tax Journal*, Vol. 41, pp. 61-74.

Erard, B. and Feinstein, J. (1994a), 'Honesty and Evasion in the Tax Compliance Game', *Rand Journal of Economics*, Vol. 25(1), pp. 1-19.

Erard, B. and Feinstein, J.S. (1994b), 'The Role of Moral Sentiments and Audit Perceptions in Tax Compliance', Supplement to *Public Finance*, Vol. 49, pp. 70-89.

Everson, M.W. (2004), Commissioner, Internal Revenue Service, Statement before the Subcommittee on Oversight of the House Committee on Ways and Means, February 12, http://waysandmeans.house.gov/hearings.asp?formmode=printfriendly&id=1164, accessed 20 September 2004.

Falkinger, J. and Walther, W. (1991), 'Rewards versus Penalties: on a New Policy Against Tax Evasion', *Public Finance Quarterly*, Vol. 19, pp. 67-79.

Feige, E.L. (1989), *The Underground Economies: Tax Evasion and Information Distortion*, Cambridge University Press, New York.

Feinstein, J.S. (1999), 'Approaches for Estimating Noncompliance: Examples from Federal Taxation in the United States', *Economic Journal*, Vol. 109, pp. F360-69.

Fischer, C.M., Wartick, M. and Mark, M. (1992), 'Detection Probability and Taxpayer Compliance: A Review of the Literature', *Journal of Accounting Literature*, Vol. 11, pp. 1-46.

Gordon, J.P.F. (1989), 'Individual Morality and Reputation Costs as Deterrents to Tax Evasion', *European Economic Review*, Vol. 33, pp. 797-805.

Grant, R.M. (2002), *Contemporary Strategy Analysis: Concepts, Techniques, Applications*, 4th ed., Blackwell, Oxford.

Hasseldine, D.J. and Kaplan, S.E. (1992), 'The Effect of Different Sanction Communications on Hypothetical Taxpayer Compliance: Policy Implications from New Zealand', *Public Finance*, Vol. 47, pp. 45-60.

Hickey, J.J.B. (2000), 'The Fiscal Challenge of E-Commerce', *British Tax Review*, pp. 91-105.

Hite, P.A. (1989), 'A Positive Approach to Taxpayer Compliance', *Public Finance*, Vol. 44, pp. 249-66.

Holz-Eakin, D. (1995), 'Should Small Businesses be Tax-Favoured?', *National Tax Journal*, Vol. XLVIII(3), pp. 387-95.

House of Commons Committee of Public Accounts (2004), *Tacking Fraud Against the Inland Revenue*, First Report of Session 2003-04, HC 62, London: The Stationery Office Limited.

Internal Revenue Service (1991), *Compliance 2000, Report to the Commissioner of Internal Revenues*, Washington DC: IRS.

Jackson, B.R. and Milliron, V.C. (1986), 'Tax Compliance Research: Findings Problems and Prospects', *Journal of Accounting Literature*, Vol. 5, pp. 125-65.

James, S. and Alley, C. (1999), 'Tax Compliance, Self-Assessment and Tax Administration in New Zealand: Is the Carrot or the Stick More Appropriate to Encourage Compliance?', *New Zealand Journal of Tax Law and Policy*, Vol. 5(1), April, pp. 3-14.

James, S., Murphy, K. and Reinhart, M. (2004), 'The Taxpayers' Charter: A Case Study in Tax Administration', *Journal of Australian Taxation*, Vol. 7(2), pp. 336-356.

James, S. and Nobes, C. (2004), *The Economics of Taxation: Principles, Policy and Practice*, 7th ed. revised, Pearson Education, Harlow.

James, S. and Sawyer, A. (2004), 'Globalisation and International Trends in Taxation', *Asia-Pacific Journal of Taxation*, Vol. 8(2), pp. 49-67.

James, S. and Wallschutzky, I. (1997), 'Tax Law Improvement in Australia and the UK: The Need for a Strategy for Simplification', *Fiscal Studies*, Vol. 18(4), pp. 445-60.

Klepper, S. and Nagin, D. (1989), 'Tax Compliance and Perceptions of the Risks of Detection and Criminal Prosecution', *Law and Society Review*, Vol. 23, pp. 209-39.

Lewis, A. (1982), *The Psychology of Taxation*, Blackwell, Oxford.

Lyssiotou, P., Pashardes, P. and Stengos, T. (2004), 'Estimates of the Black Economy Based on Consumer Demand Approaches', *Economic Journal*, Vol. 114, pp. 622-40.

McCrae, J. and Reinhart, M. (2003), *Non-filers: What we know*, Centre for Tax System Integrity Research Note 1, Australian National University (http://ctsi.anu.edu.au).

Mintzberg, H. (2004), *Managers Not MBAs: A Hard Look at the Soft Practice of Managing and Management Development*, Berret-Koehler, Publishers, San Fransisco.

Nayak, P.B. (1978), 'Optimal Income Tax Evasion and Regressive Taxes', *Public Finance*, Vol. 33(3), pp. 358-66.

New Zealand (2003), *Report of the Inland Revenue Department for the year ended 30 June 2003*, Inland Revenue, Wellington.

OECD Committee of Fiscal Affairs (1990), *Taxpayer Rights and Obligations – A Survey of the Legal Situation in OECD Countries*, OECD, Paris.

OECD Committee of Fiscal Affairs Forum on Tax Administration (2003), *Taxpayers' Rights and Obligations – Practice Note*, GAP002, 2003, available from the OECD website and accessed on 6 May 2004.

OECD (2004), *Managing and Improving Tax Compliance*, Centre for Tax Policy and Administration, OECD, www.oecd.org/dataoecd/61/8/32069634.pdf, accessed 17 September 2004.

Payne, J.L. (1993), *Costly Returns: The Burdens of the US Tax System*, ICS Press, San Francisco.

Pencavel, J.H. (1979), 'A Note on Income Tax Evasion, Labour Supply and Nonlinear Tax Schedules', *Journal of Public Economics*, Vol. 12, pp. 115-24.

Pommerehne, W.W., Hart, A. and Frey, B.S. (1994), 'Tax Morale, Tax Evasion and the Choice of Policy Instruments in Different Political Systems', Supplement to *Public Finance*, Vol. 49, pp. 52-69.

Richardson, M. and Sawyer, A.J. (2001), 'A Taxonomy of the Tax Compliance Literature: Further Findings, Problems and Prospects', *Australian Tax Forum*, Vol. 16, pp. 137-320.

Roberts, M.L. (1994), 'An Experimental Approach to Changing Taxpayers' Attitudes Towards Fairness and Compliance via Television', *Journal of the American Taxation Association*, Vol. 16(1), pp. 67-86.

Sawyer, A.J. (1999), 'Electronic Commerce: International Tax Policy Implications for Revenue Authorities and Governments', *Virginia Tax Review*, Vol. 19(1), pp. 73-113.

Sawyer, A.J. (2003), 'An Electronic Transactions Act for New Zealand at Last!', *Journal of International Banking Law and Regulation*, Vol. 18(4), pp. 151-9.

Sawyer, A.J. (2004), 'Regulations now in place for NZ's Electronic Transactions Act', *Journal of International Banking Law and Regulation*, Vol. 19(2), pp. 45-8.

Schmölders, G. (1959), 'Fiscal Psychology: A New Branch of Public Finance', *National Tax Journal*, Vol. 15, pp. 184-93.

Schmölders, G. (1970), 'Survey Research in Public Finance: A Behavioural Approach to Fiscal Theory', *Public Finance*, Vol. 25, pp. 300-06.

Soos, P.E. (1997), *The Origins of Taxation at Source in England*, IBFD, Publications Amsterdam.

Strümpel, B. (1969), 'The Contribution of Survey Research to Public Finance', in A.T. Peacock (ed.), *Quantitative Analysis in Public Finance*, Praeger, New York, pp. 13-32.

Wallschutzky, I.G. (1993), 'Achieving compliance', Proceedings of the Australasian Tax Teachers' Association, Christchurch, New Zealand, January.

Index

Albania 93, 94
Algeria 95, 96
Angola 95, 96
Argentina 91, 92
Armenia 93, 94
audit threat, and tax compliance 50-1
Australia
    Australian Business Number (ABN)
      245-6
    cash economy 56-67
    Cash Economy Task Force (CETF)
      244, 251-73
      building partnerships 256-8
      communication strategy 256
      compliance model 254-5
      reports 252-4, 259-72
    Goods and Services Tax (GST) 243,
      244
    Medicare tax levy 43-5, 245
    Pay-As-You-Go taxation 41, 44, 45,
      245
    tax authorities, perceived legitimacy
      46-51, 248-50
    tax compliance 256-8, 261-2, 266-8,
      270-1
      specific industries 258, 264-6
    tax evasion 31
      countermeasures 250-1
    underground economy
      business structure 246-7
      household transactions 247
      size 39, 85-6
Austria 84, 85-6
Azerbaijan 92, 93, 94

Bangladesh 87, 88
Belarus 93, 94
Belgium 84, 85-6
Benin 95, 96
Bhutan 87, 88
Bolivia 90-1, 92
Bosnia & Herzegovina 93, 94
Botswana 95, 96
Brazil 91, 92

Bulgaria 93, 94
Burkina Faso 95, 96
business structure, underground
    economy 193-4, 246-7

Cambodia 86-7, 88
Cameroon 95, 96
Canada
    regulations burden 161
    self-employment 195-6
    tax burden 160-1
    underground economy
      causes 160-3
      MIMIC model 163-9
      sitcom about 157
      size 84, 85-6, 157-8, 163, 169-70
cash economy
    Australia 56-67, 244
      attitudes to 57-9
      database 57
      earnings 63
      managers/professionals 65-6
      participation 58-62
      purchasers 65-6
      size 56
      social demographic groups 62-6
      and tax morale 60-2
      trade/clerical staff 66
    OECD, size 56
    see also underground economy
Central African Republic 95, 96
Chad 95, 96
Chile 91, 92
China 97
Colombia 91, 92
commodity substitution, and the
    underground economy 189-90
Congo
    Democratic Republic 95, 96
    Republic 95, 96
consumption tax 182-3
    see also retail sales tax
corruption, OECD 133, 134-5, 136
Costa Rica 91, 92

Cote d'Ivoire 95, 96
Croatia 93, 94
Crowding Theory 25
currency demand approach
    objections to 77-8
    regression equation 76-7
    underground economy, calculation
        76-8, 85, 89, 99, 139
Czech Republic 92, 93, 94

Denmark 85-6, 131
Dominican Republic 91, 92
DYMIMIC model 74, 79, 84, 85, 89, 99

e-commerce 279-80
econometric analysis, tax evasion 148-53
Ecuador 91, 92
Egypt 95, 96
El Salvador 91, 92
Estonia 93, 94
Ethiopia 95, 96

fairness
    perceptions of 42
    and tax compliance 41-2
    and tax non-compliance 40
Fiji 89-90
Finland 85-6
France 85-6

Georgia 92, 93, 94
Germany 84, 85-6, 126, 131
Ghana 95, 96
Grabiner Report (UK), underground
    economy 233-40
Greece 84, 85-6
Guatemala 91, 92
Guinea 95, 96
Gutmann Curve 129

Haiti 91, 92
hidden economy *see* underground
    economy
Honduras 91, 92
Hong Kong 87
Hungary 93, 94

India 87, 88
Indonesia 87, 88
Iran 87, 88
Ireland 84, 85-6

Israel 87, 88
Italy 84, 85-6

Jamaica 91, 92
Japan 85-6
Jordan 87, 88

Kaufmann-Kaliberda Method,
    underground economy, calculation 82
Kazakhstan 93, 94
Kenya 95, 96
Kiribati 89-90
Korea 87, 88
Kuwait 87, 88
Kyrgyz Republic 93, 94

Lackó Method, underground economy,
    calculation 82-3
    equations 82-3
    problems 82-3
Laffer curve 127-8
Lao PDR 97
Latvia 93, 94
Lebanon 87, 88
Lesotho 94-5, 96

Macedonia FYR 93, 94
Madagascar 95, 96
Malawi 95, 96
Malaysia 86-7, 88
Maldives 89-90
Mali 95, 96
market segmentation 280
Marshall Islands 89-90
Mauritania 95, 96
methodologies, underground economy,
    calculation 74-83
    currency demand approach 76-8, 85,
        89, 99, 139
    Kaufmann-Kaliberda Method 82
    Lackó Method 82-3
    MIMIC model 79-82, 159, 163-9
    monetary methods 76-8
    national accounts 75-6
    physical input method 82-3
    tax auditing 75
    transactions approach 78-9
    voluntary surveys 74-5
Mexico 91, 92
Micronesia 89-90
MIMIC model, underground economy,

calculation 79-82, 159, 163-9
equations 80
problems 81-2
Moldova 93, 94
monetary methods, underground
economy, calculation 76-8
Mongolia 87, 88
moonlighting 1, 124
Morocco 95, 96
Mozambique 94-5, 96

Namibia 94-5, 96
national accounts, underground economy
size 75-6
Nepal 87, 88
Netherlands 85-6
New Zealand 85-6, 244
Nicaragua 91, 92
Niger 95, 96
Nigeria 94-5, 96
Norway
tax evasion, econometric analysis
148-53
tax functions 156
underground economy
data 142-6
findings 140-2
questionnaire 154-6
size 85-6, 131
surveys 139-53, 154-6

OECD countries
cash economy, size 56
corruption 133, 134-5
economic freedom 133, 134
institutions, quality of 133, 134
regulations' burden 131-2
tax burden 127-32
underground economy
causes 127-36
size 84-6, 185-6
working time reduction 131-2
Oman 87, 88

Pakistan 87, 88
Palau 89-90
Panama 90-1, 91, 92
Papua New Guinea 87, 88
Paraguay 90-1, 91, 92
Pay-As-You-Go taxation 43
Australia 41, 44, 45, 245

personal identities, vs social identities 44
Peru 90-1, 92
Philippines 87, 88
Poland 93, 94
Portugal 84, 85-6
Public Choice Theory 128
Puerto Rico 91, 92

retail sales tax, vs VAT 187-9
Romania 93, 94
Russian Federation 93, 94
Rwanda 95, 96

Samoa 89-90
Saudi Arabia 87, 88
self-employment
Canada 195-6
and the underground economy 194-6
Senegal 95, 96
Serbia & Montenegro 93, 94
shadow economy *see* underground
economy
Sierra Leone 95, 96
Singapore 86-7, 88
Slovak Republic 92, 93, 94
Slovenia 93, 94
social identities
and tax compliance 50, 51-2
taxpayers 42-5
vs personal identities 44
Solomon Islands 89-90
South Africa 94-5, 96
Spain 84, 85-6
Sri Lanka 87, 88
Sweden 85-6, 131
Switzerland
direct democracy 30
tax evasion 17-34
underground economy, size 23-4, 84,
85-6
Syrian Arab Republic 87, 88

Taiwan 87, 88
Tanzania 94-5, 96
tax auditing
underground economy size 75
US 203
tax avoidance, tax evasion, difference
276
tax burden
Canada 160-1

OECD 127-32
and underground economy 127-32,
160-1
tax compliance 15-16, 17
age/income factors 49
attitudes to 285
and audit threat 50-1
factors 40-1
and fairness 41-2
model 254-5
and social identities 50, 51-2
strategies 276-87
see also tax non-compliance
tax enforcement, US 204-5
tax evasion 180, 283
Al Capone 275
Australia 31
econometric analysis 148-53
Switzerland 17-34
and democracy 29-31
determinants 24-31
early accounts 17-20
and economic policy 33-4
levels 20-4, 26-9
tax avoidance, difference 276
UK 275-6
US 275
tax loss, and the underground economy 3
tax morale 16, 25, 31-2
and cash economy activity 60-2
definition 59
measurement 60, 61
and tax non-compliance 59
tax non-compliance 39-52
behaviour analysis 281-3
economic factors 39-40
and fairness 40
measurement 280-1
risks 279-81
significance 51
and tax morale 59
UK 226-33
US 203-20
see also tax compliance
tax payers, respectful treatment of 32
tax policy
purpose 180
and the underground economy 180-97
tax system
aims 278
income vs consumption 182-3

perceived legitimacy 43, 45-6, 52,
281
Australian study 46-51
and the underground economy 184-7
taxpayers
perceived injustice 43
social identities 42-5
Thailand 86-7, 88
Togo 95, 96
Tonga 89-90
transactions approach, underground
economy, calculation 78-9
Tunisia 95, 96
Turkey 87, 88

Uganda 95, 96
UK
illegal immigration 225-6
tax
credit fraud 234
evasion 275-6
tax non-compliance
action on 226-39
alcohol fraud 238-9
confidential help line 234
detection 228-31
deterrence 232-3
fraud assessment 234
information disclosure 229-31
legitimacy incentives 226-8
prevention 228, 275
sanctions 231-2
self-employment help 234-5
VAT fraud 237, 239
tobacco smuggling 224-5, 238
underground economy
consequences 224-6
estimating 107-22
Grabiner Report 233-40
size 85-6, 131
welfare benefits fraud 225, 235-7
Ukraine 92, 93, 94
underground economy
African countries 94-6, 99
Asian countries 86-7, 99
business structure 193-4, 246-7
Central & South American countries
90-2, 99, 100
and commodity substitution 189-90
Communist countries 96-7, 99
consequences 3-7, 98-9, 179-80, 223-6

and corruption 133, 134-5, 136
data distortion 3-4
definitions 124-5, 158-9
driving forces 123
East & Central European countries
    92-4, 100
and economic efficiencies 5
estimates 118-21, 191-2
    conclusion 115-16
    criticism of 107
    data sources 116
    empirical results 112-15
    framework 108-9
    MIMIC model 79-82, 159, 163-9
    model/methods 109-11
Grabiner Report (UK) 233-40
and income distribution 5
international comparisons 84-99
literature 73, 81
measurement
    methodologies 74-83, 159
    problems 73
Middle Eastern countries 87-8, 99,
    100
OECD 84-6, 99, 127-36, 185-6
Pacific Island countries 89-90, 99,
    100
positive outcomes 6, 180, 190
sectors 125
and self-employment 194-6
significance 2, 73-4
and tax burden 127-32, 160-1
and tax loss 3
tax morality 4
and tax policy 180-97
and tax system 184-7
unfair price competition 4
and unregulated activities 5
welfare effects 4

see also cash economy; individual
    countries
United Arab Emirates 87, 88
Uruguay 91, 92
US
    tax
        auditing 203
        enforcement 204-5
        evasion 275
        gap 206-7, 209-12
        self-assessment 205-6
    tax non-compliance 203-20
        causes 208-9
        flow-through screening 217-18
        future directions 219-20
        offshore abuses 215-16
        reduction 215-19
        research program 212-14
        size 205-14
        tax credit screening 218-19
        tax shelter abuses 216-17
        trends 209
        unreported income scoring 218
    tax payers, obligations 206
    underground economy, size 84, 85-6
Uzbekistan 93, 94

Vanuatu 89-90
VAT, vs retail sales tax 187-9
Venezuela 91, 92
Vietnam 97

welfare effects, underground economy 4

Yemen Republic 87, 88

Zambia 95, 96
Zimbabwe 94-5, 96